The School Curriculum

The School Curriculum

Arthur K. Ellis
Seattle-Pacific University

James A. Mackey
University of Minnesota

Allen D. Glenn
University of Minnesota

Allyn and Bacon, Inc.
Boston   London   Sydney   Toronto

Copyright © 1988 by Allyn and Bacon, Inc.
A Division of Simon & Schuster
160 Gould Street
Needham Heights, Massachusetts 02194-2310

Ellis, Arthur K.
    The school curriculum / Arthur K. Ellis, James A. Mackey, Allen D.
Glenn.
        p.   cm.
    Bibliography: p.
    Includes index.
    ISBN 0-205-11172-6
    1. Public schools—United States—Curricula.   2. Curriculum
planning—United States.   3. Curriculum evaluation—United States.
4. Teachers—Training of—United States—Curricula.   I. Mackey,
James A., 1937–   . II. Glenn, Allen D. III. Title.
LB1570.E45 1987
375′.00973—dc19   87-15760
                                                              CIP

Series editor: Susanne Canavan
Production administrator: Annette Joseph
Production coordinator: Helyn Pultz
Editorial-production service: TKM Productions
Cover administrator: Linda K. Dickinson
Cover designer: Lynda Fishbourne

Printed in the United States of America

10 9 8 7 6 5 4 3 2 1   92 91 90 89 88 87

Brief Contents

Complete Contents

Preface

The goal of this book is to develop a synthesis of the diverse elements of the school curriculum. The curriculum, the course of study in its most literal sense, is a complex educational structure composed of subject matter, teaching, and learning. The day-to-day reality is that these elements function in an integrated fashion, and there is always something contrived about our efforts to measure them independently. We contend in this book that the reader is best served by a presentation that develops these seemingly separate entities in a way that leads to their ultimate integration. If we are successful, we will have expanded the reader's concept of the curriculum beyond the conventional horizon. We have attempted to explore the linkages among the issues, the ever-expanding knowledge base, the people who teach and learn in school settings, and the course of study itself.

Jean Piaget wrote that the goal of education is to create possibilities for people to invent and discover. It is in that spirit that we have addressed the academic, social, political, and philosophic dimensions of the school curriculum. We have developed these various dimensions of educational thought and practice in a context of how teachers perceive their task and how they might perceive it. We have explained the structure of the school curriculum not only in terms of what it is, but what it might become. In that regard, we have placed major emphasis on two overriding goals of education: literacy and critical thinking. Entire chapters are devoted to these crucial topics because they exemplify the kinds of themes that ought to be the curriculum's point of synthesis.

A theme throughout the book is the role of the teacher as a decision maker. The cumulative effects of teachers' decisions have been greatly underestimated and underexamined as a force influencing the conduct of the school curriculum. Planning, organizing, instructing, and evaluating are among the key elements of teachers' decision making that we have addressed as major topics.

Our specific objectives for the readers of this book are:

1. To develop a research-based understanding of the various forces that come together to create the idea of the school curriculum.
2. To create a synthesis of the interactions that occur between teachers and students in the social-constructed environment called *school.*
3. To articulate a philosophy of curriculum and instruction that represents considered opinion built on a knowledge of the field.

Our hope is that the readers of this book will assume an active role and that they will perceive the ideas contained in these pages not as material to be "set in a notebook, learned, and conned by rote," as Shakespeare noted of so much of what passes for learning, but as a challenge to come to terms with a complex set of processes called *curriculum* and *instruction*.

We wish to thank several people whose efforts have made this a better book. William Joyce of Michigan State University, James R. Johnson and Mary Jo Henning of The University of Toledo, Robert McNergney of The University of Virginia, Ron Wheeler of The College of William and Mary, Candace Wells of Wichita State University, Arthur Garner of Memphis State University, Nicholas Georgiady of Miami University of Ohio, and JoAnne Herbert of The University of Virginia provided us with thoughtful manuscript reviews. We thank Deborah Appleman of Carleton College for several helpful editorial suggestions. Our editor at Allyn and Bacon, Susanne Canavan, was a model of patience and leadership throughout the course of this project. Karen Ellis and Deda Jenkins did much of the word processing for which we are very grateful. And we wish to thank the many students we have enjoyed teaching over the years.

A. K. E.
J. A. M.
A. D. G.

The School Curriculum

Part I

Social Context

1

Toward a Definition
of School Curriculum

▶————————————————————————————
————————————————————————————◀

INTRODUCTION

▶ The curriculum is a mirror that reflects America's dreams for its next generation. It is through the school curriculum that Americans attempt to translate their values into reality. Therefore, no area of this nation's schooling has such a difficult, complicated, and dramatic history as the school curriculum.

The term *curriculum* is derived from the Latin word *currere,* which, in its most literal interpretation, means a running course. In recent years, as our society has placed increasing responsibility on its schools, the image of the running course has become less appropriate. The curriculum of the American school has come more to resemble a labyrinth, replete with serpentine twists and turns, and less a well-designed track.

This transformation of the American school curriculum can be attributed to two general sets of factors. The first of these is the increase in the complexity of society, requiring that individuals know more to survive in a technologically sophisticated environment. Second, in the last half of the twentieth century a tide of rising expectations has swept over all aspects of our country's life, necessitating that the schools and their curricula be more elaborate and accountable with each passing year. Each of these sets of factors has made the curriculum much more involved that it has been in the past.

Before we continue, we need to define the term *curriculum*. This book, after all, concerns the school curriculum and its accompanying instructional processes, which, we will argue, are the vital center of the American school. We begin by examining the school curriculum and its importance.

WHAT IS THE CURRICULUM?

▶ There are many definitions of *curriculum,* both formal and informal, that we could offer, but let us start by drawing a concrete picture of what *curriculum* means. If the curriculum, as we claim, is indeed reflective of the current trends, values, and occurrences of the society whose schools it defines, then an examination of the current state of that society, as represented in its newspapers, should exemplify some aspects of that curriculum. Hence, our analytical question is, Will a coherent picture of American school curriculum emerge from studying four issues of a large metropolitan newspaper? Is there enough material in one-half of a week's newspapers to illustrate, however imperfectly, the scope and the pervasiveness of the school curriculum?

We begin by arbitrarily selecting four days out of the period of March 1 to March 11, 1986, and then carefully scrutinizing those copies of the *New York Times* for articles that pertain to the school curriculum. We selected the *New York Times* because it has become essentially a national newspaper. It is not our intention to provide complete accounts of the news stories, only to summarize what is said about the school curriculum in this national forum.

▶ *News Item (March 1):* In a sixty-six page booklet entitled "What Works: Research About Teaching and Learning," the Department of Education presented President Reagan with a list of "what works" in the public schools. The report, claims the Secretary of Education, is an effort to "tell the American public what we know how to teach." The report embraces phonics as the best method of teaching reading, encourages the teaching of core subjects such as math, supports the assignment of homework, and emphasizes the teaching of history (E. G. Fiske, p. 1).

▶ *News Item (March 4):* Two students whose parents were born in Asia tied for first place in the annual Westinghouse Science Talent Search Competition. The students, a boy and a girl, provide further evidence for the noticeable trend in recent years: the domination of science awards by students who are the sons and daughters of Asian immigrants (Barbara Garmarekian, p. 15).

▶ *News Item (March 4):* An incredible demand for philosophers is developing because the artificial intelligence industry needs people who "can take vaguely formed problems and find ways to make them precise enough to be programmed." Claiming that philosophically trained individuals can perform these intellectual tasks, but that most programmers cannot, a spokesman outlined a plan to marry philosophy and high technology (Elizabeth Fowler, p. 54).

▶ *News Item (March 10):* Private industry has stepped up its aid to New York City schools because a large number of students are unprepared for the city's rapidly changing job market. Concerned that more students be trained to work in the service and finance industries — the fastest growing sectors of the local economy — many companies have begun to contribute money to the school system. It's either pay now or later, one industrial spokesperson asserted (Alexander Reid, p. 36).

▶ *News Item (March 11):* Educational Testing Service (E.T.S.) announced a fifteen-year $30 million effort to "develop a new generation of tests" that are less concerned with absolute answers and more concerned with establishing what the test taker knows and does not know. The demands of E.T.S. customers and the desire to devise exams that relate to specific occupations are behind the change, the head of the test development corporation asserted (Jonathan Friendly, p. 10).

Other articles in the four days of newspapers traced an attempt to test Texas teachers, described senior citizens assisting in the schools, and profiled colleges that were affected by changing high-school enrollments. Our armchair analysis implies that increasingly the business of America is education, and that the school curriculum is the anvil upon which many of education's most crucial and volatile issues are hammered out. What do these events say to you about the link between school and society?

Does this admittedly informal analysis help us define curriculum? It does provide us with an approximate definition. Furthermore, it suggests that curriculum is what schools teach, which is directly affected by changing social conditions and the demands of an attentive American public.

DEMANDS OF AN ATTENTIVE PUBLIC

▶ Americans have always had high expectations for their schools. The country emerged "in an age of exuberant faith in the power and possibility of education," wrote educational historian Lawrence Cremin. "The [Americans'] goal was nothing less than a new republican individual, of virtuous character, abiding patriotism, and prudent wisdom, fashioned by education into an independent yet loyal citizen" (quoted in Toch, 1984).

Over the years the relative emphasis may have changed, but the basic design set down by the early Americans has remained unaltered. There are, of course, many ways of examining the expectations that Americans have for their educational system; one could visit PTA meetings, interview individuals on a street corner, and consult with expert witnesses on public opinion and educational policy. Using these sorts of data-gathering tools, we would find out how Americans feel, in general, about educational matters. In a book on curriculum and instruction, we search for more specificity. We want to document the nature of the specific demands Americans place on their school's curriculum. Can we determine this?

One educational researcher, John Goodlad, attempted to examine what Americans want from their schools. After first determining that there were four broad areas of development that make up most curriculum — intellectual, personal, social, and vocational — Goodlad asked a sample of individuals, which included parents, teachers, and students, to rate on a scale ranging from "very unimportant" to "very important" each of these general goals (1984). Table 1–1 presents Goodlad's results.

As Table 1–1 reveals, the results are inconclusive. While there is slight difference between teachers and parents over the importance of intellectual goals, and slight disagreement among the three groups about the importance of social goals, what leaps off the table is the fact that American people — parents, teachers, and students — want the school to accomplish all the goals.

What the American people are saying in this study, Goodlad contends, is "We want it all" — intellectual, vocational, personal, and social — and most citizens believe that the school can and should provide it all.

Is it possible to be more specific about our nation's demands on its school curriculum? How do these orientations change over time? What are the catalysts for change in the American viewpoint about school curriculum? What new forms are these questions likely to assume?

THREE MAJOR INFLUENCES ON EDUCATIONAL POLICY

▶   Most educational historians contend that the struggle for the control of school curriculum is based on a disagreement over the allocation of which values will dominate curriculum decision making. In these

TABLE 1-1   School Goals Preferred by Students, Teachers, and Parents

	Intellectual	Personal	Vocational	Social
Students	47.1%	17.3%	21.8%	13.8%
Elementary School	38.0	18.3	30.3	13.4
Jr. High/Middle School	27.3	25.6	31.1	15.9
Teachers				
Elementary School	48.9%	33.5%	3.5%	14.0%
Jr. High/Middle School	46.7	29.3	10.1	13.9
High School	45.6	29.7	14.8	9.9
Parents				
Elementary School	57.6%	24.5%	8.6%	9.3%
Jr. High/Middle School	51.1	21.1	18.2	9.5
High School	46.5	19.3	25.5	8.7

Source: John I. Goodlad, *A Place Called School: Prospects for the Future* (New York: McGraw-Hill), p. 39. Quoted in Michael W. Kirst, *Who Controls Ours Schools: American Values in Conflict* (New York: W. H. Freeman, 1984).

Intellectual development: instruction in basic skills in mathematics, reading, written and verbal communication, critical thinking, and problem solving.

Personal development: instruction that prepares students for employment, develops skills necessary for getting a job, and fosters awareness of career alternatives.

Vocational development: instruction that prepares students for employment, develops skills necessary for getting a job, and fosters awareness of career alternatives.

Social development: instruction that helps students learn to get along with other students and adults, prepares students for social civic effectiveness, and develops students' awareness and appreciation of their own and other cultures.

After rating the four areas on a scale ranging from "very unimportant" to "very important," respondents selected one preferred goal from among the four.

value disputes, three values seem most frequently at issue: pragmatic efficiency, egalitarianism, and individualism or freedom of choice (Kirst, 1984, p. 59). At any given time, only one of these three values can be ascendant.

The three values cannot be maximized at the same time because they conflict with one another. American educational history is, therefore, like a pendulum, swinging across an arc from one of these values to another. This cyclic path is not arbitrary, but is directly affected by social events and the sensibilities of each particular historical epoch, some of which are relatively short in duration. For example, during the 1960s the momentum of the Civil Rights Movement swung the pendulum toward egalitarianism; in the early 1970s freedom of choice was the vogue; and in the 1980s efficiency seems again dominant.

The rapidly swinging pendulum places American curriculum policy in a state of constant tension as these three values vie for dominance. The best way to envision these competing values is to imagine them as three hot air balloons poised on a launching pad preparing for a race. Each of the three balloons is well prepared and bedecked for the competition, and each possesses a strong case for ascendancy, but each is unable to move forward until hot air is released into its balloon. (One realizes that there is more than a little danger in creating metaphors between educational policy and hot air.) When bursts of air are pumped into each respective balloon, it leaps ahead of the others. As soon as the pressure is reduced, that particular balloon slips back and is surpassed by another balloon. This situation is illustrated in Figure 1-1.

► Efficiency

Of the three values, the one with the most staying power has always been efficiency. The idea of efficiency is demonstrated by rigorous, carefully organized curriculum and competency tests for teachers and students. The general idea is that the schools can be improved if they are better run. Implicit in the efficiency scheme is the belief that schools

FIGURE 1-1 Three Basic Values That Determine Curriculum Conceptions

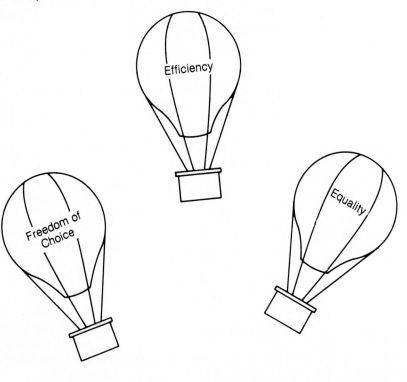

are just like businesses and large organizations, and that sound business practices can be used to improve them.

Efficiency is illustrated by the following kinds of school practices:

- ▶ centralized policy making
- ▶ accountability
- ▶ performance objectives
- ▶ competency-based programs
- ▶ mastery learning
- ▶ criterion-referenced testing

As a mechanism for making the differences among the three values clear, let us return to the medium that we used to introduce the term *curriculum*, and this time employ newspaper headlines to illustrate each of the three values. Newspaper headlines have a unique style — they are cryptic, abbreviated, and dramatic. Above all, the purpose of newspaper headlines is to grab the reader's attention. That is why we use the device here.

HEADLINES — EFFICIENCY

Schools Use New Ways to Be More Efficient and Enforce Discipline

Schools Try to Raise Effectiveness with New Methods

'Effective' Teaching Stresses High Goals and Rules That Are Clearly Defined

(*Wall Street Journal*, December 15, 1983)

Speeding Up Research on Education Issue

(*USA Today*, July 15, 1985)

Schools Can Learn from Businesses

(*Minneapolis Star-Tribune*, September 8, 1985)

Tightening the Agenda for U.S. Schools

(*Christian Science Monitor*, April 12, 1986)

Competency Tests Are Vital to Reform

(*St. Paul Pioneer Press-Dispatch*, January 9, 1985)

California Battles Educational Mediocrity

(*Minneapolis Star-Tribune*, October 29, 1985)

▶ **Egalitarianism**

Egalitarianism most dramatically dominated American—especially federal governmental—curriculum policy during the 1960s. Central to egalitarianism is the belief in equal opportunity, which is placed into operation by allowing pupils equal access to all aspects of education. Antidiscrimination and desegregation laws are the most well-known examples of ascendant egalitarianism, but the range of issues in its orbit extends along a path from gender equity on athletic teams to ways of attracting minorities and women to careers in science. Although the belief in egalitarianism is founded upon the bedrock of the American creed, in recent history this value has only been dominant when the federal government lends its strong support to programs that embody equal opportunity. As soon as federal support lessens, egalitarianism erodes somewhat.

Egalitarianism is exemplified by the following kinds of school practices:

▶ equal opportunities
▶ mainstreaming
▶ busing
▶ desegregation
▶ compensatory and remedial programs
▶ human relations

HEADLINES—EQUALITY

Study Cites Dire Results of Ignoring Poor Students

(*New York Times,* October 19, 1985)

U.S. Educ Office Warns of Possible Cut Off of $30 Million in Fed Aid Unless Chicago System Acts to End Alleged Racial Bias in Accordance with '64 Civil Rights Act

(*New York Times,* October 3, 1967)

Governor 'Choice' Is Pro-Student

(*Red Wing Eagle,* March 26, 1985)

Can Bilingual Education Do Its Job?

Education Programs in Many Languages Offered

Bilingual Plan Thrives Among Ruins of Bronx

Who, What and How Long?

In Bilingual Education: Even Experts Are Confused

> (*Los Angeles Times,* September 4–6, 1980)

U.S. Supreme Court Rules That Federal Law Entitles Handicapped Children to Public Education from Which They Can Derive 'Some Benefit'

> (*New York Times,* June 29, 1977)

Principals at City's Academically Elite Hss. Strongly Oppose Fed Govt's Investigation into Possible Discrimination Against Girls and Minority Group Members

> (*New York Times,* November 7, 1977)

▶ **Freedom of Choice**

Freedom of choice is the third basic curriculum value. With regard to school curriculum, freedom of choice has been present from the beginning of the American educational experience. In its contemporary guise, freedom of choice manifests itself in the idea of the independent school district with a highly individualized school curriculum, and in parents' rights to send their children to the kind of public school that best approximates their values. Educational vouchers, one of the most volatile issues in education today, is an almost ideal representation of freedom of choice. Vouchers involve the issuance of a government check to qualified parents that can be cashed in at the school of the parents' choice, and of course, used only for the child's schooling. In most instances, freedom of choice works only when some support, generally federal or state, is withdrawn from an educational program, and the monies or resources and the responsibility is allowed to trickle down to individual taxpayers. Various tax referenda limiting school taxes illustrate this process.

Freedom of choice is ascendant when the following kinds of school practices are dominant:

- ▶ community control
- ▶ privatization of services
- ▶ magnet schools
- ▶ tuition tax credits
- ▶ electives
- ▶ alternative schools

HEADLINES—FREEDOM OF CHOICE

S D Offers Small Schools Limited Open Enrollment

(*Minneapolis Star-Tribune*, April 11, 1985)

In a New Report Educator Urges "Personalized" High Schools

(*Time*, August 16, 1985)

Report Says Censorship Increased 37% in Public Schools During Year

(*Minneapolis Star-Tribune*, August 16, 1985)

School-Choice Plan Leaps Crucial Hurdles

(*St. Paul Pioneer Press-Dispatch*, March 28, 1985)

Two Observers of State Education Evaluate 'Free Choice' Plan

Schools and Teachers Are Motivated When They Know Students and Parents Have Chosen Them

Competition Will Hurt Schools Ex-MEA Leader Says

(*St. Paul Pioneer Press-Dispatch*, March 21, 1985)

As can be seen, the curricula of the schools is not a peripheral aspect of our society, but an integral and broad strand in the fabric of American life. What we present in this book is a systematic examination of curriculum by first providing several contexts—social, historical, and professional—in which the school curriculum can be understood, and then examining some specific elements of the courses of study in which our schools are engaged.

HOW THIS BOOK IS ORGANIZED

▶ This book has four parts: Social Context, Instructional Orientation, Curriculum Perspectives, and Emerging Concerns. The first section sets the scene for a discussion of curriculum and instruction. This initial chapter is a sketch of the social landscape in which the curriculum exists. The second chapter offers a definition of the crucial issues that influence the school curriculum, and includes three case studies that place the school curriculum in a social environment. Chapter 3 draws a social profile of the American teacher.

Part II, entitled Instructional Orientation, is the most detailed portion of the book. Chapter 4, which delineates how teachers think about teaching and their curriculum, explains the unique thoughtways that teachers use to organize their teaching. Building upon this perspective, Chapter 5 details a series of instructional tactics that can assist a teacher in preparing and planning to teach. Chapter 6 presents a creative synthesis of the instructional techniques that teachers use, and describes three general instructional strategies—classical, discovery, and changed structures—that teachers employ in their teaching. Chapter 7 explores the curriculum that teachers receive in their own teacher education programs, describing the scope and sequence of American teacher education, and evaluating the strengths and the weaknesses of teacher education in the United States. The final two chapters in Part II, Chapters 8 and 9, present the special case of teacher effectiveness. Arguing that there are existing teaching strategies that can assist teachers in organizing their classroom instruction, the chapters outline and assess three dimensions of the research on what is commonly referred to as *teacher effectiveness.*

Curriculum Perspectives, Part III, contains three chapters. The foundational components and underlying concepts of the school curriculum are identified in Chapter 10. Chapter 11 presents some basic issues that underline the formal curriculum of the American school. Arguing that although the United States does not have a centralized national school curriculum, in the same sense that France does, it is, nevertheless, possible to trace out distinct commonalities in this country's curricular orientation and structure. Chapter 12, entitled Hidden Curriculum, probes beneath the explicit school curriculum to examine some of the underlying regularities that organize classroom life which are deliberately taught but seldom explicitly articulated.

Part IV presents four emerging concerns for the school curriculum as the American educational estate heads toward the twenty-first century. The four issues we delineate are literacy, critical thinking, evaluation, and technology. Chapter 13 documents the urgent need for a new and more comprehensive definition of what is entailed to be literate in a highly technologically oriented society. Chapter 14 presents a synthesis of the issues and research in critical thinking and provides clues for the teacher interested in using critical thinking in the classroom. The role of assessment and evaluation in curriculum and instruction is discussed in Chapter 15. Chapter 16 examines how technology is affecting the process of schooling in the United States. Chapter 17 considers the teacher as a professional.

SIX CURRICULUM ISSUES

 This book covers the subject of curriculum and instruction from several perspectives—social, instructional, and curricular. Through our discussion, we hope to shed light or expand the dialogue on several major curricular issues. Since the ambiguous nature of curriculum often leads to murky and confusing discussions, it is important that we employ an efficient method to portray the most urgent curricular issues. Therefore, in our initial discussion at least, we limit our discussion to six crucial issues that capture the most essential dialectics in curricular thought. We deliberately employ the term *dialectics* (from the Greek word for *dialogue*) because we intend to promote the relentless questioning that continues to inform the concept (Heilbroner, 1980, p. 31). The six curricular issues include the following:

▶ *Issue one: General education versus tracking.* Should school curricula be constructed along egalitarian lines to promote excellence for everyone or should curriculum concentrate on the more efficient strategy of providing a high-quality education for the highly talented youth and tracking the remaining pupils in programs commensurate with their abilities?

▶ *Issue two: Real versus contrived curriculum.* Does the school curriculum—math, social studies, science, and so forth—constitute the groundwork of what a pupil ought to learn in school or are the school subjects merely vehicles to assist pupils in learning to learn? Is the process or the product more essential in school curriculum?

▶ *Issue three: Small versus large schools.* Does the abrupt change of scale that characterizes American schools—moving from many small independent units to fewer well-endowed operations—affect how well pupils perform? Is it still possible to have freedom of choice for parents and their children and promote equality in a large, efficient school organization?

▶ *Issue four: Graded versus ungraded curriculum.* Should curriculum be developed to permit students to be grouped according to their interests, aptitudes, and abilities, and then moved through school at their own pace irrespective of any grade placements, or are the efficiencies garnered by the graded curriculum—sorting and classifying students and subdividing knowledge—sufficient to warrant the continuance of that curricular form?

▶ *Issue five: Professional versus bureaucratic.* Have recent attempts to make teachers more efficient and accountable inhibited teacher independence and denied them the freedom and flexibility that is the hallmark of a diligent professional? Can it be demonstrated that these bureaucratic structures produce more effective teaching and learning?

▶ *Issue six: Sources of information—Uniform versus varied.* Is it possible to develop pervasive curricula that meet the needs of all American youth simultaneously—as illustrated by textbooks and other attempts at national curriculum—or ought the biography and the social structure surrounding the individual be paramount in the determination of a school curriculum?

In the next chapter, we explicate and discuss these crucial issues in greater detail. But before we do, we think it would be useful to know how you feel about each of these issues. The method that we have chosen to obtain this information is called a *semantic differential,* which is a measurement device developed by social psychologist Charles Osgood. After you have read this curriculum book and have debated its points with yourself, your classmates, and your teachers, we intend to ask you—as a part of the summary chapter—to retake a similar version of this information instrument. This will enable you to determine the impact of the ideas in this book. Complete the semantic differential instrument on page 16 before going on.

We have presented six issues for your examination using the semantic differential. How did you come out? Did using the strategy give you a clearer understanding of your feelings on the issues? If you found the tactic to be useful, perhaps you would like to try it yourself on issues that you feel are important. We hope that the analysis you have just done will help when you read the next chapter on crucial issues.

SUMMARY

▶   This chapter constructed a map of the terrain of the school curriculum. In the bare outlines that our map traced, we attempted to pique your interest in the territory of the curriculum. As the book continues to unfold we intend to chart, much more carefully, the dimensions of school curriculum and draw out the issues that are related to that subject. In the end, we hope that the pathways we construct will help inform your curriculum and instruction choices.

ACTIVITIES

1. Why have our concerns about school curriculum increased in the last quarter of the century?
2. Predict which of the three values–pragmatic efficiency, egalitarianism, or individualism–will ascend next, given the clues provided by the current state of our society. Defend your prediction.

Semantic Differential

Directions: Look at the six numbered words below; get an idea (image) of each word in your mind.

Below the word you will find several words that describe the image. Between the words with opposite meaning are seven spaces. Fill in the space that best describes your feeling about the image word.

1. TRACKING

Good	—	—	—	—	—	—	—	Bad
Smart	—	—	—	—	—	—	—	Stupid
Hard	—	—	—	—	—	—	—	Easy
Educated	—	—	—	—	—	—	—	Uneducated
Interesting	—	—	—	—	—	—	—	Uninteresting

2. PROCESS-ORIENTED CURRICULUM

Logical	—	—	—	—	—	—	—	Illogical
Meaningful	—	—	—	—	—	—	—	Meaningless
Hard	—	—	—	—	—	—	—	Easy
Important	—	—	—	—	—	—	—	Unimportant
Useful	—	—	—	—	—	—	—	Useless

3. LARGE SCHOOL ORGANIZATION

Good	—	—	—	—	—	—	—	Bad
Smart	—	—	—	—	—	—	—	Stupid
Educated	—	—	—	—	—	—	—	Uneducated
Ashamed	—	—	—	—	—	—	—	Proud
Important	—	—	—	—	—	—	—	Unimportant

4. GRADED CURRICULUM

Interesting	—	—	—	—	—	—	—	Uninteresting
Proud	—	—	—	—	—	—	—	Ashamed
Happy	—	—	—	—	—	—	—	Sad
Clean	—	—	—	—	—	—	—	Dirty
Important	—	—	—	—	—	—	—	Unimportant

5. BUREAUCRATIC ORGANIZATIONAL STRUCTURES

Logical	—	—	—	—	—	—	—	Illogical
Meaningful	—	—	—	—	—	—	—	Meaningless
Hard	—	—	—	—	—	—	—	Easy
Important	—	—	—	—	—	—	—	Unimportant
Useful	—	—	—	—	—	—	—	Useless

6. NATIONAL TEXTBOOKS

Proud	—	—	—	—	—	—	—	Ashamed
Important	—	—	—	—	—	—	—	Unimportant
Powerful	—	—	—	—	—	—	—	Weak
Meaningful	—	—	—	—	—	—	—	Meaningless
Uneducated	—	—	—	—	—	—	—	Educated

3. Why has efficiency been the most popular of the three values we described? Is there something characteristically unique about Americans' admiration for efficiency?
4. This chapter identified six major curriculum issues. In your opinion, which of these issues is the most important? Why?
5. Four areas of emerging concern are outlined in the chapter—literacy, critical thinking, evaluation, and technology. Can you identify any additional emerging concerns for school curriculum?

REFERENCES

Fiske, E. G. (March 1, 1986). U.S. Education Department study reports best ways to teach. *New York Times,* p. 1.

Fowler, E. (March 4, 1986). Philosophy majors in demand. *New York Times,* p. D25.

Friendly, J. (March 11, 1986). Standardized test makers shift course in response to critics. *New York Times,* p. 10.

Garmarekian, B. (March 4, 1986). Two students share top science prize. *New York Times,* p. 15.

Goodlad, J. I. (1984). *A place called school: Prospects for the future.* New York: McGraw-Hill.

Heilbroner, R. L. (1980). *Marxism: For and against.* New York: W. W. Norton.

Kirst, M. W. (1984). *Who controls our schools: American values in conflict.* New York: W. H. Freeman.

Reid, A. (March 10, 1986). Industry aid to school rises. *New York Times,* p. 36.

Toch, T. (1984). America's quest for universal literacy. *Education Week, 4,* L3.

SUGGESTED READINGS

Boyer, E. (1983). *High school: A report on secondary education in America.* New York: Harper and Row.

Goodlad, J. (1984). *A place called school: Prospects for the future.* New York: McGraw-Hill.

Hacker, A. (April 12, 1984). Schools flunk out. *New York Review of Books.*

A nation at risk: The report of the national commission in education. (1983). U.S. Department of Education.

Ravitch, D. (1983). *The troubled crusade.* New York: Basic Books.

Sizer, T. (1983). *Horace's compromise: The dilemma of the American high school.* Boston: Houghton Mifflin.

2

Critical Issues in
the School Curriculum

▶──────────────────────────
──────────────────────────◀

OVERVIEW

▶ This chapter presents the key issues facing the school curriculum. Since we defined the school curriculum very broadly to include what the schools do, some of these issues involve textbooks and courses of study, others concern the current structure of education, and still others touch on larger issues of public philosophy and ideology. As the quality of public schooling increasingly becomes a primary concern of most Americans, school curriculum issues become evermore complex and arguable.

To disentangle this complex web of curriculum issues, we will use two analytical devices. The first of these, briefly outlined in Chapter 1, presents the central concerns of curriculum and instruction in American schools in terms of six dualisms or contrasts. The second device employs three case studies of curriculum decision making as a method of seeing these issues in their actual social context. Whereas neither of these techniques will yield the definitive portrait of the crucial issues facing the school curriculum, each is presented as a means of introducing some measure of clarity and order to an incredibly complex process.

Throughout the discussion, it is important to bear in mind that the final school curriculum—the course of study, the lessons plans, the textbooks, and the teaching activities that the student experiences—is the result of a series of deliberate value choices by various actors and agencies. Concrete images of conflicts and compromises, and successes and failures are etched into the contemporary consciousness. In this chapter, we hope to show that school curriculum is in the end a vital part of the struggle for the control of public policy that is, and ought to be, carried on continuously in a democratic society. Let us move now to a discussion of the six crucial issues.

SIX CRITICAL ISSUES IN CURRICULUM AND INSTRUCTION

► Issue One: General Education versus Tracking

Should all students receive the same education during their years in public school or should the curriculum be varied for different students? The answer to this question has been a matter of long-standing debate. Advocates of general education believe that emphasis should be placed on academic subjects and that all students, irrespective of "ability" or "aptitude," should receive instruction in a core of subjects, usually including English, mathematics, science, history, and the arts. Proponents of general education argue that by giving all students a general education it is possible to afford them the ultimate freedom of choice to pursue lifelong formal and informal learning. Consequently, advocates of general education make no accommodation for such courses as home economics, driver's training, or industrial arts. Such specialization, whether it be professional, academic, or trade, is something one chooses after the completion of high school. By allowing students to be placed in tracks too early, opportunities for continued, lifelong growth are limited.[1]

In contrast, tracking systems provide a means of separating students, if not individually, at least by groups of similar ability or aptitude. The purpose of tracking is to offer these selected students an education appropriate to their intellectual needs and place in society. Advocates of tracking feel it is misleading and unrealistic to ignore the vast differences in student abilities. By separating students according to their levels, schools are better able to prepare students to assume productive roles in society.

Tracking may be found at both the elementary and secondary school levels. In the elementary school, students are divided into reading and mathematics ability groups quite early in the school experience.

---

1. For example, students who wish to attend the University of Minnesota will be required to have completed four years of English, three years of mathematics, three years of science, and two years of a single foreign language in high school. This is typical of the trend toward ever-increasing requirements for advanced study.

While movement in and out of groups may change during the year, different expectations are present for each group. Advocates of grouping suggest that these ability distinctions allow teachers to meet the individual needs of students with similar learning needs. Critics suggest that some students are branded early as being not as capable as others and receive a weaker education. During the secondary years, students are often guided into the traditional college preparation curriculum or the vocational track. This tracking has led to the establishment of a curriculum that has certain characteristics such as "practical versus academic," "lower achieving versus higher achieving," and so on.

Tracking systems are evident in most schools. The basic question for consideration at this point is, What are the implications for curriculum design and instructional strategies of a tracking educational policy versus a general education policy? What do you think?

► **Issue Two: Real versus Contrived Curriculum**

In preliterate societies all learning is "real" in the sense that children's play is merely rehearsal for such activities as hunting, gathering, and food preparation that make up daily life. All learning in such societies represents imitation of basic survival skills. Such imitation still exists today, for example, in the ritual play of youngsters who pretend to mow lawns, drive cars, and play house.

The formal school curriculum, however, has been designed to provide a separate reality from that of the home. It concentrates on academic skills and knowledge that are cumulative and increasingly complex. The purpose of the curriculum is to prepare the individual to cope with a sophisticated, complicated society. Many school experiences have little immediate use but are designed to pay off in the long run. The school curriculum often exists devoid of any context, save its own. For example, third graders practicing math do not apply the math in any way except in rare circumstances. They are taught how to perform an algorithm such as adding fractions, and are expected to practice what they are taught. Applications, except for a few "story problems," are not considered part of the process.

In this context the teacher must provide substance and structure. Paul Brandwein, an advocate of the formal approach, notes that the teacher provides the context and gives "the children experience — not random experience, which is endless, but experience that is in search of meaning" (1969).

There are those educators who argue that the formal curriculum organized around reading, math, English, science, history, and other disciplines is an incredibly inefficient means of teaching the young. Such critics suggest that teaching these subjects outside a context of real problems with real applications is largely wasted energy. Learning merely goes in one ear and out the other. The answer, of course, is to provide students with problems from real life and to teach them the skills and knowledge of the academic subjects in order to solve the problems. Thus, if students were to plan and maintain a garden or build a product, they would have endless reasons to use reading, math, science, and other subjects. This perspective is best represented by John Dewey who wrote:

> Abandon the notion of subject-matter as something fixed and ready-made in itself, outside the child's experience; cease thinking of the child's experience as something hard and fast; see it as something fluent, embryonic, vital; and we realize that the child and the curriculum are simply two limits which define a single process (Dewey, 1963, p. 6).

The formal curriculum and the instructional strategies used in schools are influenced by the tensions between these two positions. Throughout the history of education the popularity of each position has gained favor and then lost ground, although admittedly the center stage has been and is presently held by the formalists. The key question at this point is best stated in the following manner: Should the school curriculum be subject-centered or student-centered?

► Issue Three: Small versus Large Schools

How large should a school be? How many students should there be in a classroom? What role does size play in expediting or limiting the school-based learning experience? Although numerous attempts have been made over the years to answer these questions empirically, it may in fact be the case that these are philosophical or possibly economic questions. And because teaching and learning are interactive and dynamic by their very nature, it is difficult to isolate any given variable and successfully attribute larger scale effects (such as achievement) to it alone. Nevertheless, the issue is worth examining because opinions have ranged from one extreme to another over the past two decades.

In his book, *The American High School Today,* James B. Conant argued that a senior high school with a student body of fewer than 500 students simply could not offer the diversity of specialized faculty and material resources such as library and laboratory facilities needed to furnish a quality education for students entering a modern, complex society. This point of view was well received in the 1960s, a period during which more new schools were built in America than at any other time in the nation's history. To a great extent, schools were merely part of a social system that tended to equate bigger with better.

Consolidation became the byword, and the rural school almost disappeared from the map. Many small towns went together in pairs to build joint high schools. Whether in the case of the newly consolidated rural school or the newly racially integrated urban school, students began to spend more time traveling greater distances just to get to and from these larger educational structures. In the period from 1968 to 1978, for example, the St. Paul, Minnesota, Public Schools collapsed the number of their elementary schools from sixty-three neighborhood schools to nineteen newly constructed magnate/consolidated schools. Elementary school size in the district changed from an average student population of 300 or so to schools of 600 and more. This trend was typical of the changing pattern of school size across urban America.

But a turning of the tide occurred. Just as cities and corporations backed away from the bigger-is-better mentality, so did people looking at opportunities (rather, the lack of them) for student involvement and affiliation begin to question the wisdom of larger schools. More recently, research literature indicates a climate can exist for higher student achievement in smaller schools (Hawley and Rosenholtz, 1984; Walberg, 1984). Confounding the picture somewhat, however, is the fact that high-achieving Japanese elementary and secondary school classes often have from fifty to sixty students.

Noting that it is not impossible, but simply more difficult to have a good large school, Goodlad (1984) writes:

> What are the defensible reasons for operating an elementary school of more than a dozen teachers and 300 boys and girls? I can think of none. . . . I would not want to face the challenge of justifying a senior, let alone junior, high of more than 500 to 600 students. . . .

Whether or not the advocates of smaller schools will have an impact on educational policy cannot be determined at this time. Many factors are involved, including economics, athletics, and racial equity.

Size has implications for the quality of the formal curriculum and the various extracurricular activities such as sports and music programs. Size also relates to community identity and financial conditions. And, size of schools will be drastically influenced by such demographic factors as the growth and decline of student population. The key question for consideration at this time is stated in the following manner: What number of students is needed to ensure a quality school and education?

► **Issue Four: Graded versus Ungraded Curriculum**

In early America few people went to school. Those who did generally did not stay for very long. The exceptions to this were the children of the wealthy who were instructed by tutors. Under the tutorial system of learning, an individual commenced his or her education whenever it was deemed appropriate. The pace of the instruction varied with the individual and subject matter being studied. How many years of tutoring one received depended on one's potential and on the depth of study that seemed appropriate. Thus, one child's formal studies might vary by a length of several years from that of another child's.

As the national will extended to public-supported education for all young people, a tension developed as to how best to educate the young. A tutorial system could not be used because it would cost too much and there would not be enough tutors to teach all the students. Horace Mann, Henry Barnard, and other nineteenth-century educators favored the age-graded system of education that they had seen successfully employed in the German province of Prussia. By 1864 Chicago's superintendent of schools, William Wells, had divided all students in the school system into age-related grade levels. Needless to say, the age-graded system was used widely in the United States and continues to dominate public education, well more than a century later.

With the creation of age-related student groups and time schedules for determining how long a child must study a topic, fundamental differences rose between those who favored an ungraded system versus those who favored an ungraded, individualized curriculum.

Advocates of the graded system acknowledge the need for individualized efforts but contend that in order to ensure that all students receive an education, a more efficient system must be employed. Although the system is not perfect, children do develop in a similar manner, and if instruction is varied, individual differences can be accommodated.

Proponents of an ungraded curriculum suggest that individualized instruction is a much more effective way to enhance student achievement. They argue that most students spend too much of their time waiting, either because the material is too easy or too difficult. Three methods are usually suggested as viable alternatives: programmed instruction, computer-assisted instruction, and individualized educational plans (IEPs).

Programmed learning is a step-by-step, incremental learning process based on the reinforcement ideas of B. F. Skinner. Programmed learning modules take the learner through a series of readings, questions, and feedback activities. After a short reading, the learner is asked a series of questions and is given feedback on each answer. The small amounts of information are used to develop broader ideas or skills. Programmed instruction materials, however, have failed to achieve a significant niche in the school curriculum in spite of their seeming promise in the 1960s. Poorly written, austerely packaged, unimaginative materials, nearly exclusive reliance on print as a medium, and teachers unused to managing the educational environment contributed to its lack of success.

Technological advances have brought important changes to programmed instruction materials and have enhanced their potential for improved individualized instruction. Computer technology, for example, has allowed programmed instruction materials to become more interactive and more sophisticated in quality. Chapter 16 discusses the role of technology; it is sufficient here to say that the growth of programmed instruction via the computer has not yet made a significant impact on the schools.

A final strategy for individualization of instruction that has gained popularity is the Individualized Education Plan (IEP). IEPs are an integral part of Public Law 94–142 enacted in 1975 by the United States Congress. The intent of the law is to provide the "least restrictive environment" for learning in the case of handicapped students. IEPs are to include:

▶ the student's present educational achievement level
▶ appropriate educational goals for the student—both annual and short
▶ specification of special services to achieve or implement the goals
▶ the extent to which the handicapped student can be placed in a regular classroom
▶ an annual review of instructional goals, progress, and implementation plans

Advocates of individualized learning suggest that the use of IEPs in the regular classroom would provide significant changes in the manner in which students are educated, particularly in light of emerging information on learning styles and brain function.

The tensions between these two points of view are obvious. The question may be stated in the following manner: How much individualization is possible in a public school system that seeks to educate all students?

▶ **Issue Five: Professional versus Bureaucratic**

Whatever cynics might say, idealistic thought is a leading factor of choice for many who enter teaching. Teachers are, by definition, helping persons. They bring to their chosen career a desire to share their knowledge, skills, and values with students. Much of the reward structure is based on helping students learn. A teacher's day is typically one of interacting with students through modeling, motivating, exhorting, praising, and managing. Thus, good teaching involves leadership, determination, and continuous self-examination toward an overriding goal: student growth and development.

But this reality is viewed apart from the larger context of any given teacher's interaction with peers, administration, and the community. It is often the case that the larger reality is a reason why a disproportionate number of academically talented and apparently effective teachers leave the profession.

Kathy H., who left teaching for the business world after ten years in the classroom, stated:

> When I started teaching, I couldn't get enough of it. I'd get to school early and leave late. I took papers home to read on most nights. But I began to want out after my third year or so. I guess I had this idea of creative people working together to build happy lives for children. Instead of that, you hardly interact with adults at all. As far as sharing ideas, everyone seemed more interested in keeping them to themselves. The principals, I had three in ten years, seemed only to look at the management side of things. You could be teaching almost anything and as long as there was no noise or complaints, everything was fine with them. Excellence, which you hear about a lot today, was a term without meaning, and I doubt it still does. I know now that if I went back [into teaching], I'd want to be in a small school or a private school where each person, student, or teacher would have more influence. But even then, why work at a job where you're never rewarded or supported for being caring or creative or whatever?

This disillusioned teacher represents a single piece of the larger picture of those who leave teaching. In fact, research in longevity in the profession has shown that those who stay in teaching longest and who enjoy teaching the most are the least capable as measured by college grade point averages.

The question of what happens to early idealism is not unique to teaching, and it is not easy to trace any single reason that might apply across the board. One source of conflict, not unique to educational institutions, is that of bureaucracy versus professionalism.

Bureaucratic institutions are hierarchical structures. The hierarchy generally takes the form of a pyramid, with a few powerful people at or near the top and many less powerful people at the base. Figure 2-1 illustrates the bureaucratic layering of a typical school district.

A variety of alternatives have been proposed to the hierarchical structure of schools. Some advocate the use of quality circles where small groups (without regard to status) periodically meet to try to define and solve problems. Such an approach would provide a "flatter" struc-

FIGURE 2-1 Typical Bureaucratic Layering of a School District

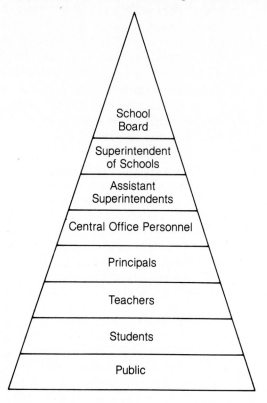

ture and would promote democracy in the schools' organizational environment. Others advocate a system of career ladders for teachers that permit a change in role during a teaching career. The goal, in either case, is to increase the professionalism of the teacher.

Adding to the tension are issues brought by national teacher organizations and society's demands for improvement in the quality of teaching and schooling. The question at this point is: What can be done to lessen the bureaucratic structure of the school?

► **Issue Six: Sources of Information–Uniform versus Varied**

The formal curriculum is composed of the specific planned instructional material and activities for students. The forum of the formal curriculum is the individual classroom where basic knowledge and skills are taught. The mainstay of the classroom is the textbook. In his book entitled *A Place Called School,* John Goodlad (1984) notes the importance of the textbook by writing:

Curricula continue to be determined largely by the editorial staffs of publishing houses and the subject matter specialists and writers chosen by them.

In addition to textbooks, curricular goals and objectives are usually formally prescribed by state guidelines and district goals. These materials provide additional sources of information for the teacher.

The reliance by most teachers on textbooks and, to a lesser extent, on state and district guides focuses the conflict between uniform sources of information and varied sources geared to the needs of individual students and locations.

Advocates of a uniform curriculum suggest that in a public school system all children need to have an opportunity to learn similar content and skills. They suggest there are basics in the curriculum that should be taught in much the same way in all schools. General education advocates point to the importance of having all students acquire fundamental knowledge and skills, and the best way to do that is to systematize the materials that are used in the classroom and to have similar goals across each discipline.

People who favor a systematic approach note two important points. First, they relate a story that goes something like the following:

> Carlos attends a large urban district. Half way through the semester, his parents moved to a different home in a nearby district and Carlos had to change schools. When Carlos attended his first social studies class, he found that instead of studying American history as in his other school, he now was studying world geography. He had studied world geography the year before and with a different textbook. Now, Carlos had to study geography again, but he would not get a chance to finish studying American history. How can students attending schools in different districts study different courses in the same year? Carlos's parents told the principal of the new school that they might just as well have moved across the country because the curriculum varied so much within the same state.

A uniform curriculum would avoid such problems, but individual differences need not be sacrificed merely because a uniform course of study exists. Schools and teachers could adjust materials to individual and community needs. Variation can exist to a considerable degree within a uniform curriculum. Advocates of a uniform curriculum say there is room for varied materials within any standardized curriculum but that standardization is one means of ensuring equal educational opportunity from region to region.

Those educators who favor the use of more varied materials contend that undue reliance on commercial textbooks and set curriculum guides leads to blandness and sterile learning. Critics of textbooks point to the commercial nature of texts. Commercial publishing companies exist to make money. In order to make money, companies must sell as many books as possible; therefore, large states such as Texas and California, where the textbook adoption stakes are the highest, often dictate to the whole country what should and should not appear in textbooks. Companies often avoid controversial issues and present bland, watered-down views of the world. Advocates of a more varied curriculum approach question the effectiveness of thirty students all reading the same two paragraphs from the same text on the Battle of Lexington. They suggest that it would be much better if everyone in the class read from different sources. Students in today's information age need to realize early in their scholarly career that a wide range of information is available for the study of almost any subject.

Tensions are created when the goals of a mass education system interact with the needs of individuals. The question is: What techniques can be used to bring about an appropriate level of curricular uniformity (indeed, what is an appropriate level?) in such a way that the unique needs of individuals and local communities are not sacrificed?

CASE STUDIES IN CURRICULUM

▶ Our intent in bringing these issues to your attention is to present some of the underlying complexities of the curriculum. These issues, however they are resolved from community to community and across the nation, represent the heart and soul of the school curriculum. We will press the issues a little farther by turning to three case studies that are designed to bring life to otherwise abstract philosophical positions. These case studies are the Boston, Massachusetts, plan for school desegregation; the South East Alternatives Curriculum Program of the Minneapolis, Minnesota, Public Schools; and the decision of the California State Board of Education not to adopt any of a group of recommended biology textbooks. As you read the case studies, apply them to the dilemmas we have just posed. Also, think of applications of curricular philosophical viewpoints within your own sphere of experience and influence.

Each of these cases describes a decision or series of decisions that led to some contention between at least two of the parties in the case. Sometimes the dispute in the case involves sweeping social issues, at other times the events are less monumental. All of the events in the cases are real; nothing has been altered. We offer these cases in their social milieu to demonstrate that most curriculum decision making involves issues that are more complicated than any abstract description could capture.

► Obtaining Racial Balance in the Boston Schools[2]

For most of the course of American educational history, the Boston schools were at the forefront of educational reform and innovation. Renowned as the site of the first publically supported secondary school, and the home of Horace Mann, the Boston schools in the mid-1960s seemed secure and immune from many of the problems that plagued most public school systems, when suddenly they were plunged into the midst of a crisis.

Throughout 1964 and the early part of 1965, a committee appointed by the Massachusetts legislature had been at work investigating racial imbalance in the Boston schools. In April 1965 their final report revealed a rigidly segregated school system where half of the black pupils attended twenty-eight schools that were at least 80 percent black. In addition, the report found that sixteen schools in the heart of the black community were 96 percent black. Maintaining that racial imbalance does serious damage to all children, the authors of the report began by encouraging legislation to compel the Boston schools to eliminate the racial imbalance and proceeded to recommend a series of specific steps to remedy the segregation. These recommendations included open enrollment programs, the closing of some extremely segregated schools and their relocation at sites chosen to promote integration, and the exchange of students between their school buildings.

Although the evidence of segregation seemed incontrovertible, within hours of the release of the report, the Boston school committee rejected it, contending that the report was the "pompous proclamation of the uninformed," and that it proposed actions that were "undemocratic, un-American, absurdly expensive, and diametrically opposed to the wishes of the parents of the city." The school committee claimed that they represented the will of the people and were determined to resist any attempt to alter the composition of the Boston schools.

The Massachusetts legislature responded by quickly passing a bill outlawing school segregation. For the next nine years, the Boston school committee and the Massachusetts legislature found themselves engaged in an intricate joust where each attempt by the legislature to enforce its decree was parried by a counterthrust in the form of a lawsuit from the Boston school committee.

2. The information in this case study was derived from the following sources: J. Anthony Lukas, *Common Ground: A Turbulent Decade in the Lives of Three American Families* (New York: Alfred A. Knopf, 1985); Robert Dentler and Marvin Scott, *Schools on Trial: An Inside Account of the Boston Desegregation Case* (Cambridge, Mass.: Abt Books, 1981); and Geraldine Kozberg, personal conversation, June 1986.

This impasse ended abruptly in April 1974 when an all-day rally took place where 25,000 supporters of repeal paraded across the Boston Commons, waving banners with slogans like "No Forced Busing" and "Down with Unjust Laws" while chanting "Never! Never!" In June 1974 the state legislature, influenced by the public outcry and the frequent delays surrounding the enforcement of the Racial Imbalance Act, reconsidered their earlier decision and voted to repeal the Racial Imbalance Act that they had passed in 1965.

The Massachusetts governor quickly vetoed the repeal of the Racial Imbalance Act, but in the statement explaining his decision, he shocked his supporters by revealing that he intended to replace the old law with one that employed voluntary and "freedom of choice" measures to obtain integrated schools. Even the most die-hard integrationists realized that the Massachusetts government would no longer energetically foster racial integration. This left the supporters of integration with a single option—the federal courts.

The case that entered the federal court, representing fifty-three black plaintiffs as a "class," became *Tallulah Morgan* vs. *James Hennigan* (after one of the plaintiffs and the chairperson of the school committee). The plaintiffs' argument contended that racial imbalance in the Boston schools was not accidental and innocent; rather, it had been purposefully reinforced and maintained over the years by the Boston school committee through such techniques as manipulated district lines, site selection policies, and other pupil assignment practices. The plaintiffs attempted to make their case from verbatim stenographic accounts of school committee meetings where the segregationist techniques were introduced and explicated. Judge W. Arthur Garrity, Jr., found that the Boston school committee had violated the constitutional rights of the plaintiff class.

To compensate for the violation of the black students' constitutional rights, Judge Garrity required the school committee to present a comprehensive plan outlining their segregation policies by December 1974. The school committee selected an administrator to write a desegregation plan. When he submitted the plan, the committee promptly rejected it because it involved a busing stipulation. Arguing that the school committee was unable to develop a workable plan, Judge Garrity moved to take control of the Boston public schools.

In this unprecedented role, Garrity appointed a team of experts to assist him and charged them to gather evidence from public hearings and then write a desegretation plan. In May 1975 the experts' plan was put into effect.

Almost immediately, the attempt to integrate South Boston High School produced a series of riots. Each morning the school buses from black neighborhoods arrived amidst a hail of stones and bricks. Inside the school, the situation was equally grim, with assaults and planned disturbances occurring with monotonous regularity.

Judge Garrity responded by placing the school into receivership, which meant that for the first time a federal court had taken over both the administration and the responsibility for the day-to-day operation of an American public school. Garrity's three administrators began to reconstruct the teaching and learning at South Boston High. They abolished the rigid course schedule, replacing it with a variety of programs created to generate student-centered learning activities, established an arts program, and formed a school within a school. Later the new administrators developed programs that enabled students to move beyond the confines of the school, desegregated most athletic teams, and created new team sports for girls. Garrity himself transferred some of the most overtly racist teachers to other Boston schools.

As the new programs took hold, student altercations declined, and the two holding rooms for suspended students were converted into a snack room. After a time, even the school buses began to arrive in relative safety.

Two of Garrity's experts—both professors of education—claimed that what finally changed the school was:

> The injection of a fundamentally different approach to curriculum and instruction, an approach that seriously considered the needs and expressed interests of the students and their teachers (Dentler and Scott, 1981, p. 179).

This case of "Obtaining Racial Balance" underscores several important questions about the curriculum decision-making process:

1. How do we determine whose values are likely to dominate the school curriculum?
2. Should the school curriculum be an agency that maintains society or should the curriculum try to change society? Why?
3. What kind of painful dislocations are likely to result from curriculum changes?
4. Are conflicts and clashes the only way that the curriculum can change?
5. What are the central values that school curriculum rests upon?
6. In what ways does the school curriculum shape who gets what, when, and how in American society?

The previous case asked whether the citizens of Boston had the right to decide fundamental issues of curriculum for themselves. This second case takes a somewhat different tack.

▶ How to Start an Open School[3]

Reform was in the air in Southeast Minneapolis, Minnesota, in the fall of 1970. Starting with a series of evening meetings organized by mothers from a cooperative nursery school, separate groups of parents from the neighborhoods around the University of Minnesota began pressuring the Minneapolis school board to provide an open school alternative to the curriculum programs currently available to their children.

After all, the parents reasoned, the time was ripe for innovation as each of the five public schools in "Southeast" experimented with some new programs ranging from two schools paired for desegregation to an ungraded "continuous progress" program in a third elementary school. The change had been even more dramatic in the area's single secondary school. After merging with the University's laboratory school, the combined school had enlisted community involvement by establishing a board to help administer the new organization, installed "a school without walls" to accommodate the more rebellious members of the student body, and began efforts to attract students from outside the area to their "magnet" program. The parents argued that open education programs should be available to elementary students as well.

The ideas inherent in open education were not new, but in the experimentally fertile soil of this time the loose bundle of ideas came together into a clearly identifiable ideology—often at odds with traditional public educational programs.

According to one observer of open education programs, the ideology has several key issues: the teacher is a facilitator and experimenter; children are organized to work in interest groups; ungraded classrooms where students are expected to learn as much from older students as their teachers prevail; there is a wide variety of instructional materials; and rigid schedules, fixed periods, and bells are abolished. Overarching all other ideas in the open school ideology is the presumption that the pupils, however young, should make their own decisions (Lukas, 1985, p. 331).

In many instances, pleas for open programs are not well received by educators. This was not the case in Southeast where several teachers were already moving in this direction.

---

3. The information in this case study was derived from the following sources: Anthony J. Morley, *Southeast Alternatives: The Final Report* (Minneapolis, Minn.: Minneapolis Public Schools, 1976); Elizabeth Mason Mackey, personal conversation, June 1986; and J. Anthony Lukas, *Common Ground: A Turbulent Decade in the Lives of Three American Families* (New York: Alfred A. Knopf, 1985).

Generally speaking, the superintendent felt that attempts to solve educational problems are undertaken in either a piecemeal fashion or as a part of some fad. He believed that muddling through was often inefficient because the effect on the overall learning environment was difficult to locate.

The more the school officials discussed their plan, the stronger it appeared. The superintendent, in particular, was convinced that significant renewal would come only from risking new approaches and applying research findings on a fairly large scale. The superintendent encouraged the Southeast parents, telling them that he would provide support in every way he could.

Through the remainder of the winter and the spring, the preliminary planning for the open school moved steadily forward. When school concluded in June, the pace quickened. By the fall, the planners intended to have an open school in operation.

The principal and the teachers, working closely with several of the concerned parents' groups, began constructing the new roles and changed environment that an open school required. Sometimes the ideas came from the plan originally developed by the concerned parents. More frequently, the new pedagogical format sprung out of the imagination and experience of the classroom teachers. Throughout the summer, these plans were systematically examined, and either revised or cast aside. The common sense of both teachers and parents often seasoned the original idea.

Early in their curriculum development, the group realized that the new rules and the presence of many parents in the building necessitated new communication patterns. As a remedy, the group conducted ten sessions to practice new patterns among themselves. When the planners grew frustrated with the one-shot consultants, they rented a bus and visited an ongoing open school. Although this was more useful, what proved to be most helpful to the teachers was the three-week pilot school they ran for themselves in the middle of the summer, which gave them some concrete experience.

As summer ended, and school opening loomed, the open school people were worried that they weren't fully prepared, yet they approached the new school term with excitement and guarded confidence.

The case of "Starting an Open School" raises several questions about the process of curriculum change:

1. How can individual citizens influence the school curriculum? Can they contribute to the way a school system is organized?
2. What is the key curriculum value that underlies the parents' behavior in this case? What do the parents want from their schools?
3. What methods do teachers use to change the curriculum? Do they seem to prefer action to theory in their curriculum change activity?

4. How does the curriculum change in this case differ from the change process in the Boston school case?
5. How can principals and teachers enlist parents' interest in the school without giving them control of the curriculum?
6. Critics of American education, and some teachers, claim that teachers have little responsibility for the conditions of their working lives. Did anything happen in this case that changed this circumstance?

Teaching that depends primarily upon a textbook was known as the "American system" in the nineteenth century. Schools relied on textbooks because there were few well-trained teachers in the rapidly growing country. The conventional wisdom held that even an ill-trained teacher could prosper if he or she followed a comprehensive textbook.

Social conditions and teacher training have changed in this century, but the school's dependence on the textbook remains, and texts continue to be the most important window through which American students view their subject matter. In this case study we describe a textbook controversy in California and ask some questions about textbook adoption. How are textbooks selected? Who are the most important agents in the process of textbook selection? In the final analysis, how do textbooks influence the curriculum?

▶ How to Make Textbooks Smarter[4]

On September 13, 1985, in Sacramento, the California Board of Education rejected every science textbook submitted for use in the seventh- and eighth-grade curriculum, claiming that the books inadequately depicted evolution and human reproduction. The board's decision was not a complete surprise to the citizens of California because at every step in the state's adoption process there had been ominous rumblings of dissatisfaction.

Not all states have a formal textbook adoption process, but the two largest purchasers—Texas and California—do, and they have a booming voice in the process which strongly affects all the others. The statewide adoption process that is probably the biggest influence in shaping textbooks for good or ill is used by twenty-two states. In the adoption states, a single office does the textbook buying for all the school districts in the state.

---

4. The information in this case study was derived from the following sources: Elizabeth Fernandez, "New Science Texts Flunk Initial Review State Likely to Order Changes," *Sacramento Bee*, August 23, 1985, p. A01; Elizabeth Fernandez, "Honig Hails Common Goal Says Private, Public Schools Serve Knowledge," *Sacramento Bee*, August 23, 1985, p. B4; and Keith Henderson, "California—A State with Clout—Speaks Up on Textbook Quality," *The Christian Science Monitor*, October 24, 1985, p. B4.

In California, the adoption process is complex, including suggestions from the education field and the public. According to Francie Alexander, head of textbook development for California, the process has three essential parts: First, a citizen panel appointed by the state board checks the "social content"; for example, how women and ethnic groups are represented. Next, various experts are recruited to examine the textbooks for each subject area and present their results to the Curriculum Development Commission which assesses the educational quality of the books (Henderson, October 24, 1985). Throughout, the public is given the opportunity to review the texts at instructional materials display centers scattered throughout the state. Finally, decisions about textbooks are made at public hearings held by the State Board of Education.

At its September 1985 meeting, the state board, in a strongly worded opinion, rejected all the science books under consideration, claiming that they had been "dumbed down." Bill Honig, the State Superintendent of Public Instruction, said that the science books were too superficial and too bland. "Because evolution is controversial, I think the publishing companies tried to duck it," Honig said.

> Superintendent Honig went on to assert that: . . . science is a great story. If you're going to teach the theory of evolution, you've got to explain the theory itself—the evidence. Darwin going to the islands *[sic]*. You've got to give it flesh and blood. From these books, you wouldn't have any idea of what it's about. They have to come up to standards or we're not going to allow them in California (Fernandez, October 26, 1985).

The state board's decision, coupled with the fact that California's 1,029 school districts must spend at least 80 percent of their instructional funds from the state on state-adopted books, demonstrates the power of the education board with the major publishing companies. Alexander said, "It has been the state's experience that, when a publisher is faced with the choice of changing their texts to make them marketable to the state public schools or not changing them and losing that market, the changes will be made."

Although the media portrayed the state board's decision as yet another skirmish in the seemingly endless battle with religious fundamentalists over creationism, Superintendent Honig, a month later in an address to the Association of Christian Schools International, stressed that quality education was the issue, not religion. During his talk, Honig stated:

> We may disagree about evolutionism versus creationism, but it's crucial that we give our young people a realistic view of the world. When we see a narrow curriculum, reduced curriculum, we are putting our young people at a tremendous disadvantage (quoted in Fernandez, October 26, 1987).

Soon after this textbook rejection, the California case became a national example as editorials and articles nationwide praised the California State Board's insistence on academic excellence for students.

This case of "Smarter Textbooks" shows several important questions about curriculum change:

1. Who are the various groups that contribute to the context and format of school textbooks?
2. What kinds of controversies are likely to erupt over textbooks?
3. How are these controversies settled? Are there specific mechanisms to accomplish this conflict resolution?
4. Does any one group have a disproportionate influence in the textbook selection process?

These case studies depict three paramount social influences upon the American school curriculum. From the involvement of federal courts in the Boston schools, to the state decision of California, to the stubborn insistence on curricular alternatives by a group of teachers and parents in Southeast Minneapolis, one catches a glimpse of how social values shape the curriculum of American schools.

SUMMARY

▶ This chapter described some crucial issues that influence the school curriculum. We employed a dialectial technique to present these issues. The six dualisms raised several important questions. The first asked if school curriculum should aim at providing high-quality education for everyone or should it teach students according to their abilities. The second speculated about whether process or product is more essential to a successful school curriculum. The third wondered if it is possible to promote equality in large school organizations. The fourth examined curriculum policies that permitted students to move through school at their own pace and asked whether this is a sound curriculum policy. The fifth, dualism, investigated whether increasingly bureaucratic school structure produces more effective teaching and learning. The sixth asked if it is possible to develop a school curriculum that meets the needs of all American youth simultaneously.

As a means of bringing these somewhat abstract curriculum issues into sharper focus, the second half of the chapter presented three case studies that illustrated curriculum decision making. These cases, which concerned global curriculum issues, were presented to demonstrate that, in the final analysis, curriculum is a product of the American public's deliberate values choice. These values choices are often untidy and frequently filled with conflict. The next chapter examines the most important agents in the school curriculum process—the teachers.

ACTIVITIES

1. Identify and clarify a controversial issue that will have an impact on the curriculum of the schools in your own community.
2. To what extent is educational experimentalism alive today? Do a sufficient number of curricular/instructional alternatives exist in your opinion?
3. How are the controversial issues addressed in this chapter treated in other nations, for example, Japan, England, and Canada?
4. Given the harsh measure of criticism that school textbooks continue to receive, what do you think needs to be done to improve them?

REFERENCES

Berliner, D. C. (1984). The half-full glass: A review of research on teaching. In P. L. Hosford, *Using what we know about teaching*. Alexandria, Va.: Association for Supervision and Curriculum Development.

Brandwein, P. (1969). *Toward a discipline of responsible consent.* New York: Harcourt, Brace, Jovanovich.

Conant, J. B. (1959). *The American high school today: A first report to interested citizens.* New York: McGraw-Hill.

Dentler, R., and Scott, M. (1981). *Schools on trial: An inside account of the Boston desegregation case.* Cambridge, Mass.: Abt Books.

Dewey, J. (1963). *Experience and education.* New York: Collier.

Ellis, A. K.; Cogan, J. J.; and Howey, K. R. (1986). *Introduction to the foundation of education* (2nd ed.). Englewood Cliffs, N.J.: Prentice-Hall.

Fernandez, E. (October 26, 1985). Honig hails common goals—Says private, public schools serve knowledge. *Sacramento Bee.*

Goodlad, J. I. (1984). *A place called school.* New York: McGraw-Hill.

Hawley, W., and Rosenholtz, S. (1984). Good schools: What research says about improving student achievement. *Peabody Journal of Education, 61,* 4.

Henderson, K. (October 24, 1985). California—A state with clout—Speaks up on textbook quality. *The Christian Science Monitor,* p. B4.

Lucas J. A. (1985). *Common ground: A turbulent decade in the lives of three American families.* New York: Alfred A. Knopf.

Trachtenberg, D. (1974). Student tasks in text material: What cognitive skills do they tap? *Peabody Journal of Education, 52* (1), 54–57.

Walberg, H. J. (1984). Improving the productivity of America's schools. *Educational Leadership, 41,* 19–27.

SUGGESTED READINGS

Boyd, W. L. (1978). The changing politics of curriculum policy-making for American schools. *Review of Educational Research, 48,* 577–628.

Britzman, D. P. (November 1968). Cultural myths in the making of a teacher: Biography and social structure in teacher education. *Harvard Educational Review, 56,* 442–456.

Koerner, J. (1968). *Who controls American education?* Boston: Beacon Press.

Lukas, J. A. (1985). *Common ground: A turbulent decade in the lives of three American families.* New York: Alfred A. Knopf.

Tyack, D. B. (1974). *The one best system: A history of American urban education.* Cambridge, Mass.: Harvard University.

Rosenholtz, S. J. (January 1985). Political myths about educational reform: Lessons from research on teching. *Phi Delta Kappan, 66,* 349–355.

3
The Social Context of Teachers' Curriculum Decisions

OVERVIEW

▶ This chapter sketches a profile of those individuals responsible for orchestrating the school curriculum—the American classroom teachers. The following account employs a description of the workday week of a hypothetical teacher to set the stage for an examination of classrooms in general, and then presents a demographic portrait of American teachers.

After outlining a general picture that contends that the quest for efficiency that dominates the contemporary school scene has caused a reduction in teacher's freedom of choice, subsequent sections detail some of the social forces that influence teachers, examine the sources of teachers' rewards, and delve into the processes of teacher selection and socialization.

A PROFILE OF AMERICAN TEACHERS

▶ At 4:30 P.M. on a wintry Friday afternoon, a forty-one-year-old woman loaded down with books and papers trudged toward her car in the teachers' parking lot of an elementary school. Reshuffling her load, she searched for her car keys, opened the door, threw the papers in the backseat and let out an involuntary sigh.

Nearly twenty years after she began her teaching career, Michelle Comstock had completed yet another week of teaching filled with frustration, accomplishment, cynicism, and hope.

During the familiar route home, Michelle replayed in her mind the week that had just passed. In addition to the typical Monday blues, the first day of the week presented an unexpected challenge to Michelle.

Early that morning, her principal had appeared in her doorway and asked if she would consent to adding Ted to her class list. Ted was a small, exotic-looking boy who had arrived at the beginning of the school year. Since his arrival, Ted had become notorious for his ability to disrupt classroom order. He repeatedly picked fights in class and ruined the papers and products of his fellow classmates. When confronted about misbehavior, Ted's predictable response was the violent tantrum that included kicking and throwing furniture. The boy's mother admitted that she was virtually powerless in controlling Ted's outbursts and begged the school to help her control him.

Now sheepishly the principal implored Michelle to take on Ted. "You do this so well," he claimed. "You're so good with these kinds of kids." Michelle responded to the challenge, and not knowing how to decline, agreed to let Ted join her class. For the first two days there were no incidents, and on the third day Ted had been absent. But on Friday the trouble began, and Ted's behavior had become inappropriate. In correcting Ted, Michelle had gotten angry and shouted at him. She had felt ashamed. Over the weekend Michelle knew that she must devise a plan for dealing with Ted or risk having a seriously disrupted classroom.

On Wednesday a second troubling incident occurred without warning. Michelle had asked her student teacher to tutor a student in the small anteroom she shared with Dina, the teacher in the room adjacent to her own. Carelessly, Michelle had forgotten the carefully negotiated schedule she had worked out with Dina. Even so, Michelle was both embarrassed and angry when Dina stormed into her room to inform her of the error. The incident had chilled the interaction between the long-time associates. Dina's diatribe made Michelle very uncomfortable.

As her mind drifted to another topic, Michelle recalled that in recent weeks, she had been plagued by the nagging feeling that there must be an effective pedagogical tool to teach the idea of borrowing in math. Although she felt that most of her pupils learned the algorithms, they did it mechanically. Most of them seemed unaware of what they were actually doing.

At educational conferences when she tried to discuss her problem with mathematics educators, they either seemed uninterested or unable to comprehend her problem. By and large, she felt, they were more interested in how children reasoned about the content of mathematics and less interested in basic classroom teaching problems and they were completely unable to take the position of the child. Still, Michelle wished that she could devise some instructional tactic to make the ideas underlying the concept of borrowing clearer to her pupils.

As Michelle approached the turnoff leading to her street, she smiled as she remembered how well a recent class project had gone. This year she resolved to make her students' oral reports worthwhile. To that end she devised a method to make the reports a game, limited them to five minutes in length, and constructed a gong that resembled the one used on the old "Gong Show."

Students were drilled in ways of presenting information, encouraged to be succinct, and cautioned against the use of tired phrases like "you know" and "he was sittin' there" and other slang that ordinarily peppered their speech patterns, and finally, they were told that if they were really long-winded, they might be gonged into silence.

Most of Michelle's pupils had responded magnificently. They seemed to enjoy the game-like situation and more appeared to have actually read the assigned books than was generally the case. Michelle remembered other surges of pleasure she had when she felt that she had reached her students and they had learned. Nothing that she could think of in teaching gave her more pure satisfaction.

As she pulled into her driveway, Michelle was still smiling, and remembered that she had forgotten to go to the Thank-God-It's-Friday meeting sponsored by her teachers' association.

Michelle's week is typical of what professional life is like for nearly 2,000,000 people that make up the teaching profession in the United States. Who are these individuals? What kinds of general statements can we make about American teachers?

Two-thirds of the teachers that comprise the faculties of our nation's 16,000 schools are women. The majority of the teacher work force are women, but there is a great difference in their representation in the various types of schools. Although 85 percent of America's elementary teachers are women, only 38 percent of high-school staffs are female. According to the *Metropolitan Life Survey of the American Teacher* (Harris, 1984), the average American teacher is nearly forty-one years of age, making him or her about five years older than the typical American worker. About one-quarter of teachers are under thirty-five years of age, and only 1 percent are under age twenty-five.

Nearly half (48 percent) of all teachers have taught for at least fifteen years. Some 78 percent of the teachers belong to a teachers' organization. As a group, teachers are hardworking, with the average teacher reporting that he or she spends nearly fifty hours a week either teaching or preparing to teach. The average teacher receives slightly over $23,000, with a median household income of the American teacher being $30,000, which is approximately the same as the average American college graduate's household (Friendly, 1985). Unfortunately, in the last decade, teachers' incomes, when compared to comparable professions, has declined 13.7 percent, while other college-trained occupations have increased 17 percent.

Thus, while teachers' salaries are no longer meager, the income of teachers has declined against every other occupation. The dramatic decline in teachers' income is illustrated in recent a study that found:

In absolute terms the purchasing power of the average annual salary for teachers peaked in 1972–73 but declined thereafter; by 1979–80 the average teacher had lost more than $1,000 in real purchasing power. To take another measure, the ratio of the average teacher salary to the "intermediate family budget" (as set forth by the Department of Labor) declined steadily from its high point to 88.9% in 1972–73 to 78% in 1979–80. Likewise, a recent study comparing teachers' salaries with those of all production workers and specifically with steelworkers and auto workers found that differentials had shrunk steadily through the seventies so that the salary advantage that teachers enjoyed in the early seventies had disappeared by 1978. Even in comparison to other full-time state and local government employees, teachers' salary advantage had shrunk from 25% in 1971 to 19.5% in 1978 (Sykes, 1983, p. 92).

As a group, teachers appear to be receptive to changes and reforms in their profession. The Metropolitan Survey shows that 97 percent favor a renewed emphasis on such basics as reading, writing, and mathematics. A vast majority are also in favor of broadening the curriculum to include such areas as computer literacy and more foreign language instruction. In addition, teachers overwhelmingly support giving outstanding students special incentives, establishing minimum competency for graduation, and devising ways to fire incompetent teachers.

Most teachers strongly favor trends toward increased professionalism. Almost all are willing to have their performance evaluated by administrators. The vast majority accept peer evaluation, and a majority even accept the somewhat controversial use of standardized tests of student skills as a means of evaluating teacher performance. Louis Harris, who conducted the 1984 Metropolitan Life's national survey of American teachers, claims that his report "depicts a group of serious professionals, not wedded to the status quo, and willing to make personal sacrifices to improve the quality of education" (Harris, 1984, p. 3). Harris goes on to say, "A question that must be raised is whether the rest of the country—school administrators, parents, politicians, national leaders, and others—is willing to take the challenge laid down by teachers to meet new standards of excellence and accountability."

Harris's comment graphically documents the contradictory tendencies that have vividly stood out throughout the entire period of American educational history. No other country has verbally committed so much to its schools for so long, yet no other has been so resolute in its refusal to financially support its schools in the manner that is needed.

In many ways, the unwillingness of Americans to extend their respect to teachers and the teaching profession is at the heart of the educational estate's most crucial dilemma—the large-scale retreat of competent and capable men and women from teaching. What began as a trickle has become a flood that threatens to erode the teaching enterprise. Nowhere is this attitude toward their work illustrated better than in the amazing declaration of 36 percent of the teachers in the Harris survey, who contended that they would probably not select teaching as a career if they had it to do again. This refusal is five times greater than the number of teachers who responded similarly twenty years ago. Thus, throughout the entire American teaching profession, this kind of dissatisfaction and regret is increasing exponentially.

Although there are many reasons for teachers' dissatisfaction, among the more significant are plunging public respect for teaching, widespread dissatisfaction with teacher training, declining salaries, and the growing necessity to devote time to administrative duties (Kirst, 1984).

Unlike most professions, where those who depart are apt to be individuals who are either poorly prepared or ill suited to the profession, dropouts from teaching tend to be among the most talented. At least half leave after only seven years, and it is the most academically able who are most likely to leave. Michael Kirst cites a North Carolina study that cites "teachers earning higher scores on the National Teachers Examination are almost twice as likely to leave teaching than all others who have been teaching the same length of time" (1985, p. 146).

As a means of illustrating this dilemma, witness the following:

> In the fall of 1984, as a segment of an American Broadcasting Company television special entitled "To Save Our Schools, to Save Our Students," three teachers who had expressed a desire to leave teaching were profiled. The story of Rex Thomas, a twenty-five-year veteran of teaching at Monroe High School in Los Angeles was especially poignant. Like our hypothetical teacher, Michelle Comstock, Thomas's story is also illustrative of several general characteristics of those who leave teaching.
>
> Thomas, a stocky, energetic, and demonstrably creative history teacher, claimed, "If I were to start my life over again as to a career, I would not ever consider teaching." Later in the interview Thomas asserts, "I have two sons of my own and I have threatened them that if they ever consider education, I would disown them." The tragedy of Mr. Thomas's case is not that he is a bitter burnt-out case, but rather that this vital man who is, from all evidence, at the peak of his power, is leaving the teaching profession.
>
> As evidence of Thomas's teaching prowess, we see him teaching a riveting lesson on witness identification. His virtuosity in the classroom is clearly irrefutable. Yet the delights of teaching for Thomas have paled as he is increasingly overcome by the sense of defeat that is driving him away. More and more, he claims that he returns home each evening and asks himself, "Did I do anything or was I just a clerk occupying space?"

THE WORKADAY WORLD OF CLASSROOM TEACHERS

 We have just painted a portrait of those who make up the teaching profession and have shown how some feel about their chosen career.

Now let us look a bit more closely at some of the day-to-day considerations of all teachers—thinking about their work, planning their lessons, and dealing with behavior problems. We will draw heavily from recent studies that have shed much light on the workaday world of the public schools.

How do teachers plan for their work? At first blush, this appears to be a difficult question. There are, after all, over two million American teachers working in a variety of instructional settings. Yet research from a variety of orientations reveals that there are predictable paths down which teachers proceed when they work at teaching. In one of the earliest studies of teacher behavior, Dan Lortie, a sociologist at the University of Chicago, attempted to discover the beliefs that undergird teachers' behavior (1967). He did this by employing an imaginative construction which argued that if we know what makes a teacher ashamed, we can develop an understanding of the day-to-day operation of the public schools.

▶ Teachers' Shame

Lortie's inquiry, part of a larger study, employed a single question. He asked teachers, "Most of us have some occasions, hopefully rare, when we feel ashamed about something we have done. What kinds of things have happened which you regretted having done?" (Lortie, 1967, p. 158). Lortie then sought to explore what he termed the negative end of the moral spectrum, calculating that if he could locate behavior that made teachers ashamed, he would learn their belief systems.

We begin our examination of a somewhat negative account for three distinct reasons: Lortie has produced a report of pristine clarity; the subject matter is dramatic; and, most importantly, error analysis has a rich heritage in social scientific research, dating back to the early work of Jean Piaget.

At first Lortie's question appears amorphous, guaranteed to yield a wide variety of idiosyncratic responses, but in the study the question allowed Lortie to obtain a serendipitous result. His striking finding was that one response category—behavior involving anger—contained the majority of teacher answers. Angry behavior, mainly involving verbal atacks of one kind or another on students, made teachers ashamed more than any other of their remembered behaviors. In fact, anger was mentioned by four times as many teachers as the next two "shame" producers, behavior connected with disciplining action and inadequacies in instruction.

Lortie reasoned that teachers strongly regret their anger because it affects the most vital point of contact in their work—the quality of their relationships with pupils. Angry behavior, teachers feel, "threatens prestige and thus their leadership role, causes students to draw away from them, and it may disrupt weeks of careful work or close out the possibility of further rapport" (Lortie, 1967, p. 163).

Teachers feel remorse over anger because they view their anger as destructive and are ashamed because of the trouble that they have brought upon themselves. Their ideology is captured in the words of a teacher who had a belligerent but popular boy expelled from her class. After the expulsion, the teacher said:

> That class would do nothing for me. They didn't know the whole story either and he was a leader to them. From that time on they just sat. They wouldn't ask a question. They wouldn't speak to me. That went on for the rest of the year which was a couple of months (Lortie, 1967, p. 170).

But there is more to the teacher's commitment than pragmatic considerations. There is a deeply held moral position that is a much more important basis for teacher behavior. Lortie found this in a set of beliefs he called "norms of client responsibility." Simply put, this means that the teacher realized that she is involved in an unequal relationship with her pupils who essentially have no way of transcending unfair or arbitrary behavior, and thus, the teacher has two distinct responsibilities: (1) to behave in a just fashion, and (2) to never use her authority in a way that hurts or harms her charges. You may recall how ashamed Michelle felt after she shouted at her problem student. Losing one's temper in the midst of teaching is seen as more than bad form, it is perceived by most teachers as a violation of a trust.

That all of these themes have become part of America's folklore of teachers is evidenced by an incident on the syndicated television program "The White Shadow." Ken Reeves, the white basketball coach at a largely black school, has had generally good relationships with his players. Into this generally harmonious atmosphere enters a transfer student named Marcus who tries out for the basketball team. Although Marcus is tall, burly, and talented, Reeves feels compelled to cut him from the team because he is a source of constant disruption. Marcus leaves the team apparently unconcerned, but his pattern of belligerent behavior continues.

One day Reeves, alone in the gym waiting for his players, encounters Marcus. They exchange bitter words. As Reeves turns to walk away from the acrimonious exchange, Marcus strikes him in the face, knocking him to the gym floor. With Marcus looming over him, seemingly ready to renew the attack, Reeves stumbles to his feet and returns the blow. Because he is very large, very skilled, and extremely angry at Marcus's punch, the fight is quickly over. As his players enter the gym, Reeves is seen taking Marcus to the principal's office.

The remainder of the program focuses on the aftermath of the fight. Even though Reeves was merely defending himself from a vicious attack, he is racked by self-recrimination and shame. In his mind, there is never a justifiable reason for striking a pupil, and he has abused his responsibility. Reeves's great inner turmoil is compounded by the withdrawal of his players' allegiance. Even though each of them had an unpleasant encounter with Marcus, they retreat from their coach. The players cannot accept Reeves's violation of his responsibility. Even though Reeves's fellow teachers vocally support his behavior, and tell him that he did the right thing, they too retreat from him as if they are ashamed for him.

In the end, in the way of television programs, there is a clear resolution to the problem as Marcus is apprehended while attempting to rape a female teacher and is taken off to jail. In the teachers' world, however, the resolution is always more tenuous and the aftereffects of the incident linger.

These kinds of incidents have a profound effect because teachers believe that reaching students is the key to teaching. In the incident we have just described, Ken Reeves did not reach Marcus, and he feels that he has failed.

▶ Teachers' Rewards

Now that we have examined the negative end of the teachers' moral spectrum, let us consider the kinds of rewards that teachers obtain from teaching.

Quickly we find teaching to be a diverse and contradictory occupation. Although teachers are public employees enmeshed in school systems that are monolithic, hierarchical, and concentrated, in the most important aspects of their role teachers have great autonomy. They possess this freedom because, by and large, their most important rewards come from the small universe of their classrooms.

According to another set of Lortie studies, there are three kinds of rewards available to teachers: external, ancillary, and intrinsic. External rewards, such as money, prestige, and power, are present in such low valence in teaching that they are not important to most teachers. Ancillary rewards, such as security, the work calendar, and the physical environment, are quickly taken for granted by teachers once they secure a position. It is the third classification, intrinsic rewards, that is important to teachers. Intrinsic rewards result from interactions with students and hence are subjective and idiosyncratic. Varied as they are, Lortie found that for 86 percent of the over 3,000 teachers in his studies, the single most important reward teachers mention is "knowing that I have 'reached' students and they have learned" (Lortie, 1969, p. 32).

Recall the great pleasure that Michelle's "gong show" routine gave her. The most important aspect of that activity was that it reached her students. Remember also the pain that Reeves felt over his failure to reach Marcus.

Those outside education find it difficult to comprehend that the most important satisfaction a teacher would receive from his or her work is reaching a student, but the evidence from both formal research and anecdotal accounts clearly establishes that this is the case. Reaching students goes beyond altruism; it is simply the benchmark of a teacher's feeling of success.

One of the authors recalls a conversation overheard between a secondary physical education teacher and an adolescent student with a long record of miscreant behavior in school. When the student told his teacher that he could obtain an after-school job that was thirteen miles from his home but had no way to get there, the teacher, without a pause, said, "I'll take you until you get a car." Because intrinsic rewards are the most important source of teacher satisfaction, teachers are more likely to be sensitive to their students and less concerned about their colleagues and administrators. It is their pupils that are primary sources of teachers' rewards and frustrations.

This orientation tends to make teachers somewhat immune from administrative actions. Skillful administrators, usually former teachers themselves, realize this and concentrate their energies on managing those matters that are not directly related to classroom instruction. Similarly, teachers who are immersed in the daily demands of the classroom are relatively indifferent to the organizational affairs of the school, which they gratefully relegate to the school principal.

Lortie, for example, presented the teachers in his study with a hypothetical situation where they were magically granted ten additional hours and asked to choose how they would use them. By a ratio of nine to one, the teachers chose to use the time on core teaching tasks rather than organizational matters (1969, p. 35).

Because most teachers work alone, and because teaching has an unfinished quality that makes it necessary for each teacher to define acceptable teaching outcomes, most teachers resent any interference with their teaching. For example, teachers are unlikely to be enthusiastic about administrative interruptions or supervisory visits. With regard to other outsiders, teachers want them in their classroom only after a "request for assistance." Teachers know that they must solve their own problems. When they do consider asking for outside assistance, they are likely to ask another teacher (Lortie, 1969, p. 38).

Recent attempts to control teaching more carefully through legislation, competency-based curricula, and state-wide testing has also made teachers uncomfortable because it violates their definition of teaching. In school systems where these kinds of directives are rigorously enforced, teachers feel torn between appeasing bureaucratic requirements and meeting their students' needs. One teacher characterized her dilemma in the following fashion:

> You're supposed to accomplish a, b, c and whatever in the day. That really is unrealistic because it depends on the class. It depends on how prepared the students come to class (Darling-Hammond and Wise, 1985, p. 324).

Another anecdote illustrates teachers' resistance of attempts to limit their autonomy. Margaret J. Lathlaen, who was selected to join the National Teachers in Space program in 1984, and was reluctant to leave her job because it was so challenging and rewarding, claimed that she is not sure she wants to return to her old job. Lathlaen told the governors' association that she feels her state legislature has taken the fun out of teaching. "I no longer have autonomy over what is taught" she claimed, and then asserted, "I don't even have a lot of choice about how I teach" (Friendly, April 1, 1986, p. 18). These kinds of complaints have become more frequent as state governments become increasingly involved in the day-to-day activities of the schools.

THE SELECTION AND SOCIALIZATION OF TEACHERS

▶ The readers who have followed our argument might be inclined to ask, If teachers are indeed autonomous, then why are they so predictable? Why are teachers generally conservative in their outlook and practice? Why are educational observers able to provide relatively accurate estimations of teacher behavior?

Scholars who have attempted to answer these kinds of questions have employed a variety of conceptual schemes, ranging from psychodynamic theories to common sense explanations. But in the final analysis, the most useful schemes are those that seek to explain how teachers are selected and socialized.

▶ Selection

Some of the devices used to select teachers are atypical for our achievement-oriented society because they require the candidate to suspend or control some aspect of his or her behavior, generally energy or upward mobility. For most careers those kinds of ambition are seen as necessary ingredients for success.

From the very beginning of our republic, American people have possessed a clear idea of the kinds of individuals they wanted to teach in their schools. Although it is not possible to characterize exactly, it does seem that a somewhat muted temperament has always been seen as a highly desirable personal attribute in a teacher. In a variety of ways, the people controlling schools have used that quality as a screen to winnow out undesirable candidates. As an example of the tight control communities exercised over their teachers, let us look at the following information.

When the males who predominated in the schools of the early republic began to assert themselves in the middle of the last century, the composition of teaching staffs gradually shifted so that by 1900 American public schools were essentially female enclaves (Hofstadter, 1963, p. 325). By the 1920s, as males began to reenter public school teaching in significant numbers, they encountered schools that were resolutely feminine.

When we label the schools *feminine,* we do not mean to call them *effete;* rather, we mean that schooling in our country has long been seen and has continued to be regarded primarily as a woman's job, not offering men the stature of a fully legitimate male role (Zeigler, 1976, p. 12). This feminization of teaching is unique to the United States. In most European countries, for example, the role of the teacher is a high-status one. Richard Hofstadter aptly described the American situation:

> The American belief that education and culture are feminine concerns is thus confirmed, and no doubt partly shaped, by the experiences of boys in school . . . the boys grew up thinking of men teachers as somewhat effeminate and treat them with a curious mixture of genteel deference (of the sort due to women) and hearty male condescension. In a certain constricted sense, the male teacher may be respected, but he is not "one of the boys" (Hofstadter, 1963, p. 320).

Into this atmosphere enter young men and women who are generally of a nonrebellious, perhaps conforming temperament. But before these men and women become teachers some rather effective mechanisms of self-selection have been at work.

Self-selection remains the most important screening device for potential teachers. By the time most people make the decision to become a teacher they already have a very clear idea of the dimensions and demands of the profession. They have this clear perception because they have witnessed at least 10,000 hours of teaching in their own schooling.

Few enter the teaching field blindly. Most know exactly the kinds of aptitudes required. In no other occupation is such prescience possible. Yet, although all beginning teachers have been recipients of the service they will perform, many experience considerable disillusion at the realities of teaching. This is especially true of teachers who begin their careers in inner-city schools (Mackey, 1970).

After self-selection, the next element of the selection process that is encountered by the aspirant teacher is the teacher-training institution. (Teacher education will be discussed more expansively in Chapter 7.) Whether located in an education department, or housed in a separate college of a large university, or residing in a separate college or university devoted entirely to teacher training, these academic outposts isolated for teacher training have probably received more criticism than any other institution in American society, with the exception of the Internal Revenue Service. One recent essay, for example, referred to schools of education as "the biggest running joke in higher education where would-be teachers all too often waltz as if they were signing up for intramural softball" (*Newsweek,* September 24, 1984, p. 64).

It is in one of these much maligned institutes for education where most teachers receive their pedagogical training. This training is generally divided into three essential parts: foundation courses, which involve various education theories; methods courses, which emphasize teaching techniques, and direct experience courses, which tend to be some variant of fieldwork, most often practice teaching.

Although numerous criticisms have been leveled at teacher-training programs, the central charge is that they are not rigorous in their selection procedures, and that rarely does anyone who applies for admission to a teacher-education program get rejected (Feistritzer, 1984). In addition, critics contend the course work in education programs is boring, derivative, easy, and unrealistic.

Less hyperbolic and more reflective criticism of teacher training revolves around the contention that schools of education are too reflective of the status quo and too apt to produce candidates whose primary concern becomes working harmoniously within the educational system. In other words, schools of education do not serve to inspire educational change or promote educational progress. This process is accused of muting personal idiosyncratic characteristics, deemphasizing intellectual aspects of learning and teaching, and homogenizing new teachers.

The third essential component of the selection process is the hiring mechanisms of the public schools. Here the emphasis appears to be on selecting individuals who will not create a stir within either the schools or the community, rather than probing for distinguishing intellectual characteristics. Frequently, selection is based on the teaching candidates' personal contacts, poise in personal interviews, and anecdotal reports on their character and practice-teaching experience. Ultimately, the school principal selects the candidate that he or she likes and believes will best fit in the school climate, with little evidence or knowledge of that person's intellectual characteristics.

In recent years, however, the selection process for teachers has probably been affected more by the vast expansion of occupational choice for young women than by any other single factor. Historically, education was one of the few occupations that was entirely open to women, and many intellectually superior women were attracted to teaching. In the past fifteen years, this has dramatically changed as other vocational occupational choices (management, law, and medicine) have opened up for bright young women. Thus, the bright women who so enriched the intellectual cadre of the public school have virtually disappeared from school employees' personnel files. Statistics cited by Kirst bear this out. He reveals that in one state "the proportion of men scoring well on the National Teachers Exam has remained fairly stable, but the portion of women scoring well has dropped sharply" (Kirst, 1984, p. 139). After revealing that in one year (1977) over 100,000 women were lost to education, he concludes by ironically noting that "sexism once helped preserve quality in the public schools" (Kirst, 1984, p. 139).

In sum, self-selection guided by the aspirant teacher's prior knowledge of education, the educational institute's failure to impose rigorous criteria, and administrators' penchant for weeding out colorful candidates all contribute to the increasing homogeneity of the teaching profession.

▶ Socialization

The word *socialization* refers to the set of norms, rules, and rituals a person learns as she or he becomes part of a particular culture. Occupational socialization concerns itself with the methods by which an individual is inducted into a career, craft, or profession. This occupational socialization occurs for teachers as well, yet the process is unlike that of any other professional group in several distinct ways.

First, it is remarkable in its casualness. Most professions take few chances with newcomers and insist that neophytes submit themselves to years of scrutiny, indoctrination, internship, and formal testing, but entrance to the teaching profession is based on the simple possession of a teaching license, which seldom involves any demonstration of competency. It is casual because it does not matter where a person receives his or her teacher training. Receiving training in an elite school seems to confer no additional prestige to the beginning teacher.

Second, socialization to teaching appears to be emulative rather than culminative in its form. By this, we mean that most teachers learn their craft by modeling the behavior of some teacher who taught them in the past, rather than learning from master teachers. More relevantly, it appears that pedagogical training does not alter a person's earlier perception about teaching. In preparing for teaching, even the final apprenticeship, student teaching, is a relatively casual affair (Lortie, 1975, p. 79).

This system leads to a glacial pace of change in the teaching profession, encourages safe and traditional instructional techniques, and, in general, fosters a conservative outlook among teachers. For example, the structure of work in the area where there is the heaviest concentration of teachers—elementary schools—has not changed appreciably in this century. A teacher from 1910, for instance, would have little difficulty recognizing school classrooms today because then, as now, teachers work in self-contained classrooms organized in much the same way, using the same essential curricular materials.

Third, teachers develop their basic pedagogical practices in an idiosyncratic fashion because they work in an isolated environment and seldom visit other teachers at work. Most teaching practices are predicated primarily on an "whatever works" ethic. This kind of perspective, when coupled with the rapidity of behavior in the typical classroom, tends to work against sustained reflection and contributes to the intuitive pedagogical orientation that characterizes the outlook of so many teachers. With relentless similarity, teachers testify that they employ a particular pedagogical technique in their classroom because "it feels right."

Fourth, teacher isolation contributes to another facet of their behavior—their susceptibility to educational trends. The kinds of new ideas that appeal to the individual in this vulnerable position must work. Abstraction and experimentation are too risky. Therefore, teachers who reluctantly accept new curricula and instructional materials do so only if they can clearly see they will work. Materials that are presented to teachers in a carefully orchestrated package have a greater chance of acceptance. It goes without saying that these acceptable materials are not likely to be much of a deviation from past pedagogical devices.

Finally, socialization to teaching is highly truncated because it is not founded on well-developed and highly agreed upon occupational norms. Simply put, teachers do what their teachers did, and the profession does not change rapidly. Change takes place slowly because the emerging bodies of knowledge do not appear relevant to the majority of teachers who deprecate most research findings as theoretical and impractical. The rigors of teaching incline beginning teachers toward caution, which frequently becomes habit as the teacher is further socialized to his or her conservative craft.

SUMMARY

► This chapter profiled the social world of the teacher. After establishing the teacher milieu, we examined the results of opinion polls of teachers' beliefs. We found that teachers were somewhat older than the popular image holds, and they appear receptive to efforts to improve their teaching.

Most teachers possess a somewhat similar set of social beliefs: they desire, above all, to reach students, and achieve great satisfaction from the intrinsic rewards of teaching. Most teachers also have a similar conception of client responsibility. When they feel that they have violated this trust, most teachers are ashamed.

At present, some teachers feel threatened by state governments' efforts to improve education through legislation. This chapter claimed that the social disposition of teaching is predictable because nearly all teachers experience similar selection and socialization processes.

ACTIVITIES

1. Does the description of Michelle Comstock provide any clues about why she became a teacher? Why do you think she chose the teaching profession?
2. What are some of the implications for school curriculum from an increasingly older cadre of teachers?
3. What are the most important reasons that Rex Thomas is leaving the teaching profession? Is his case typical? List some ways you could find out why others have left. Propose a strategy that you believe would keep Mr. Thomas teaching.
4. Why does the American public have so much difficulty understanding teachers?
5. List some rewards that teachers obtain from their work that were not described in this chapter.

REFERENCES

Darling-Hammond, L., and Wise, A. E. (January 1985). Beyond standardization: State standards and school improvement. *The Elementary School Journal, 85,* 315–336.

Feistritzer, E. (1984). *The making of a teacher.* Washington: National Center of Education Information.

Friendly, J. (August 31, 1985). After lag, teachers start to catch up on pay. *New York Times,* p. 1.

Friendly, J. (April 1, 1986). Teacher autonomy at issue. *New York Times,* p. 19.

Harris, L. (June 1984). *The Metropolitan Life survey of the American teacher.* New York: Metropolitan Life Insurance Company.

Hofstadter, R. C. (1963). *Anti-intellectualism in American life*. New York: Vintage Books.

Kirst, M. W. (1984). *Who controls our schools*. New York: W. H. Freeman.

Larson, L. (1976). Review of a school teacher. *Teachers College Record, 77,* 642–643.

Lortie, D. C. (Summer 1967). The teachers shame: Anger and the normative committment of classroom teachers. *School Review, 75,* 155–171.

Lortie, D. C. (1969). The balance of control and autonomy in elementary school teaching. In A. Etzioni (Ed.), *The semi-professions and their organization*. New York: Free Press.

Lortie, D. C. (1975). *School teacher: A sociological study*. Chicago: University of Chicago Press.

Mackey, J. (Fall 1970). New strategies of social inquiry for ghetto schools. *High School Journal, 53,* 133–141.

Sykes, G. (October 1983). Contradictions, ironies and promises unfulfilled: A contemporary account of the status of teaching. *Phi Delta Kappan, 65,* 87–93.

Ziegler, H. (1976). *Political life of American teachers*. Englewood Cliffs, N.J.: Prentice-Hall.

SUGGESTED READINGS

Becker, H. (1954). The career of the Chicago public school teacher. *American Journal of Sociology, 57,* 470–477.

Dreeben, R. (1970). *The nature of teaching*. Glenview, Ill.: Scott, Foresman.

Elsbree, W. S. (1939). *The American teacher*. New York: American Book Company.

Feiman-Nemser, S., and Floden, R. E. (1986). The cultures of teaching. In M. C. Wittrock (Ed.), *Handbook of research on teaching* (3rd ed.). New York: Macmillan, pp. 505–527.

Lortie, D. C. (1975). *School teacher*. Chicago: University of Chicago.

Sarason, S. B. (1982). *The culture of the school and the problem of change* (2nd ed.). Boston: Allyn and Bacon.

Waller, W. (1932). *The sociology of teaching*. New York: Russell and Russell.

Part II

Instructional Orientation

4

The Curricular and Instructional Perspective of Classroom Teachers

▶───────────────────────────────◀

OVERVIEW

▶ This chapter describes the nature of teachers' thinking. As a means of illustrating teacher cognition, we again employ Michelle Comstock as our prototype teacher. Following this analysis, the narrative depicts the nature of the relationship between teachers and their colleagues. We will then characterize teachers' professional organizations. The final section describes the most pressing current teacher-related issue — teacher evaluation.

The work individuals do causes them to behave in a particular way, which in turns shapes the work itself. This is true of butchers, bakers, and teachers. But describing how teachers think is difficult in two respects. First, it is presumptuous to generalize about two million individuals who teach in a variety of school environments. Second, since everyone has been to school and therefore believes that he or she knows the purpose of schooling, the craft of teaching seems obvious. Yet, because conflict about the goals of education is endemic and has swirled around the enterprise from the beginning, it is important that we do generalize. Although the goals of education are, in the final analysis, the basic goals of society and are therefore necessarily complex and provocative, at least some of the strain and tension between the education profession and the public is caused by the latter's unwillingness to comprehend how teachers think about teaching.

Since the primary objective of this chapter is important yet elusive, it is useful to begin the chapter with a concrete activity. We hope that the exercise on teachers' thinking will bring the subject into clearer focus. Our method toward this end is to select some data from the researcher whose work dominated our last chapter, Dan C. Lortie (1975), and organize some of his findings for our own purposes. Some readers may note that much of the Lortie work that we use is relatively dated. (Our most recent reference to Lortie's work was published in 1975.) It is our contention, however, that the kinds of characteristics that Lortie's research located are not transitory and will endure the test of time.

In April 1986 a team of researchers published the first results of their attempt to test the various Lortie hypotheses (Kottkamp, Provenzo, and Cohn). Although the three researchers' replication found that over the course of nearly twenty years some changes did occur, Lortie's study, in the main, stood the test of time. His research conclusion has remained in place.

You recall that Lortie attempted to build a comprehensive sociological profile of the American school teacher. Although our intentions differ from Lortie's, his data are as invaluable as his work is magisterial. Our exercise is titled *Teachers' Goals*. Please complete the exercise before you go on.

TEACHERS' THINKING

► Until recently, most of what we knew about teacher thinking was based on anecdote and personal testimony. Novels such as *Blackboard Jungle* and *Up the Down Staircase* seized the popular imagination with their graphic, dramatic, and sensationalized accounts of teachers' thinking about and working at their craft.

During the past decade, this has begun to change as scholars from a variety of disciplines have produced some systematic research on the subject. In the case of our hypothetical teacher, Michelle Comstock, many of the problems that teachers encounter are personal and internal. Some of Michelle's concerns are intellectual in nature, as in her desire to find a better way to teach borrowing; others involve thoughts about group solidarity; still others concentrate on particular students, as in her quest for a way to deal with Ted—the boy with the serious behavior problem.

We will not argue here that Michelle represents all teachers, or even that all teachers possess a common ideology. What we do claim is that there is an essential core of beliefs that make up the inner world of most teachers. We call this set of core beliefs *the teacher's curricular and instructional perspective* or *pedagogical perspective*.

Teachers' Goals (Exercise)

Dan C. Lortie selected a small sample of teachers and then asked the question, "I know it's not easy to state clearly, but would you try to explain to me what you try most to achieve as a teacher? What are you really trying to do most of all?" Listed below are eight of the responses teachers gave to Lortie.

Assume that you are a teacher. From that perspective, read the eight teacher responses and then rank them in the order of their importance to you as a teacher. Place a number 1 by the most important variable, a number 2 by the second most important, and so on through number 8, the least important.

_____ A. Trying to make them think on their own; be independent. To me, it's fine if they can learn chemistry, but in examinations I want to see if they can take it down and think it out clearly.

_____ B. I like to think I try to make them like school.

_____ C. To develop pupils who will become wholesome individuals in society.... They will respect not only the teacher but have respect for others.

_____ D. Every spare minute I try to stress good citizenship, and if anything comes up in the classroom, the subjects are dropped and I go into that particular thing.

_____ E. You have to prepare them for life. I don't care if they don't know how to typewrite, they have to be individuals first. Instill a love of learning from within–not learning for the sake of bettering one's economic status but the love of education for the sake of education.

_____ F. Basically, I want them to learn to be eager to want to learn things.

_____ G. I'm trying to get every kid to read as well as he can. Until every kid that I can touch can read what he's supposed to, I'm not happy.

_____ H. I'd say a background of workable English. They give themselves away when they speak. While they make themselves understood, they all classify themselves when they say, "Do you want me to put them letters in the post box?" You know what they mean but they won't be as comfortable among different kinds of people if they are not familiar with their native language.

The most obvious property of Michelle's thinking is her intense concern for the needs of students. To contend that most teachers are child-centered is to understate the case. For example, it is of utmost importance to Michelle that she reach Ted, understand him, and make him comfortable. Only after these affective concerns are dealt with, will she worry about his academic shortcomings.

In her thinking about Ted, Michelle will not categorize him as a behavior problem, but think of him as a unique individual with unique problems. Teachers are not attracted to pigeonholing categories, such as Ted's problem is X, he is suffering from Y. When subgroups within the profession (special education teachers, for example) attempt to apply a quasi-psychological vocabulary to their students, most classroom teachers do not take their description seriously.

Michelle will probably not consult any technical literature that discusses children like Ted, because she does not think that answers to Ted's problems reside in books where students are discussed in general. Even if she discusses Ted with another teacher or a principal, she will not use a technical vocabulary to describe her dilemma, in the fashion of a psychologist or a physician or even a special education teacher. Michelle's approach will be entirely idiosyncratic, probably somewhat analogous to that of an artist.

One observer of the educational scene, Philip Jackson, applied the term "romantic temperament" to demonstrate the similarities between teachers and artists. Jackson's argument is worth quoting at length:

> A closer analogy might be drawn between the teaching situation and the problems facing the creative artist. As a painter, for example, goes about his work he is surely involved in making decisions—whether to add a dab of color here, alter a contour there, change this highlight or that, and so on. He may even be a hypothesis-tester in the sense of making a guess about what will work, trying it, and observing whether or not his guess was correct. Yet when we describe his work in these rational terms we run the risk of making it appear to be more cerebral than it truly is. More important, the artist himself would probably not recognize our description. In all probability he would claim that he did not *feel* much like a decision maker as he went about his work. Indeed, if queried about a particular decision he might well be completely at a loss to explain why he acted as he did. Instead of outlining for us the pros and cons that led him to choose from among many alternatives, he is more likely to refer in veiled terms to his intuitive powers by saying something like, "It just felt right to do it that way" (Jackson, 1971, p. 19).

Jackson's conceptual scheme would lead us to assert that Michelle is not likely to be very interested in the cause of Ted's misbehavior because teaching does not afford one the luxury of the analytical approach and because the immediacy and depth of caring that characterizes most teacher-student interaction mutes the analytical point of view (Jackson, 1971, p. 20). Michelle's task is to cure Ted, not to understand his background.

But the primary motivator for Michelle is her desire to help students like Ted and her belief, based on both experience and instinct, that such problems can be addressed in a useful and positive way. Michelle really believes that she can create a learning environment in which Ted will be almost magically turned into an acceptable student. She has done it before and she believes that it can be done with Ted. Michelle knows that her experiment with Ted may fail but, like most teachers, it is in the direction of optimism. In the end, she believes she will reach Ted, and he will learn.

Dwarfing all other aspects of Michelle's inner world is her almost mystical allegiance to intuition. Although she does a good deal of planning in preparation for her instruction, in the end she believes that effective teaching:

> . . . seems to call for doing what comes naturally and feeling one's way. The techniques that work well with one student fail with the next. The well-prepared lesson falls flat and the *ad lib* activity is an unqualified (and unexpected) success, the discussion that was dragging along for several minutes suddenly, for no apparent reason, comes to life. Experiences such as these (and they seem to be exceedingly common in most classrooms) serve to reinforce the intuitive basis of the teacher's actions and encourage her to think of teaching as far more of an art than a science (Jackson, 1971, p. 20).

Instinct may hold primacy in Michelle's instructional orientation, but she is highly unlikely to belittle the role of scientific explanation or expertise in solving her classroom problems. This attitude is best illustrated with her problem in teaching the math concept of borrowing. As you recall, because she felt that she was not reaching her pupils, she sought the advice of an expert in mathematics education. Her frustration in this pursuit does not cause her to disparage scientific explanations of teaching; rather, it serves to illustrate Michelle's emphasis on students rather than subject matter.

It is probably this aspect of teachers' thinking — their belief in their intuition — that most often escapes the public imagination. Thus, when there is some sort of educational crisis, the predictable public response is get tough and teach more content.

Michelle and her colleagues sense that pedagogical problems are never that simple. Unfortunately, for the most part, teachers seem to lack the self-assurance and confidence necessary to articulate the correctness of their beliefs. Jackson claims that attitudes of "doubt and defiance . . . comprise an integral part of the teacher's pedagogical perspective" (1971, p. 23). He goes on to assert that teachers' defensiveness about their practice is revealed in their vulnerability to criticism (when attacked, most teachers assume a defensive posture, seldom fighting back) and their misgiving about the quality of their performance.

This strange combination of vulnerability, confidence, instinct, and formal training help color the pedagogical perspective of the teacher. The idiosyncrasy of a teacher's perspective influences the next aspect of a teacher's life that we will examine—intercollegial relationships.

TEACHERS AND THEIR COLLEAGUES

▶ Most teachers believe that colleagues play a minimal role in their work. When teachers interact with their peers, the conversation seldom moves beyond talk of family, gossip, or sports. When they do discuss school, it is generally restricted to complaints about salary, working conditions, or students.

Much of this unwillingness to discuss teaching can be attributed to the fact that teaching lacks a well-developed technical culture, and it is difficult to discuss a subject without a common vocabulary. But teachers' recalcitrance goes deeper than that.

Teachers do not share because, to a large extent, they are antagonistic cooperators. That is, the norms of teaching demand sociability and cooperation, but there is no built-in reward for such behavior. All the rewards from teaching come from the classroom, away from the eyes of any colleagues. Therefore, despite the cooperative ethic, teachers compete with one another on several levels.

At one level, teachers compete with one another for various measures of popularity. Labels such as *most popular, best liked,* and *most competent* (as perceived by the administration and parents) are highly sought after. This competition remains covert and the struggle muted because the stakes, and the rewards, appear to be intangible. Nevertheless, the competition for these reputations is often considerable. Because of the flat status hierarchy and the fact that teaching takes place away from other teachers, no teacher is actually sure if his or her colleagues are effective or not. In this uncertain situation, it is not uncommon for an individual to take upon herself or himself the appellation of great teacher, and by his or her demeanor and personage behave in a way appropriate to that station. All of this is without others actually seeing the individual teach.

At another level, teachers compete with one another over pedagogical materials. Whereas this kind of pedagogical territorialism is more prevalent at the upper levels of schooling, the process exists at all levels and causes teachers to hoard their ideas and "trade secrets."

The same process, in a slightly altered form, is at work when some members of a school staff declare that they have control over a particular aspect of the school's curriculum. This kind of "proprietary" behavior is at work when English teachers declare that they have a right to certain pieces of literature, or when science instructors lay claim to a particular piece of equipment even though they do not technically own the apparatus.

The fact that teachers claim hegemony over particular parts of the curriculum and refuse to cooperate or share their ideas is understandable in terms of the enormous amount of time that stretches before every teacher. Each minute of this time must be either accounted for or filled with activities by the teacher. Secondary teachers, in particular, find themselves constrained within a one-hour universe that repeats its orbit five times a day. Thus, when teachers find a lesson or some activity that works for them, they develop a proprietary instinct about that pedagogical device.

TEACHER ISOLATION AND THE NEED FOR COLLABORATION

▶ Should teachers be the Robinson Crusoe-like figures we have just described? Are there any compelling reasons for teachers to abandon their islands of isolation and begin to collaborate? Since recent research evidence clearly affirms these questions, and even contends that the quest for teaching excellence is impeded by the failure of teachers to work together, it is important to explicate the primary reasons supporting teacher collaboration.

First, behaving like Robinson Crusoe forces teachers to rely entirely on trial and error learning. Lacking models or teaching without professional dialogue makes it unlikely that teachers will try any innovations. Second, working alone makes teachers dependent on their ability to locate problems and to select solutions. Unless they are eternally sensitive, ceaselessly analytical, and never tired or careless, they are apt to develop some habits that impede the learning of their pupils. Third, since they possess few models of excellence because of their isolation, teachers are likely to fall back on methods they recall from their past. This deprives them of the benefits that can be gained from the advice, excellence, and expertise of their colleagues (Rosenholtz, 1985).

Collaboration yields other benefits. When teachers begin to discuss their craft with others, they are likely to see that they share common problems which suggest common solutions. Common problems and solutions contribute to the development of common school goals. When all the teachers in a school strive toward common goals, the school is inclined toward greater effectiveness. The two groups of individuals most likely to gain from greater collaborations are beginning teachers and highly skilled teachers. Beginners gain because the "reality shock" of the classroom often forces them into a survivalist stance which bends their efforts toward punitive group management methods. Taking the custodial view detracts the teacher from the students, and as their frustration increases, their enthusiasm wanes. A collaborative setting can change this downward spiral because beginners can get support and guidance from more experienced mentor teachers. The mentor advice "enables the beginners to both manage and teach students successfully (Rosenholtz, 1985, p. 343).

The mentor teachers, in turn, benefit from collaboration in a variety of ways. They see themselves as influential and skilled, which enhances their self-concept, and they come to have more pride in themselves and in the craft of teaching. In the end, the development of better collegial relations enhances both student and teacher learning.

TEACHERS' ORGANIZATIONS

▶ The extent of the attempt of the profession to establish collegial ties lies predominantly in the artificiality provided by interest groups such as teachers' unions and subject area organizations. The two kinds of organizations differ markedly from one another with regard to membership, purpose, and influence.

The ranks of subject area organizations include individuals from specific disciplines such as mathematics, science, or social studies. These organizations serve several purposes: First, they elevate the day-to-day concerns of subject area teaching into a coherent organization with a consistent philosophy and clearly articulated goals and objectives; second, they provide an outlet for the exchange of teaching ideas through subject area journals and professional meetings; and third, they provide a formal link between university professors who research the subject area and the classroom teacher. The influence of these organizations is minimal because most teachers do not choose to affiliate themselves with one of them. In addition, professional subject area organizations have little influence over the workaday world of the teacher.

Although membership in subject area organizations has remained relatively constant over the past thirty years, the influence of teachers' unions has increased dramatically. There are two major professional interest groups: the American Federation of Teachers and the National Education Association. Although the two organizations differ slightly from one another in membership, general philosophy, and operating tactics, they are similar in their concern for teachers' economic welfare and job security. As interest groups, the two organizations transmit the demands of their member teachers to the various agents of the political system.

The National Education Association (NEA) is the larger and older of the two groups. Founded over 125 years ago, NEA functioned, for most of its history, as a national teachers' association striving to remain above politics. With that perspective, the NEA focused its concern on standards and ethics, research and dissemination, and technical assistance to local affiliates (Wirt and Kirst, 1972).

In recent decades, taking its cues from its younger though traditionally more strident sister organization, changes in the laws regulating political activity, and the rise of more militant teachers, the NEA has concentrated its efforts more on bread-and-butter issues, such as salaries, job security, and working conditions. In the process of this transformation, the NEA has abandoned the ethic that teachers should avoid collective action to obtain their political demands and has actively entered into the struggle for the control of public policy.

Every state in our country has its own branch of the NEA, which functions as a virtually autonomous unit. Frequently, these state organizations are very potent lobbying groups. The state NEA affiliates differ considerably in the amount of political pressure they exert.

The other teachers' union, the American Federation of Teachers (AFT) is younger, smaller, more urban, and—historically at least—more militant than its sister organization. The AFT was born out of the conditions that produced trade unionism in general, and as a result, continues to show the lines of its parentage, the AFL-CIO.

Until the highly publicized New York teacher strikes of 1968, and the rise of Albert Shanker as a leader of national stature, the AFT was a series of loosely aligned local teachers' unions without a strong central leadership. For most of the history of the organization, the idea of a centralized union made most old-line unionists nervous (Braun, 1972). As a result, national conventions tended to be fratricidal quarrels between the New York and midwestern contingents. Then, as now, the AFT was essentially an urban organization with minimal representation outside the orbit of large cities.

The twin tactics of negotiations and collective bargaining were the chief unifying instrument for the AFT. Using these strategies, the AFT has attempted to improve the status of teachers economically, socially, and politically (Shanker, 1985).

The current situation finds teachers more likely than ever to belong to large unions that are increasingly well organized. The rapid growth of teachers' unions has produced many benefits for teachers: more autonomy in their workplace, higher salary, and better working conditions. But these gains have been realized at considerble expense because teachers can no longer claim that they occupy the special position above politics. Nowadays, the various political agents with whom they struggle over the control of public policy regard them as one more pressure group whose claim must be balanced against other claims (Kirst, 1984).

In the wake of the tidal waves of criticism that have inundated teachers, many political agents, reacting to sentiment from their constituents, want to combine the revenue they give to schools and teachers with more control over the teaching profession. In the next section we will examine the movement to control both teachers and the schools through mandated teacher evaluation, or as Wise (1979) calls it, *legislated learning.*

TEACHER EVALUATION

► Teacher evaluation is a difficult subject to explicate because researchers and writers have produced a vast mountain of scholarship on the subject. Although there is much disagreement between the many writers and educational observers who have tackled this complex subject, two major issues emerge: Teacher evaluation is both necessary and controversial. For example, although a series of recent Gallup polls (1985) have shown that the American public overwhelmingly supports teacher evaluation, the ranks of teachers bristle at the prospect of government-controlled accountability.

Rather than attempting to burrow into that mountain of often conflicting information, we will scale teacher evaluation indirectly, first, by showing how the changes in teacher evaluation policies have affected our hypothetical teacher, Michelle Comstock, in her day-to-day work, and then by discussing teacher evaluation in general.

When Michelle began teaching in 1965, teacher evaluation was a relatively simple affair. Several times each year Michelle's principal dropped into her classroom (generally unannounced), observed her teaching for a short period of time, made a few superficial notes, and then left, generally without comment. Sometime in the early spring, Michelle scheduled an appointment with her principal to discuss these observations and to evaluate her teaching.

Each of the yearly evaluation conferences proceeded similarly. After some initial small talk, the principal produced a document upon which he or she had recorded comments about the classroom visitations. Generally, the principal recorded more visits than Michelle remembered. While Michelle read the typed form containing the observations, the principal embroidered the written record with some general comments such as, "Your class control seems better this year." In general, the written document tended to be much more formal and detailed than were the principal's comments.

After a perfunctory discussion about the document, the principal would attempt to bring the meeting to a close by asking Michelle if she had any additional comments. This ritual would end as Michelle signed the evaluation and was told that she would be rehired. Michelle was granted tenure after three consecutive years of positive evaluations. After that, she remembers that the yearly teacher evaluations became even more casual and sporadic.

When Michelle looks back, her own evaluation of her teaching was much more important to her development. But that, too, was relatively casual. Michelle's self-evaluation proceeded in various ways. It was either precipitated by some instructional dilemma or from an idea acquired from an article or education course.

Once when she was worried that she was dominating classroom talk, she remembers using classroom interaction analysis—a measuring device that traces the patterns of teacher-student dialogue—and then performing several analyses on audiotaped recordings. On another occasion, Michelle and her friend observed one another's classes and shared what they had seen.

Whatever the origin of Michelle's inspiration, the results were predictably similar. After examining that aspect of her instruction that concerned her for a time, she would abandon the process because she had either answered her question or had reached an impasse. Although Michelle did not think about it much, if she were asked, she would maintain that her self-evaluation frequently resulted in the improvement of her teaching.

Sometime after Michelle began teaching, the conventional wisdom about teacher evaluation began to change. The change was brought about for a simple reason: The federal government entered education. Although Michelle was dimly aware of it at the time, the entrance of the federal government was to profoundly alter the way that she and other teachers would be evaluated.

► A Brief Historical Background to Teacher Evaluation

The federal government entered teacher evaluation indirectly when the Supreme Court jarred the American tradition of strict local control of schooling by ruling against the segregated school system of Topeka, Kansas, in 1954. In their historic decision, the Court held that segregation denied equal educational opportunity to black pupils.

For a decade after that decision, the federal government actively pursued desegregation, and launched a series of initiatives designed to improve the equality of opportunity for minority pupils (Wise, 1979). The culmination of the federal effort at equalizing educational opportunity was the enactment of a series of laws in 1965. The most important of these laws was the Elementary and Secondary Education Act (ESEA), which through its key provision, Title I, has allowed the federal government to pour $42.4 billion of financial aid into American schools in the last two decades. The primary goal of ESEA was to overcome disadvantages that stood in the way of education, and, through education, to overcome poverty (Maeroff, September 30, 1985).

The apparent success of the early efforts at educational improvement encouraged even more federal activity. In rapid succession, the federal government conducted a vast survey—popularly referred to as the *Coleman Report*—to examine the precise status of equal opportunity; entered into an agreement with the Education Commission of the States to create the National Assessment of Educational Progress (NAEP) to "examine achievement in 10 learning areas . . . (and) to apply the implications of these changes to national educational policy" (Tyler, 1975, p. xi); and charged the National Institute of Education (NIE) to help solve the problems of American education.

The extensive federal involvement has redefined the conventional wisdom about the control of public education and changed the face of the American schools. The repeated rebuffs by the Congress to the Reagan administration's attempt to reduce federal aid to education illustrates the widespread acceptance of the federal government's vital role in education.

Incontestably, the federal involvement has influenced schooling in another important area—as an impetus for more state involvement in education. As the federal portion of the total revenues of the school has fallen from a high of 9.2 percent in 1980 to the current 6.2 percent, the state's role in all aspects of education, but especially in the area of teacher evaluation, has increased markedly (Maeroff, September 30, 1985). Originally employed to strengthen their educational regulatory agencies, federal funds are increasingly used as a means of springboarding the states into the center of the educational stream.

Although it is impossible to generalize precisely about the activity of fifty distinct political entities, it appears that most state governments have shown more concern for ensuring educational achievement than for providing educational opportunity. To satisfy this mandate for accountability, the states, especially state legislatures, have imposed managerial schemes from industry on the schools and asserted that the schools would realize better results from management science (Wise, 1979, p. 12).

With their emphasis on productivity as opposed to equity, the states have introduced a variety of schemes to evaluate teachers' practice and, in the process, abandoned the old consensus that "education could be improved without improving the quality of teachers" (Wise et al., 1985, p. 62). Thus, techniques such as teacher-proof curriculum, test-based instructional management, and student competence testing are no longer at the forefront of educational reform.

Replacing the preceding strategies as the center of the educational orbit are a series of techniques that focus the spotlight directly on teachers, and that seek to evaluate the quality of their teaching. According to evaluation expert, Linda Darling-Hammond and her colleagues of the Rand Corporation, standards for teacher evaluation can be subsumed into three general categories: competency-based teacher certification, test for certification, and test for recertification (1985). In the next section we will examine each of these general categories in detail.

In summary, the movement of the federal and state governments into an area formerly reserved for the local community has changed the nature of teacher evaluation in distinct ways, making the procedure more remote, bureaucratized, and tighter, and placing teachers under more careful scrutiny and making them more accountable.

LEGISLATING LEARNING

► Since the recent rash of reports that have lamented the state of our nation's education, most American state legislatures and departments of education have stepped up the process of devising methods for the improvement of instruction through various kinds of teaching. As we claimed previously, three general methods have been employed: competency-based teacher education (CBTE), initial certification testing, and recertification testing. This section describes each of the three systems and provides an illustration of each.

► Competency-Based Teacher Education (CBTE)

CBTE is the most well-developed, comprehensive, and enduring of the three methods of teacher evaluation. CBTE is an idea whose time has come several times throughout the course of American history (Callahan, 1962). In its present embodiment, the model is very carefully defined and articulated.

The basic idea behind CBTE holds that there are a finite number of competencies, defined in terms of knowledge, skills, and behaviors, that teachers must possess to succeed. These competencies are not normative or ideological, but are based on what teachers actually do in the classroom. Advocates of this methodology contend that it is possible to make these competencies explicit and public and to measure teachers' performance in terms of them. Unlike most other systems of teacher certification, in competency-based teacher education, progress is determined by the achievement of the competencies rather than by the completion of courses or other traditional academic requirements. In the final analysis, advocates of CBTE claim that they can specify the tasks that a person must be able to perform to teach effectively, and that they can train teachers in the execution of them.

The Virginia Beginning Teacher Assistance Program (BTAP) illustrates CBTE. The program responds to a rule enacted by the state board of education to improve teaching and to ensure that all beginning teachers possess minimal teaching competency. The curriculum that emerged from the Beginning Teacher Assistance Program is contained in a volume entitled *Assisting the Beginning Teacher* (McNergney, 1985), which identifies fourteen skill areas and provides self-instructional material and competency tests to access mastery in each of the areas.

The editor of the curriculum package claims in his introduction, "It is important to emphasize that a competent beginning teacher is one who demonstrates certain professional knowledge and attitudes in the performance of his or her job" (McNergney, 1985, p. iv). He goes on to assert that each of the competencies has evolved from the research literature, and argues that while that is not a fail-safe for success in the classroom, at least this scheme will define the basic outlines of competent teaching.

Each of the chapters in the BTAP follows the same general format. A definition of the competency is followed by the purpose of the chapter which, in turn, is followed by a section entitled "Background Knowledge" where research findings on that competency are detailed. The heart of each of the fourteen chapters is the activities section where the students are introduced to the nuts and bolts of the respective competency. At appropriate points in these passages, the student takes checkup tests.

Although nowhere is a complete program of competency-based certification fully in place, most teachers tend to approach the concept with suspicion. In general, teachers doubt that the skills embodied in CBTE could be compiled, oppose the concept because of the standardization of teaching implied, and believe that teaching is too complex to be reduced to such a narrow definition. In a study of teachers' responses to CBTE, one teacher argued, "[teaching] is not an area of skill like learning how to use a power saw." Another claimed, "It would be absolutely impossible to set down in some kind of curriculum all the things a teacher had to be able to do to be competent" (Darling-Hammond and Wise, January 1985, p. 327).

Teachers also assert that advocates of competency programs have yet to address "the most meaningful aspect of teaching—the ability to make appropriate judgments about what to do in specific instances" (Darling-Hammond and Wise, January 1985, p. 327).

▶ **Initial Certification Testing**

The idea of testing teachers' knowledge of their subject matter as a prerequisite for initial certification is not new. The National Teachers Examination (NTE) has existed since 1940. What is new is the great enthusiasm with which state legislatures and departments of education embrace the idea of testing beginning teachers (Harris, 1981).

The logic in favor of the widespread acceptance of teacher testing is easy to trace. The standardized paper and pencil test is the most available and inexpensive remedy extant for the failure of an educational system. Immediately after enacting a teacher testing bill, a legislative body can report that it has begun to reform education in its respective state. Thus, in the last decade, an increasing number of states have chosen the elixir of initial teacher testing as an antidote for educational decay.

Although most of the states that have legislated learning in this fashion have chosen to use the NTE as their test for certification, a few have manufactured homegrown versions (Harris, 1981). The most comprehensive statewide system of initial teacher testing is in Georgia which, through its *Teacher Area Criterion Referenced Tests,* has developed seventeen tests that are currently being administered to candidates for initial certification in thirty-two teaching fields.

The Georgia Board claims that the tests, each of which takes three hours to complete, were developed because "there is a need to assess teachers so that certification is based on demonstrated performance, assuring that educational personnel have the competencies essential to facilitate the intellectual, social, emotional and physical growth of learners" (Georgia Dept. of Education, 1979, p. 10).

Most states restrict their teacher tests to a candidate's mastery of reading, writing, mathematics, and the area in which the potential teacher requests certification. A recent Minnesota statute, for example, states, "The examination must measure academic knowledge only and not teaching theories, methodology, skills of teaching and other areas traditionally associated with teacher education programs" (Minnesota Laws, 1985, section 125.03).

According to many educational observers, including Darling-Hammond (January 1985), teachers are divided in their views about the usefulness of paper and pencil tests for certification. Most feel such a test might screen out the poorly educated, but are skeptical as to whether such a test could predict actual teaching performance. In general, teachers support subject matter tests, but oppose tests of pedagogy on the grounds of feasibility and practicality.

► Recertification Testing

Requiring licensed teachers to submit themselves to a test as a condition of continuing employment is probably the most explosive issue in American education today. In this conflict over testing for recertification one can clearly discern the central elements of the legislating learning controversy. At odds are two formidable opponents. On one side are governors and members of state legislatures united in their efforts to improve education by enacting a series of laws that will make teachers more accountable. Arrayed on the other side are America's teachers — the best organized workers in the country — maintaining that their shortcomings are overemphasized and that legislated learning represents only an illusion of progress.

Nowhere is the struggle between teachers and the politicians being played out more hotly than in Arkansas. The struggle first began in 1983, when Arkansas governor, Bill Clinton, pushed through a series of state reforms, including a pay raise for Arkansas teachers. He engineered a 1 percent sales tax hike to pay for the reforms, which the taxpayers enthusiastically approved. As a condition for this reform, however, the governor demanded a guarantee on teacher quality, which he claimed could be measured by a literacy test that would be used as part of the process of recertifying veteran teachers. Clinton's idea became law. By 1987, all Arkansas teachers had to take the test and pass or lose their license to teach (Frady, 1984).

A storm of criticism followed the passing of the testing for recertification bill. A teacher who appeared on a widely publicized network television special seemed to capture the prevailing mood of Arkansas teachers by stating, "I will not take that test. I will quit my job first." The testing bill still stands despite the enormous effort on the part of Arkansas teachers, who, through their teacher organization, have spent a great deal of money on an anti-test media blitz.

Elsewhere, teacher opposition to this kind of legislation is equally vehement, if somewhat less visceral, than it is in Arkansas. In the main, teachers stress the necessity to assess classroom performance. One teacher in the Darling-Hammond study (1985) argued, "Testing a teacher because of his knowledge in mathematics and because of what he knows about how to teach is not going to ensure that he is a good teacher at all." Another teacher gave qualified support to the idea, but only if a crucial distinction were made. He said, "I distinguish between understanding and performance. What you know, I think, can be tested in a standardized way. What you can do has to be evaluated personally" (Darling-Hammond, January 1985, p. 330).

According to the available research on teacher effectiveness, this teacher's distinction is entirely appropriate because studies have shown no consistent relationship between test scores on a measure of teacher competency and teachers' classroom performance (Andrews, Blackman, and Mackey, 1980). In the end, testing teachers for recertification may have public appeal, it may present the illusion that the state's politicians are working to reform education, and it may even raise the status of teachers in the eyes of the public, but it does not signify what teachers can or will do in their respective classrooms, and thus it is a seriously flawed mechanism to improve teaching.

Finally, teacher evaluation is essential to effective teaching. The three methods of teacher evaluation we examined are the current responses to ineffective teaching. We examined each of these methods and found that although each of them represents a sincere effort to improve American education, each method is somewhat flawed. In teacher evaluation, as in most areas of their work, teachers must feel empowered, rewarded, and must be honored for their achievement. If they are not, then no amount of testing, whether mandatory or voluntary, will improve their performance.

SUMMARY

▶ This chapter examined teachers at work, and found that there was a common set of beliefs that most teachers held and similar kinds of rewards that teachers obtain from their work. Since many of these strains and rewards are intrinsic, we claimed that teachers are not well understood by the public and that teachers are not particularly efficient at arguing their point of view. Our account of teachers suggests that Americans value education but do not respect teachers.

Our examination of teaching revealed that the teaching profession has entered a crisis of sorts and that the commonplace solution for the problem, legislating more rigorous teacher evaluation, is not popular with many teachers.

In the end, we found teaching to be an imperiled profession that is seriously in need of reform. Needed reform, however, will come about only after additional status is granted to American teachers, because, as noted educational observer Ernest Boyer maintains, they are the heart of the educational enterprise. No amount of new rules and regulations will improve teaching unless we replace our perspective of teaching as a second-class semiprofession filled with lackluster personnel with a perspective of teaching as a respectable profession filled with empowered teachers. Nothing less will improve the conditions of American teachers.

ACTIVITIES

1. List the qualities of a good teacher. Remember a good teacher from the past. What qualities from the list does that teacher possess?
2. Do you think teachers, as a group, are resistant to change in schools? What can be done to facilitate change in schools? What types of changes need to be made?
3. In your opinion, what is the value of teacher organizations? How might they better serve the profession?
4. What are the three methods of teacher evaluation? What are the advantages and drawbacks of these three methods?
5. How can teachers be "empowered, rewarded, and honored for their achievement"?

REFERENCES

Andrews, J. W., Blackman, C. R., and Mackey, J. A. (1980). Pre-service performance and the national teacher examinations. *Phi Delta Kappan, 61,* 358–359.

Braun, R. J. (1972). *Teachers and power: The story of the American Federation of Teachers.* New York: Simon and Schuster.

Callahan, R. E. (1962). *Education and the cult of efficiency: A study of the social forces that have shaped the administration of the public schools.* Chicago: University of Chicago Press.

Darling-Hammond, L., and Wise, A. E. (January 1985). Beyond standardization: State standards and school improvement. *Elementary School Journal, 85,* 315–337.

Feistritzer, E. (1984). *The making of a teacher.* Washington: National Center of Education Information.

Frady, M. (September 7, 1984). To save our schools, to save our students. New York: American Broadcasting Company.

Friendly, J. (August 31, 1985). After lag, teachers start to catch up on pay. *New York Times,* p. 1.

Gallup, A. M. (September 1985). The 17th annual Gallup Poll of the public's attitudes toward the public schools. *Phi Delta Kappan, 67,* 35–47.

Georgia Department of Education. (1979). *Registration Bulletin 1979–80 — Georgia teacher certification testing program.* Atlanta.

Harris, L. (June 1984). *The Metropolitan Life survey of the American teacher.* New York: Metropolitan Life Insurance Company.

Harris, W. U. (1981). Teachers command of subject matter. In J. Millman (Ed.), *Handbook of teacher evaluation.* Beverly Hills: Sage Publications.

Hofstadter, R. C. (1963). *Anti-intellectualism in American life.* New York: Vintage Books.

Jackson, P. W. (1971). In G. E. Lessor (Ed.), *Psychology and educational practice.* Glenview, Ill.: Scott Foresman.

Kirst, M. W. (1984). *Who controls our schools.* New York: W. H. Freeman.

Kottkamp, R. B., Provenzo, E. F., and Cohn, M. M. (1986). Stability and change in a profession: Two decades of teacher attitudes, 1964–1984. *Phi Delta Kappan, 67,* 559–567.

Lortie, D. C. (Summer 1967). The teachers' shame: Anger and the normative committment of classroom teachers. *School Review, 75,* 155–171.

Lortie, D. C. (1969). The balance of control and autonomy in elementary school teaching. In A. Etzioni (Ed.), *The semi-professions and their organization.* New York: Free Press.

Lortie, D. C. (1975). *School teacher: A sociological study.* Chicago: University of Chicago Press.

Mackey, J. (Fall 1970). New strategies of social inquiry for ghetto schools. *High School Journal.*

Maeroff, G. I. (September 30, 1985). After 20 years, education programs are a solid legacy of great society. *New York Times,* p. 24.

McNergney, R. (1985). *Assisting the beginning teacher.* Richmond: Commonwealth of Virginia.

Minnesota Laws. (1985). Ch. 12, Article 8, Section 21.

Rosenholtz, S. J. (1985). Political myths about educational reform: Lessons from research on teaching. *Phi Delta Kappan, 66,* 349–355.

Shanker, S. (Fall 1985). The making of a profession. *American Educator, 9,* 10–17.

Sykes, G. (October 1983). Contradictions, ironies and promises unfulfilled: A contemporary account of the status of teaching. *Phi Delta Kappan, 65,* 87–93.

Tyler, R. (1975). Foreword to *Update on Education.* Denver: Education Commission of the States.

Why Teachers Fail (September 24, 1984). *Newsweek.*

Wirt, F. M., and Kirst, M. W. (1972). *The political web of American schools.* Boston: Little, Brown.

Wise, S. E. (1979). *Legislated learning: The bureaucratization of the American classroom.* Berkeley: University of California Press.

Wise, S. E., Darling-Hammond, L., McLaughlin, M. W., and Bernstein, H. T. (September 1985). Teacher evaluation: A study of effective practices. *The Elementary School Journal, 96,* 61–121.

Zeigler, H. (1967). *Political life of American teachers.* Englewood Cliffs, N.J.: Prentice-Hall.

SUGGESTED READINGS

Cuban, L. (1984). *How teachers taught: Constancy and change in American classrooms: 1890–1980.* New York: Longman.

Elbaz, F. (1983). *Teacher thinking: A study of practical knowledge.* New York: Nichols.

Feistritzer, C. E. (1983). *The American teacher.* Washington, D.C.: Feistritzer Publications.

Jackson, P. (1968). *Life in classrooms.* New York: Holt, Rinehart and Winston.

Lightfoot, S. L. (1983). The lives of teachers. In L. S. Shulman and G. Sykes (Eds.), *Handbook of teaching and policy.* New York: Longmans, pp. 241–260.

Ryan, K. et al. (1980). *Biting the apple: Accounts of first year teachers.* New York: Longman.

5

Curricular and Instructional Planning

In the story, *Alice's Adventures in Wonderland,* Alice encounters a Cheshire cat who is perched in a tree above her, grinning from ear to ear. Because she is confused and lost, Alice asks the cat which of several diverging roads she ought to take. "That depends on where it is you would like to go," the Cheshire cat answers.

"I'm not sure which way I should go. You see I'm quite lost," Alice replies.

"Then it really doesn't matter which way you go," said the Cheshire cat.

Planning for curriculum and planning instruction ideally begins with a long-range plan based on a set of ideas about subject matter and students. This plan should represent your ideas about what you think ought to be learned by your students and how they ought to learn it. In fact, teacher planning transforms curriculum into instruction. Teaching affords little time for reflection once it's underway; therefore, unless you have a clearly articulated goal structure, you will inevitably fall into the trap of doing activities at best, and worksheets and pages from the text at worst. A goal structure gives you a map to use to guide and chart your progress. It helps you stay on course because you know what the course is. It prevents you from digressing into trivialities because it keeps you focused on your purpose and destination. And keep in mind that a goal structure helps you to maintain your enthusiasm because you know whether your results have meaning. The act of teaching is the most obvious and visible element of instruction, but if teaching is not preceded by careful organized planning, its effectiveness will be greatly diminished. To return to Alice for a moment, a good plan ought to be based on where you want to go.

PHILOSOPHY OF CURRICULUM AND INSTRUCTION

▶   Recently we were involved in a conversation with some people who are greatly concerned with the progress and development of art in the schools. They pointed out what was to them an obvious fact: In a given school district, school, or classroom, there exists either a conceptually based, systematically designed, sequentially taught, teacher-directed fine arts curriculum, or there exists a more random, nondirected, naturalistic, Rousseauistic approach to artistic expression in which children are left free to develop largely without teacher intervention. Although the two approaches are antipodal to one another, they hold a basic principle in common: Each approach is rooted in a definite philosophy of teaching, learning, and human development.

We suggested to our thoughtful conversationalists that perhaps a third possibility existed: Art as a subject is given short shrift in our schools because it is not perceived by teachers, administrators, and the public as "basic," and, owing to that perception, it has become an occasional area in the curriculum with less attention being paid either to skill development or to freeing the child than to such craft projects as Thanksgiving turkeys cut from paper plates and Easter bunnies made from cardboard egg cartons. Although they seemed to resist this suggestion, our artist acquaintances allowed that this was certainly a third though distinctly less desirable possibility.

With a view toward the larger picture of the total school curriculum, it is at least a possibility that some or all of what transpires daily in classrooms is, like our third possibility in the art curriculum, a theoretical or "common-sense" approach.

Teaching, like bricklaying, is a practical activity. It is a job that must be performed on a daily rather than inspirational basis, and to do it well takes a great deal of insight and ability. The work demands much of its practitioners, and it is typical for people inside and outside the profession to cite patience and tolerance as requisite virtues to the task.

Teachers in the United States and Canada are well prepared for their vocation in a formal sense. The days when people taught without college degrees are over. In fact, in a number of states, a majority of public school teachers hold advanced degrees. Thus, the idea that in order to teach a certain level one must have successfully completed the level immediately above it has passed into history. It is worth noting that in pedagogical history, the chief qualification for teaching a subject is a minimal knowledge of the subject.

Today much more is asked of teachers. In addition to mastering the specific content of their teaching area, teachers are expected to have a working knowledge of psychological theories of learning and human development, of teaching methodologies, and of group and individual management techniques. We could add to this list, but the illustrations provided here ought to make clear the proposition that effective teaching requires rather sophisticated personnel who are able to perceive the complexities inherent in human learning and who are able to plan programs, make decisions, and solve problems with a considerable degree of flexibility. In this sense, our analogy between teaching and laying bricks breaks down in spite of the fact that both are practical activities that require great skill when they are done well. The difference is found in the dynamic quality of teaching versus the comparatively static quality of brick laying. It is certainly true that bricklaying involves problem solving (for example, building a wall on a sloping hillside versus flat ground) and flexibility in dealing with untoward weather conditions, shipment delays, and unpredictable customers. However, the teacher not only instructs a number of differentially motivated, skilled, and informed students, but plans and assesses as well.

The individual teacher and his or her responsibilities in planning the curriculum are a piece of a larger picture. Except in rare cases, teachers certainly are not expected to invent the curriculum they will teach. Much of it comes preplanned. Their primary mission is to implement it once they understand and agree with the precepts. First of all, bear in mind that in the United States there is no national curriculum. Because of our system of local control, any two teachers teaching the same subject from the same book may well teach it differently, with varying pacing, style, and emphasis. Each school district provides its teachers with guides to the various subject matter areas of the curriculum. Larger districts sometimes develop their own, modeled on state-developed guidelines, and smaller districts generally use state department of education guides. On an even larger scale, most state or district planning guides are based on the thinking of the various subject matter guidelines set forth by the respective national professional organizations. The goal structure established by the National Council of Teachers of Mathematics (NCTM) is provided here in order to furnish you with an example of the planning of curriculum and instruction that takes place at the larger, strategic levels for implementation at state, district, and classroom levels.

A GOAL STRUCTURE FOR CURRICULAR AND
INSTRUCTIONAL PLANNING

Adapted from the National Council of Teachers of Mathematics (1977)

1. *Problem Solving.* The principal reason for studying mathematics is to solve problems by applying previously acquired knowledge to new situations. Problem-solving strategies include: posing questions, analyzing situations, translating results, illustrating results, drawing diagrams, and using trial and error. Students must be able to apply logic to arrive at correct conclusions, determine relevant data, and draw conclusions based on their information base. Solving world or story problems is one form of problem solving. However, students should be given real-life problems to solve as well.

2. *Applying Mathematics to Everyday Situations.* The use of mathematics is interrelated with all computation activities. Have students take situations, translate them into mathematical expressions, solve the equations, and interpret the results as they relate to the situations.

3. *Alertness to the Reasonableness of Results.* Sometimes mistakes are made in computational work. Students should learn to check their results for "reasonableness" of their answer in relation to their original problem. With the increased use of electronic calculating devices, this skill is particularly important.

4. *Estimation and Approximation.* Students should have the ability to work out rapid calculations by rounding off numbers. They should also have skills in estimating quantity, length, distance, and weight. They also must be able to decide when a particular estimate is precise enough for the situation at hand.

5. *Appropriate Computational Skills.* Students must have skills in single-digit (decimal and whole number) addition, subtraction, multiplication, and division. They must be able to recognize and manipulate common fractions and percentages. Mental arithmetic is a valuable skill for students to have. However, it must be recognized that long, complicated calculations in today's world are generally done with a calculator.

6. *Geometry.* Students should learn the geometric concepts necessary to function in a three-dimensional world. Concepts such as point, line, plane, parallel, and perpendicular are important to know. Students should know the basic measurement and problem-solving properties of simple geometric figures, and they should be able to recognize similarities and differences among objects.

7. *Measurement.* As a minimum skill, students should be able to measure distance, weight, time, capacity, and temperature. Measurement of angles and calculations of simple areas and volumes

are also essential. Students should have knowledge in both the metric and customary systems.

8. *Reading, Interpreting, and Constructing Tables, Charts, and Graphs.* Students should know how to read and draw conclusions from simple tables, charts, maps, and graphs. They should be able to condense numerical information into more meaningful terms by creating tables, charts, and graphs.

9. *Using Mathematics to Predict.* Students should know how future events, such as election forecasts, are predicted by the use of probability. They should be able to identify situations where an immediate past experience would not affect the likelihood of a future event.

10. *Computer Literacy.* Students should be aware of the many uses of computers in society, such as in teaching / learning situations, financial transactions, and information storage and retrieval. The increased use of computers by government, industry, and business demands an awareness of computer uses and limitations.

LONG-RANGE PLANNING

▶ Perhaps one of the most persistent problems in teaching is the failure on the part of teachers to develop long-range instructional plans during the early part of the school year. This is understandable because teaching has a sense of immediacy. The demands placed on teachers by students are many and there is little time for reflection in the typical day. Although we can readily concede these realities, we can also observe that long-range planning is crucial to the pursuit of excellence whether in teaching, automobile production, or operating a home.

The failure to develop long-range plans in that week before the students arrive often leads to needless repetition, gaps in content coverage, inability to finish the prescribed course of study in a year's time, and lack of meaningful attention to individual differences.

The obvious time to develop long-range instructional plans is prior to the beginning of the school year. That is the time to begin talking with fellow teachers who teach at the levels preceding and following yours in order to find out what kinds of things they emphasize. Thus, if third-grade teachers are told by second-grade teachers that they *introduce* the topic of research reports, and fourth-grade teachers say that they emphasize certain "advanced" research skills, then there is definitely a need to emphasize basic research report skills with third graders throughout the year. The same idea would apply to other topics such as paragraph construction, dictionary skills, critical thinking, and so on.

Teachers who develop an outline of major topics that they will be teaching during the year have a discussion list to take to the teachers who teach the levels above and below them. They can indicate, for example, if they (1) do not teach a given topic, (2) introduce the topic, (3) teach the topic at something deeper than an introductory level, and (4) expect the topic to have been learned in most cases.

The simple two-step process of outlining the topics that will be covered during the year and talking with the teachers who work with the students who precede and follow a given level will go a long way toward articulating a long-range goal structure.

UNIT INSTRUCTION

► Having thought through the scope and sequence of a curriculum for the entire year, a teacher is ready to break down that very large block of time into several smaller blocks of time called *units*. A unit is a teaching sequence of several weeks' duration in which instruction is based on a central or organizing theme. Whereas unit titles and subtitles may correspond to the chapter titles and subtitles of textbooks, teachers may wish to make certain modifications that reflect their own personal strengths or interests or that are more suited to a particular community. For example, one teacher who is an amateur history buff taught a Research / Reporting / Writing unit around the theme of "Backyard Histories." By doing this the teacher not only (1) accommodated her own interests (a very important dimension in teaching since teacher enthusiasm is a key variable in achievement), but she also was able to (2) work within the context of the local community, and (3) integrate her language and social studies teaching. In most instances, however, units will probably bear considerable likeness to those prescribed by the text.

► Unit Overview

At this point, let us turn our attention to an outline format for unit development. Here is an example from a unit on *Listening and Speaking:*

TOPICS FOR LISTENING AND
SPEAKING UNIT

Listening	Speaking
for sequence	giving directions
to directions	discussion

TOPICS FOR LISTENING AND
SPEAKING UNIT (Continued)

Listening	Speaking
to rules	formal and informal speech
to fact and opinion	describing
to detail	story telling
for main idea	oral reading
for appreciation	to groups
courtesy	reporting
interviews	interviews

Once the key topics that will be covered in a unit are listed, the next step is to develop a *unit overview,* which provides (1) a rationale for instruction, (2) a central theme or generalization, (3) a list of key concepts, and (4) a set of block plans that includes a list of instructional activities.

A sample of each follows:[1]

LISTENING AND SPEAKING:
UNIT OUTLINE

1. *Overview:*

This unit focuses on the process of communication, with particular emphasis on listening and speaking. In the Language section of the unit, the students learn some practical techniques for listening in class, conducting a formal meeting, making introductions, conducting interviews, and presenting oral reports. The Study Skills section enhances communication as the students study synonyms and antonyms as well as use a thesaurus. In the Composition section, the students write friendly and business letters. Letters from E. B. White to a group of sixth graders comprise the Literature section.

2. *Central Theme:*

Listening and speaking skills are useful and necessary to conduct our everyday

---

1. Adapted from Level 6, *Language for Daily Use* (New York: Harcourt, Brace, Jovanovich, 1983), pp. T312, 313.

3. *Key Concepts:*
   a. *Language:*

lives. They are basic skills that all students must acquire.

Instructions, directions, main idea, details, parliamentary procedure, chairperson, secretary, minutes, treasurer, recognize, motion, second, introduction, interview, oral report

   b. *Study Skills:*

Opposite, similar, antonym, thesaurus, synonym

   c. *Composition:*

Friendly letter, heading, greeting, body, closing signature, envelope, sender's address, receiver's address, ZIP code, business letter, inside address, edit

   d. *Literature:*

Letters, theme, main ideas

4. *Block Plans*

Monday	*Tuesday*	*Wednesday*	*Thursday*	*Friday*
1 Sharing ideas	2 Listening in class	3 Listening in class	4 Speaking in a small group	5 Speaking in a small group
6 Speaking in class	7 Speaking in class	8 Conducting a meeting	9 Resource speaker	10 Review session
11 Making introductions	12 Interviewing people	13 Oral history	14 Oral history	15 Preparing a report
16 Preparing a report	17 Reporting to class	18 Reporting to class	19 Presentation to other classes	20 Review session
21 Review session	22 Unit test			

LESSON PLANS

► Once a framework for a unit instruction has been established, the next step is to articulate the daily lessons themselves. Thoughtfully developed lesson plans are crucial to the enterprise of excellence. There is a widespread belief that writing lesson plans is merely an exercise for the undergraduate to do in order to pass a course in educational methods. Nothing could be farther from the truth. Outstanding teachers invariably write lesson plans for their instruction. The fact that mediocre teachers do not write lesson plans (they don't do a number of things that would obviously raise achievement standards) ought not to be considered a useful argument against their development. Perhaps the most persistent problem that arises from the failure to write articulated, sequential plans is the tendency for a teacher to fall prey to doing random activities rather than achieving instructional obejctives in an ordered, systematic way.

▶ Lesson Plan Theory and Practice

Madeline Hunter has developed a useful procedure for thinking about and acting on the planning variable in the instructional process. Essentially, she identifies three aspects of teaching: (1) what will be taught, (2) how the students will behave, and (3) how the teacher will behave. See Figure 5–1. Hunter (1982) writes:

> The first decision of teaching is based on content, the *what* of teaching, its complexity as well as the rate and degree at which the content will be taught. The second decision is directed to the *student behavior* that makes learning

FIGURE 5-1 Instructional Events Related to Quality Instruction (1982)

```
Presentation                                          ┐
  Overview                                            │
    Review                                            │
    What?                                             │
    Why?                                              │
    Explanation                                       │
    Students demonstrate understanding                │
                                                      │
Feedback                                              │  FEEDBACK
                                                      │
Practice                                              │
  Guided/Controlled                                   │
  Independent                                         │
                                                      │
Performance                                           │
  Daily work                                          │
  Unit tests                                          │
  Periodic review                                     ┘
```

TABLE 5-1 Madeline Hunter's White Sauce Recipe— or Eight Steps for Effective Instruction

1. *Anticipatory Set:* Set the stage. Focus student attention on the topic. This is the teacher behavior that causes the student to attend. It can build on previous learning.
2. *Behavioral Objectives:* A description of a pattern of behavior (performance) you want the learner to be able to demonstrate.
3. *Purpose:* Why are you doing this? Why did you establish this objective?
4. *Input:* Introduce the material. Use visual and auditory modes of learning. Spend time here if you want the students to work independently.
5. *Modeling:* Should be used with *every* lesson. Demonstrate what is expected of the students. *Show* them.
6. *Check for Understanding:* Student(s) tell *you* what is expected. Don't ask, "Does everyone understand?" Ask something like, "Can you tell me what we will do, Jim?"
7. *Guided Practice:* Students are guided by you as they work through one or two problems, and/or the students begin working while teacher circulates, assisting those who need help.
8. *Independent Practice:* Student completes task alone. Spend time and effort on steps 5, 6, and 7 to make this a successful task. If a child practices incorreclty, you will have to *undo* it and reteach.

Adapted from Hunter (1982).

possible, the student's *how* of learning. There are two aspects of a student's learning behavior. One aspect is focused on the input modalities the student will use to acquire knowledge or skill. That is, will (s)he read, discuss, listen, observe, do? *There is no one best way to learn,* and use of a combination of these input behaviors usually is more effective than relying on one. The third decision is about teacher behavior. It asks, "What will you do during the lesson?" Will you lecture, ask questions, model behavior, etc.?

Hunter's instructional model, which she calls a "White Sauce Recipe," or "Eight Steps to Effective Instruction," provides a clear summary of a lesson schematic. Her model, illustrated in Table 5–1, is followed by examples of three lessons that utilize Hunter's approach in slightly different formats.

▶ Lesson Plan Models

There is, of course, no one right format for writing lesson plans. They can be written in a variety of ways. The important thing to bear in mind is that they should be useful and practical. Typically, however, they are written to include an objective, a procedure for the teacher and students to follow, and a practice session, which may be guided or independent, sometimes in the form of homework.

Sample Lesson Plan One

Name _____ School _____

Subject _____ Grade Level _____

No. of Students _____ Date/Time _____

Lesson Generalization: The predicate of a sentence may consist of a transitive verb, which requires a direct object, or an intransitive verb, which does not.

Lesson Behaviors: Given a list of sentences, students will be able to identify those that contain transitive verbs and those that contain intransitive verbs.

Lesson Component	Procedures	Specific Resource Time
1. *Anticipatory Set*	Ask students to try an experiment. I will write the following words on the board: swam slept hiked built borrowed threw Students use their own names in front of each of the words (for example, Tim swam) to see which could be complete sentences. Ask why some of the words complete a sentence and why some do not.	5 min
2. *Input*	Show transparency that contains List A (sentences with intransitive verbs) and List B (sentences with transitive verbs) and ask how the lists are different.	5 min
	Introduce terms: *transitive, intransitive, direct object.* Define them and show examples from sentences in a story (on transparency).	10 min
3. *Modeling*	Return to original list on board and write sentences using teacher's name. Explain how transitive verbs require direct objects and intransitive verbs do not.	10 min

Sample Lesson Plan One (continued)

4. *Check for Understanding*	Ask for definitions:
	
	transitive verb
	direct object
	intransitive verb
	
	Ask for volunteers to complete the following orally:
	
	Teresa
	  ran sold
	  saw spilled
		5 min

5. *Guided Practice*	Give students worksheet that calls for identification of type of periodicals. Work the first three examples together.	3 min
6. *Independent Practice*[*]	Students complete worksheet.	12 min

*Slow learners work with teacher
Vocabulary words: *transitive verb, intransitive verb, direct object*
Additional resources: transparencies
Enrichment level: Find examples of types of predicates in science and social studies books.

Sample Lesson Plan Two

Name _____ School _____
Subject Mathematics: Counting Grade Level (K–1)
No. of Students _____ Date/Time _____

Lesson Generalization: Students will be counting objects up to 10 and developing skills in the basic areas of adding and subtracting.

Objective: Given up to ten objects, the students will be able to count the appropriate numbers of objects as requested by the teacher. Students will understand the concepts of *more, less, add, take away, left behind,* and so on.

Setting the Stage: Tell the students that they are going to play a new counting game. Each student is given a cinnamon juju bear. (Don't eat it yet!) They are told that they are living in a dark forest and they must get prepared to hibernate, because winter is coming fast. Each student is given ten Fruit Loops: four "cherries," three "lemons," and three "oranges."

Sample Lesson Plan Two (continued)

Lesson Procedures: Each student will be sitting on the floor as a part of a large circle. Students are told to cup their left hand as if it were a "bearcave." The cinnamon bear must go out into the forest and find two "cherries," one "lemon," and two "oranges" and bring them back to its cave. The students then get two red, one yellow, and two orange Fruit Loops and slide them into the "bearcave." (Ask the students how many the bear has in its cave.) The bear then goes back out to find more fruit. While the bear is gone, a badger sneaks into the cave and steals (takes away) one "orange" and one "lemon." (Ask the students how many the badger left behind in the cave.) Continue presenting as many different combinations using the concepts of *add, take away, left behind, more, less,* and so on, as time allows. When students understand the concepts, stop the lesson.

Summary: At the end of the lesson, ask students which flavor their bear liked best. Develop a chart with the following format:

My bear liked this fruit flavor the best:

Cherry	Lemon	Orange

Students sign their name under the flavor that their bear liked the best. If they have not eaten their objects yet, let them do so.

Evidence of Learning: Students will be able to demonstrate *more, less, add, take away, left behind, and so on.*

Time: Approximately 15–20 minutes.

Specific Resources: Fruit Loops, cinnamon juju bears, and a chart.

Sample Lesson Plan Three

Name _____ School _____

Subject Economics: Consumer Research   Grade Level _____

No. of Students _____ Date/Time _____

Lesson Generalization: The analytical skills of product testings and decision making are useful and directly applicable in our society.

Lesson Behaviors: Students will work in groups of four to test various brands of paper towels.
1. Decide on appropriate tests.
2. Analyze and test products.
3. Record results.
4. Synthesize and report findings.

Sample Lesson Plan Three (continued)

Lesson Component: Product tests of five brands of paper towels. Purpose of test is to determine rank ordering of products from best buy to worst buy.

Procedures:
1. Motivation: Seek examples of consumerism from students.
2. Students will work in small groups assigned the task of testing paper towels.
3. Students will use at least four test procedures to develop their rankings.
4. Each group will be responsible for developing and conducting its own tests.
5. Groups will report their findings to class.
6. Teacher summary.

Specific Resources: Five brands of paper towels, testings materials, including measuring cups, eyedroppers, and rulers.

Time: Two social studies periods.

Evidence of Learning: Group cooperation, decision making, tests, reports.

Additional Resources: Paper towels, graph paper, and measuring instruments.

► ## Instructional Objectives

More than two decades ago, Robert Mager (1962) wrote a book titled, *Preparing Instructional Objectives.* Using ideas from behavioral psychology, Mager stressed that in order for teaching objectives to be clear and meaningful, they would have to address the following three questions: (1) What should the learner be able to do? (2) Under what conditions will the learner to be able to do it? and (3) How well must it be done? Mager (1975) thus established explicitly the criteria for instructional objectives. They are:

1. *Performance.* An objective always says what a learner is expected to be able to *do.*
2. *Conditions.* An objective always describes the important conditions (if any) under which the performance is to occur.
3. *Criterion.* Whenever possible, an objective describes the criterion of acceptable performance by describing how well the learner must perform in order to be considered acceptable.

Take a moment to consider the following two language arts objectives. Determine whether they meet the three criteria for instructional objectives.

CLEAR VS. UNCLEAR VERBS FOR WRITING OBJECTIVES

Unclear Verbs		Clear Verbs	
enjoy	realize	list	demonstrate
value	become aware of	identify	describe
know	understand	classify	write
appreciate		select	define
		construct	measure
		compare/contrast	

1. Students will develop a clear understanding of topic sentences in paragraphs and will be able to recognize them.
2. Using a worksheet containing six brief paragraphs, students will underline the topic sentences in at least five of the six paragraphs.

Objective number one is not clear about what students are to *do,* it does not specify conditions under which students will perform, and it does not establish the criterion for success. Objective number two tells us what students will do (underline topic sentences), how they will do it (on a worksheet), and the measure of successful performance (five out of six correct).

A note of caution: Behavioral objectives are helpful because they specify what students will do with their time and to what extent they must perform to be judged successful. While this ensures accountability of instruction, it cannot, of course, guarantee the quality and ultimate purposefulness of instruction. It is well to remember that teaching is as much art as it is science, and that not everything you teach your students needs to be accounted for in strict behavioral terms. This is not a way of saying that accountability and precision in teaching/learning are trivial matters. Rather, we are saying that good teaching, which is a very complex enterprise, is the outcome of a variety of approaches.

CURRICULAR AND INSTRUCTIONAL REALITY

▶ One way to determine what teachers have in mind when they plan curriculum and instruction is to look at outcomes. The manner in which time is actually spent in classrooms furnishes us with clues to teachers' sense of priorities. If one were to deduce teachers' planning priorities from John Goodlad's data, the obvious conclusion is that elementary teachers plan and carry out more seatwork than anything else. Secondary teachers, on the other hand, plan and carry out more explanations/lectures than anything else. Table 5–2 illustrates Goodlad's findings of how school days are typically spent.

TABLE 5-2 Snapshot Data: Rank Order of Activities by Probability of Students Having Been Observed Participating in Each at Any Particular Moment

Early Elementary Activity	Percent	Upper Elementary Activity	Percent
Written work	28.3	Written work	30.4
Listening to explanations/lectures	18.2	Listening to explanations/lectures	20.1
Preparation for assignments	12.7	Preparation for assignments	11.5
Practice/performance-physical	7.3	Discussion	7.7
Use of AV equipment	6.8	Reading	5.5
Reading	6.0	Practice/performance-physical	5.3
Student nontask behavior–No		Use of AV equipment	4.9
assignment	5.7	Student nontask behavior–No	
Discussion	5.3	assignment	4.8
Practice/performance-Verbal	5.2	Practice/performance-Verbal	4.4
Taking tests	2.2	Taking tests	3.3
Watching demonstrations	1.5	Watching demonstrations	1.0
Being disciplined	0.5	Simulation/role play	0.4
Simulation/role play	0.2	Being disciplined	0.3

Junior High Activity	Percent	Senior High Activity	Percent
Listening to explanations/lectures	21.9	Listening to explanations/lectures	25.3
Written work	20.7	Practice/performance-physical	17.5
Preparation for assignments	15.9	Written work	15.1
Practice/performance-physical	14.7	Preparation for assignments	12.8
Taking tests	5.5	Student nontask behavior–No	
Discussion	4.2	assignment	6.9
Practice/performance-verbal	4.2	Taking tests	5.8
Use of AV equipment	4.1	Discussion	5.1
Student nontask behavior–No		Practice/performance-verbal	4.5
assignment	3.6	Use of AV equipment	2.8
Reading	2.8	Reading	1.9
Watching demonstrations	1.5	Watching demonstrations	1.6
Simulation/role play	0.2	Simulation/role play	0.1
Being disciplined	0.2	Being disciplined	0.1

Study Table 5–2 carefully to see what hypotheses you can make from it. Here are two hypotheses to get you started:

1. It would appear that teachers plan lessons that encourage (require?) a passive, seatbound student role in learning.

2. It would appear that the modern technology (AV equipment, computers, etc.) play a very minor role in teachers' planning for curriculum and instruction.

3. _____

4. _____

5. _____

Table 5–2 tells us how things are (in this very large sample of classrooms) and not necessarily how they ought to be. A reading of John Dewey, Jean Piaget, Jerome Bruner, and John Goodlad (1960) would lead one quickly to a rearrangement of these priorities in curriculum and instruction toward more involved, creative, and conceptually oriented classroom environments. It is well to keep in mind Goodlad's observation that:

> . . . the teacher is the central figure in determining the activities, as well as the tone of the classroom. The teachers is *virtually autonomous* with respect to classroom decisions—selecting materials, determining class organization, choosing instructional procedures, and so on (Goodlad, 1984).

Thus we return to a familiar refrain in the sage of American public education: local control. The classroom teacher works within a framework of broad parameters and few constraints when he or she plans for and carries out curriculum and instruction on a daily basis.

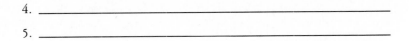

Individual and Groups

There is an old story that the ideal curriculum and teaching environment for learning politics consisted of nothing more than political boss and sometimes tutor Mark Hanna and his budding pupil and future president Teddy Roosevelt sitting on either end of a log. The mythical picture of the sage old mentor and the bright and eager pupil represents in all our minds the best in teaching and learning. It's all there: wisdom, motivation, knowledge, informality, intimacy, the teachable moment, the simple setting, the caring teacher, and the adoring learner. The romantic effect is heightened even further by what isn't there: no bells, no walls, no administrators, no required degrees and certificates, no state department, no mindless textbooks, no unmotivated teachers and students. Other similar examples come to mind: Helen Keller reaching for the stars because of the patient goodness of her tutor Anne Sullivan; young George Washington hanging on to every word uttered by his older brother Lawrence; Martin Luther King, Jr., learning compassion, oratory, and a vision from his daddy. In Mexico, a whole nation learned to read by employing the principle of "each one teach one." Perhaps in your own life you have been fortunate enough to share such an experience. If so, you know how privileged you are.

But these are fanciful notions of curriculum and instruction against the backdrop of formal education in the United States and Canada today. It doesn't work that way except perhaps in a few unusual cases. Most teachers have to plan their curricular and instructional efforts with class sizes of twenty-five to thirty-five students in mind. They have, in fact, little time for planning. In spite of this reality, there remains the abiding notion of individualized instruction as the way students *should* be learning. Teachers are bombarded with questionable (in terms of any kind of classroom application) "research" about learning styles, personality types, temperaments, sex differences, and hemispheric lateralization of the brain, the point of which is to enable them to plan a curriculum that customizes learning to fit the needs of any given individual student or subgroup of students.

Deviations from whole-class instruction are theoretically based on something similar to a doctor-patient model where the student is diagnosed (say in terms of reading ability) and given a prescription or treatment (assigned work at a certain group or level). The reasons why teachers break whole classes into groups are several. One reason is tradition. Do you know *anyone* who attended first grade who wasn't placed into an ability-related reading group? The groups are usually given names that reflect anything except what they are, which are high-, medium-, and low-reading groups. They might be called the Skylarks, the Gobots, the Hobbits, or the Green Group, but everyone knows these are ability groups. There is virtually no comprehensive research base in support of this procedure, but tradition is a powerful force and so that's the way it is. When asked to defend this procedure, teachers will argue that it is a way to accommodate differences in individuals by ability. But here is a case where the cure is probably worse than the disease. Einstein, for example, could not read until he was nine years old, so he would have been placed in a low group (or referred to special education). The resultant effect of such typecasting has no doubt served to lower the self-image of countless children over the years whose ultimate success in life was something less than Einstein's, but more to the point, was less than it might have been.

Another reason teachers group students is for interactive purposes. Studies of classroom interaction indicate that teachers plan for classrooms to be quiet places dominated by seatwork and by teacher-led presentations. Even the small reading groups found at primary levels are not convened in order to facilitate student-to-student interaction. Thus, some teachers try to allow individuals a greater opportunity to express themselves by placing them into small discussion groups or committees. When the task is clear and planning has been made for acceptable group behavior, this method can indeed accomplish the goal of increased active student participation.

The theory of individualized instruction is that each student moves at his or her own pace. One of the more notable attempts at individualized instruction was Individually Guided Education (IGE), developed in Wisconsin. At the present time, a small number of church-sponsored private schools use a completely individualized curriculum called Accelerated Christian Education (ACE). In an ACE school, a student completes a sequential series of workbooks in each subject area and moves forward at his or her own pace. But individualization of instruction is a rare commodity in the public schools of today. As Goodlad and others have observed, the classroom of today resembles, for the most part, the classroom of 1900—one teacher in front of thirty pupils.

But just as a study by the University of Arizona Health Science Center showed that as many as 35 percent of medical prescriptions are never even filled and of those that are filled 30–60 percent are incorrectly administered, so is a massive breakdown of this seemingly appropriate pedagogical procedure obvious to any discerning observer. Worse yet is the "cure" itself. As certain researchers have pointed out, placing students in high, medium, and low academic categories early in their school courses exacts a great price.

DIFFERENTIATING ASSIGNMENTS TO ACCOMMODATE INDIVIDUAL DIFFERENCES

▶ There are at least two reasons why teachers might wish to differentiate certain assignments: students have different abilities and students have different interests. Providing options for a class of twenty-five to thirty students doesn't mean developing that many differing options. It would be quite helpful for a teacher to provide, say, three levels to an assignment. Thus, slower, middle, and advanced students could be accommodated. Take a few moments to examine the activity cards shown in Figures 5–2 through 5–4. Notice that the activities become progressively more complex. Notice also that they provide such interest options as reading a picture, reading printed source material, drawing a diagram, making a map, creative writing, technical writing, coloring, construction, and student-conducted research.

Slower students might complete only Activity Card #1. Higher achievers might be led to select different activities from among the three cards. The strength of this approach is that everyone can reach his or her limits while the entire class studies the same topic. Thus, class discussions will make sense when you bring the entire class together to deliberate on a given topic.

FIGURE 5-2 Activity Card #1: The Fur Trade

1. Copy these sentences and fill in the missing words.

The time of year in the picture is _____. The traders are preparing

the fur post for the _____ season. Two _____ are paddling a

canoe in the _____. A woman tends the garden where _____

and _____ are grown. Other Indians are making _____.

2. Study the picture for a moment. List at least five activites you see.
3. Which of the jobs in the picture would you like to do? Tell why.
4. Draw a diagram of the fur post. Label all parts and sizes of it.
5. Use popsicle sticks, clay, glue, cardboard, and construction paper to construct a model of the fur post.

Drawing by Chet Kozlak; reprinted from *A Great Lakes Fur Trade Coloring Book/Les Fourrures et les Grands lac Cahier a colorier,* Copyright 1981 by the Minnesota Historical Society.

FIGURE 5-3 Activity Card #2: The Fur Trade

1. Read the first ten pages of the book, *With Pipe, Paddle, and Song*. It will tell you many things about the fur trade. You may wish to read further.
2. Write a short story that explains the purpose of the fur trade. Include the following in your story:
   Where did the fur trade take place? When?
   Who was involved in the fur trade?
   What did people do with the furs in those days?
   How were the furs trapped and taken to market?
3. Imagine you are in charge of a fur post. Make a list of supplies you will need for the winter.
4. Draw and color a picture of a fur post as you think it might look in winter.

Drawing by Chet Kozlak; reprinted from *A Great Lakes Fur Trade Coloring Book/Les Fourrures et les Grands lacs Cahier a colorier*, Copyright 1981 by the Minnesota Historical Society.

FIGURE 5-4 Activity Card #3: The Fur Trade

1. Make a map showing where the furs will be shipped from the fur post.
2. Find at least three books in the library to use in writing a two-page report on the fur trade.
3. Imagine you are a traveler who visits the fur post in summer. Write a letter to a friend in New York describing life at the post. Explain to your friend how life here is different from life in New York.
4. How did the establishment of the fur trade change the Indians' way of life? Tell how you feel about the changes.

Drawing by Chet Kozlak; reprinted from *A Great Lakes Fur Trade Coloring Book/Les Fourrures et les Grands lacs Cahier a colorier,* Copyright 1981 by the Minnesota Historical Society.

► **Three Goal Structures for Planning**

It is an oversimplification of complex realities to assume that what teachers teach is necessarily what students learn. Much of what is taught (and presumably learned) is designed to help students interact with *ideas* and *materials*. Teachers are encouraged to facilitate students' learning by involving them in intellectually stimulating situations where they use manipulatives, make original charts, play games, gather data, construct tables and graphs, and so on. This, of course, is all to the good. It is a way of learning that is supported by a larger and ever-growing body of research. But there is another dimension, often overlooked, that bears examination as well. That dimension is the classroom *goal structure* that teachers create.

Johnson and Johnson clarify the meaning of classroom goal structure by posing the question, "How should students interact with each other?" The basis on which students interact with each other is something that teachers determine. Who gives them such power? Actually, the choice is theirs by default. It is important to remember that while teachers are often told *what* they must teach, they are seldom told *how* they must teach it.

Johnson and Johnson (1975, 1984) suggest that the basic generalization about goal structuring is that *how the teacher sets up the learning goals determines the teacher-student and student-student interaction patterns.*

The Johnsons identify three types of classroom goal structures: competitive, individualistic, and cooperative. They note that each has its merits and that a teacher should probably use all three goal structures over the course of a year. But their own research and the related research of other investigators that they have reviewed has led them to the conclusion that the greatest potential academic and social good accrues from a cooperative goal structure. Curiously though, it is seldom employed by teachers simply because they do not understand how to implement it, or because they have the mistaken idea that a cooperative goal structure makes it impossible to reward individual achievement. The following overview of the three basic goal structures is intended to show you how they work.

Competitive Goal Structure
In a competitive situation (whether academic, athletic, or whatever) one person can attain his or her goal only if others fail to obtain theirs. Thus, a negative correlation exists among goal attainments. In other words, if I win, you lose. And if you win, I lose. In this type of goal structure, each individual strives toward the highest marks. Evaluation is comparative or norm-referenced. Grades are often based on a curve. Winners are rewarded. Losers are not exactly punished, but one wonders whether they know that.

The game of croquet provides an interesting illustration of an extreme competitive goal structure. You are not only trying to hit your own ball through the wicket, but you are also allowed to drive your opponent's ball away from the course. Closer to the classroom. John Goodlad (1984) has suggested that the natural outcome one might suspect in the typical school situation is the tendency on the part of the students to want to cheat, perhaps because they are too often put in a competitive win/no-win situation.

All this is not to say that competition is inherently evil. All of us have enjoyed and benefited from certain types of competition. But you must learn to distinguish between appropriate and inappropriate competition. School learning, for example, is not a scarce resource that is available only to a few. All students can and ought to learn.

Individualistic Goal Structure

In a individualistic situation, each person's goal attainment is unrelated to the goal attainment of others. No correlation among goal attainment exists. There is no linkage and therefore no support from one student to another. Each person is rewarded for his or her own product. Evaluation is based on set standards; therefore, everyone could, conceivably achieve "mastery" or the criterion of success. In this respect, individualistic learning is criterion-referenced. If, for example, 90 percent correct is the criterion for a grade of "A," it is possible that all students, some students, or no students might achieve this criterion.

This pattern is quite common in classrooms. It is seen in spelling and other subjects where there are lists, dates and so on, to learn. In mathematics, if everyone memorizes all the basic addition and multiplication facts, they receive an "A" on the facts test. If everyone is able to complete a problem-solving test at a certain level, they all pass the test. A curious form of individualistic learning occurs in group work when each student does a particular piece of work and receives his or her own reward.

Cooperative Goal Structure

In a cooperative learning environment, when one person achieves his or her goal, all others achieve their goals. Therefore, a positive correlation exists among goal attainments. People sink or swim together.

In a cooperative goal structure, rewards are linked. For example, students may be given a common grade for a group project. But more than that, they may help each other in an interactive way. Cumulative research findings that favor cooperative learning include the following points:

1. Higher achievement, better retention
2. Growth in moral and cognitive reasoning

3. Enhanced motivation to learn
4. Greater liking for school and school subjects
5. Improved attitude toward teachers
6. Enhanced self-esteem
7. Greater liking for each other regardless of individual differences

The Johnsons make two other arguments, which no teacher can afford to ignore:

1. Back to basics? There is nothing more basic than working successfully with others.
2. The single most common reason why people are fired from their job is failure to get along with others.

To illustrate the three goal structures, let's examine the following problem. The task is to count the number of triangles found in Figure 5-5.

▶ *Competitively:* Put your students in groups of three and have the students in each group compete to see who can count the most triangles.

▶ *Individualistically:* Tell your students to count as many triangles as they can. Anyone who counts at least 90 percent of the actual total succeeds at the task.

▶ *Cooperatively:* Put your students in groups of three. Ask each group to find as many triangles as they can. Encourage them to help each other because success depends on each person's help.

How many triangles did students find working alone? With someone? Generally, higher quality results evolve from cooperative group efforts.

FIGURE 5-5 Triangles: How Many Can You Find?

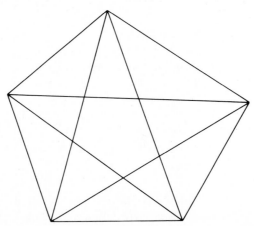

The purpose of this brief overview of classroom goal structures is to stress the importance of the *affective* environment in learning. (The term *affective* refers to attitudes and feelings.) Teaching math, English, or any subject is much more than exposing students to new content. The concepts of individualistic, competitive, and cooperative learning provide insights to the "hidden" processes of instruction, which in the long run are equally as important as *what* we teach.

SUMMARY

▶ In this chapter we attempted to make a case for the crucial nature of planning and organizing the curriculum. Teachers need to articulate a philosophy of curriculum and instruction based on their own thinking and the carefully considered goal statements of the various professional curricular organizations. In most cases, districts either develop their own set of curricular and instructional objectives or depend on state department of education guidelines. Despite this patchwork mix of input from individual teachers, there is remarkable homogeneity in terms of how units, lessons, and instructional strategies are brought to bear on a daily basis. If one were to deduce what teachers plan from what they do, we could reasonably assume they plan primarily for seatwork and teacher presentations. In addition to these observations, we offered strategies for unit and lesson planning, for grouping, and for academic/social goal structures.

ACTIVITIES

1. Identify any two subject areas of the school curriculum and compare and contrast the goal statements of their respective professional organizations (e.g., International Reading Association, National Council for the Social Studies, etc.).
2. Interview a public school teacher and ask: (1) to what extent he or she is guided by a philosophy of curriculum and instruction, and (2) if so, what is that philosophy?
3. Examine Table 5-2, which documents John Goodlad's findings of how students spend their day. What changes would you recommend?
4. The issue of meeting individual needs within a group (classroom) structure is indeed a challenging one. What ideas can you come up with in this regard?

REFERENCES

Bruner, J. (1960). *The process of education*. Cambridge, Mass.: Harvard University Press.

Fenstermacher, G. A., and Goodlad, J. I. (Eds.). (1983). *Individual differences and the common curriculum*. Chicago: University of Chicago Press.

Goodlad, J. I. (1984). *A place called school*. New York: McGraw-Hill, p. 123.

Hunter, M. (1982). *Mastery teaching*. El Segundo, Calif.: ITIP Publications, p. 5.

Jackson, P. (1968). *Life in classrooms*. New York: Holt, Rinehart, and Winston.

Johnson, D. W., and Johnson, R. T. (1975). *Learning together and alone*. Englewood Cliffs, N.J.: Prentice-Hall.

Johnson, D. W., and Johnson, R. T. (1984). *Circles of learning*. Washington, D.C.: ASCD.

Mager, R. F. (1962). *Preparing instructional objectives*. Belmont, Calif.: Fearon.

Mager, R. F. (1975). *Preparing instructional objectives* (2nd ed.). Belmont, Calif.: Pitman Learning, p. 21.

Slavin, R. (1986). *Educational psychology: Theory into practice*. Englewood Cliffs, N.J.: Prentice-Hall.

Squires, D. A., et al. (1983). *Effective schools and classrooms: A research-based perspective*. Washington, D.C.: ASCD, p. 20.

Tyler, R. W. (1949). *Basic principles of curriculum and instruction*. Chicago: University of Chicago Press.

Whitehead, A. N. (1929). *The aims of education and other essays*. New York: MacMillan.

SUGGESTED READINGS

Clark, C. M., and Yinger, R. J. (1979). Research on teacher thinking. *Curriculum Inquiry, 7,* 279–394.

Elbaz, F. (1983). *Teacher thinking: A study of practical knowledge*. New York: Nichols Publishing.

Goodlad, J., and Klein, M. F. (1970). *Behind the classroom door*. Worthington, Ohio: Charles A. Jones.

Jackson, P. W. (1968). *Life in classrooms*. New York: Holt, Rinehart and Winston.

McCutcheon, G. (1980). How do elementary teachers plan? The nature of planning and influences on it. *Elementary School Journal, 81,* 4–23.

Shavelson, R. J., and Stern, P. C. (1981). Research on teachers' pedagogical thoughts, judgements, decisions, and behavior. *Review of Educational Research, 51,* 455–498.

6

Three Categories of
Instructional Strategy

OVERVIEW

▶   This chapter concentrates on instructional strategies, which are defined
as the pedagogical techniques that are available to a teacher. Three
distinct modes of instruction are introduced: classical, where the student receives knowledge passively; discovery, where the student learns
inductively through activities; and changed structure, where the
classroom environment is altered to facilitate learning.

Since the models of instruction are somewhat abstract, the chapter
concludes with a very detailed account of a teacher using each of the
models in his secondary school classroom.

INSTRUCTIONAL STRATEGIES

▶   If teacher planning is the architectural drawing that traces the basic
curricular design, then the instructional strategy provides the support—
the joists and girders, not obvious but indispensable—that underlies
the curriculum. In this chapter we will discuss three instructional
strategies by viewing teaching from several perspectives and examining the various models, styles, and approaches to teaching that are currently available to teachers. Since the chapter proposes to separate

elements of instruction that are not easily separated, and as a result runs the risk of becoming a bit abstruse, we believe that the clarity of our argument will be enhanced if we approach our subject matter somewhat gingerly by employing a medical analogy as a way of introduction.

Let us imagine that we want to examine the effectiveness of medical practice. Although there are numerous ways of accomplishing our task, there are four obvious directions in which we could proceed. First, we could investigate the doctor-patient relationship by asking patients to list the characteristics of effective physicians. Second, we could explore the training that future doctors receive in medical education. Third, we could observe physicians' performance by listing actual behaviors and relating them to outcomes such as the recovery or mortality rates of their patients. Finally, we could review the alternative modes and strategies that are available, given particular medical problems. It is to this latter consideration — available strategies — that we direct our attention in this chapter.

For this discussion, at least, we contend that it is beneficial for teachers to imagine instruction as a set or repertoire of behaviors that are available to them, given the specific desired educational outcome. In essence, the chapter will present the inventory of a general store of instruction, and encourage the teacher to shop for an appropriate technique. In our general store of instructional strategies, we will demonstrate that there is at least one appropriate strategy for any given teacher's instructional needs.

▶ Categories of Instructional Strategies

These categories are based on the differences in kinds of learning behavior that students are likely to be engaged in when these instructional strategies are employed. That is, we will delineate three distinct modes in which students can be taught. We call these modes *classical, discovery,* and *changed structure.* The pupil experiencing classical instructional strategies, a lecture for example, is treated as if his or her mind is an empty bucket into which knowledge can be poured. In the discovery mode, the circumstances are different because it is assumed that the pupil possesses or can actively acquire a repertoire of knowledge and skills to apply to, for example, the resolution of a problem or the discovery of a generalization. The changed structure approach, exemplified by role playing, simulation games, and group process, alters the classroom environment to facilitate learning. Table 6–1 presents this conceptual scheme a little more crisply.

A more complete description of each of these approaches will

TABLE 6-1 Categories of Instructional Strategy

Teacher-Centered Classical	Discovery Approaches	Changed Structure
* Lectures	* Problem solving	* On-site learning
* Readings	* Case studies	* Small groups
* Demonstration	* Inquiry teaching	* Role playing
* Guided discussion	* Experiments	* Simulation
* Textbook recitation		* Group investigation

demonstrate their characteristics as well as their relative strengths and weaknesses as instructional strategies.

Classical Mode / Teacher Centered

In this mode of instruction, the teacher is seen as an authority who is the sole possessor of a particular body of knowledge. The function of the teacher is to funnel information down to naive learners and to decide entirely what direction the class will take. The communicative mode for this style of teaching is mainly teacher talks and students listen.

Classical instruction is product-oriented rather than process-oriented. That is, teachers who employ classical instructional strategies are more interested that their students learn a body of knowledge than they are concerned that their pupils acquire a particular intellectual skill or examine particular values or attitudes. Inevitably, classical instruction is accompanied by a series of obligatory techniques such as assigned readings, questions at the end of chapters, whole class discussions, and the assumption that no interaction between teachers and students is necessary. The lecture is the signal technique of this kind of teaching, although several other methods such as textbook recitation, demonstrations, and guided discussion are well within the confines of the classical mode.

The classical mode has several strengths. Dwarfing all others, of course, is the predictability of the approach. Since teachers have nearly complete control, they can anticipate what will happen down to the smallest detail, and plan for nearly every kind of contingency. Teachers can know exactly what they are going to teach and how they are going to approach each issue. In addition, classical modes are easy to evaluate because every student has virtually an identical learning experience. This teaching mode permits teachers to be elaborately prepared and to take their classes along routes dictated by the teachers' greatest strength.

Most classical mode approaches, especially the teaching that characterizes lectures, allow teachers to cover a great deal of information rapidly. The efficiency that this approach embodies is, in fact, limited only by the energy, organization, and knowledge of the teacher.

Inherent in the classical mode of instruction is that it is expected by most students because they are accustomed to receiving their lessons this way. Therefore, pupils are unlikely to be confused by this instructional mode. By the same token, most teachers are probably comfortable with classical modes because most of their own instruction has emanated from this style.

Both the physical and social architecture of the schools are conducive to classical approaches to instruction. Physically, classrooms are constructed as small squares that naturally present teachers to their students frontally. The teacher who wants to alter this environment has to rearrange the furniture of the classroom. Socially, classical methods please administrators because they allow teachers to present the appearance of control and diligence; the structure of this approach pleases other teachers because the method fosters a quiet atmosphere and makes one's teaching unlikely to disturb fellow teachers.

Although the advantages of the classical mode are significant, this method does have liabilities. Transcending all others is student passivity. Practitioners of classical methods assume that their students are in the position of the learners described over a century ago by Charles Dickens as "inclined planes of little vessels then and there arranged in order to have imperial gallons of facts poured into them until they were full to the brim" (Dickens, 1854/1972, pp. 15–16).

In addition, the carefulness and completeness of the teacher's script precludes ad libbing and improvisation by the student. By disallowing the unique contribution by one's students to the examination of the topic at hand, practitioners of classical approaches risk throttling potentially useful insights on the subject and prematurely capping the knowledge that can be explored.

In the same vein, the approach does not allow for individual learner characteristics in its planning process. Thus, for some teachers who employ this technique, the route of their course is mapped out before they see their students, and they are reluctant to change their pedagogy to match their learners' characteristics. Ironically, the learner becomes an obstacle to the teachers' goals. The orientation of the course becomes a linear progression from the teachers' knowledge to the presentation of content. In some schools, it is nearly possible to predict the season of the year by the emergence of particular learning materials.

Classical modes of instruction, then, are familiar, predictable, and efficient, but they are restrictive and likely to miss nuances and mute differences between students.

Discovery Mode

The teacher using the discovery mode is likely to act in an encouraging and accessible manner; he or she encourages class members to interact with one another, is willing to admit several answers to each question, and talks only a little bit more than the students.

Discovery modes of instruction tend to be process-oriented. The bulk of the responsibility for learning is placed on the students. Because teachers employing this model are more interested in students' thinking process than they are in correct answers, the discovery approach depends on extensive teacher-pupil interaction. Problem solving, case studies, and inquiry teaching are among the representations of discovery modes.

Discovery modes have several strengths. Overarching all is the assumption that the learner is not a blank slate, but the possessor of enough knowledge and analytical ability to contribute to a discussion of the issues under examination. In fact, the discovery approach promotes the possibility that the students may even introduce new issues for the class to examine. Discovery methods present the illusion, at least, of independence. By virtue of the fact that the discovery mode is oriented toward process, these methods provide practice in thinking, and present the possibility of using the newly acquired concepts to analyze and sort the students' surroundings.

Discovery approaches also help students translate knowledge into their own ways of thinking. Many cognitive psychologists, especially those who scrutinize students' acquisition of reading skills, stress the importance of the prior knowledge or *schemata* that a student possesses. These observers of the learning process claim that students are likely to make greater cognitive gains when the material presented can be easily subsumed into preexisting mental constructs (Anderson and Pearson, 1984).

While helping students translate knowledge into their own mental constructs, the use of this approach also serves to motivate students to search for knowledge. In doing so, students often come face-to-face with the validity or lack thereof of their own ideas. Discovery modes, and the confusion that accompanies the process, subject pupils' ideas to a vigorous examination which, if they take the quest seriously, "will scatter their ideas like chaff or if they have any real substance, root them more strongly" (Wain, 1981, p. 251).

Although the siren song of the discovery mode appears difficult to resist, it is possible that a well-motivated yet unprepared teacher's pedagogy can crash on the shoals of despair. Discovery modes are often difficult to implement, nearly impossible to predict outcomes for, prone to lurch out of control at the slightest provocation, and are maddeningly subject to pupil impatience.

Some of the weaknesses in the discovery mode are inherent in the methods, others are in the social-psychological properties of the teachers and the situation. Let us examine some of the social-psychological characteristics first.

Most teachers are better at explaining than they are at eliciting. As the aphorism goes, "Scratch a teacher and you find a preacher." Much of the thrust of teacher preparation, coupled with the generally outgoing dispositions of those who chose to teach, conspire to make the spectator and facilitator stance difficult to adapt. The delay and the detachment necessary for discovery teaching are thus difficult for many teachers to sustain.

More serious, perhaps, is the loss of control that resides in discovery modes. Here, the teacher, although still nominally in charge, is asked to be one in a community of learners. Many steeled to command find ambiguity uncomfortable and are inclined to abandon discovery modes at the first sign of something that smacks of serendipity.

The central weakness of the method itself is the likelihood that the learning session will degenerate into chaos. In addition, children and adolescents have limited experience in pursuing argument, and are very likely to see a discussion of an issue as an opportunity to put down or ridicule their peers. They are also equally likely to perceive the teacher's purposeful distancing as an abdication of control.

When this tendency is combined with the general lack of clear and easily interpretable models for discovery approaches like case studies and problem solving, it is relatively easy to see why efforts to use these techniques frequently go awry.

In summary, discovery-oriented approaches possess great potential for expanding the horizons of young people's thinking, but the paths of these models are strewn with obstacles and various other intellectual debris.

Changed Structure

Changed structure approaches tend to be experimentally oriented. They seek to exemplify the contrast between traditional school learning and the kind of learning that takes place in much of life outside of school. By and large, these modes emphasize action and the modeling of real-life situations.

The changed structures model incorporates the notion that the traditional environment is often too sterile, artificial, and confining to promote real-life learning. Teachers using these models are more interested in preparing students to accept adult responsibilities than they are concerned with covering traditional school content.

Although the variety of instructional approaches embodied by the changed structures approach stretches along a lengthy continuum—proceeding from various kinds of community involvement on one end to small group activities, role playing, and simulation on the other end—the essence of the approach is relatively simple.

The purpose is to create a dislocation in students' thinking by changing the prescribed order of instruction.

Whereas most information assimilation approaches, such as the classical and discovery modes, proceed from the reception of information to the understanding of general principles to the inference of a particular application of the principle, and finally to the sphere of action, the changed structure approach turns this instructional cycle upside down. Changed structure approaches reverse the order by introducing action first, and encouraging the pupil to see the effect of action, and then proceeding to understanding the elements of the particular case before making any kind of generalization. The final step in this approach is to attempt to apply the warranted generalization to a new circumstance (Coleman, 1972).

In the changed structure approach, the role of the teacher defies categorization because it changes with the demands and new constraints that are presented by each new learning situation and environment. Generally speaking, the communication mode of the changed structure approach is primarily student to student, and often not directly about subject matter.

Changed structure approaches have several advantages. The first of these is the increase in interest that these kinds of activities can create, especially among students in the later stages of childhood and early adolescence. Because children at this time are beginning to acquire the ability to think about their own thinking, they tend to be extremely self-centered and egocentric. These students are in a continuous process of self-assessment and self-definition. Thus, the kinds of activities that most appeal to them are likely to be lessons that increase feelings of competence or enhance a sense of self-worth. These sorts of activities are integral to changed structure approaches such as role playing and small group activities. Seeing these kinds of instructional approaches as personally profitable, students are likely to be very interested in them, and their motivation to participate in them is likely to be intensified.

An additional point favoring changed structure approaches is that they provide a more accurate mirror of reality than most school work, which by its very nature is abstract and remote from everyday life and the students' personal concerns.

As our world—illustrated by electronic technology and increasingly complicated forms of social organizations—becomes more difficult to understand and penetrate, students need practice, in school, in the kinds of experience that reflect the goings on of the larger society. It is no longer an acceptable practice to view the school years as a time for a sociological moratorium from the real world. Schools are in increasing danger of being regarded as a static artifact, an artificial institution in a world whose concerns and procedures bear little resemblance to our high technological and information laden environment.

Another consideration favoring the changed structure approach is its potential for increasing the students' role-taking ability. A central developmental task of adolescence ought to be the acquisition of the ability to literally "walk around in somebody else's shoes." This ability makes possible a better understanding of a wide array of social scenarios; places cooperation, negotiation, and other conflict-resolution skills in the hands of the pupils; and reduces the dichotomous sense of the we/they situation that tends to characterize so much of our social relations today.

Still further, the pedagogical dimensions of changed structure approaches make it possible for teachers and schools to use a much wider range of untapped resources than traditional instructional approaches. Using community involvement as an example, changed structure approaches makes it possible for the pupils to get into the community, but in a protected way. Perhaps of equal importance, changed structure activities afford the various institutions of the community opportunities to get into the school, potentially contributing to both understanding and rapport between sometimes opposing groups.

The primary weaknesses of the changed structure approaches tend to be tactical. They require immense energy and imagination, and often appear to both students and parents to be impractical.

Because these kinds of instructional approaches are uncommon, students tend to misunderstand them, perceiving them as recreation or a waste of time. Since the ultimate goals of such activities are inclined to be abstract and long range (i.e., "This will help you understand society when you are an adult") from the students' viewpoint, many representations of changed structure approaches may seem like a meaningless string of abstractions because the goals are so far in the future.

In addition, because of the unconventionality and inherent self-revelatory nature of this kind of instructional approach, it is likely to meet with vigorous opposition from parents, administrators, and school boards. Part of this opposition is due to misunderstanding the purpose of changed structure activities, but a more important component of this is part of the vigorous campaign against anything labeled "valuing" that has been sweeping across the country.

Teachers ignore this social force at their peril. The movement is part of the widespread social interest of citizens in the workings of their social institutions. More specifically, however, the movement against any instructional approaches that teach about evolution, value clarification and self-evaluations, sexuality, or globalism has gained momentum in recent years.

CONCEPTUALIZATION OF TEACHING METHODS

▶ The three instructional strategies we have just described take into account, in varying ways, certain dimensions that can be perceived as interacting continuums that represent distinct and significant facets of the complex teacher-learner-student interaction.

As we saw in our examination of the instructional strategies, there appear to be three major variables that determine the nature of the students' learning experience: (1) the extent to which learning activities are planned by the teacher rather than being left to the spontaneous dynamics of student interaction, (2) the extent to which the student's role in the learning process is active and participatory rather than passive and uninvolved, and (3) the degree to which the content and methodologies have empirical grounding in the real world rather than being artificial creations designed for school consumption only. Figure 6–1 illustrates these three variables in three-dimensional space.

FIGURE 6-1 Three Categories of Instructional Strategies

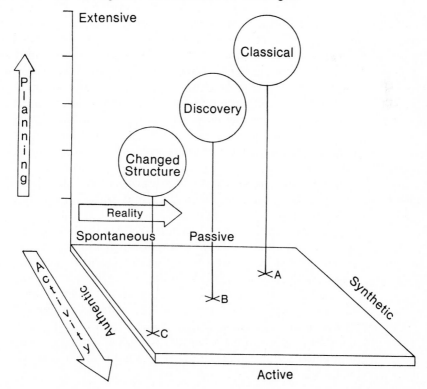

Each of the instructional strategies previously discussed represents a different configuration of these variables. We will further examine each teaching strategy, first by describing its relative position on the intersecting continuums, and second by discussing how that configuration affects the specific way that the strategy is employed in the classroom.

As previously suggested, the classical mode is best characterized by predictability, control, and product orientation. Using Figure 6–1, the classical mode would probably be plotted at about Point A. (A brief explanation of how the different dimensions contribute to the construction of this particular strategy will follow.)

The classical mode is positioned on the extreme side of the passive component. This reflects the minimal degree of active student participation that is generally a part of this model. On the spontaneous/planned dimensions, the classical mode falls heavily into the planned region. An effective lecture, for example, must be rather carefully planned. Serendipity has no place in this mode of instruction. On the reality dimension, the classical mode is very close to the synthetic side of the configuration because it is almost entirely the creation of the lecturer's imagination and, as such, tends to be artificial in its dimensions. In other words, the classical mode is generally more concerned with traditional school subjects than real-world experiences.

The discovery mode is characterized by spontaneity, independence, and self-direction. Upon examining Figure 6–1, one sees that the discovery mode would be plotted at about Point B.

The discovery mode is on the active side of that dimension, reflecting the great amount of activity involved in participation in this kind of instruction. On the spontaneous/planned dimension, the discovery mode lies between the poles. Discovery learning instruction requires minimal planning in order to direct students toward a general objective. An undue amount of planning would tend to stifle this kind of activity.

Changed structure modes are postited in the lower left corner of Figure 6–1, at about Point C. These instructional strategies tend to be experimentally oriented.

Placing the changed structure strategy in the extreme corner of the activity pole reflects the fact that strategies of this mode are action-oriented. It is from the activity that the lesson is generated. On the planning dimension, too, this mode is clearly in an extreme position because after an initial scenario, this mode of instruction takes on a life of its own, making planning difficult if not impossible. With regard to the third dimension, reality, the position is again at the edge of its respective continuum because its entire rationale is calculated to stimulate real-life conditions as much as is possible in the artificial world of the classroom.

► **From the Classroom**

Since the depiction of instructional strategies has thus far been somewhat abstract, some concrete classroom illustration is absolutely necessary to clarify the strategies. By looking directly at the teaching of a specific topic, the distinctions among the three strategies will, hopefully, emerge.

Imagine a hypothetical teacher named Barney Watson who teaches world history to tenth graders in a large urban high school in the northeast. As we enter his classroom we discover that Barney—a tall, fast-talking individual—has been teaching his students nearly a semester and feels that while his pupils generally accept him and his instructional techniques, most are not enthusiastic about the study of history.

As we approach Barney, he tells us that he wants to begin a two-week teaching unit stressing the general idea of twentieth-century man's search for political and social order. Doing this, Barney claims, will show his students the different kinds of political regimes that people have lived under during this time. In addition to teaching his pupils factual information about the history and ramifications of the different forms that social order takes, Barney claims he wants to give his students a sense of what nondemocratic regimes feel like. "I guess that I think these kids will be less susceptible to authoritarian, quick-fix solutions if they can experience what they feel like," Watson argues.

Let us step back and see how Barney actually employs the strategies we've talked about to accomplish his instructional goals. He begins with a changed structure approach.

Changed Structure
It must be kept in mind that the fundamental requirement here is for Barney to shake up his students. In order to accomplish this, he must simultaneously alter both the students' sociological perspective and the structure of their classroom. What Barney needs is a dramatic lesson that will at once hook his students into the subject matter and shock them out of their habitually apolitical stance.

The way to do this, he decides, is to begin by turning his classroom into a showcase for fascism, the most vicious of the nondemocratic social orders. Watson wants to put students in the identical position that the German people were under in the late 1930s. Let's look at what the first part of Barney's changed structure class looks like (*Behavior Today*, January 25, 1971).

He begins by using half truths and outright lies in presentations that glorify militarism. For example, he claims that authoritarian governments have much to offer over democracy. Next, he concocts a mythical great leader using books about Stalin, Hitler, and Mussolini. Democratic heroes like Washington, Lincoln, and Jefferson are denounced as antimilitary and weak wimps. Various terrorists and assassins are praised for eliminating "peacemongers." When students disagree, they are offered no opportunity to verbalize their opinions and are berated for daring to disagree with the "leader."

After about a half hour of this arbitrary treatment, Barney expects that there will be a student revolt, where the more outspoken members of the class will arise, decry his procedure, and demand some sort of explanation for his unsettling treatment of them. Watson hopes that it will be possible to show by the changed structure he has created what it feels like to live under such a political regime. He also hopes that behaviors of this kind will foster an interest in the usefulness of a democratic political orientation and develop an abiding interest in the political process in general at the conclusion of his changed structure lesson. Barney plans to spend a good deal of time debriefing his students, and then change his instructional strategy to a classical mode.

Classical Mode

Now that Barney has "hooked" his students with the dramatic and unconventional opening lesson, he reverts to a more traditional approach to convey a good deal of factual information about social and political order. "We need to cover some ground," he asserts.

He, therefore, decides to present information in a relatively straightforward fashion. He claims that readings, discussions, and what he calls "teacher talk" (really a form of casual lecture) are appropriate. Barney feels now that the students have a personal stake in the various political and social orders, and have internalized some of the concepts and feelings that swirl around them, they are more likely to be receptive to more classical and formal presentations of subject matter.

We visit Barney in the middle of his three-day classical instructional approach. He has assigned his students a chapter from the class text entitled, *Social and Political Order in the Modern World*. For his presentations he has relied on a chapter called "Waiting for Hitler" from Paul Johnson's *Modern Times* (1983). Yesterday, to the students' amazement, Barney passed out photocopies of part of an old *Classics* comic book, *Pitcairn Island*. In brief, this comic tells what happens to Fletcher Christian and his fellow mutineers after they have set Captain Bligh adrift in the South Pacific. Barney has employed this comic book because it shows the condition and problems that are present in a very elementary social order. He hopes that the relative simplicity of the situation will clearly illustrate the basic problem all societies face.

Watson begins his classical instruction strategy (in this case, textbook/comic book recitation) with the question, "What problems will the mutineers face once they land on Pitcairn Island?"

At first there is no answer. Then, a girl offers tentatively, "There are so many possible problems that it is hard to decide."

"What about the women?" Watson says.

"Compared to what?" the class clown reliably shouts. The class laughs and Watson's mouth withers into a disapproving frown.

"C'mon, what about the women?"

A male student slouched in the back of the classroom answers, "There are not enough women—thirteen men and eight women. There will be fighting over them. All fights are caused by women."

Feminine hisses arise, but Watson ignores them and asks, "Well, how does a society go about solving problems like this?" There is no answer.

"What is a society?" Watson asks. "Is this classroom a society?"

"Yes," a girl responds.

"Why?"

"Because it has an organization and rules."

"What kinds of rules? Give me an example."

"Big Barn talks, we listen," shouts one of the boys. The class hoots in agreement. Watson smiles, nods, and continues to write on the chalkboard, and asks, "Who makes these rules anyway?"

Soon the class is occupied with the task of listing some of the ways in which law and order is made in their classroom. Several point out that although Watson is a partisan for democratic ways, he often engages in undemocratic practices under the guise of a teacher's prerogative.

Before long, most of the recitation has ceased and Watson is lecturing on the conditions in Weimar, Germany, that led to the rise of Hitler. He is generally knowledgeable, often witty, and anecdotal. Most of the students automatically take out their notebooks and begin to write in them. For a few students a thin glaze settles over their eyes, their chins slump, and their mouths gape. As the bell rings, a quick reading assignment is made. The class leaves with the promise that tomorrow the discussion will shift a little south, to examine conditions in another totalitarian state, Italy, in the 1930s.

As the students file out, Watson observes that tomorrow he will tell them about the time he met Mussolini as he strolled down the Via Venadee searching for a men's room. The students arch their eyebrows at one another and exchange knowing nods. Barney proceeds toward the teachers' lounge.

Discovery Mode

Inside the teachers' room, Barney pours himself a large cup of coffee and settles his huge body into a chair. Sitting, he exclaims, "Now we're getting those kids into the subject matter! I've tried to get them to feel what totalitarianism was like with the role play. That sort of confrontation is useful because it arouses curiosity and forces students to speculate and raise questions. But it isn't useful to stay on this kind of stuff too long. My classroom is not a damn circus."

After the visitor asks when a teacher should alter his or her instructional strategy, Watson, seeming to avoid the question, sips his coffee and says, "Explaining that's what I like whether it's lecturing, demonstrating, or discussing what I've assigned the kids to read. I just feel comfortable with those kinds of tactics. It's probably why I became a teacher. Besides, it seems to me that these kinds of instructional strategies lead to the development of knowledge and intellectual skills in a way no other strategy can. They're like great works of art or military tactics, classical moves."

Asked again if he will soon shift his instructional strategy, Barney smiles and says, "Another day with Mussolini—an amazing guy, did you know that as a kid he was twice expelled from school for stabbing classmates in the butt? Hot-tempered little bugger! Anyway, I'll finish up *Il Duce,* and try some discovery learning. I'll use discovery modes of learning because it will help me to see if the students have learned anything."

Pausing to stare expansively out the lounge window, he asserts, "What I want to know is, are they able to discuss the various aspects of political order in an intelligent way? Can they make important distinctions? My bottom line, I guess, is can they apply what I've taught them to other situations?

"Hey, why don't you come in and see what I'm going to do?"

Two days later, as we approach Watson's classroom, he is in the midst of a discovery learning lesson. Previous to today's class, Watson approached four of his students and asked them to participate in the present lesson. He briefed those students about a hypothetical incident that he wants to stage for his pupils. The purpose, he claims, is to dramatically drive home the generalization that totalitarian states attempt to direct the behavior of their citizens by maintaining control over all sources of information.

The account that follows describes how Barney created such an incident before his class. As you read the account of the incident, keep in mind that Barney is trying to facilitate the discovery of certain facts of totalitarianism by this particular instructional strategy (Mehlinger, 1965).

A TOTALITARIAN OCCURRENCE[1]

Ten minutes after the bell rings, four boys arrive late. The last of these students is a small, frail boy who wears thick glasses. Although he is

---

1. This incident is a dramatized version of a lesson plan that appeared in H. D. Mehlinger's *The Study of Totalitarianism: An Inductive Approach* (Washington, D.C.: National Council of Social Studies, 1965). Reprinted from *Social Education* with permission of the National Council for the Social Studies with the author's permission.

rumpled and appears to have been in a fight, it is almost impossible to imagine him fighting. As the three other boys, named Charles, Bob, and Richard, reach their seats, Watson speaks to them.

"Boys, why are you late?" There is no answer.

"Boys, I have to have a reason for your tardiness." Hesitantly, Richard leans forward and mumbles, "I stopped to watch a fight outside the building."

"What fight? There wasn't any fight. I know when there is a fight in this school. What about it, class? Was there any fight?"

There is virtually no response from the class. Watson places his right leg on a chair and leans his body on his legs, and stares at Richard, then slowly states, "You just don't seem to have much support for the fight excuse. So, who was fighting?"

Richard, studying the back of his hands, says, "I ain't no narc, but I didn't do nothing. John was one of them." The students laugh. They view John, the frail boy, the least likely student to be involved in a fight.

John leaps out of his seat and yells, "The hell I was! What are you saying that for?"

From across the room, Bob casually says, "There's no point lying about it. I saw you." Charles, the last of the late arrivals, glares at Bob and says, "John was not fighting. He was with me."

Watson looks at all four boys and, appearing depressed, excitedly says, "Wait a minute. Were you guys fighting or not? What do you think about it, class? Was John fighting or wasn't he? Let's put it to a vote."

Some of the class appears bewildered, others laugh, and still others drop their heads and look out of the top of their eye sockets at one another. From the back of the room, one boy whispers softly, "Man, what is goin' on? It is like a vaudeville show in here today."

Watson conducts the vote. The result is inconclusive. Most of the students appear to find it difficult to believe that John is a fighter.

Just as the vote concludes, another teacher frames the doorway. Although he speaks only to Watson, most students hear him say something about a fight. As he moves to leave, the other teacher is heard to say, "I didn't see who, but I think some of your boys may be involved."

As the other teacher leaves, he nearly collides into a young woman carrying a message for Watson. The young woman announces that the principal wants to see John.

As John leaves, Charles appears stricken and quickly he blurts out, "Look, I lied, I didn't know if John was fighting or not. I just didn't want him to get in trouble. I can't believe he would fight."

Watson's response to Charles's declaration is to begin to rave a bit about the importance of telling the truth. Most of the students do not appear very interested. Soon Watson stops his diatribe and the students return to work. After about five minutes they are interrupted by the voice of the principal coming over the public address system. "Mr. Watson, John will be returning in a few minutes to get his books. He has been suspended for three days for fighting."

Soon John returns to the room, looking somewhat disturbed. He picks up his books and walks toward the door. Abruptly, he stops and returns to Watson's desk. Looking down at the floor, he says, "Mr. Watson, I'm sorry that I lied to you. I didn't want to get suspended. Sorry."

As the door closes, Watson asks the students to put aside their books.

"Something interesting has happened and I think we should explore it. Take out a piece of paper. I want you to answer some questions."

Below is an exact copy of Barney Watson's lesson plan. Examine it as if you were one of Barney's pupils.

BARNEY'S LESSON PLAN

1. Were you aware that there had been a fight before class? Did you see it or hear it before you came to class?
2. Did you believe at first that John had been fighting?
3. At what point did you decide John had been fighting?
   a. When the boys arrived late?
   b. When you learned there had been a fight?
   c. When you saw John's rumpled clothes?
   d. When Richard said John had been fighting?
   e. When the teacher said there had been a fight and the four boys might be involved?
   f. When the secretary called John to the office?
   g. When Richard confessed that he did not know whether John was fighting or not?
   h. When the principal said John was being sent home for fighting?
   i. When John confessed?
4. If you still do not believe John was fighting, what would it take to convince you? (Mehlinger, 1965, p. 63).

After the students have responded to the questions, Barney collects their papers and has several students read the responses from each paper while he tabulates them on the board. After the results are posted, Watson suddenly announces that there had never been a fight and says that the whole incident was a hoax. He proceeds to compare the results posted on the board with the actual facts of the case.

The astute observer might claim that this scene that Barney staged changes the structure of the classroom and may more properly belong to a previously discussed strategy. However, the purpose of this lesson is to have students discover some predetermined "truths" about totalitarian systems and, therefore, is more of a discovery approach in nature.

This does, however, point out the close interrelationships between all three of the strategies that we have discussed in this chapter. Like Barney Watson, creative teachers would do well to experiment with all three strategies in various combinations in the hopes of maximizing their instructional goals.

SUMMARY

▶ This chapter examined instructional strategies — the teaching methods or techniques that teachers select to realize their desired goals. Three general modes of instructional strategy were identified and explicated in terms of their strengths and weaknesses. We argued that the advantages and disadvantages depended on the unique teaching situation and the particular teacher's objective.

The three identified instructional strategies were labeled *classical, discovery,* and *changed structure.*

Classical modes were described as strategies where the teacher was an authority whose responsibility was to pass the information down to essentially passive students. The circumstances in the discovery mode differed from classical modes because it was assumed that learning was optimized when the student actively resolved the problem. Changed structure approaches were described as more activity-oriented with a changed prescribed order of instruction.

The content of each of these modes was then described in terms of three criteria, each of which ranged along a continuum which, in turn, represented the amount of the ingredient present in the technique. The three criteria were planning, activity, and reality.

As a means of clarifying and crystalizing these somewhat abstract conceptions, the chapter concluded with a detailed case study of a single teacher employing each of these modes of instructional techniques in his history class.

ACTIVITIES

1. Why do many teachers rely so heavily on classical instructional approaches?

2. Are discovery approaches difficult to install in most school curriculums? Why?
3. Make a chart depicting the differences in student and teacher behaviors across the three categories of instruction: classical, discovery, and changed structure.
4. Develop three different lesson plans using the same objective or objectives that reflect the three different modes of instruction.
5. Can you describe another category of instructional strategy other than the three presented here?

REFERENCES

Anderson, R. C., and Pearson, D. P. (1984). A schema theoretic view of basic processes in reading comprehension. In P. D. Pearson, R. Barr, M. L. Kamill, and P. Mosenthal (Eds.), *Handbook of research in reading.* New York: Longman.

Coleman, J. S. (February 1972). The children have outgrown the schools. *Psychology Today,* 72–75.

Dickens, C. (1954/1972). *Hard times.* London: Collins.

Johnson, P. (1983). *Modern times: The world from the twenties to the eighties.* New York: Harper and Row.

Medley, D. (1979). The effectiveness of teachers. In P. Peterson and H. Walbery (Eds.), *Research on teaching: Concepts, findings and implications.* Berkeley, Calif.: McCutchan.

Mehlinger, H. D. (1965). *The study of totalitarianism: An inductive approach.* Washington, D.C.: National Council for the Social Studies.

Staff (January 25, 1971). Fascism in the classroom. *Behavior Today,* 1.

Wain, J. (1981). C. S. Lewis as a teacher. In J. Epstein (Ed.), *Masters: Portraits of great teachers.* New York: Basic Books, 251.

SUGGESTED READINGS

Ausubel, D. P. (1963). *The psychology of meaningful verbal learning.* New York: Grune and Stratton.

Bloom, B. S. (1976). *Human characteristics and school learning.* New York: McGraw-Hill.

Bruner, J. (1961). *The process of education.* Cambridge, Mass.: Harvard University Press.

Cooper, J. M. (ed.) (1977). *Classroom teaching skills: A handbook.* Lexington, Mass.: D. C. Heath.

Joyce, B., and Weil, M. (1986). *Models of teaching.* Englewood Cliffs, N.J.: Prentice-Hall.

Orlich, D. C. (1985). *Teaching strategies: A guide to better instruction.* Lexington, Mass.: D. C. Heath.

Shulman, L. S., and Keislar, E. R. (eds.) (1966). *Learning by discovery: A critical appraisal.* Skokie, Ill.: Rand McNally.

Weinstein, C. E., and Mayer, R. E. (1986). The teaching of learning strategies. In M. E. Wittrock, *Handbook of research on teaching* (3rd ed.). New York: Macmillan, 315–327.

7

The Curriculum
of Teacher Education

OVERVIEW

▶ Central to the discussion of teacher education in this chapter is the curriculum that teachers receive in their training. We emphasize teacher education in this, a book on curriculum, because the structure and the nature of the curriculum prospective teachers receive in their training inexorably affects their curricular and instructional practice throughout their teaching career. Teacher education curriculum is described at length, but instead of beginning with a discussion of this curriculum, we start with a brief history of teacher education in America. We believe that this exposition will bring some of the present issues and problems into clearer focus. After this background, we approach the content, the problems, and the promises of American teacher education in a relatively straightforward fashion. The chapter concludes with five recommendations for the improvement of teacher preparation.

TEACHER EDUCATION

▶ In this chapter, we explore the issue of American teacher education by carefully examining its rambling structure as if it were a large, old mansion that is under continuous reconstruction. We portray the old house as a place of feverish activity where new rooms are endlessly being added, while many old ones are left unmaintained and unrepaired, affording the winds of criticism and complaint ample opportunity to blow nearly unobstructed through the building, often damaging unprotected conceptions and other valuables. We go on to claim that compounding the poor maintenance of the mansion is the constantly changing interior decor of the large house, where the motif often changes without any apparent reason or forewarning. We conclude our exposition with a discussion of the prospects for renewing the historic and valuable but vulnerable structure of teacher education. We begin with a discussion of the origins of American teacher education.

HOW DID AMERICAN TEACHER EDUCATION DEVELOP?

► For most of recorded history, the chief source of a child's education was his or her family. The child knew and believed what his or her parents taught and made available. With the early Americans, this process was intensified because their unique values had driven them to the New World, and they tried to ensure that those values were instilled in their offspring. In addition, almost every early American lived within a large extended family in a small community who shared the same values and perspectives on life in their new country.

As early as 1642, Massachusetts passed a law requiring parents to teach their children to read. The Puritans insisted that the children read in order to ensure their religious welfare, because, as Edmund Morgan recalls, "One chief project of that old deluder, Satan, [was] to keep men from the knowledge of the Scriptures" (1944, p. 14). Since the belief that ignorance leads to sin was the impetus for education, those communities with ardent religious beliefs tended to be more highly educated. Nowhere was religious belief stronger than in New England, which, in turn, became the best educated region of colonial America.

Thus, although education was not necessarily simple, it was a relatively straightforward process, because it was conducted in a self-contained community without the interference of outside influences or expectations. Unfortunately, the simplicity of early American education was shortlived. When it became clear that after-supper lessons would not suffice for the bridling growth of the new order, parents sent children outside the home for their lessons.

When the families sought formal education for their children, they were confronted with schools that extended along a bewildering spectrum of choices. At one end of the continuum were Latin Grammar schools where the teachers were college educated. In some smaller communities, parents enlisted the aid of young men to serve as teachers while waiting for better occupational prospects to break, but in the main, schools were staffed by the "low bred" clown about whom Noah Webster complained so bitterly (Tyack, 1967, p. 413).

Historian Richard Hofstadter claimed, "Men permanently fixed in the role of schoolmaster seem often to have been of indifferent quality and extraordinarily ill-suited for the job" (1963, p. 313). Generally speaking, early American school keeping seemed to have attracted more than its share of drunkards, rascals, and incompetents. But since the needs of the society were simple, this disgraceful situation did not attract widespread attention until late into the eighteenth century.

Sometime after the end of the Revolutionary War, around the beginning of the nineteenth century, the structure and mobility of American society began to change. In increasing numbers, the people of America began to abandon their rural way of life and move to the cities. This emigration required a new kind of schooling, which in turn demanded a new kind of teacher. It also augured a different form of teacher education—one that was more formalized than the casual socialization that had previously characterized the process.

At first, the commonsense solutions were applied to the problem of teaching pupils how to read and write. The initial plan was some version of the Lancastrian or monitorial system of instruction, by which a single teacher ruled a very large classroom containing children of all ages. In this system, the teacher functioned as a sort of foreman who assigned "older pupils, some of whom were in training to become Lancastrian teachers themselves, the lessons of each day for each grade, and sent them off to pass it on in various sections of the room" (Mayer, 1961, p. 38). (See Figure 7–1.)

There was a certain utilitarian logic in the Lancastrian system, but there was also a massive problem. Many pupils were unable to spend time on their own lessons because they were spending the majority of working hours instructing their younger classmates. Therefore, the older children received only minimal instruction time. Soon the parents of the school children began to demand a more efficient teacher training.

In the early years of the nineteenth century, two new ideas evolved. The first of these was the graded primary school, adopted largely from the Prussian school system. The most important aspect of the graded primary school was that it created a demand for new teachers and made possible the emergence of women teachers. Previously, the conventional wisdom held that the large class sizes that characterized the Lancastrian system created discipline problems that could not be resolved by female teachers. Now, the common belief argued, smaller classes would allow women to teach, and would eliminate the necessity of hiring from the pool of generally low-quality male candidates.

FIGURE 7-1 A Lancastrian Schoolroom

Ellwood P. Cubberley, *Public Education in the United States* (rev. ed.), page 130. Copyright
© 1962 by Houghton Mifflin Company.

The normal school was the second important idea to emerge out
of the educational climate of the early nineteenth century. Once the
monitoring system was discredited, there was no longer a way an individual could learn to become a teacher other than trial and error.
As Martin Mayer notes in *The Schools,* it is difficult to set up a true
apprenticeship in teaching. Although others may supervise a teacher's
work and offer suggestions for improvement, true teaching only occurs when an individual assumes full classroom responsibilities. Teachers
are not like lawyers or carpenters who can learn their duties slowly under
the supervision of a master (1961, p. 407).

At first, reformers attempted to raise teachers' prowess with short
institutes—intermittent meetings somewhat like present-day teachers'
conventions—but they quickly realized that this approach was inadequate, and they moved to create teacher training institutions which
came to be called normal schools.

The first state-supported normal school began at Lexington,
Massachusetts, in 1839. Borrowing ideas from American academies,
as well as German and French teacher preparation schools, normal
schools had but a single purpose—to train teachers for elementary
schools. (Until well into the twentieth century only a minuscule percentage of Americans attended any kind of secondary school.) Throughout
the nineteenth century, normal schools became the American way to
prepare teachers and to socialize the flood tide of new citizens, both
from within and from outside the United States.

In the normal schools, the largely female clientele acquired the bare rudiments of an education before they served their meager knowledge to their own pupils. Normal school education was largely secondary and remedial in nature because most of the students possessed only an elementary school education themselves. The curriculum of the normal school comprised mainly academic subject matter. Students learned pedagogical methods from the instructional models their own teachers employed. (See Table 7-1.)

At no time during the long course of the nineteenth century did more than 20 percent of the nation's teachers receive their training in a normal school. For the preponderant bulk of teachers, the way they learned was through trial and error on the job.

Although the normal school was the primary method of teacher training for the bulk of the 1800s, after the Civil War, as industrialism gained a stranglehold on the nation's life, the demand for better trained teachers gained momentum. At first this demand reflected the gradual growth of American universities in general, and was not strident. Soon, however, as the emergent industrial nation entered the last decade of the nineteenth century, Americans began to feel increasingly uneasy about their schools and about their teachers.

TABLE 7-1 Course of Study in Castine Normal School, Maine, 1890

| | FIRST YEAR | |
F Class	E Class	D Class
Arithmetic, from percentage	Arithmetic, methods	Algebra
Grammar	Grammar	Geometry
Geography	Geography	Physics
School economy	Algebra	Physical geography
Reading	Physiology	Drawing
Writing, one-half term		
Elementary music, one-half term		

| | SECOND YEAR | |
C Class	B Class	A Class
Geometry	Psychology	Didactics and history of education
General history	Chemistry	Practice teaching
Physics	United States history	English literature
Rhetoric	Civil government	Astronomy
Botany	Moral philosophy	Geology, one-half term
Bookkeeping, one-half term	Practice teaching	

Source: "Catalogue and Circular of the State Normal School at Castine, Maine, 1890," in *Report of the Commissioner of Education, 1898–1899*, Vol. II, p. 2301.

The response to industrialism may have sparked the demand for reform in teacher education, but three specific historical events fueled the fire for change: a series of journalistic accounts about American schools, new ideas about how to understand and instruct children and adolescents, and the rapid growth of publicly supported high schools.

The muckraking investigations of schooling, primarily by Joseph Mayer Rice and Jacob Riis (discussed in considerable detail in Chapter 8), focused Americans' attention on their schools. Rice's exposé, in particular, replete with dramatic imagery and telling anecdote, made an immediate contribution to the demand for changes in the way teachers were prepared.

The emerging revolution in educational thought, well underway at the beginning of the 1890s, was a second contributor to the general quickening of interest in a more professional education for American teachers. Generally speaking, the movement in education was a part of the societal wave against formalism that swept across the United States around the turn of the century. The specific pedagogical formalism the educators objected to was represented by sterile and unimaginative methods of teacher preparation. In increasing number, American scholars such as John Dewey, William T. Harris, G. Stanley Hall, and others began a search "to see if there was not some better way" (Cremin, 1961, p. 172).

That better way was represented by the New Educational Psychology enunciated by all of these scholars, but best captured by Dewey, the chairman of the Department of Pedagogy at the recently established University of Chicago, who claimed that all education must take as its starting point, "the instinctive, impulsive attitudes and activities of the child." In order to possess the requisite skill to enable children to discover these kinds of problems, and to help the pupils to answer them through disciplined activity, required more highly trained teachers (Ginger, 1958, p. 207). Teachers needed to be able to understand children as well as subject matter because children were more than inert balls of clay. This, in turn, called for a more sophisticated system of teacher education. The best place for this kind of education, they claimed, was a four-year college.

The rapid growth of secondary schools was the third contributor to the demand for a change in teacher education. Although publicly supported secondary schools became possible after 1874—when the courts held that taxes could be levied for their support—it wasn't until about 1900 that enough pressure began to build to demand that teacher training for these secondary schools be conducted in four-year colleges. The development of regional school accreditation agencies that certificated secondary schools made it virtually impossible for normal schools to continue to prepare high-school teachers in any significant number.

In many cases, the normal schools ceased to exist; in other instances, especially state-supported normal schools, they were converted into four-year teachers' colleges. By 1920, this transition was essentially complete, as single-purpose four-year teaching training institutions became the modal way to educate teachers.

Some students who were preparing to become primary school teachers did continue to receive two-year certificates at teachers' colleges. The crush of students after World War II, and the baby boom of the 1960s dramatically increased college enrollments at all levels, which caused many of the teachers' colleges to change their names to state colleges and the like. In spite of the fact that America's research-oriented universities (which previously eschewed teacher education) became more involved in teacher training, the essential course of teacher education has remained largely unchanged throughout the twentieth century.

The changes that have occurred in teacher education in the last sixty years have been more in the nature of either fine-tuning or responding to the immediate educational trend of the moment. (Chapter 8 will provide more elaboration on American educational history in this century.) Let us look at a general profile of the characteristics of teacher education.

WHO, WHERE, WHAT, AND HOW
IN AMERICAN TEACHER EDUCATION

▶   American teacher education is gigantic. There are 1,287 institutions of higher education that train and recommend teachers for certification. The National Center for Education Information reports that this represents an increase of 115 percent over the course of the past decade, even though the number of students enrolled in training programs was down by 33 percent during that period (Feistritzer, 1985, p. 81).

The training institutions are widely diverse. About 40 percent of these institutions are small senior colleges with less than 1,000 students and a small number of pedagogical instructors (Smith, 1980, p. 81). The remaining institutions—municipal, private, and state colleges and universities—tend to be multipurpose, involved in many activities other than teacher education. At the apex of the pyramid of colleges are the approximately 30 research-oriented universities where nearly all teacher education research is conducted, and where many of the most advanced programs are housed.

New York state has the largest number of teacher training institutions, numbering ninety-six, followed by California with seventy-nine, and Illinois with fifty-eight. The states of Wyoming and Nevada have the smallest number, with one and two institutions, respectively. The ubiquitousness of teacher training institutions is illustrated by the thirteen teacher training facilities in South Dakota, a state with less than 700,000 people.

It is this slow-moving system that has caused teacher training in the twentieth century to be under nearly constant fire, as a virtual hundred-year war has been waged against the American system of teacher training. Thus, before we describe the course of study in colleges of education, it is appropriate to examine what is it about teacher training that makes people so angry.

WHY NEARLY EVERYONE IS ANGRY AT TEACHER TRAINING

▶ What kind of education do students actually receive when they become teachers? Perhaps a closer examination of the typical course of study in teacher training institutions and colleges of education will bring into sharper focus the nature of current teacher training as well as the source of many of the critics' misgivings.

The college training of most potential teachers comprises two streams: liberal and technical. Most problems with teacher education originate over the composition and flow of these two opposing streams.

▶ Liberal Arts Training

The first of these, the liberal arts rivulet, commences the moment a student enters college. To fulfill the general education requirements that make up the bulk of the liberal arts course work, students are expected to select from the total college curriculum a portion of each of several of the liberal arts, typically history, humanities, the arts, and science.

The rationale for the liberal arts sequence is that it gives breadth to the students' education, enabling them to be more sensitive toward cultural diversity, and introducing them to the various heritages and cultures, while tracing out the basic historical, mathematical, literary, and scientific forces that undergird the contemporary world. As a result of this segment of their collegiate experience, students are expected to obtain more meaning from their experiences and to develop the conceptual thinking necessary to help them critically examine the more technical parts of their education without — at least in the early stages of their curriculum — possessing detailed and specialized knowledge of the various subject matters.

For students enrolled in secondary teacher training programs, their general education stream has an additional tributary that flows into it, especially in the later part of their program—their academic major. This major concentration, while still largely an academic liberal education, tends to be more specific and prescribed than for elementary education students. However, even elementary education students are expected to undertake an area of concentration in their program of study.

The academic major constitutes approximately one-third of the teacher trainees' total college work. As a result of majoring in a field of study, a student is expected to demonstrate specific and detailed knowledge of a specific subject matter. For an individual majoring in science, this would mean broad and comprehensive knowledge of all the sciences and of scientific modes of inquiry, and highly sophisticated and technical comprehension of one of the sciences, physics for example.

Although the teacher is not supposed to be an expert in his or her major, it is assumed that the individual is funded with the detailed knowledge of what makes up the discipline and, perhaps more importantly, that he or she has acquired the capacity to think "inside the subject matter." A student majoring in English, for example, would be able to specify standards for literary excellence and apply them to an examination of a novel such as F. Scott Fitzgerald's *The Great Gatsby;* a history major would be able to employ, in the examination of an historical document, the analytical questions and mode of inquiry that characterize historical investigations.

Hence, the liberal function of education is to make certain that teacher trainees develop perspectives about the problems of living, including their professional ones. The intention of this enhanced perspective is to enable teachers to view problems in the broadest sense possible.

▶ Technical Training

The composition and flow of the technical stream in teacher education is entirely different. Education is said to function technically when it is aimed at the cultivation of skill in the actual performance of a previously determined task. In a technical education, these tasks are reduced to a set of effective routines. The technical components of most professional programs are considered their core and are seldom the subject of controversy, much less public comment. But in teacher education, the technical aspects produce a flood of criticism and denunciation. The reasons for the criticism could be summarized under five broad headings.

First, teaching is concerned with a series of complex intellectual phenomena directed at young and often immature learners. Because of those factors, teachers frequently fail to achieve their declared objectives. These failures often become public knowledge because the fiscal support for schools comes from the citizenry, which is of a consensus that education is vitally important. With the widespread coverage that characterizes public affairs in a democratic society, when there is a loud and well-documented failure of any publicly supported enterprise, someone has to be blamed. Teachers and their seemingly questionable training are conveniently at hand.

Thus, when foreign competition brings economic woes to American business, it is not the executives who run the American corporations that are blamed; instead, it is school systems—organized and managed by allegedly poorly trained teachers—that have put the nation at risk. This is, of course, not fair to teachers, and places that at a very awkward disadvantage, but it is a scenario that has been replayed several times in recent American educational history.

A second significant reason that teacher training is so often attacked has to do with the phenomenon of the lay expert. There is a tendency and a willingness of people to criticize teachers and their training because they feel that they had a level of experience with schooling that exceeds their knowledge of any other social institution. Many adults—often subconsciously—harbor resentment about what happened to them during their school days, and demonstrate an overweening desire to overcome these supposed injustices in their own children's education.

In addition, the school years are important in the formation of our social attitudes. Novelist Kurt Vonnegut, Jr., for example, commented about this experience:

> When you get to be our age, you all of a sudden realize that you are being ruled by people you went to high school with. You all of a sudden catch on that life is nothing but high school. High school is closer to the core of American experience than anything else I can think (Vonnegut, 1970, p. xii).

Another reason that makes people angry at teacher education is the apparent lack of rigor in the admission standards for teachers. The criterion that most Americans employ in this comparison is medical school. Because medical school standards are rigorous, and it is difficult to get in, the conventional wisdom holds that it is only the extraordinarily well qualified that enter medical school. There is, at least in the public mind, a strong support for the generalization, "All doctors must be smart because it is so difficult to be admitted to medical school." No amount of contrary evidence seems likely to dislodge that belief. When this is combined with the fact that nearly everyone knows a teacher who does not seem to be very bright, we have a powerful argument against teacher education admissions standards.

A fourth reason why teacher education is so often criticized is the pervasive perception that teacher training courses are not intellectually respectable, but rather a collection of "how-to" courses that teach students useless techniques that are not connected to the "content" of the school. Reading through attacks on teacher training from the last fifty years reveals the frequency of that argument repeatedly (Bestor, 1953; Conant, 1964).

Part of the reason for these attacks is that many education courses are sometimes amorphous, directed at irrelevancies and empty of content. Another part of the argument originates from the American academies' disdain for the "useful arts." Whether the issue has been the introduction of engineering curriculum into our state universities' curriculum (Noble, 1979, pp. 20–27) or moving teacher training out of normal schools into four-year teachers' colleges, the resistance from professors in the established disciplines to vocationally oriented curriculum has been fierce.

In the end, the principal reason why teacher education makes people so angry is that nearly everyone concerned—both supporters and opponents—tends to oversimplify a very complex process.

In the most comprehensive history of American teacher education, Merle Borrowman argued a generation ago, "The problem is to organize the pre-service experience of potential teachers so efficiently that maximum understanding and control of the forces at work in educational situations are achieved along with a safe margin of technical skill" (1956, p. 229). This seems simple, but for over a hundred years of formal American teacher education, it has been demonstrated to be achingly difficult and has created a nearly intractable problem for teacher educators.

Borrowman goes on to contend that the accomplishment of this difficult task will take place only when teacher education maintains the exquisite balance between the liberal and technical views of teacher training. To this point, organizing instruction so that it serves both liberal and technical ends is an aspiration that has remained elusive. Nevertheless, it is a goal that teacher education must continue to strive for. As a means of seeing how successful teacher educators are in their quest, we will now examine the nature of curriculum in teacher education.

WHAT IS THE CURRICULUM IN TEACHER EDUCATION LIKE?

► The curriculum that comprises teacher education is divided into three parts. The first group, called *foundations,* consists mainly of history, philosophy, and behavioral science courses; the next sequence contains how-to-teach courses, commonly called *methods;* and the third group, whether referred to as *clinical experiences, student teaching,* or *practicum,* refers to direct teaching experience in the elementary and secondary classroom.

► ## Foundations Courses

Foundations courses are perceived as the bedrock upon which the rest of the teacher training program rests. These courses comprise two somewhat arbitrary categories: those that deal with the meaning and purpose of education and its relationship to society and culture, which are called *social foundations;* and courses that give students information about the learner and the learning process, which is called *educational psychology.* Courses in the former category are most akin to the courses students take in the liberal arts and go by labels such as History and Philosophy of Education, Sociology or Politics of Education, and School and Society.

Developers of social foundations courses claim that they differ from their liberal arts counterparts by taking a more functional, activistic, and problem-solving approach to American social problems. The authors who first traced the basic principles for these courses asserted, "Social foundations as a field, is concerned with those aspects and problems of society which need to be taken into account in determining educational policy, especially as this policy concerns the social policy of the school, and in determining broader social issues which affect educational policy" (Anderson et al., 1951, pp. iv–v).

Typically, these courses are at some distant remove from the actual teaching-learning process, and are taught by professors who are more likely to be directly involved with their respective academic disciplines than they are entwined in the day-to-day machinations of the elementary and secondary classrooms. The social foundations professor is likely to do research on issues outside the "guts" of schooling, concentrating on subjects such as the social compositions of school boards, the impact of school busing, the history of educational institutions in colonial America, and the economics of special education.

Some critics of social foundations courses claim that the demand that what is studied must be of direct and immediate utility to practitioners is an "abomination" and very difficult to realize (Cohen, 1976, p. 305). Others claim that the general orientation that characterizes social foundations courses can "serve the narrow purposes of indoctrination and vocationalism" (Bestor, 1953, p. 144). Although assertions that social foundations courses engage in indoctrination have lessened in recent times, no year passes without at least one clarion call for the abolition of foundations courses. Demands that foundations courses be streamlined are legion.

Eductional psychology is the label used to describe the second, and largest, group in the foundations division of the colleges of education. This group also probably has the highest status among the various professors of education. Educational psychology, for example, is the benchmark against which other educational research is compared. The basic elements of educational psychology are the heart of the process of education. Among many other subjects, educational psychologists investigate how children grow and think, compare various models of learning and teaching, and most recently, devise conceptions of effective pedagogical practice.

Much of the course content of educational psychology is based on research findings from the various fields of psychology. All educational psychology courses start from the premise of the learning process as a psychological phenomenon, and proceed down intellectual pathways that investigate psychologically oriented topics such as motivation, incentives, individual differences, perception as it relates to learning, and the uses of measurement (Woodring, 1957).

Course titles in educational psychology range across a wide spectrum, extending from offerings in Introductory Child Psychology to Methods of Conducting Research with Senior Citizens, and along the way covering courses as varied as Statistical Analysis and Measurement, Counseling Procedures, Education of the Visually Handicapped, and Human Relations.

Criticisms of educational psychology are generally not unduly harsh, claiming only that the courses are often too theoretical, infrequently confuse fact and opinion, and, finally, cram so many different points of view into the class that they become confusing to the students. Few critics appear inclined to debate whether or not the discipline of psychology ought to be the basis for most pedagogical practice. In many ways this is strange because the question, Should educational practice be based on the positivistically oriented psychology or on one of the more interpretative studies?, would have far-reaching effects for teaching in America. In most European countries disciplines other than psychology have a much more important place in teacher preparation. In British teacher training, for example, sociology plays a significant role in teacher preparation; yet Russian educators feel that only by using the historical approach can teachers understand present social phenomena.

▶ Methods Courses

This second major subdivision of courses is the most representative and the most infamous of all the offerings in the college of education. These courses, called "those terrible methods courses" by James B. Conant (1964) in his classical study, *The Education of American Teachers,* would appear to be the essence of teacher training because among course offerings in the university, they are most directly involved with actual techniques of teaching. Some of the methods courses involve general methods of teaching and are not restricted by subject matter; others are devoted exclusively to the subject matter of a particular academic discipline. Examples of the former include courses on Curriculum Construction, Analysis of Teaching, and Techniques of Instruction; examples of the latter, content-specific courses, include Methods of Teaching Social Studies, Planning and Assessing Foreign Language Instruction, and Methods of Teaching Arithmetic to Slow Learners.

Methods teachers are more likely than foundations instructors to have had teaching experience in either elementary or secondary schools. Central to the methods courses is the idea of planning and organizing for teaching. Among the many and varied topics that students encounter in methods courses are How to Write Objectives and Lesson Plans, Classroom Management, and Curriculum Development.

As a means of illustrating methods courses, let us present a content outline from a methods of instruction course.

AN INTRODUCTION TO SECONDARY SOCIAL TEACHING

1. What is social studies?
2. Thinking about social studies teaching
3. Mode, strategy, and method
4. Planning goals and objectives
5. How to develop a lesson plan
6. What is competency-based instruction?
7. What are expository and discovery lessons?
8. Teaching the use of concepts
9. Teaching the use of hypotheses
10. Teaching values
11. How to conduct a classroom discussion
12. A strategy for integrating lessons in social studies
13. Evaluating student learning: How to make a test

As the course outline reveals, methods courses directly confront the basic issues of teaching. If teaching is difficult and complex, then the issues that methods courses confront must be complicated. The subject matter of methods courses is, in fact, so complex that these courses bring to mind Samuel Johnson's dictum concerning another phenomena about which he said, "It is not that they do it well that is impressive, it is that they do it at all that is amazing."

When methods courses are competently taught—and this occurs much more frequently than the critics of the courses contend—they employ repeated acts of analysis and synthesis, with the methods students being called upon to first break the dimensions of teaching to smaller parts and then to reassemble them. The methods process is similar to repairing a watch. It is exacting work requiring careful attention, but with careful supervision and a desire to learn the craft involved, it is possible to acquire the requisite skills.

As you observed from the content outline, methods courses devote more time to the nontutorial aspects of designing, selecting, and organizing activities than to the tutorial aspects. That is, more time is spent studying planning, in its various plumages, than is spent in actual instruction. The dimensions of planning are probably more easily contained within the walls of a classroom, especially when the classroom is jammed with students. The tutorial or actual teaching aspects are, therefore, concentrated upon in the direct experience component of the teacher training programs.

Methods courses are particularly susceptible to the fads that swirl around the educational landscape, and are thus likely to change their direction without a good deal of forewarning. During the last decade, for example, methods of instruction courses have been dominated by behaviorally oriented strategies such as competency-based instruction and other similar schemes. Issues like programmed learning, instructional packets, mainstreaming, and discovery learning were also subjects of intense interest for a short period before they either declined or faded somewhat. Computer-assisted instruction is currently the most emergent issue in methods courses. Only research and time will tell whether the reach of this innovation has exceeded its grasp.

A central explanation for the volatility of methods courses is that they attempt to abstract a clinical experience—the various components of the process of teaching. Since this is a kind of methodological reductionism, the components sometimes do not make sense to the students in the classes because the parts are fragmented. Some critics of methods classes claim that because of the uncertainty in teaching, generally, the methods classes are empty bull sessions where students contribute to a pool of ignorance (Silberman, 1970). Other critics claim that it is impossible to teach pedagogical techniques without the content itself being present. Nowhere more so than in the methods courses is the tension between the liberal and the technical divisions of the teacher training process greater. In fact, many special methods courses, such as teaching literature or second languages, are taught outside of the education college by professors who are trained in the particular subject matter rather than in methods teaching.

In the past decade, students have been required to take more education courses than in the past. The national average, for example, shows that the prospective elementary teacher is required to take sixty-two semester hours of liberal studies, and fifty-two hours of professional studies, seventeen of which tend to be in clinical experience.

The balance is somewhat different for secondary teachers who are re-quired to take slightly more in the area of liberal studies and markedly fewer education courses (Feistritzer, 1985).

▶ ## Direct Experience

When education graduates are asked to evaluate their training, with no known exceptions, it is the direct experience component of their education that they claim was the most valuable. Even when their direct experience has been unpleasant or poorly executed, the students are likely to count it as valuable (Silberman, 1970).

Direct experience takes many forms, extending from assisting a classroom teacher for a very short period, to a practicum where the student is held responsible for teaching a few very carefully monitored class sessions, to full-time student teaching where the neophyte teacher is largely responsible for the entire classroom.

For most students, the single-most important course of their en-tire teacher training is their internship or student teaching. It is in stu-dent teaching where they finally get the feel for what it is like to be a teacher. Faced with a classroom filled with real pupils — not their peers pretending to be students or a brief sojourn in another teacher's class — student teaching tests their mettle.

Practice teaching for most students proceeds in a similar fashion. After completing all or nearly all of the proscribed teacher training curriculum, the prospective student teacher is presented with a list of schools that have an opening for a student teacher. The student makes his or her choice and is assigned to work with one teacher. This cooperating teacher familiarizes the student with the school and the class, assists the beginner with planning, and models appropriate teaching techniques.

After observing for a time, the neophyte gradually assumes greater responsibility for teaching the class. Toward the end of the experience it appears to an outside observer that the student teacher has assumed total control of the cooperating teacher's class. We say *appears* because even though the student teacher is doing most of the teaching in the class, he or she is still working along the lines set up by the cooperating teacher, who is still in control even when absent.

When there are disagreements or disputes in student teaching, they generally involve conflict over the autonomy given the student teachers. Most failures in student teaching occur for three reasons: the student teacher lacks commitment to teaching and is unwilling to in-vest a sufficient amount of energy into the activity; the student teacher lacks the skills necessary to manage the classroom; or the cooperating teacher and the student teacher are unable to negotiate a satisfying working relationship. (When there is a dispute, the nature of the system generally dictates that the student teacher will have to lose, and either change his or her mode of operating, be reassigned to another teacher, or drop out of the program.)

In fact, however, few student teachers do fail; most succeed, making the experience generally a competence-building exercise. Thus, when they look back, most teachers claim that more student teaching would be better.

Central to almost all reform proposals for the improvement of educational practice throughout the entire course of American educational history have been pleas, by teachers themselves and reformers from outside the educational estate, to expand, extend, or enlarge the student teaching experience. The current reform movement is no exception, showing increased faith in student teaching as a panacea for the improvement of teaching.

There is reason to be somewhat suspicious of more student teaching as the panaceas of all educational problems. First, teaching is ultimately a complex craft that must be siphoned from a reservoir of analytical concepts. If the inferential frame of mind, as well as the affective skills, are not present in the teacher before student teaching, then the aspiring teacher may imbibe a large draught of unexamined dispositions from the practical experience. According to David Berliner, an authority on effective teaching, oftentimes student teaching results in "decreased attitudes toward teaching and a reduction in the display of the teaching behaviors taught at the training institution" (1985, p. 2).

Without belaboring weaknesses of what is undeniably a uniquely valuable experience, it is important for us to recognize that there is no royal road to effective teaching, and that improvement will not occur merely from the simple practice of requiring students to do more practice teaching. In the final analysis, student teaching will be only as valuable as the concepts that are placed into the mind of the student teacher in the class work that undergirds student teaching. (More will be said about this subject in the next section.)

HOW CAN AMERICAN TEACHER EDUCATION BE IMPROVED?

▶ Since the very beginning of organized teacher education in America, there has been a nearly continuous clamor demanding that the system be improved, changed, or abolished. This should be expected in a nation that accepts the proposition that the success of the republic depends upon the kind of education that is available for its children (Cremin, 1980, p. 135).

Earlier in this text, we claimed that demands for change and reform resemble a swinging pendulum traveling along an arc, moving from a high point to a low point and then back again to the peak of the arc. Presently, American society appears to have returned to the peak of the pendulum's arc with regard to criticisms of teachers and their education.

Although the varieties of criticism and suggestions for improvement are infinite, we will examine five kinds of recommendations that have been put forward as a means of improving teacher education. We have not defined the complete list, but only a series of serious arguments for the reform of teacher education that are abroad in contemporary educational circles. We will now discuss each of the recommendations.

1. *Teacher education will improve when there is a closer coordination between the liberal and the technical dimensions of the training process.*

Fragmentation is the signal feature of teacher education programs. Early American educationists accepted the dichotomy of liberal and technical out of expediency. There were two reasons for their compromise. First, the educationists, in their zeal to organize a professional sequence, overemphasized the technical dimension of teaching at the expense of the liberal side. Not incidentally, this led to the "widely cited obsession of teachers with the tricks of the trade" (Borrowman, 1956, p. 229). The scorn, even the outright contempt, of the liberal arts faculty for the technical side of teaching caused the educationists to avoid working with these academicians whenever possible. Since the academicians were not particularly interested in teacher education, they allowed themselves to be cut off from the teacher training process. If teacher training is to improve, this gulf between the liberal and technical sides must be bridged.

Merely returning teacher training to the liberal arts division or forcing students to take more courses in their subject matter will not suffice. A spate of recent research demonstrates that just "knowing one's subject does not necessarily make one a good teacher" (Evertson, Hawley, and Zlotnik, 1984, p. 30). In an extensive review of this question, David Berliner (1985) presents findings from a series of studies that essentially reveal a low correlation between measures of subject matter competency and student achievement, and even shows no consistent relationship between a teacher's knowledge of subject matter and student achievement. He proceeds to assert, "Hopes that an increased level of subject matter competency on the part of the teachers will result in increased student achievement seems naive, except at the advanced frontiers of the subject" (p. 30).

Educationalists, too, must be wary of the gulf between themselves and the liberal arts. Although their zeal to forge professional education impelled them at first, as time went on, they tended to draw increasingly inward and deliberately cut themselves off from the liberal arts. As education historians have shown, this often led educationists to create castles in the air and abstract programs without a basis in the world around them (Katz, 1968, p. 215).

Each of these groups could begin the rapprochement with a small step toward one another. For example, meetings could be held between the groups to coordinate expectations for students and to work toward providing provisions for would-be teachers in academic courses and for students with academic majors who are interested in sampling education courses.

> 2. *Teacher education can be improved by imposing more stringent exit and certification requirements.*

The most important change in teacher education in recent years has been the development of exit tests. Although the majority of teacher training institutions do not yet require exit tests, the movement is clearly in that direction. There is almost unprecedented agreement about the importance of exit tests. What debate that does exist is between advocates of a national teacher examination and proponents of separate tests for each state. At present, the state-by-state test idea is more popular.

Although the demand for teacher testing has brought about some change in teacher education, the real complexity in teacher education is over the process of certifying teachers. The present methods are a Byzantine intrigue, with each state having a slightly different system. In general, most states follow some version of the "approved program" route for certifying teachers. What this means is that any graduate of a program approved by that state's department of education automatically is eligible to receive a teaching certificate if he or she applies.

The primary differences in this process are relatively easy to perceive. Larger, more affluent states with more substantial state departments of education can more readily police the colleges and universities that train teachers, and more importantly, these states can be more rigorous in setting standards for certification.

According to C. Emily Feistritzer (1985), certification requirements have changed greatly in the last two years. All but twenty-two states have altered their requirements during that short period. The direction of almost all of the changes has been toward more rigor. Many states have introduced a basic skills test as a part of their certification process.

New Jersey, for example, introduced a certification requirement in 1984 that brought about a fundamental change in the process. To become a teacher in New Jersey one must graduate from an approved college or university, student teach for one year, and pass the National Teachers Examination specialization test for secondary teachers. At this time, this trend in the certifying process has not been subjected to any analysis. Nevertheless, it presents a real and present danger to all teacher training institutions, which can be countered only by systematic and detailed explorations of entrance and exit tests for prospective teachers. With regard to exit tests, it is therefore imperative that education schools move first, before laws are passed that restrict their behavior.

The need for colleges of education to support changes in the certification process was given further impetus by the recently released report by the prestigious Carnegie Forum on education and the economy. Among several other recommendations, the forum proposed the establishment of a board that would set nation-wide professional teaching standards for certification (1986).

> 3. *Teacher education will improve when the training program is extended to five years.*

The notion of a five-year teacher training program is one of those persistent ideas whose time never seems to come. Part of the reason for this is the understandable reluctance of teacher educators to alter their basic organizational structures, which they contend have been carefully constructed over a considerable period of time. A second reason may be that five-year programs are often seen as opportunistic ventures by small, largely undistinguished liberal arts colleges to increase their enrollments. Although a five-year teacher training program, mainly in the form of the master of arts in teaching (MAT), has been frequently discussed and even sometimes implemented in the period since the second world war, the idea itself has never really generated much enthusiasm in large teacher training institutions.

The notion of a five-year training program idea has recently been energized somewhat by the activities of the so-called Holmes Study Consortium. This group, which comprises representatives from America's research-oriented universities, aims to improve the condition of teacher education programs (Johnson Foundation / Racine Foundation, 1985). Among several ideas that they have submitted for discussion is the five-year program proposal. The Holmes group claims that four years is an insufficient time to mount an effective program because it prevents prospective teachers from taking sufficient work in their subject matter and it crowds their program unnecessarily.

To say that the Holmes group proposal has been greeted with less than enthusiastic support is an understatement. The Holmes plan was condemned almost as soon as it was introduced to education faculties. Faculty members object to the five-year plan because they feel their programs are already cumbersome and unarticulated; what they need is more organization not more courses, they argue. Even within the Holmes group itself, there is substantial disagreement, and an opposing group arguing against the idea has recently surfaced (Feistritzer, January 1986). This group of dissenting deans claims that the fifth-year idea is without strong foundation, will alienate education faculty, and will drive away prospective students who will be estranged from a program that approaches the duration of highly paid professionals in length without offering comparable salaries.

The Carnegie Report supports the proposal to end undergraduate education degrees, requiring instead a baccalaureate in the liberal arts prior to a master's degree in teaching. In addition, the Carnegie Forum suggests a dramatic rise in teachers' salaries (1986).

4. *Teacher education will improve only when better students are attracted to teacher training programs.*

Teacher training institutions are impaled upon the horns of the dilemma of raising admissions standards. On the one hand, teaching has dramatically lost its appeal for America's young people, and the number of academically able students applying for admission to colleges of education has declined markedly (Darling-Hammond, 1984). On the other hand, it is crystal clear that the first step in improving teaching is a more academically able student population for teacher education programs. How can this be done?

First, colleges of education, public schools, and government bodies must cooperate in the development of career ladders for teachers (Johnson Foundation / Racine Foundation, 1985). At the initial stages of induction into teaching, candidates would proceed through a series of carefully supervised steps. They would move from being a teacher candidate in the school of education, to an intern teacher in a public school—working half time and studying half time—and then to the position of a novice where they would assume primary teaching responsibilities while still receiving intensive supervision from both the college and the school's personnel. Finally, they would move into the position of a career teacher where they are considered fully qualified. In this version of the career-ladder approach, the teacher, after considerable experience and study, could ultimately be eligible for the position of professional career teacher, where he or she has more status, responsibility, and, not incidentally, more pay. The career teacher title would not be a formal certificate like a CPA, but more an informal appellation like the CLU label that highly qualified insurance agents receive as a reward for exemplary performance.

Second, teacher training institutions must loosen their rigid, lockstep programs. They must be willing to accept individuals with a variety of educational and experimental backgrounds. If, for example, a prospective teacher training candidate has worked in a school as a teacher aide, then that person should be permitted to submit that experience as a part of the requirements for a teaching degree. If another prospective teacher, for example, has a bachelor's or master's degree, then that candidate should not be admitted into the training program in the same way as a nineteen-year-old undergraduate. Of course, several versions of each of these improvements are already at large in teacher preparation programs, but they need to be much more pervasive. The hallmark of a teacher training program that will attract able students is flexibility and willingness to negotiate with attractive candidates with idiosyncratic credentials.

A third mechanism that teacher education programs could use to attract better students simply involves the application and refinement of some traditional recruitment techniques such as attracting and distributing more money for scholarships. This is an area that teacher training programs have not done very aggressively.

5. *Teacher education programs will improve when they become more clinical in their orientation.*

In the end, teaching is doing. A teacher is called upon to perform. When a teachers fails, it is his or her performance that is inadequate. The improvement of teaching, therefore, comes from improving one's performance.

The area of the teacher education curriculum where performance can be practiced is the clinical part of teacher training. Teacher educators have never dealt very creatively with this dimension of their training process. To illustrate, consider the following dilemma described by David Berliner (1985) who identified the concept of "wait time" (the length of time from the end of a teacher's question until the student is called) as an important research finding — one that has been known for at least twenty years by educators, and which, he claims, produces wonderous things for the teacher who uses the technique. Berliner speculates about why wait time is not a part of most teachers' repertoires. His disarmingly simple answer is that most teachers do not use wait time in their work because they only know about the idea intellectually from books or class presentations or articles. They literally have not internalized the process. In their training, most teachers are given little opportunity to practice wait time or any other similar clinical conception. Ironically, then, given the common image of teacher training, the idea of wait time is not a part of a teacher's common practice because the teacher learned the concept in a way that was too bookish and semantic.

How often would teachers be required to practice wait time in order to have internalized the process? No one is exactly sure, but it is possible to speculate that a great deal of overlearning is simple but not obvious. In teaching, events transpire so rapidly that teachers' responses must be reflexive to a large extent. In order for a technique to be reflexive it has to be either natural or endlessly practiced. Although the basic idea of wait time is elementary, the patience that comes with practice is not.

What would a completely clinical program look like? The premise behind such a program is that it would be concerned with the reconstruction of an individual's teaching experience. This means that a prospective teacher would have assimilated a battery of analytical concepts before beginning any teaching, and this array of concepts would be relentlessly examined whenever he or she taught. In our hypothetical clinical program, the amount of seminar time—where teacher trainees examined their teaching with other similarly placed individuals—would equal or even exceed the amount of time that the student engaged in actual classroom teaching. In the end, the teaching time would be more valuable because it was carefully scrutinized.

The most important result of the program would be to produce teachers that thought in terms of a series of concepts that pertained to teaching. These concepts would be hammered out in the seminar room as a result of argumentation with other neophyte teachers, and tempered by the experience of actual classroom practice. With regard to the classroom practice part of the teacher training program, it appears that a great deal of instruction could result from assigning groups of students to classrooms.

SUMMARY

▶ This chapter explored the curriculum of teacher education. After describing the history of American teacher education, the chapter presented a profile of the current teacher education scene. We found that American teacher education is a gigantic enterprise that comprises a vast array of training institutions. In answering the question, Why is nearly everyone angry at teacher training?, we found the most tangible to be the bifurcation of teacher training in American colleges and universities, and the tendency of Americans to oversimplify the processes of teaching and teacher preparation.

The middle part of the chapter presented a description of the character and dimensions of the curriculum of teacher education. We saw that the curriculum of teacher education has three essential parts: foundations, methods, and direct experience. Each of these elements of the curriculum has a unique disposition and flavor.

The final part of the chapter appraised a series of arguments and plans that have been put forward for the improvement of American teacher education. It was abundantly clear that changing the landscape of American teacher education will be very difficult because the terrain is so extensive and the number of interests are firmly rooted. We saw that aspirations of Americans are the single-most important element in American teacher education, and that when these desires and dreams are high, the support of teacher education is high. We seem to be in the midst of such a period, making this a propitious time to institute reforms in teacher preparation.

In the final analysis, teacher education in our country remains a stately and valuable mansion. If it often appears somewhat down at the heels and in the need of maintenance, the disrepair is due more to overuse rather than to neglect. The kind of activities that take place in the mansion are vital to the workings of American society.

ACTIVITIES

1. What three historical events are given as the cause of reform in teacher education during the last decade of the nineteenth century? What vestiges of these reforms can be seen in present-day teacher education curriculum?
2. Reflect on your teacher education experiences and discuss the tension you have seen or felt between the liberal arts strand of teacher education and the technical / methodological strand of education.
3. What can teacher training institutions do in terms of public relations to reduce public anger in reference to teacher training?
4. What special interest groups block change or reform in American teacher education? What can be done to remove these blocks?
5. What reforms in teacher education would you, as a student, like to see?

REFERENCES

Anderson, S. W., Stanley, W. O., Smith, B. O., Benne, K. D., and MacMurray, F. (1951). *The theoretical foundations of education: Historical, comparative, philosophical and social.* Urbana, Ill.: Bureau of Research and Service.

Berliner, D. C. (November–December 1985). Laboratory settings and the study of teacher education. *Journal of Teacher Education, 75,* 2–8.

Bestor, A. E. (1953). *Educational wastelands*. Urbana: University of Illinois Press.

Borrowman, M. L. (1956). *The liberal and technical in teacher education: A historical survey of American thought*. New York: Bureau of Publications, Teacher College, Columbus University.

Carnegie Forum on Education and the Economy. (1986). *A nation prepared: Teachers for 21st century*. New York: Carnegie Foundation for Educational.

Cohen, S. (August 1976). The history of American education, 1900–1976: The uses of the past. *Harvard Educational Review, 46*, 298–325.

Conant, J. B. (1964). *The education of American teachers*. New York: McGraw-Hill.

Cremin, L. A. (1961). *The transformation of the school: Progressivism in American education, 1876–1957*. New York: Vintage Books.

Cremin, L. A. (1980). *American education: The national experience, 1783–1876*. New York: Harper and Row.

Darling-Hammond, L. (July 1984). *Beyond the commission reports: The coming crisis in teaching*. Santa Monica, Calif.: Rand Corporation.

Darling-Hammond, L., and Wise, A. E. (January 1985). Beyond standardization: State standards and school improvement. *The Elementary School Journal, 85*, 315–336.

Evertson, D., Hawley, W., and Zlotnik, M. (August 1984). *The characteristics of effective teacher preparation programs: A review of research*. Nashville, Tenn.: Peabody College, Vanderbilt University.

Feistritzer, C. E. (1985). *The condition of teaching: A state by state analysis*. New York: The Carnegie Foundation for the Advancement of Teaching.

Ginger, R. (1958). *Altegeld's America: The Lincoln ideal versus changing realities*. Chicago: Quadrangle Books.

Hofstadter, R. C. (1963). *Anti-intellectualism in American Life*. New York: Vintage Books.

Johnson Foundation / Racine Foundation. (June 10, 1985). New goals and initiatives for teacher education recommended by Holmes group consortium. *News Release*.

Katz, M. B. (1968). *The irony of early school reform: Educational innovation in mid-nineteenth century Massachusetts*. Cambridge, Mass.: Harvard University Press.

Lanier, J. E. (May 1985). Goals for educating teachers as professionals: Holmes Group working paper, unpublished.

Mayer, M. (1961). *The schools*. New York: Harper and Brothers.

Morgan, E. S. (1944). *The Puritan family: Religion and domestic relations in seventeenth-century New England*. New York: Harper and Row.

Noble, D. (1979). *American by design: Science, technology and the rise of corporation capitalism*. Oxford, Eng.: Oxford University Press.

Silberman, C. E. (1970). *Crisis in the classroom: The remaking of American education*. New York: Random House.

Smith, B. O. (October 1980). Pedagogical education: How about reform? *Phi Delta Kappan*.

Tyack, D. B. (1967). *Turning points in American educational history*. Waltham, Mass.: Blaisdell Publishing.

Vonnegut, K. (1970). *Introduction*. In J. Birmingham (Ed.), *Our time is new*. New York: Progu Publishing.

Woodring, P. (1957). *A faith of the nation*. New York: McGraw-Hill.

SUGGESTED READINGS

Borrowman, M. L. (1965). *Teacher education in America: A documentary history.* New York: Teachers College Press, Columbia University.

Carnegie Task Force on Teaching as a Profession. (1986). *A nation prepared: Teachers for the 21st century.* New York: Carnegie Forum on Education and the Economy.

Conant, J. B. (1963). *The education of American teachers.* New York: McGraw-Hill.

Feistritzer, C. E. (1986). *The making of a teacher: A report on teacher education and certification.* Washington, D.C.: National Center for Educational Information.

Hoffman, J. V., and Edwards, S. A. (1986). *Reality and reform in clinical teacher education.* New York: Random House.

Howey, K. R., and Gardner, W. R. (1983). *The education of teachers: A look ahead.* New York: Longman.

Koerner, J. D. (1963). *The miseducation of American teachers.* Boston: Houghton Mifflin.

Lanier, J. E., and Little, J. W. (1986). *Research on teacher education.* In M. E. Wittrock (Ed.), *Handbook of research on teaching* (3rd ed.). New York: Macmillan.

Tomorrow's teachers: A report of the Holmes group. (1986). East Lansing, Mich.: The Holmes Group, 527–568.

8

What Is Teacher
Effectiveness?

OVERVIEW

▶ This chapter introduces, analyzes, and interprets a framework for looking at the research on classroom teaching that has emerged in the last
fifteen years. The chapter first defines teaching, then briefly traces the
nature of teaching reform in this century, and finally narrows its focus
to the concept of teacher effectiveness. In the process, some insight
into the nature and the structure of educational research will be gained.

INTRODUCTION

▶ At least since Aristotle enrolled in Plato's academy in the third century B.C., teaching has been treated with a strange combination of
mistrust and wonder. For most of us, capturing the essence of effective teaching is nearly as difficult as seizing hold of a handful of smoke.
Although almost everyone can distinguish good teaching from bad
when experiencing it firsthand, most people resist the demand to define
it.

Because teaching is often viewed as mysterious and immune to
change, until recently it seldom served as a benchmark for educational
quality. Instead, a series of empty symbols, such as the characteristics

of the staff, various aspects of the school's physical plant, and the ethnic and socioeconomic characteristics of pupils, were employed to assess differences among teachers and schools. The result of these indirect inquiries was that, although educational researchers frequently found differences in student achievement, they were unable to explain the contribution of teaching to these differences (Spady, 1982).

In the last ten years much of this has changed as a group of educational researchers, after groping through a fog of complexity, have begun to discover the nature of effective teaching. This chapter describes that exploration on which the group of researchers searched for a definition of effective teaching, and upon discovering such, attempted to explore the territory surrounding the elusive definition.

As we journey toward a cognitive map of effective teaching, we start with a definition of teaching, move on to probe the social forces that have propelled educators toward a search for greater teacher effectiveness, and then proceed to examine the various tactics and strategies that characterize exploration of teacher effectiveness. In the next chapter, we conclude our account with a creative synthesis of research findings that have emerged from our explorations.

We hope to demonstrate that although the label *teacher effectiveness* may be premature—perhaps even hyperbolic—the term does signal a disposition, a movement in a direction that seems to be yielding an accumulating catalogue of knowledge that possesses the potential to improve dramatically the process of education. Before we plunge into the research, let us provide a generic definition of the act of teaching. As you shall see, it is not as easy as it appears at first blush.

WHAT IS TEACHING?

▶ Imgine for a moment that you are an observer in an interaction that involves more than one person. What clues would you look for, i.e., what behaviors, attitudes, or statements need to be present in order for you to conclude logically that teaching is taking place in this interaction? Try to describe the teaching characteristics in the space below.

_____

_____

_____

_____

To make our definition a little more realistic, examine the following interactions. Your task is simply to read the description and see if you can discover which of these interactions qualifies as teaching as you now think of it. Indicate your choice by circling either the yes or the no that follows each description.

1. A woman shows two adolescent boys how to beat egg whites. YES   NO
2. A manager of a baseball team approaches the pitching mound. YES   NO
3. Mr. Rogers tells his viewers to be wary of strangers.   YES   NO
4. A woman in a white coat explains to another woman how to apply makeup.   YES   NO
5. Ted Koppel looks directly into the camera and describes the nature of the Arab-Israeli conflict.   YES   NO

Look carefully at the situations you decided characterized teaching. What do these situations have in common? In other words, what are the main characteristics of that which we have come to recognize as an act of teaching? Describe below.

———————————————————————————————————

———————————————————————————————————

———————————————————————————————————

———————————————————————————————————

Now that you have tried to develop a definition of teaching, let us try to reconstruct the central features of that definition with the most elementary model possible, one without any unnecessary elaboration. We want to know, What are the bare essentials of teaching? To help us in our task, we will rely on the scholarship of Gary Fenstermacher who has engaged in extensive linguistic analyses of teaching (1986).

According to Fenstermacher, teaching comprises irreducible components. The components of teaching are contained within an interaction between at least two persons who are engaged in a particular way. There is an imbalance in the interaction because one of the individuals, the teacher, "knows, understands or is able to do something that he is trying to share with the other person" (1986, p. 38). The teacher intends to convey the knowledge to the student. The reason that the individuals are together is to convey the information. The association ceases, at least momentarily, when both persons possess the content.

Immediately, several problems emerge from this definition. Although Fenstermacher recognizes four, there could be others as well. For example, does the student have to want to know in order for teaching to take place? Must at least two people be involved? What about self-study? Is there a difference between teaching and telling (between a presentation on *Nova* and one of Dan Rather's news reports)? How well must the teacher know the content in order to teach it (have it all in his or her head or merely have access to it)?

Fenstermacher contends that additions to the definitions are extensions or elaborations to the generic concept, and not necessary for the root concept to be a complete definition. He claims that there are several ways of elaborating the basic definition.

> One might do so organizationally by examining the concept within the context of schooling. The concept might be elaborated behaviorally which is what educational psychologists do when they study the concept. Or it could be elaborated morally, as educational philosophers are want to do. Anthropologists make cultural elaborations, sociologists make structured elaborations, and so it goes for many different approaches to the study of teaching (Fenstermacher, 1986, p. 38).

Notice that to this point, we have not presented a definition of effective teaching, nor have we identified a set of conditions that must exist before effective teaching can take place. The development of a definition of effective teaching is the central task of this chapter. We plan to do this by degrees. Imagine that a definition of effective teaching lies at the center of a maze. We want to reach that center, but before we are able to do so, we must carefully explore the outer fringes. We will start with a brief description of the social conditions that propel American education toward school reform and increased teacher effectiveness.

CYCLES OF EDUCATIONAL REFORM

▶ Our nation's attention to public issues moves in a cyclical fashion. First, a series of events combines to push an issue into preeminence. Then the issue is intensely debated and widely publicized, and after a time, it begins to retreat from center stage and fades into the background until the cycle repeats itself (Downs, 1972).

Sometimes, if the issue is especially close to a large number of people, the heightened level of concern lasts for a considerable length of time. The recent widespread upsurge of interest in public education and the state of American schools is an indication that we are in the midst of such a cycle.

Although Americans are never uninterested in their schools, from time to time, generally during periods of domestic crisis, our concerns reach a sharper pitch. One historian claims that Americans' "persistent, intense, and sometimes touching faith in the efficacy of popular education" is the preeminent characteristic of our national experience

(Hofstadter, 1963, p. 299). Another contends that where the European reaction to great social unrest is revolution, the American response is to organize a course on the subject (Cremin, 1965).

During the past hundred years, there have been at least three distinct occasions when Americans not only organized courses but rallied around the flag of educational reform: just before the turn of the century, in the late 1950s, and in the early 1980s. In each of these episodes, the alleged ineffectiveness of teachers occupied a central position.

The similarities between the three reform movements are striking. All were begun by individuals from outside the schools who, despite proclaimed impartiality, initiated their investigations from a negative position. "What's wrong with our schools?" is a key refrain in all the reform rhetoric. None of the reform movements seemed much interested in what the schools were doing right. In assessing the blame for the "failure of the schools," each group chided teachers for being antiquated, wasteful, inefficient, and ineffective. In general, all three movements were born of frustration and nurtured by larger events in the society, and the tone of all was shrill.

The first of these reforms resulted from a series of articles published by Joseph M. Rice, a pediatrician-turned-journalist, that described the sorry state of American schools (Rice, 1893/1969). Journeying across the country in the first half of 1892, Rice visited schools in thirty-six cities, talked to 1,200 teachers, and then wrote eight articles in *The Forum,* a widely read mass-circulation magazine.

Rice was appalled by most of the teaching he observed. In his view, most school work was very formal with pupils learning to read, write, and cipher mechanically without acquiring any new ideas. The majority of the teachers, he contended, provided mechanical instruction because they lacked any other pedagogy. He argued that teachers were poorly trained, lacked competence in all but the most elementary subject matter, and seldom possessed anything even approaching a professional spirit.

Although Rice was not universal in his denunciation of teachers and schools, he did find most teachers to be so little advanced "that they may be regarded as representing a stage of civilization before the age of steam and electricity; largely mechanical, laborious, uninteresting and of little educational value" (1893/1969, p. 218).

Two central elements for improvement were proposed by Rice. First, he insisted that teachers must begin to lead children to the acquisition of ideas and teach them to clearly express themselves in written language. Second, Rice insisted that there indeed was a science of education, which teachers must learn if their performances were to improve. As a means of encouraging this kind of practice, he proposed "direct, thorough, and scientific supervision," and, one might add, the watchful monitoring by an aroused public of its schools.

The national debate on the quality of American teachers resumed again in the 1950s. For some time America's discontent with its schools had smoldered. When the Russians launched Sputnik into space on October 4, 1957, the national shame at having been beaten ignited and sparked the flame of reform. The intellectual ignition for the upsurge of interest in the quality of teaching was provided by a series of books and articles by James B. Conant, former president of Harvard and ambassador to West Germany. Like Rice before him, Conant's position was that, by and large, American teachers had failed to provide our children with a quality education (Ravitch, 1983).

Although Conant was convinced that the current practices of American teachers were ineffective, he did not suggest what they should do to improve their classroom teaching. Schooling would improve, Conant claimed, if teacher education programs became more demanding and school curricula made more rigorous.

Conant's orientation reflected an outlook common to reformers of this era. At its core, the argument held that it was possible to change teacher behavior and classroom performance by replacing idiosyncratic curriculum with more standardized learning. The attempt was to nudge teachers away from telling and recitation toward a more subtle discovery learning approach, as was currently being touted by psychologist Jerome Bruner.

The primary appeal of this argument was its efficiency. It was possible to bring together subject matter specialists and curriculum designers and, in a relatively short time, produce a nearly "teacher proof" curriculum package. Unfortunately, teachers, who were denied participation in most of the curriculum development and were therefore largely unprepared in the use of the materials, were apt to abandon them after initial interest. The effect of the lack of teacher involvement muted the expected pedagogical revolution before it gathered much momentum.

Although teacher inattention contributed to a gradual decline in interest in teacher reform, what ultimately drowned the movement was the tidal wave of the civil rights revolution in the mid-1960s. Diane Ravitch explains what happened:

> The expected pedagogical revolution in the schools was not to be, however. It was swept aside by the onrush of the racial revolution, which presented a forceful challenge to the political, social, and economic basis of American schools: Between 1963 and 1965, the nation's social fabric suffered a series of jolts. . . . Civil rights leaders in North and South brought their demands for integration, equality and justice to the doors of the public schools; in the context of such transcending demands, the pedagogical revolution was no revolution at all (1983, p. 233).

The present wind of educational reform was fanned by the growing awareness in the early 1980s that schools had once again become ineffective. As with previous reforms, the movement originated from outside the schools and tended to single out the ineffectiveness of teachers as the principal cause of the schools' failure. In the summer of 1980, Secretary of Education T. H. Bell sent a letter to the president to "call attention to an alarmingly persistent decline in the quality of education" (Hechinger, August 25, 1981, p. 15). Bell went on to establish a National Commission on Excellence in Education which he charged with producing a report that would recommend changes and improvements. Bell claimed that the report would be directed "to the American academic community, to governing boards, to state legislative bodies, and to others responsible for general support and supervision of schools and colleges."

After eighteen months of deliberation, the committee issued a report which claimed:

> Our nation is at risk. Our once unchallenged preeminence in commerce, industry, science, and technological innovation is being overtaken by competitors throughout the world. . . . [Education is] only one of the many causes and dimensions of the problem, but it is the one that undergirds American prosperity, security, and civility . . . the educational foundations of our society are presently being eroded by a rising tide of mediocrity that threatens our very future as a Nation and a people (National Commission on Excellence in Education, 1983, p. 1).

A Nation at Risk proceeded to paint a pessimistic portrait of American schools. Among the several areas of weakness documented by the report was the quality and effectiveness of teachers. In general, the report asserted that teachers lack competence in both teaching and subject matter knowledge. The report claimed, for example, that half of the newly employed mathematics, science, and English teachers were not qualified in these areas, and that more than two-thirds of high school physics courses were taught by unqualified teachers.

The overwhelmingly negative tone of this government report sent educational researchers scurrying for empirical evidence of this apparent educational crisis. The subsequent quest for possible solutions to shortcomings of the schools has sparked interest in a new body of research about effective teaching. Before we move to explicate the results of research on effective teaching, it is imperative that we describe, in some detail, how this research is conducted.

HOW RESEARCH ON TEACHING IS CONDUCTED

▶ In various places throughout this book we have alluded to the enormous complexity that characterizes teaching. In the past this complexity made it difficult for researchers to examine classroom instruction in any depth. Thus, for most of the history of professional education, research findings on teaching resulted from inquiries that examined teaching in an indirect way. One analyst of the phenomenon contends that the research has passed through three distinct but overlapping phases. Each of these phases was characterized by a dominant method of looking at teaching, and each of the methodologies moved closer to the direct observation of classroom interaction (Rosenshine, 1979).

The first research phase sought a definition of effective teaching in the personality of teachers. Investigators attempted to find which personality characteristics were most highly related to student achievement gain. This kind of research was easy to do since it consisted mainly of surveys and did not require that the researcher observe any classrooms. Unfortunately, a teacher's personality does not necessarily reflect what he or she does in the classroom. The gulf between one's declared instructional intentions and actual teaching behavior is often wide.

In the second phase, researchers entered the classroom in search of the teaching characteristics that distinguished effective teachers from less effective teachers. Like Ponce de Leon seeking the fountain of youth, they were single-minded in their quest for a definition of an effective teacher. That is, the researchers thought that they could locate an all-purpose list of the characteristics of an effective teacher, regardless of what or where that individual taught. Whereas these researchers arrived at some suggestive conceptions, in the end, they were forced to conclude that there is probably not a singular definition of an effective teacher.

Neither of these two orientations produced much that was useful to classroom teachers. Most teachers felt that reading these kinds of research findings was like eating liver, probably good for them but not worth the aggravation that accompanied the effort.

No single incident triggered the third—and as we will argue, more useful—phase of research on teaching. Three events combined to bring about this latter phase. First, several individuals attempted to capture the main ideas about research on teaching by writing textbooks on the subject. (The development of a text is important for a field because it is a signal that the field is maturing.)

The most important of these texts, *Handbook of Research on Teaching* (Gage, 1963) was notable for the manner in which it laid out a foundation for research results that it reported. The message of the majority of the chapters in the handbook may be framed as follows: Although we as yet do not have much evidence about effective teaching, this is the way we should proceed if we want to obtain that evidence. Where the first *Handbook of Research on Teaching* laid the foundation for more effective research on teaching, a series of subsequent works traced the rough dimensions of the research agenda. The first handbook was followed by a series of texts that began to construct a body of knowledge.

The second event that made the field of research on teaching more robust was the decision by the National Institute of Education (NIE) to support research on teaching in a small number of locations. This decision led to the development of what Lee Shulman calls an invisible college—a group of individuals endlessly examining, probing, and debating about their own and other members of the colleges' research on teaching (1986).

The third signal event contributing to a change in the orientation of research on teaching was the gradual abandonment of the search for a universal definition of effective teaching, and the general acceptance that effective teaching was a function of the circumstances that surround teaching, which, in turn, depends on the interests, capabilities, and motivation of the teachers and students in that particular context.

These three events did not, by themselves, transform the ugly outbuilding that had previously housed research on teaching into a majestic mansion. Instead, they served to construct a rude but serviceable structure that with care and hard work could be developed into a high-quality edifice.

At present there are countless strategies or models for the study of teaching. Each of these models differ from one another, sometimes profoundly; more often, however, the difference is a matter of degree. What each of the models holds in common is a commitment to inquire into the puzzles of teaching, and a set of fundamental terms of analysis.

Every research orientation defines two primary participants—teachers and students—who are seen as working jointly at thinking and acting. Three attributes of these actors determine the effectiveness of their teaching and learning. These determinants are the capacities, actions, and thoughts of the teachers and the students. Teaching and learning are nested in a number of contexts, or "surrounds," which are the milieu in which teaching occurs. These surrounds include individual, group, class, school, and community settings (Shulman, 1986, p. 8).

The researchers study two sorts of transactions that comprise the essence of classroom life: the formal and the hidden curriculum. The formal curriculum consists of the clearly visible or manifest aspects of the school curriculum such as academic tasks, school assignments, and classroom content; the hidden curriculum is composed of latent functions such as the interactional, social, and managerial aspects of classroom dynamics. In the old educational aphorism that still holds, school is a place where children learn to sit still and learn why Spot jumps; the sitting still is the hidden curriculum, and the Spot segment illustrates the formal curriculum.

Since this conception is a bit abstract, let us make our discussion more concrete by examining a classroom. Ask a friend or colleague if you might enter her or his classroom to examine one aspect of classroom life. Assure the person that you are not going to make a judgment about the quality of his or her teaching. Claim only that you are going to look at a single aspect of the class—classroom motivation. Because our purpose here is to get your hand into classroom observation and not to make you a measurement specialist, we are going to provide the observation tool which is printed below.

To use the device, just observe the classroom for fifteen minutes or so, then answer the questions using a narrative.

Examining Classroom Motivation

1. How explicit and public are the learning rules in the class? What is and is not allowed in the class?
2. To what extent do students participate in making the rules? To what degree can students influence the class rules?
3. How many ways are there to score points in the class?
4. How are the major decisions regarding space, sequence, tactics, and strategy for learning made?
5. Describe the major motivational processes that you have observed in this visit.

Suggested by Alschuler, 1973.

This kind of analytical tool is an example of a high-inference observational instrument; that is, a measuring tool that allows for some interjection of the observer's opinion, while severely limiting the number of categories the observer examines. By restricting the number of categories to a manageable proportion, the observer can hopefully make sharper distinctions among the wide variety of classroom events. It is the difference between using a search light to illuminate the entire classroom, and focusing a bright spotlight on a small sector of the classroom.

The task you have just performed is an accurate simulation of research on teaching. You isolated one area for study, selected a tool to obtain information, and proceeded to gather data. Although actual classroom research would be somewhat more sophisticated (using larger and more representative samples, and constructing more detailed observational instruments), your experience at learning to look in your friend's classroom approximated most classroom research, except for a notable difference. Most recent research compares the results of the classroom observation with some other psychological characteristic. Frequently that variable consists of student achievement scores, generally test results from a standarized achievement test.

What the research seeks to determine is, How does one dimension of teacher behavior, such as the level of classroom questions or the number of misbehaviors, contribute to a rise in test scores? Rather than employing the raw achievement scores, the analyst generally is inclined to use a measure that indicates how much progress the pupils have made since the teacher began to use the behavior under study. These measures are called *student gain scores*.

If all of this seems elementary, it is this kind of intellectual construction that makes scientific progress possible, because inquiry must start with a simplified model of human behavior and gradually move toward more complexity. It is as one Nobel prize winner noted, "The capacity of the human mind for formulating and solving complex problems is very small compared with the size of the problems whose solution is required" (Simon, 1957, p. 199).

Although the models for studying classrooms remain as yet unsophisticated, there are clear differences of opinion among researchers. Since this chapter is neither an encyclopedia entry nor a statement on the philosophy of social science, a complete exegesis of the differences is inappropriate here. In the next chapter, we will attempt to make clearer distinctions between the varieties of research on teaching.

SUMMARY

► This chapter constructed a framework to examine teacher effectiveness. The task involved several incremental steps: first, we sought the simplest possible model of teaching; second, we established some background for the current interest in teacher effectiveness by examining the main currents in the stream of educational reform in the last century; and third, we provided a detailed account of the process of educational research. This chapter provided the footing and laid the foundation for Chapter 9, which describes the research on teacher effectiveness in more specific detail.

ACTIVITIES

1. Read *A Nation at Risk* and analyze the report in terms of the American values discussed in Chapter 1: equity, efficiency, and choice. Which of these three values seems to be the most prevalent in the report? Document your choice.

2. How are the three cycles of educational reform different from one another?
3. Reflect on your own high-school experience, and identify the formal curriculum and the hidden curriculum in your high school.
4. Compile a list of motivational processes you have observed in schools. Speculate about what the various motivational processes teach children either explicitly or implicitly.
5. In your opinion, why is educational research such an inexact science?

REFERENCES

Alschuler, A. S. (1973). *Developing achievement motivation in adolescents. Education for human growth.* Englewood Cliffs, N.J.: Educational Technology Publications.

Cremin, L. A. (1965). *The genius of American education.* New York: Vintage Books.

Downs, A. J. (Summer 1972). Up and down with ecology — The issue-attention cycle. *The Public Interest, 28,* 38–50.

Fenstermacher, G. C. (1986). Philosophy of research on teaching: Three aspects. In M. C. Wittrock (Ed.), *Third handbook of research on teaching.* New York: MacMillan.

Gage, N. L. (Ed.) (1963). *Handbook of research on teaching.* Chicago: Rand McNally.

Hechinger, F. M. (August 25, 1981). New approach: A forum of ideas. *New York Times,* p. 15.

Hofstadter, R. C. (1963). *Anti-intellectualism in American life.* New York: Vintage Books.

National Commission on Excellence in Education. (1983). *A nation at risk: The imperative for educational reform.* Washington, D.C.: U.S. Department of Education.

Ravitch, D. (1983). *The troubled crusade: American education, 1945–1980.* New York: Basic Books.

Rice, J. M. (1893/1969). *The public school system of the United States.* New York: Arno Press.

Rosenshine, B. (1979). Content, time, and direct instruction. In P. Peterson and H. Walberg (Eds.), *Research on teaching: Concepts, findings, and implications.* Berkeley, Calif.: McCutchan.

Shulman, L. S. (1986). Paradigms and research programs in the study of teaching: A contemporary perspective. In M. C. Wittrock (Ed.), *Third handbook of research on teaching.* New York: MacMillan.

Simon, H. A. (1957). *Models of man: Social and rational: Mathematical essays.* New York: John Wiley.

Spady, W. S. (November 1982). Keys to effective instruction: A response to Williams. *School Administrator,* 35–36.

SUGGESTED READINGS

Action for excellence: A comprehensive plan to improve our nation's schools. (1983). Denver: Educational Commission of the States.

City high schools: A recognition of progress. (1984). New York: The Ford Foundation.

Educating Americans for the 21st century: A plan of action for improving mathematics, science, and technology education for all American elementary and secondary students so that their achievement is the best in the world by 1995: A report to the American people and the National Science Board. (1983). Washington, D.C.: National Science Board Commission on Precollege Education in Mathematics, Science, and Technology.

Felt, M. C. (1985). *Improving our schools: Thirty-three studies that inform local action.* Newton, Mass.: Education Development Center.

Lezotte, L. W., Hathaway, D. U., Miller, S. K., Passalacqua, J., and Brookover, W. B. (1982). *Creating effective schools: An inservice program for enhancing school learning, climate, and achievement.* Holmes, Fla.: Learning Publications.

Lightfoot, S. L. (1983). *The good high school: Portraits of character and culture.* New York: Basic Books.

Making the grade: Report of the Twentieth Century Fund task force on federal elementary and secondary education policy. (1983). New York: The Twentieth Century Fund.

9

Three Orientations to Research on Teaching

OVERVIEW

► This chapter is a detailed account of three distinct frameworks for the examination of teacher effectiveness. The three perspectives are *process product*, where the researchers examine the relationship between a teaching behavior and some future student performance; *student thought process*, where the research is somewhat more concerned with the students' thinking; and *classroom ecology*, where the researcher probes the social environment of the classroom for clues to teacher effectiveness.

In a discussion of the three perspectives, we present the research findings in terms of generalizations to organize the presentation. Although there is a large body of research on teaching that at first glance seems widely varied, there are basically three distinct research programs that characterize the current research on teaching scene. Two of the research programs are rooted in psychology; the third blossomed in anthropology before it was transplanted to the field of educational research (Shulman, 1986).

Dwarfing the others with its size and influence is the process-product tradition which examines the relationship between teaching behavior and subsequent student performances. Since process-product research is the largest and the most variegated of the three research traditions, we will have the most to say about that variety.

The second research program, most appropriately described as the study of student thought processes, concentrates on "student thoughts and feelings, usually in relation to teacher actions and subsequent student actions or capacities" (Shulman, 1986, p. 16). The third research tradition, the classroom ecology program, investigates the social and cultural environment of the classroom. This model, much more interpretative and less positivistic than the previous two traditions, traces how different patterns of teacher-student interaction affect teaching and learning. In order to avoid confusion about these models, it is appropriate to begin our discussion with a diagram that displays some of the differences between them. Figure 9–1 is a diagrammatic representation of the three research programs.

Before we explicate these research traditions, it is important to make two important distinctions. First, no researcher begins from a research tradition; all start with a puzzle that they seek to answer. It is only when we reconstruct their logic that we are able to assign their research to a category. Second, each of our three categories sacrifice all encompassing presentations to purchase clarity and, hopefully, understandability. Let us move to the three traditions, each of which will be examined.

THREE VARIETIES OF TEACHER EFFECTIVENESS

▶ Process-Product Research

This variety of research on teaching grows out of the soil of behavioral psychology. Briefly, this psychological orientation takes an imperial stance toward the individuals that it studies. That is, behavioral psychologists position themselves away from, and even above, the individuals they study. Look at the vocabulary behavioralists employ in their inquiries: *subjects, controlled experiments, dependent variables, rewards,* and *reinforcements.* Behavioralists, with whom we associate process-product researchers, take the vantage point of an outside observer seeking to discover the laws that govern the observable features of the behavior being studied. By definition, process-product researchers are not much interested in unobservable human behavior such as emotions, thoughts, or feelings. In some ways practitioners from this orientation resemble the young man from an American steel town who remarked that he did not trust air he could not see.

The desired result of process-product research is a series of lawful generalizations, namely some predictions about teaching outcomes that will transfer to similar situations. Despite the fact that a great many slings and arrows have been directed at process-product research, the field has produced many useful generalizations in the relatively short period of its existence.

FIGURE 9-1 Three Orientations Toward Research on Teaching

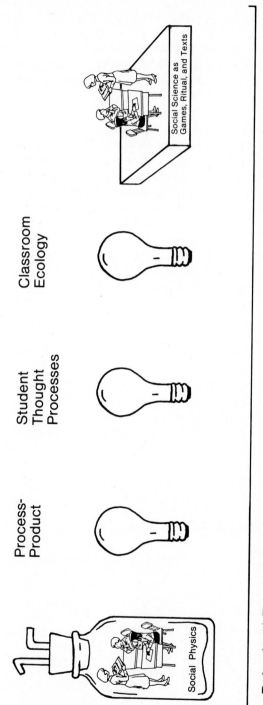

Process-
Product

Student
Thought
Processes

Classroom
Ecology

Social Science as
Games, Ritual, and Texts

Social Physics

- Behavioral Psychology
- Quantitative
- Positivistic
- Laws-and-Causes

- Cultural Anthropology
- Qualitative Methods
- Interpretative
- Cases-and-Interpretations

Shulman claims that there are four distinct reasons for the rapid success of the process-product orientation. In addition to its close affinity to the dominant school of psychological research, behavioralism, process-product approaches succeeded because their research studies were conducted in actual classrooms, the results had straightforward policy implications, and most important, the model worked. Teachers who followed the process-product directives had students with higher achievement scores than other teachers who did not follow the imperatives of the conception in research studies where comparisons between the two groups were attempted (1986).

Another characteristic of process-product research that escapes the attention of supporters and detractors alike is the scheme's breathtaking simplicity. As a means of simultaneously illustrating the simplicity of product-process design, and introducing discussion of the research, refer to Figure 9–2.

Process-product research, which is probably better known by the label attached to its prototypical instructional method, *direct instruction,* began with the work of educational psychologists John Carroll and Benjamin Bloom who initiated the concentrated focus on individual classrooms. These psychologists' research suggested that the teacher is the most powerful force affecting classroom achievement. Further, their research showed that there are certain kinds of teacher behaviors in the process-product interaction that led to effective student performance.

Process-product research shows that the effective teacher is more likely to present information actively and clearly, tends to be task focused, and is more interested in instruction and less interested in socialization than less effective teachers. According to Thomas Good, effective teachers are nonevaluative and tend to create a relaxed learning atmosphere, yet simultaneously express higher achievement norms, move at a faster pace, and have fewer behavior problems than other

FIGURE 9-2 The Process-Product Research Scheme

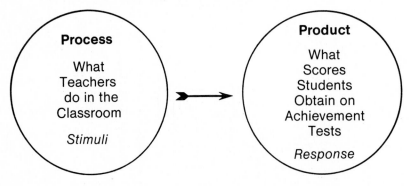

teachers. At odds with conventional wisdom, effective teachers seem to offer less student choice, use fewer small groups, and ask more lower level questions than less effective teachers (1983).

Two major implications emerge from the process-product research. The first suggests that there is a direct relationship between student achievement and time on task, and that the most crucial aspect of time on task is academic learning time — the time a student spends engaged with instructional materials or activities that are at an appropriate level of difficulty for that student. In addition, the research supports the utility of an academic focus, a structured environment, and the factual, low-level questioning technique. Simply put, difficult materials and strategies and a confusing environment appear to bewilder pupils and retard their learning (Berliner, 1979).

The second major trend emerging from the research supports the importance that the timing of tasks plays in learning. William Spady, for example, insists that "it is not the simplified notion of time spent on tasks that is important. Good timing is the key to utilization of instructional time" (Spady, 1982, p. 35). He contends that the instructional alignment composed of clear objectives, explicit teaching of the content of those objectives, and the assessment of each objective works best and produces student achievement that generally exceeds expectations.

Since we claimed that process-product research is a leviathan that looms over the landscape of research on teaching, and because the focus and methodologies of the various aspects of the research differ, we will present a creative synthesis of the results that have emerged from the body of research that will deepen and broaden the general overview that we have just outlined. Three general themes seem the most clear:

1. The teacher is the most important factor in student learning.
2. Classroom management is positively related to achievement gain.
3. Achievement gain is not necessarily related to a warm classroom climate.

Let us examine each of them in turn.

The Teacher Is the Most Important Factor in Student Learning
As we suggested previously, a variety of evidence has been accumulated to support the position that the classroom teacher is the most powerful factor affecting academic achievement. The distinguishing characteristic of the effective teacher is active teaching. The active teacher sets clear learning goals, constructs activities designed to help accomplish those goals, carefully supervises student progress, and models the learning activities for pupils. Active teachers move at a brisk pace and present material at a difficulty level that allows for rather consistent stu-

dent success. Research reveals that the combination of classroom behaviors that make up the active teaching model can be employed to differentiate relatively effective teachers from relatively ineffective teachers.

Concentrating the focus more specifically, Barak Rosenshine (1976) says the model is made up of the following:

- ▶ A clear focus on academic goals
- ▶ An effort to promote extensive content coverage and high levels of student involvement in classroom tasks
- ▶ Instructional goals and materials and an attempt to actively monitor student progress toward these goals
- ▶ Structured learning activities and feedback which is immediate and academically oriented
- ▶ An environment that is task oriented but relaxed.

Table 9–1 illustrates the central elements of direct instruction.

TABLE 9-1   A Summary of Elements in Direct Instruction

Elements	Recommended Teacher Behavior	Undersirable Teacher Behavior
Time and Activities	Time structured by the teacher	Time spent on arts, crafts, dramatic play, active play, stories
	Time spent on number and reading activities using textbooks, or in verbal interactions and on mathematics	Game-like activities
		Number of interest centers
	Time spent on seatwork with academic workbooks through which the pupils proceeded at their own pace	Large number of different, concurrent activities
		Hours of unstructured time
		Frequent socialization
Work Groupings	Students worked in groups supervised by the teacher	Free work groups
		Children working independently without supervision of teacher
Teacher Directions and Questions	Teacher directs activities without giving pupils choice of activities or reasons for the selection of activities	Teacher joins or participates in pupil's activities
		Teacher organizes learning around pupil's own problem

TABLE 9-1 A Summary of Elements in Direct Instruction (continued)

Elements	Recommended Teacher Behavior	Undesirable Teacher Behavior
	Learning is organized around questions posed by the teacher	Teacher approaches subject matter in an indirect, formal way
	Teacher asks narrow questions	Teacher encourages pupil to express himself freely
	Teacher asks direct questions that have only a single answer	Teacher permits pupil to suggest additional or alternative answers
	Adult commands, requests, or direct questions that had an academic focus	Pupil initiates activities
		Pupil has freedom to select activities
		Teacher commands and requests, nonacademic
		Teacher open-ended questions and nonacademic commands
Student Responses	Students give a high percentage of correct answers both in verbal interaction and in workbooks	Child open-ended questions and nonacademic commands
		Adult nonacademic commands or requests, or open-ended questions
	Students are encouraged to attempt to answer questions (rather than saying, "I don't know")	Child nonacademic responses
		Child general comments to adults or among children
Adult Feedback	Teacher immediately reinforces pupil as to right or wrong	Adult feedback on nonacademic activities (e.g., play, music)
	Adult feedback had an academic focus	
	Teacher asks new questions after correct answer	
	Teacher gives answer after incorrect answer	

Source: Barak Rosenshine, "Classroom Motivation," in *The Psychology of Teaching Methods,* Seventy-fifth Yearbook, National Society for Study of Education, Part I, ed. N. L. Gage (Chicago: University of Chicago Press, 1976), pp. 369–370.

To make our image of direct instruction clear, let us imagine a hypothetical fourth-grade classroom where the teacher, Mary Walker, is teaching arithmetic.

Before teaching, Ms. Walker developed a very clear lesson plan. In essence, Ms. Walker plans to structure carefully the entire class, which will, for the majority of the class period, meet in a large group. Pupils will be given little choice as to what they will study, and their expected performance will be to provide answers to Ms. Walker's questions, which will tend to be directed at a literal level that most students will be able to comprehend. After a pupil answers a question, she or he will receive immediate feedback, and Ms. Walker will pose another question. Ms. Walker will earnestly strive to keep her students engaged in arithmetic with a variety of whole class activities and individual seatwork. Because she is so tightly organized, Ms. Walker expects a minimum of disruption.

Ms. Walker begins teaching with a review of the concepts and skills of the previous night's homework. After collecting homework assignments (which she intends to carefully mark and pass back), she asks several mental computation exercises.

After about ten minutes, Ms. Walker moves on to some new work, that she introduces by focusing on the prerequisite skills and concepts, and proceeds to illustrate by using explanations and demonstrations. By frequent assessment checks, Ms. Walker determines what directions need more elaboration.

After about twenty minutes of this exposition, the pupils are given an assignment that they are allowed to practice, without interruption, for about fifteen minutes. Ms. Walker tells the pupils that their work will be checked at the conclusion of this period. Ms. Walker sustains student involvement by moving around the room to assist and supervise her pupils. When the work concludes, Ms. Walker, who has checked most students' work, makes a homework assignment and moves on to another subject.

Now that we have presented the direct instruction model, we would like to see how you feel about it. As a perception check, we have constructed an exercise on page 169.

Which of the Costs/Benefits you named in the chart would carry the most weight in the typical teacher's decision? Would it make a difference if the person was an English teacher? An elementary teacher? A science teacher? What would carry the most weight in your decision?

After reading about the research on teaching and studying a description of the instructional model that best represents that research, how do you feel about direct instruction? Is direct instruction something that you could use to enhance your teaching? Why or why not?

Cost/Benefit Analysis of Direct Instruction

Directions: Imagine that you are a typical classroom teacher. From what you have just read about the direct instruction model, how do you feel about that way of teaching? Now let us try to be a little more systematic in our analysis of your feelings. Using the schematic presented below, try to figure out what the typical teacher would have to give up and what he or she would gain by using the direct instruction model that we just described. List what the typical classroom teacher would gain that might improve his or her teaching on the *Benefits* side of the ledger and what the teacher would have to sacrifice on the *Costs* side of the schematic.

Costs	Benefits
1.	1.
2.	2.
3.	3.
4.	4.

Classroom Management Is Positively Related to Achievement Gain

During the past decade, something remarkable has happened to our knowledge of classroom management. Witness the following:

▶ Every study so far shows that classroom management is related to student achievement (Good, 1983).

▶ Effective classroom managers can be distinguished from less effective managers by their ability to prevent student misbehaviors (Good, 1983).

▶ Fewer misbehaviors occur in classrooms where students clearly understand the class rules (Brophy, 1983).

▶ The differing classroom behavior of high- and low-ability pupils calls for different systems of teacher management (Evertson et al., 1980).

▶ Explicit teaching of self-control skills lessens student misbehaviors.

In a comprehensive examination of the research findings on classroom management, Brophy (1983) presents a composite picture of the well-managed classroom.

The physical environment of the well-managed classroom is clearly and carefully organized. Students are well aware of acceptable classroom movements, the location of resources, and teacher expectations. The teacher presents carefully structured lessons at a rapid pace, making transactions to smooth discernible parts. Students attend to the teacher's directions and are responsive to the teacher's questions. The steady flow of the class works automatically with a minimum of teacher effort.

Although the smoothly running classroom seems effortless, research shows that it results from consistent teacher efforts to create, maintain, and occasionally restore conditions that foster effective learning. How does this atmosphere evolve? How can a teacher construct such an environment? Recent studies of classroom management and the behavior teachers employ to control the learning environment have sought to answer these questions. Although discipline has been a central concern of educators since the ancient Greeks first brought their students indoors and created the first classrooms, the systematic study of classrooms is of relatively recent vintage.

The systematic study of classroom management began in the late 1960s with the work of Jacob Kounin (1970), who, upon examining videotapes of classrooms, discovered that there were several differences between teachers who were judged to be good classroom managers and those deemed to be poor ones. Kounin found that the most important difference between the two kinds of teachers was that the effective teachers were able to limit the frequency with which students became disruptive in the first place. In other words, effective teachers practiced preventive discipline.

Kounin discovered that the two groups differed in the techniques they employed. Effective classroom managers seemed to possess a repertoire of techniques necessary to maintain a well-organized classroom. The most readily identifiable of these techniques was something Kounin labeled "withitness." By this, he meant the effective teachers had an almost intuitive ability to anticipate what was about to occur that could disrupt the class order, and were able to prevent trouble before it started. They could do this because they positioned themselves both physically and intellectually so that they could see all their students at all times.

The second of the different behaviors in the good managers' repertoire was "overlapping," or the ability to do more than one thing at a time. A teacher skilled in this behavior could, for example, correct papers and quiet students at the same time.

Signal continuity and momentum was the third effective behavior. This means moving at a brisk pace, and correcting students, bringing them back into the flow of the class, without losing the momentum. When there is a minimum of disruption and a continuous "academic" signal to attend to, the class operates as a smooth, well-organized system.

In addition, effective classroom managers seemed to hold students in a mild suspense, which seems to encourage them to be alert and accountable. They accomplished this in a variety of ways, the most important being throwing out challenges or randomly selecting respondents to questions.

Finally, Kounin found that effective managers tended to present assignments that possessed both variety and challenge.

According to Jere Brophy (1983), who has extended and elaborated upon Kounin's work, most of Kounin's ideas have been supported by subsequent research on classroom management. The notable exception seems to be the group-alerting technique, which holds students in suspense. It appears that this technique is easily abused and should be employed sparingly because overutilization can alienate pupils and fragment their attention.

On the whole, however, Kounin's conclusions, first postulated half a generation ago, have stood up admirably and serve as the foundation for reliable knowledge about classroom management.

Although American classrooms are probably not in the violent disarray that is sometimes suggested by politicians and the popular press, it seems clear that the presence of strong classroom management is a requisite for student learning. What emerges from the research is a constellation of teacher behaviors that can promote the presence of discipline without sacrificing the warm and accessible learning environment that many students, parents, and teachers have come to prefer.

Achievement Gain Is Not Necessarily Related to a Warm Classroom Climate

Although it remains unrecorded, Ichabod Crane probably did not care if his pupils liked school. In fact, it is not likely that he thought much about whether or not his students cared. His attitude is typical of most teachers through the history of American education who, generally, viewed their mission as twofold: to teach basic skills and to create appropriate conditions for character formation. Most students shared their teachers' attitude, and believed that they were in school because their parents made them attend and so they would not be ignorant.

This attitude largely held for the better part of two centuries. In the summer of 1966, this conventional wisdom was abruptly threatened by the release of *The Equality of Educational Opportunity*, a 737-page report that presented results from a survey of about 600,000 children and 60,000 teachers in nearly 4,000 schools (Coleman et al., 1966). Although the report included 548 pages of complex statistical explanation, the results were popularly interpreted to simply say that, with regard to the overall quality of a child's development, "schools make no difference; families make the difference." The report seemed to demonstrate that the most variation in student achievement resulted from social environment and family background than any aspect of the quality of the school or teaching.

Although James S. Coleman, the principal author of the report, has denied much of what is attributed to the report, he did steadfastly maintain that the schools seemed powerless to reduce deficits between groups of pupils. Educational leaders interpreted that statement to mean that, in classroom practice, the teacher's primary concern was the students' well-being—held in importance above the instruction of academic content. Most parents and nearly all teachers were indifferent, if not outright hostile, toward this new "unofficial" educational policy. Teachers did make a difference, they maintained, and the primary function of school was not to make students happy but to teach basic skills and promote academic achievement.

It was not until the mid-1970s that research, which attempted to describe the optimal classroom climate, began to emerge. The effort in this direction began with a review of research conducted by educational psychologist Donald Medley. Medley put the question rather starkly when he asked, "Do teachers who produce relatively rapid gains in reading do so at the expense of pupils' attitude toward school or their self-esteem?" (Medley, 1979, p. 21). In other words, can student attitude and student achievement—previously considered two separate entities—be considered together to increase our understanding of effective schooling?

Using one hundred classrooms in grades 1–12, Medley and his associates questioned the necessity of emphasizing affective objectives. He found that, although the more effective teachers selected appropriate goals, involved their students in planning, and listened to students, these teachers did not feel that they had to cultivate a particularly warm environment before they began to teach content. Indeed, Medley's study revealed that an emphasis on certain affective outcomes—undue amount of participation in decision making, overemphasis on praise and reward, and strong attention to one-to-one counseling—contributed to a decline in student achievement. In essence, Medley and his associates found that the teacher who spends a great deal of time on the affective aspects of teaching may be doing so to repair a poorly managed classroom. The teacher who has created a well-managed classroom has less need to interpret learning with affective maintenance behavior (Coker, Medley, and Soar, 1980).

In a more comprehensive search for the optimal classroom climate, Robert and Ruth Soar found that although a negative climate—one in which a teacher spends a great deal of time criticizing pupils for behavior—is undesirable for learning, there is no evidence to "support the notion that a positive or warm classroom climate does much to increase student achievement" (Rouk, 1980, p. 16).

The Soars found that the environment for learning comprised two parts: emotional climate and teacher management. With regard to emotional climate, they found that the most effective classroom seems to be neutral. The pattern of teacher management that facilitates the most student learning was composed of structures that limited pupils' freedom of choice, physical movement, and disruption. In these effective settings, there was more teacher talk and teacher control of pupils' task behavior.

What appears, then, is a clear picture of the kind of classroom climate that effective teachers prefer. It is characterized by cooperative relationships between teachers and students. The teacher in this setting is unlikely to shame or harass students, but also is not apt to spend an inordinate amount of time creating a particularly warm classroom climate. In general, the teacher who is effective is pleasant but business-like in the relationship with his or her students.

We feel it is important to offer a caveat here. While it is true that there is currently no compelling evidence to link warm and affective classrooms with strong academic achievement, there is also no evidence to suggest that the presence of a negative climate promotes academic achievement in any way. The research findings cited should not be interpreted as a license to promote cruelty or even neutrality in the classroom.

For most of the recent period of research on teaching, process-product orientations have dominated, providing the preponderant bulk of the research findings on teacher effectiveness. As educational research moves toward the twenty-first century, the process-product scheme appears to be losing its vigor (Shulman, 1986). In subsequent years, this model is likely to decline in influence, as other orientations suplant the behaviorally oriented conceptual scheme. Although, in part, the changes can be attributed to a change in fashion in the American social scientific community, there are numerous reasons why the process-product orientation is no longer the monolith that towers over the research on teaching landscape.

Four reasons appear most important. First, process-product approaches—beginning with very simple models of teaching—have accomplished their goals, and now many researchers want to move on to more sophisticated research configurations in order to deepen and extend their inquiries.

Second, in attempting to simplify teacher processes, process-product researchers have synthesized a wide variety of disparate teacher behaviors into general categories, and then claimed that these categories influence student achievement. These endeavors may facilitate conversations between members of the process-product "invisible college," but they complicate the situation for classroom teachers who are unable to use the artificial concepts in their teaching. (Can any teacher set out to teach "opportunity to learn," one of the most important of the process-product constructs?)

Third, process-product research seldom tells its readers why a particular process works. The process-product research agenda, as Shulman says, is relentlessly empirical, but alarmingly short on theoretical explanations. As we claimed in Chapter 3, teachers are most attracted to a new technique when that innovation comes enveloped in an explanation. (The United States Department of Education, for example, is so sensitive to this phenomenon that they titled a recent publication for teachers *What Works,* 1986.)

The fourth reason that this orientation's influence is declining is the widespread recognition that the product is always measured by students' scores on standard achievement tests. Nearly all teachers argue that achievement tests are a poor reflection of what happens in their classroom. More than inaccurate, they contend, using achievement tests is unfair and causes teachers to ignore higher order thinking and other difficult-to-measure pedagogical strategies (Mackey and Appleman, February 1985).

But in the final analysis, process-product research is probably losing its vigor because it fails to account for that most vital ingredient in the entire teaching-learning concept — what is in the students' heads. It is to that complex phenomena, the various student thought processes, that we now turn our attention.

▶ **Student Thought Processes Research**

The movie *The Fantastic Voyage* is a standard adventure story with a twist. Released in the mid-1960s, the film continues to enjoy a large audience because it is based on the premise that a group of people can be miniaturized enough to be injected into the bloodstream of a famous scientist who has been shot, and who alone knows a secret that can save the world. *The Fantastic Voyage* is appealing because it offers us a view into the universe within us all — the human body and brain. A consuming interest in this interior universe has always been one of people's obsessions.

Down the long corridors of human history the nature of thinking has been the central concern of both philosophy and psychology. Until recently, however, it was only possible to speculate about the dimensions of human's inner world. In recent decades, this has changed as psychologists have embarked upon a fantastic voyage to explore the inner recesses of the universe within. The collective label that has been attached to these inquiries is *cognitive science.*

For our purposes here, the most important of these sets of inquiries have been those that mediate students' learning. An appropriate way to begin is to reintroduce the diagram we employed to illustrate the process-product orientation. Figure 9–3, of course, is fundamentally different for the present scheme, but it does originate from the same foundation.

As the most cursory examination of the diagram reveals, teacher effectiveness research operating from this orientation is necessarily more complex and involved. Where process-product research concerns obser-

FIGURE 9-3 The Student Thought Processes Research Scheme

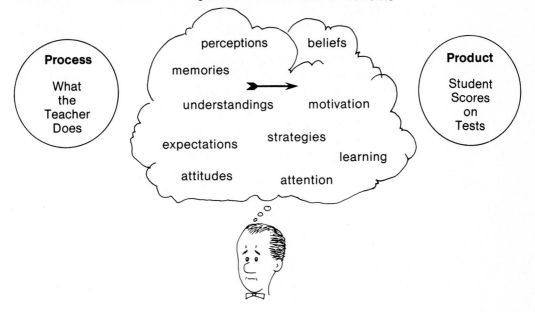

vable behavior and tends to ignore thinking and other mental representations, the student thought processes research program contends that it is not possible to understand student behaviors unless some aspect of that student's cognition is examined. Because this research deals with more complex phenomena, it is more difficult to conduct, and therefore more cumbersome to organize and report. It is like comparing the difference between growing wheat and raising orchids. Since the student thought process "orchids" are rarer, but also probably more valuable, the subject appears well worth pursuing. In our discussion of this research tradition we again organize our discussion in terms of generalizations. In this case, the research findings suggest two major generalizations:

1. Reducing complexity leads to academic achievement.
2. Different subject matter, pupil ages, and social classes demand different teaching strategies.

Reducing Complexity Leads to Academic Achievement
Perhaps the most palpable finding that has emerged from research on student thought processes is the realization of the enormous complexity of classroom life. Numerous studies of the thinking processes underlying school work show the "complex character of the operations and decisions that academic competence entails a complexity that is often

overlooked when the goals of the school are discussed" (Doyle, 1983, p. 17).

In order to be effective, a teacher must be able to encourage both basic and higher order skills in a simple and straightforward fashion. In other words, even complex learning tasks need to be presented in a noncomplicated manner. It is important to keep in mind the fact that the "stuff" of school, reading and writing, is the "most remarkable specific performance that civilization has learned in all its history" (Huey, 1908/1968).

Classrooms are complex because many activities occur simultaneously. It is estimated that each hour of classroom life comprises no fewer than ten significant instructional decisions. In a single day, teachers have over 1,500 distinct interactions with their pupils; some concern trivial incidents such as hair pulling and other misbehavior, but more involve important instructional decisions (Berliner, 1985). Amidst all these buzzing, bewildering interactions, the teacher is forced to respond reflexively, to literally shift gears as fast as a basketball player. While no one expects the teacher to be magic, the research does suggest some ways of making classrooms simpler.

The first of these ways is to realize how students think about academic work, because the difference between the teacher's curriculum and what students learn is considerable. In general, students will learn only tasks for which they are held accountable. For example, if a teacher spends a good deal of time discussing the ideas behind mathematical reasoning, but grades computational problems, the pupils will define their task as learning computation. This is because answering—whether it involves homework, class discussion, worksheets, or achievement tests—is the students' paramount responsibility in school. Students' judgments of how well they fulfill their obligation is reflected in the grades they receive. In general, pupils seldom study to acquire knowledge; rather, they labor to earn acceptable grades. Given these observations, teachers can best proceed to make their classrooms less complex by knowing their students well, both in terms of their abilities and their relatively narrow personal objectives (Doyle, 1983).

Whole class instruction is an effective medium for reducing complexity. Most reviews of classroom effectiveness show little apparent difference between whole class instruction and the deployment of pupils into small groups. Herein lies the advantage: Although teachers lose nothing in effectiveness with this configuration, they gain a great deal of strategic advantage.

Whole class instruction makes it possible to develop a single lesson plan for the entire activity. It presents much greater opportunity for the teacher to move around the class during seatwork, and it allows for many more demonstrations and discussions of complex and difficult learning material. In addition, whole class instruction, because it provides the teacher with more control, makes possible a greater congruence between the teacher's intended curriculum and what pupils actually learn (Good and Brophy, 1986).

Carefully structuring class presentations is another method to reduce complexity. Structuring means "beginning with overviews, and advance organizers; outlining the content and signal transactions between lesson parts; summarizing subparts of the lesson as it proceeds; and reviewing main ideas at the end" (Good and Brophy, 1986, p. 362). Taken together, these structuring procedures reduce complexity because they provide the student with a clearer road map to the teacher's intention, thus reducing student confusion.

Complexity can also be reduced if teachers employ the ideas inherent in the concept of academic learning time in their teaching (Berliner, 1979). As you recall, academic learning time refers to the time a student is engaged with instructional materials that are at an appropriate level of difficulty. In order for students to learn, they must experience success in the classroom. This will happen when the complexity is reduced by presenting students with materials that they understand. Although the idea appears obvious, the *Beginning Teacher Evaluation Study* (Fisher et al., 1978), a comprehensive examination of California teachers, discovered that teachers failed to do this about half of the time.

The optimal way, then, to reduce complexity is to briskly move students along a carefully prescribed path, studying instructional materials that the teacher has diagnosed as being at an easy level of difficulty. Moving with small steps and asking questions that students can answer make the complexity and confusion minimal and enhance student success, and ultimately reduce complexity.

Different Subject Matter, Pupil Ages, and Social Classes Demand Different Teaching Strategies
For some time, researchers on teaching have searched for a key to interpret the characteristics of the effective teacher. They pursued this quest with intensity, believing that if they found standard procedures of good teaching, instruction would fall neatly into place.

During the past fifteen years, research has revealed that there is no single set of characteristics that define good teaching. Simply put, the research suggests different teaching strategies for different groups. The major differences orbit around a student's background, a pupil's age, and the composition of the subject matter. Each of these differences will be discussed.

Student Background   Forty years ago, Allison Davis (1948) called attention to the effect of societal position on the students' mode of communication. He implored teachers to incorporate knowledge about students' backgrounds when developing teaching strategy, but his advice was not heeded.

Later research showed that different ethnic and social classes use language differently and that, because schools reflect the linguistic bias of the predominantly white middle-class culture, children whose language use is built on different norms and expectations are decidedly disadvantaged.

Examples of this included the work done on the concept of restricted and elaborated linguistic codes (Bernstein, 1971). Many lower-class children possess the restricted code that makes much of school puzzling, bewildering, and alienating because they do not easily use language as a method to verbally expand verbal thought. Since the elaborated linguistics style dominates most schools, these students often experience great difficulties in school.

This issue has returned to the educational forefront as research reveals that what works in a suburban school often fails in a central city school. The research confirms what most sensitive teachers have intuited: Because lower-class children have their way of doing things that is different from the school culture (which most often represents middle-class values), they feel less comfortable and confident in schools and are less likely to participate in school activities.

In order to improve lower-class students' performance, the effective teacher needs to emphasize positive affect and establish a relaxed learning climate. Because many lower-class students are reluctant to respond even when they know the answer, the teacher must elicit pupil answers. Successful teaching techniques also include the regular monitoring of activities, the careful supervision of seatwork, and the one-to-one tutoring with students who need special help (Brophy and Evertson, 1974).

In contrast, high-socioeconomic status students, who are more likely to be eager and successful, require a different treatment. Here the most successful techniques included "communicating high expectations to their students, occasionally delivering symbolic rewards when the students succeed, and on rare occasions, criticizing them when they failed due to inattentiveness or poor effort" (Brophy and Good, 1986, p. 341).

Pupils Age   Researchers have found that the pattern of teacher effectiveness varies according to age and grade level. Even the seemingly slight differences between the second and fifth grades demand different teaching strategies. Successful teachers of younger children employ many different kinds of reading materials, keep the pupils working on the task, and frequently work with the pupils individually. Class sessions tend to be strongly expository and teacher dominated. With older children, just the opposite strategy is effective. Here diverse materials hinder learning, and longer periods of give and take between teacher and pupil are important (Rouk, 1980, p. 17).

The difference, of course, is due to the kind of reading skills that are emphasized at the different grade levels. In second grade, decoding, a skill that must be practiced over and over, is emphasized. Later, as the student acquires the basic skills, reading comprehension—where the student is asked to read and evaluate, and the teacher's task is to stimulate thinking about the meaning of the text—is the central objective.

In addition to these differences, teachers of later grades spend less time in instruction of desired routines and procedures. In its place, clear explanations about teacher expectation and students' accountability become necessities. In other words, older students may know how to perform certain classroom tasks, but often must be convinced of the importance of their cooperation.

Subject Matter In addition to students' background and developmental characteristics, the intrinsic character of academic work determines what type of teaching and learning strategies will be employed. Early in their schooling career, students realize that different learning tasks demand different learning strategies and they adjust themselves accordingly. Therefore, it seems that a brief analysis of the kind of work that comprises academic learning would be a promising approach to understand how teaching effects occur in the classroom.

In the clearest exposition to date, Walter Doyle (1983) identified four general types of academic tasks:

- ▶ Memory, the reproduction of previously encountered material
- ▶ Procedural, the application of a standard formula to generate answers
- ▶ Comprehension, the ability to draw inferences from previously encountered work
- ▶ Opinion, the statement of a preference for something

Doyle claims that there are clear-cut distinctions between the tasks, and that teaching strategies suitable for one type may not be suitable for other types.

When we isolate academic work into discrete categories, we begin to learn more about the nature of academic work. For example, when teachers assign a task designed to assess a student's comprehension of material, the student is less likely to be able to reproduce the specific facts of surface features of the original text. On the other hand, rote memorization tasks do reproduce knowledge that helps students make inferences or analogies.

Similarly, being able to perform computational tasks proficiently does not necessary mean that one understands *why* it works. Conversely, understanding why something works does not necessarily lead to computational proficiency (Doyle, 1983).

As Doyle points out, "Accomplishing one task does not automatically lead to the outcomes of the other. Indeed memory procedures and comprehension processing may interfere with each other in accomplishing a given task" (1983, p. 166).

In other words, teachers must align their instructional goals with their knowledge of the specific nature of academic tasks as well as the relationship of one task to another. Failure to do so may create some unintentional interference in the learning process.

The research on the nature of academic work has several implications for improving the quality of teaching. First, it appears that students do not simply learn what is taught; they invent their own conceptual schemes to make sense of the materials. Because their schemes are their own inventions, they often contain misconceptions of the content that is taught. Teachers must be alert to the possibility of misconstrual, and be ready to provide corrective feedback.

Second, if the subject matter is well known or fully developed, direct methods of instruction are the most appropriate method of teaching. Direct instruction is particularly suitable if the pupil is young, unfamiliar with the content, or of low ability.

Third, direct instruction must not be the sole mode of teaching. This is because a certain degree of "unstructuredness" is needed to determine whether students possess the ability to apply the knowledge they have acquired to new situations. Also, direct instruction on specific skills needs to be combined with instruction in higher order skills if students are to acquire "the knowledge structure for representing tasks and selecting solutions strategies" (Doyle, 1983, p. 178).

Finally, it appears that students need a well-developed amount of knowledge about subject matter because this will allow them to better understand and represent the problems in the subject matter. If students do not possess appropriate knowledge, they are apt to rely on memorization strategies and not understand what the teacher is presenting them.

With the student thought processes program, we have come face-to-face with the awesome complexity of classroom life. We see that the researchers operating from this base have made some interesting and potentially useful forays into the cognitive universe within American students, but much more remains uncharted, unexplored, and unexplained.

As was the case with process-product models, many of the realities of classroom life are ignored by this model. The intense concentration on student thought processes forces researchers to "provide incomplete portrayals of other aspects of the teaching situation" (Shulman, 1986,

p. 16). With this in mind, let us move to the third general orientation—classroom ecology research.

▶ Classroom Ecology Research

Anthropology has always maintained a firm grasp on educators' imaginations. Although anthropologists were seldom official members of the educational research community, over the years many have established temporary residences on the grounds of the educational estate. Recently, several anthropologists appear to have permanently settled there.

The anthropological perspective that informs most classroom ecological approaches differs dramatically from either of the two previously described research orientations. Where process-product research stands above its subjects and the student thought processes approach remains distant, the ecological researchers involve themselves directly in the day-to-day routines of the students in their inquiries. In fact, classroom ecology approaches have a number of distinct characteristics that make them unique. The differences include the following:

▶ The use of careful case studies, rather than employing large and diverse groups

▶ A search for meanings through interpretation, rather than exploring for laws and causes

▶ The observation of students in face-to-face interaction, rather than depending on the tasks of classification

▶ The placement of researchers inside the experience of the persons they study, rather than remaining detached from their subjects

▶ An approach more characteristic of the humanities—akin to understanding a text, game, or ritual, or analyzing a painting—rather than straining for a version of social physics (Gardner, 1985).

Classroom ecology also differs in the results that are yielded from the research process. The two other approaches define *effectiveness* as something existing away from the immediate classroom, in the results of an achievement test for example; whereas classroom ecology approaches search for the criteria of effectiveness within the classroom. Researchers who use this approach are primarily interested in "collecting and analyzing streams of human behavior in natural settings [classrooms] and exploring what is learned from and how people learn through interacting with others" (Green and Smith, 1983, p. 357).

Although the formal conceptualization of the ecological approach took place only a little longer than ten years ago, it is nevertheless possible to locate two principal themes in the research:

1. Classrooms are communicative environments where meaning is constructed and signaled during interactions.
2. Classrooms are organized social and cultural environments where student behavior is governed by locatable sets of rules.

We will use these two generalizations to organize a brief discussion of the results of ecological research. Our discussion is necessarily brief because the developers of this approach—as is almost always the case with new intellectual schemes—have been more successful in organizing a framework than in producing a extensive body of knowledge. Nevertheless, their research results show great promise for understanding the classroom context of teacher-student interaction.

Classrooms Are Communicative Environments
Research reveals that learning is structured by classroom interaction which changes constantly because of the messages that teachers and students send to one another. (This perspective views the formal curriculum—including academic tasks and school assignments—as guides to action, with the "real" curriculum emerging out of the student-teacher interaction rather than from any written document.) From this conception, teacher effectiveness, for example, depends on a teacher's ability to simultaneously attend to his or her students' academic and social participation, while managing a variety of classroom activities. In order to succeed in this environment, students must possess more than academic knowledge; they must be aware of appropriate ways to demonstrate their knowledge.

Students frequently display their knowledge inadequately because of linguistic or participatory differences between their homes and the school. These differences also lend to misunderstandings with regard to expectations in the classroom. These differences reveal themselves through what ecologists call *clashes,* which are best understood as social or cultural misunderstandings.

Although these clashes are seldom dramatic, it is useful to observe them because it provides a window through which to view the differing expectations of the teacher and students. After understanding a clash, a teacher can adjust his or her teaching strategies and become more effective.

Understanding the classroom as a communicative environment can move teachers closer to a method for "describing the everyday events of classroom life and its effect on students' learning and participation" (Green and Smith, 1983, p. 383).

Research on the communicative environment would seem to make the following suggestions to teachers:

▶ Examine the kind of nonverbal messages you send to students and determine how they interfere with learning.

▶ Construct messages to students that help them to learn how to participate effectively in classroom interaction.

▶ Vary your discussion techniques to accommodate for differing participation styles.

Classrooms Are Rule-Governed Environments

All classrooms are complex social and cultural environments organized around a "constitution" that is composed of a detailed set of rules for governing behavior. These rules range from the general—how to talk to teachers—to the highly specific—how to gain access to the conversation in a reading group. This constitution organizes nearly all the interaction in the classroom.

Classroom rules are expectations for "how to speak, when, to whom and for what purpose" (Green, 1983, p. 203). Studying classroom rules, for instance, reveals that teachers create different environments for high-, middle-, and low-group students. In reading groups, the high group is encouraged to go for the meaning in passages; while low achievers emphasize pronunciation, grammar errors, and single-word decoding.

Ecological research also reveals that classroom rules are signaled by a variety of teacher behaviors, such as the distribution of turns, acknowledgments of student contributions, and permission to talk. Looking and responding in an apparently competent fashion sends important cues to the teacher, who is forced to make decisions about the studentship of a large number of individuals at once. In many ways the classroom is an analogue for a game where the successful participant is able to infer the correct rules for a great variety of different situations.

Differing learning tasks, of course, produce different contexts, which in turn create different sets of rules. If this construction appears complex, it is because the ecological researchers—perhaps for the first time in the history of research on teaching—have lain bare the bewildering complexity of the classroom learning environment.

Research on classroom rules makes these suggestions to teachers:

▶ Establish and enforce clear rules for classroom interaction and participation.

▶ Recognize the organizing power of classroom ritual and routine.

▶ Examine your point of view about alternative cultural expectations for behavior. (Your perception of student misbehavior may just be socially or culturally different behavior which is neither destructive of the process of learning or disrespectful.)

In the final analysis, classroom ecology research presents a daring and provocative new way of viewing the buzzing, blooming world of the school classroom. If the ambitions of researchers often exceed their accomplishments, as Shulman says, then these researchers should not be faulted for their adventuresomeness, but perhaps applauded for the great possibilities that their research suggests.

SUMMARY

▶ This chapter attempted to define *teacher effectiveness*. We argued that research on teaching has advanced beyond the era of maxims and homilies that have traditionally characterized discussions of pedagogy, to an emerging academic discipline. That research on teaching is an embryonic academic field is indicated by a growing number of text-books on the subject and the increasing consensus on the state of the art of teaching. We claimed that scholars increasingly agree about what kinds of teaching behavior and classroom climate contributes most to educational effectiveness. We went on to argue that this body of knowledge makes it possible to distinguish effective teachers from less effective teachers.

Although the research on teaching is not yet able to provide complete answers to pedagogical problems, at least researchers are putting their fingers on the pulse of teaching—the day-to-day process in the classroom—and they have observed some trends that seem to appear with enough regularity to be taken seriously. If the teacher is savvy enough to dismiss much of the overgeneralization and dogmatism that surrounds teacher effectiveness research, and is even-headed enough to resist the frantic attempt to package the results too slickly, there is much that is of benefit in the research on teacher effectiveness.

Effective teaching will remain an art; thus, like most art, it will never be completely understood. In this chapter we have argued that although teaching is an art, it can be, as the noted educational observer N. L. Gage has pointed out, informed by the findings of science-research on teaching.

ACTIVITIES

1. What are the three phases of teacher research? How do the three different methodologies go about looking at effective teaching? What are the drawbacks of each of these approaches?
2. What factors seem to affect a student's school success? What factors are beyond the control of the teacher? How influential can teachers be?

3. List the characteristics of an effective learning environment.
4. How can complexity in the classroom be reduced?
5. Take a different skill from a content area of your choice and discuss how you would go about simplifying the complex skill; for example, quadratic equations, finding the areas of polygons, making maps, using the library, writing a research paper, and so on.
6. Think about your favorite or chosen subject area. Which of the four general types of academic tasks–memory, procedural, comprehension, opinion–receives the most emphasis? Why? Where would you like to spend the majority of your teaching time?
7. How can teachers improve the communicative environment in their classrooms?
8. What does current research say about classroom rules?

REFERENCES

Berliner, D. C. (1979). Tempus educare. In P. L. Peterson and H. J. Walbert (Eds.), *Research on teaching*. Berkeley, Calif.: McCutchan.

Berliner, D. C. (1985). Laboratory settings and the study of teacher education. *Journal of Teacher Education, 36*, 2–9.

Bernstein, B. (1971). On the classification and framing of educational knowledge. In *Class, codes and control* (Vol. 1). Beverly Hills, Calif.: Sage Publications.

Bloom, B. S. (1976). *Human characteristics and school learning*. New York: McGraw-Hill.

Brophy, J. D., and Evertson, C. (1974). *Process-product correlations in Texas teacher effectiveness study: Final report*. Austin: University of Texas, Research and Development Center for Teacher Education.

Brophy, J. E. (1983). Classroom organization and management. *Elementary School Journal, 83*, 265–286.

Brophy, J. S., and Good, T. L. (1986). Teacher behavior and student behavior. In M. C. Wittrock (Ed.), *Third handbook of research on teaching*. New York: MacMillan.

Bruner, J. (1960). *The process of education*. Cambridge, Mass.: Harvard University Press.

Coker, H., Medley, D., and Soar, R. (1980). How valid are expert opinions about effective teaching? *Phi Delta Kappan, 62*, 131–134, 149.

Coleman, J., Campbell, E., Hobson, C., McPartland, J., Mood, A., Weinfield, F., and York, R. (1966). *The equality of educational opportunity*. Washington, D.C.: U.S. Office of Health, Education, and Welfare.

Davis, A. (1948). *Social class influences upon learning*. Cambridge, Mass.: Harvard University Press.

Doyle, W. (1983). Academic work. *Review of Educational Research, 53*, 159–199.

Evertson, C., Anderson, C., Anderson, L., and Brophy, J. (1980). Relationships between classroom behaviors and student outcomes in junior high mathematics and English classes. *American Educational Research Journal, 17,* 43–60.

Felt, M. C. (1985). *Improving our schools.* Newton, Mass.: Educational Development Center.

Fisher, C., Filby, N., Marliave, R., Cahen, L., Dishaw, M., Moore, J., and Berliner, D. (1978). *Teaching behavior, academic learning time, and student achievement. Beginning teacher evaluation study phase III-B, Final report.* San Francisco: Far West Laboratory.

Gage, N. L. (Ed.) (1983). *Handbook of research on teaching.* Chicago: Rand McNally.

Gardner, H. (1985). *The mind's new science.* New York: Basic Books.

Good, T. L. (1983). Classroom research: A decade of progress. *Educational Psychologist, 18,* 127–144.

Good, T. L., and Brophy, J. E. (1986). Teacher behavior and student achievement. In M. C. Wittrock (Ed.), *Handbook of research on teaching* (3rd ed.). New York: MacMillan.

Green, J. (1983). Research on teaching as a linguistic process: A state of the art. In E. Gordon (Ed.), *Review of Research in Education* (Vol. 10). Washington, D.C.: American Education Research Association.

Green, J. L., and Smith, D. (1983). Teaching and learning: A linguistic perspective. *Elementary School Journal, 83,* 353–390.

Hodgson, G. (March 1973). Do schools make a difference? *Atlantic, 231,* 35–45.

Hofstadter, R. C. (1963). *Anti-intellectualism in American Life.* New York: Vintage Books.

Huey, E. G. (1908/1968). *The psychology and pedagogy of reading.* New York: MacMillan.

Kounin, J. (1970). *Discipline and group management in classrooms.* New York: Holt, Rinehart, and Winston.

Mackey, J., and Appleman, D. (February 24, 1985). Student tests fail as worthy measure of school effectiveness. *St. Paul Pioneer Press and Dispatch,* 3G.

Medley, D. (1979). The effectiveness of teachers. In P. Peterson and H. Walberg (Eds.), *Research on teaching: Concepts, findings and implications.* Berkeley, Calif.: McCutchan.

National Commission on Excellence in Education. (1983). *A nation at risk: The imperative for educational reform.* Washington, D.C.: U.S. Department of Education.

Ravitch, D. (1983). *The troubled crusade: American education, 1945–1980.* New York: Basic Books.

Rice, J. M. (1893/1969). *The public school system of the United States.* New York: Arno Press.

Rosenshine, B. (1976). Classroom instruction. In N. Gage (Ed.), *The psychology of teaching methods.* Seventy-seventh Yearbook, National Society for the study of education. Chicago: University of Chicago Press.

Rosenshine, B. (1979). Content, time, and direct instruction. In P. Peterson and H. Walberg (Eds.), *Research on teaching: Concepts, findings, and implications.* Berkeley, Calif.: McCutchan.

Rouk, U. (Spring 1980). *What makes an effective teacher?* Educational Research and Development Report of CEMREL, Inc., St. Louis.

Rutter, M., Maughan, B., Mortimore, P., Ouston, J., and Smith, A. (1979). *Fifteen thousand hours: Secondary schools and their effects on children.* Cambridge, Mass.: Harvard University Press.

Shulman, L. S. (1986). Paradigms and research programs in the study of teaching: A contemporary perspective. In M. C. Wittrock (Ed.), *Third handbook of research on teaching.* New York: MacMillan.

Simon, H. A. (1957). *Models of man: Social and rational: Mathematical essays.* New York: John Wiley.

Soar, R. S., and Soar, R. M. (1979). Emotional climate and management. In P. L. Peterson and H. J. Walberg (Eds.), *Research on teaching.* Berkeley, Calif.: McCutchan.

Spady, W. S. (November 1982). Keys to effective instruction: A response to Williams. *School Administrator, 35–36.*

SUGGESTED READINGS

Berliner, D. C. (Ed.). (Fall 1983). Special issue: Research on teaching. *Educational Psychologist, 18,* 125–217.

Brophy, J. (October 1986). Teacher influences on student achievement. *American Psychologist, 41,* 1069–1077.

Dunkin, M., and Biddle, B. (1974). *The study of teaching.* New York: Holt, Rinehart, and Winston.

Denham, C., and Lieberman, A. (Eds.). (1980). *Time to learn.* Washington, D.C.: National Institute of Education.

Good, T., and Brophy, J. (1984). *Looking in classrooms* (3rd ed.). New York: Harper and Row.

Good, T. (March 1983). Research on teaching (entire issue). *The Elementary Teacher, 83,* 261–500.

Peterson, P. A., and Walberg, H. J. (1979). *Research on teaching: Concepts, findings, and implications.* Berkeley, Calif.: McCutchan.

Wittrock, M. (Ed.). (1986). *Third handbook of research on teaching.* New York: Macmillan.

Part **III**

Curriculum Perspectives

10

Elements of the School Curriculum

▶────────────────────────────────────
────────────────────────────────────◀

▶ When John Dewey set out in 1896 to buy desks for his new laboratory school at the University of Chicago, he could not find what he wanted. After moving from one school supply store to another, one dealer finally told Dewey, "I am afraid we do not have what you want. You want something at which children work; these are for listening."

What Dewey wanted was a way to physically organize his classrooms so his pupils "could do things, not merely sit quietly while the teacher chanted prefabricated knowledge for him/her to memorize" (Ginger, 1958, p. 204). Dewey did not, of course, claim that desks were at the center of his curriculum universe. He contended only that the architectonics of the classroom defined and constrained the possibilities of the learning environment, either enabling or preventing particular lessons from enfolding. He said, "The attitude of listening means, comparatively speaking, passivity, absorption" (Dewey, 1902, pp. 32–33). Dewey wanted more from his students. He wanted them to be active learners; therefore, even the desks had to facilitate such activities.

Many teachers would respond positively to Dewey's attempt to find something practical for his classrooms because most educators pride themselves on being practical people. They are interested in what works in the classroom and what specific things they can do to become better teachers. Most would maintain that they are exempt from theoretical influences. But in reality, they are not. John Dewey was a practical man, but his need for a specific desk was based not just on practicality but on an educational philosophy that guided his concept of the curriculum. As this chapter will point out, nearly every teacher has a series of beliefs about what schools ought to do, a set of values about the most desirable outcomes from schooling, and some very clear ideas about the kinds of graduates the school ought to produce.

Although this constellation of world views may not articulate a complete educational philosophy, it does, nevertheless, exert an influence on the kinds of instructional practices that go on in the teacher's classroom. This often ill-defined philosophy has a direct impact on the school curriculum.

The school curriculum, as we have defined throughout this book, is the sum total of all that is studied, taught, and learned in school. But what does that mean? How does one understand the factors that influence these actions? In this chapter and the next two chapters we are going to provide methods for such an examination. Before we examine the formal curriculum, Chapter 11, and the hidden curriculum, Chapter 12, a step-by-step examination of the basic elements of any school curriculum is needed.

The chapter begins by briefly presenting the origins of four dominant views of curriculum. These are critical to understanding the curriculum because they provide the philosophical underpinnings for understanding the basic elements of overall school curriculum and that of an individual classroom. By having an understanding of these basic elements of a curriculum, the teacher begins to understand the elements that influence the instructional decisions that are made.

THINKING ABOUT THE CURRICULUM

► Understanding the curriculum is a difficult task. Some parts fit together as neatly as Chinese boxes. For example, in our discussion of desks, a clear structure was unveiled. Dewey controlled the way learning was to be organized by selecting the proper kind of student desk. But it is not always so easy to understand the many elements that influence the manner in which the curriculum is organized.

An important key in gaining an understanding of a school's curriculum is to remember that fundamental decisions can generally be reduced to a question of values—what is important? In Chapter 1 we outlined three basic American values, social efficiency, equality, and freedom of choice, that have served as focal points in the organizing of the school's curriculum. The tension among the values creates discussion about what schools should be about and has led to four dominant views about curriculum.

▶ Four Dominant Curriculum Strands

Curriculum historian Herbert Kliebard (1982) has identified four dominant curriculum strands. He labeled them *humanism, developmentalism, social meliorism,* and *social efficiency.* Although these strands
are not identical to the general values we claimed underlie most curriculum decisions, it is clear that these four curriculum strands are closely
related to the three basic values. Each of these four strands represents
a different viewpoint regarding the proper nature of the curriculum.

According to Kliebard, at the turn of the century a series of
events—occurring in an almost chain reaction—conspired to produce
an alteration in the shape of American schools. The effect of the change
was to shift the educational center of gravity away from the teacher
and textbook as the sole source of knowledge to a curriculum where
the knowledge base was more remote, distant, and abstract. The ex-
ponential increase in the number of students and greater complexity
of society's demands on the school were reflected in the curriculum,
which in turn gave form to the school itself. As the curriculum assumed
greater importance, conflicting conceptions of the curriculum began
to vie with one another for ascendancy. The competition was more
than a matter of taste. The stakes were nothing less than what kind
of education is best for America's children. It quickly became clear,
however, that different interest groups emphasized different kinds of
knowledge and different curriculum forms.

Although the events that produced the crisis in the 1890s are now
distant, and America has changed dramatically since that time, the
four curriculum strands Kliebard saw congealing in the boiling caldron
of American society remain. They continue because the curriculum
is the major mechanism for determining the forms and shape of schooling. Although the immediate curriculum problems, such as how to
instruct children about AIDS without outraging the opponents of sex
education, frequently change, the bedrock curriculum issues, such as
how to initiate the young into a complex and technological world, remain constant.

Humanism
Of the four curriculum conceptions, the humanistic model is the oldest.
Throughout Western history proponents of this strand have responded
to a single challenge: How can society provide their young with weapons
against ignorance? Whatever the social circumstances, the humanist
prescription was always essentially the same: study the accumulated
knowledge of the western cultural heritage. Humanists have always
taken up the mantle of reinterpreting, perserving, and instructing the
young in the revered traditions and values amidst rapid social change.

Since the humanistic curriculum was first, other curriculum conceptions were required to describe what they found unacceptable about the humanistic strand, before they were permitted to trace out their own argument. Critics of the humanistic strand quickly became aware of the advantages of being first. They learned rapidly that whether it is breakfast cereal or educational philosophies, being there first has distinct advantages.

The specific articulation of the humanistic creed for American schools can be traced back to the commanding efforts of William Torrey Harris, superintendent of the St. Louis school system in the 1870s. Harris, who later became United States Commissioner of Education, believed that the school curriculum was nothing less than the mechanism "by which the individual is elevated into the species and becomes privy to the accumulated wisdom of the race." The classics, Harris thundered, are the only defensible course of study.

Both Harris and his most powerful associate, Harvard University President Charles Eliot, asserted that the school curriculum should not be used to emphasize direct social reform; rather, the humanistic ideal should guide the curriculum because it endows students with the power of reason, sensitivity to beauty, and high moral character. Over a century later, the humanistic vision still influences school curriculum—an academic equivalent of wing tip shoes, fashionable, immune from trends, but not wildly popular—in the hands of contemporary humanists like Mortimer Adler.

Harris's views about how the curriculum should be organized had a dramatic impact on the formal curriculum of the school. In Chapter 11, we will examine how this view of the curriculum remains dominant in today's schools.

Developmentalism

The second curriculum strand, the developmental model, was first articulated by psychologist G. Stanley Hall. The principal idea in the developmental model was that subject matter could be taught more effectively if the results of child study were first taken into account. Believing that individual behavior develops through a series of stages, Hall and other advocates of developmentalism maintained that a school be judged by the way it adapted its curriculum to the natural growth of its pupils. In the transformed school curriculum promoted by the developmentalists, the child was at the center of the curriculum.

Although developmentalism has remained near the center of the "theoretical" curriculum promoted by many college methods instructors in the form of interdisciplinary studies, inquiry learning, and active learner involvement, the orientation has seldom entered the mainstream of the school curriculum. Whether the conception was labeled the "Project Method," as outlined by William Heard Kilpatrick in the 1920s, or as "free schools," as outlined by a great array of theorists in the 1960s and 1970s, developmental curriculum frequently perished soon after blooming because the organizational structure of the schools provided sterile soil for its continued growth.

Social Meliorism
The third curriculum strand identified by Kliebard is social meliorism. This conception, first explicated by sociologist Lester Frank Ward, conceived of education as the great panacea for all social ills. Through the dissemination of information, especially scientific information, the popularization of knowledge would inevitably create widespread understanding of humans' relations with one another and with nature. Only the state, Ward argued, had the sufficiently broad means and motives necessary to sponsor his kind of schooling. The curriculum based on this conception would promote an equalitarianism that would enrich the promise of American life (Cremin, 1961).

The curriculum that evolves from social meliorism centers on human relationships. Self-development, personal growth, freedom of choice, values clarification, experimentalism, peace education, and global education are among the wide-ranging topics of concern to social meliorists.

Social meliorism was furthered by George S. Counts in his book, *Dare the Schools Build a New Social Order?* (1982). Counts's central thesis was a call for the schools to become an agent for change in society. The long series of curricular innovations that sprung from the 1954 school desegregation case are another manifestation of the social meliorism impulse in American life.

Social Efficiency
The fourth curriculum strand, social efficiency, was first clearly articulated by Joseph Mayer Rice, who raised the question, "What makes some schools more effective than others?" The answer, derived from theories of scientific management, popular in American industry around the turn of the century, is labeled by Kliebard as *school efficiency*. Social efficiency has great appeal to those who see wasted time and effort in much of what transpires at school.

Social efficiency ideas have had more influence on organization and instruction of the school curriculum. Whereas the humanist strand outlined the shape of the subject matter—tracing out the subjects students studied—the social efficiency strand defined the way the schools were run.

From the era just before World War I, when the ideas of industrial engineer Frederick W. Taylor captured the imagination of the educational administrative community with his principles of scientific management to the present, the "cult of efficiency" has been at the heart of curriculum discourse for most of this century. For example,

FIGURE 10-1 Basic Elements of the Curriculum

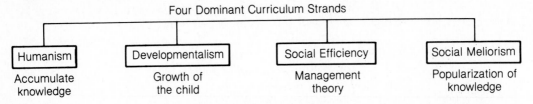

Four Dominant Curriculum Strands

| Humanism | Developmentalism | Social Efficiency | Social Meliorism |
| Accumulate knowledge | Growth of the child | Management theory | Popularization of knowledge |

social efficiency theorist Ralph Tyler's book, *Basic Principles of Curriculum and Instruction,* which presents the most cogent representation of this curriculum strand, was voted in 1981 as the most influential education book of the twentieth century (Shane, 1981). The influence of Tyler's model, and of social efficiency, is illustrated by omnipresent goal-centered teaching models in nearly every curriculum and instruction text.

Figure 10–1 illustrates how the basic strands fit into our understanding of the curriculum today. It is important to remember that the general tensions within American society over the important values will influence each of these dominant strands and determine which one may be most influential in educational thought. One's agreement with one or more of these strands thus influences how the school curriculum might be organized.

ORGANIZING A SCHOOL CURRICULUM

▶ If a person believes, for example, that humanism is the most dominant overall philosophy for organizing the curriculum, what does that mean? What are the implications? In the nineteenth century, that would mean a careful examination of the role of the teacher in the classroom and possibly an examination of the role of the textbook. Today, curriculum analysts take a broader view by examining the role of the teacher, the learner, the course of study, and examinations. These four factors interact with varying degree of emphasis.

Chapters 3 and 4 focused on the role of the teacher, and Chapters 7 and 16 focused on examinations; therefore, we will concentrate our discussion here on the course of study and the learner. How should these two areas be organized in the curriculum?

▶ Course of Study and the Learner

When James Garfield was elected president in 1880, he was asked what constituted an ideal education. His answer, remarkable in its brevity and common sense, was, "Mark Hopkins [his teacher at Amherst College] at one end of a log and me at the other end." Charming and potentially instructive though that curriculum conception may be, it is a luxury denied most twentieth-century curriculum makers. In this century, the sheer mass of students from widely divergent backgrounds and the multiplicity of expectations combine to make Garfield's ideal curriculum untenable. As a consequence, today's schools must pay special attention to organizational structures. The most dominant methods rely heavily on modern bureaucratic methods.

Under this kind of system, the learner tends to be viewed as the raw material for the school to transform into a more refined finished product. In this orientation, the student-learner appears before the curriculum as essentially a blank slate to be molded into a democratic citizen by the school curriculum.

This "raw material" metaphor was suggested in 1918 by J. F. Bobbitt:

> Work up the raw material into the finished product for which it is best adopted. Applied to education this means: Educate the individual according to his capabilities. This requires that the materials of the curriculum be sufficiently various to meet the needs of every class of individuals in the community, and the course of training and study be sufficiently flexible that the individual can be given just the things he needs (Bobbitt, p. 41).

Although the rhetoric has mellowed and become more sophisticated in modern times, the image of the pupil as a tabula rosa to be transformed into the citizen of tomorrow lingers. The end result is the creation of a bureaucratic structure that organizes students (the raw material) in such a way as to best mold them into productive citizens. How is this done?

To illustrate how a system might be organized, we will use the example of the organization of the Gary, Indiana, schools in the early part of this century. As you read about the Gary schools, keep the following questions in mind:

1. Of the four dominant strands in curriculum development, which one seems to be the most important to the developers of the Gary schools? What evidence can you cite?
2. What are the organizational elements that emerge during the process of creating the curriculum?
3. How are the various parts of the curriculum related to one another?
4. Is there some type of sequence to the development of the curriculum? Or must some things be in place before others?
5. Are there elements in the curriculum that are the most important?

With these questions in mind, read the case study of the Gary, Indiana, schools.

► William Wirt and the Gary, Indiana, Schools:
A Case Study in Curriculum Development

Today, Gary, Indiana, is a decaying steel town thirty miles east of Chicago, best known as music man Harold Hill's old hometown. Among some educators, Gary is remembered as the site of a famous experiment in education.

In 1905, the sand dunes and swamplands on the south shore of Lake Michigan were the province of foxes and muskrats, the home of the Chicago Gun and Hunt Club. Called The Dunes, the area was a place where rich merchants from Chicago came to relax on weekends and enjoy the pristine beauty of the countryside.

In 1906, a decision by the newly formed United States Steel Corporation to erect the world's largest mill in The Dunes changed the area forever. Within three years, the site had mushroomed into a community of 12,000 people, centering around the steel mill.

A city growing as rapidly as Gary had several distinct problems—not the least of which was how to organize its schools. Gary solved the school problem by hiring a thirty-three-year-old educator named William Wirt to be the school superintendent. Wirt, who had previously been in charge of the tiny Bluffton, Indiana, schools, was given a free hand in building the Gary system from the bottom up. By 1916, the Gary system had developed a school curriculum that was receiving world-wide attention. What did Wirt do?

In later years, Wirt maintained he had intended only to put John Dewey's theories into practice. Earlier, Wirt asserted his curriculum organization had but two fixed principles:

> All children should be busy all day long at work, study, and play under right conditions; and cities can finance an adequate work-study and play program only when all the facilities of the entire community for the work, study, and play of children are properly coordinated with the school, the coordinating agent, so that all facilities supplement one another and "peak loads" are avoided by keeping all facilities of the school plant in use all of the time (Wirt, 1916, p. xviii).

Wirt argued that although no set curriculum organization could possibly meet the needs of all children, it was important that any scheme include a way to departmentalize teaching—even in the elementary school—and to rotate classes so that teachers could render the greatest service with the least expenditure of energy and obtain maximum use of the school plant.

Wirt made available to each child greatly extended educational opportunities—in playgrounds, gardens, libraries, gymnasiums, and swimming pools—and he made the school the true center of the artistic and intellectual life of the neighborhood. The Gary plan quickly became known as the "platoon system" because the students were efficiently moved, in groups, from one activity to another. Every part of a Gary school was used to the maximum. Most schools were open twelve months a year, and were available to students of all ages (Cremin, 1961).

According to Cremin, every Gary school was organized as a miniature community. Elementary and secondary pupils were housed in the same buildings. There, they shared a common education and experienced similar social situations, both of which they examined together in a unique forum called "auditorium," which modeled a democratic society. In this embryonic school community, the building upkeep was supervised by the shop staff, the cafeteria was serviced by the domestic science staff, and the school records were processed by the business department.

In the formal curriculum of the Gary schools, a concerted effort was made to relate content to the students' individual and social needs. Conventional school subjects (grammar, spelling, reading, writing, and speaking), combined in an interdisciplinary language arts configuration, tied to the group activities of the auditorium. History and geography came together as instructional units, for example, "The City: A Healthful Place to Live." Science sprang from field trips and visits to mills to more systematic studies. And industrial arts progressed from instruction in mechanical skills to more general surveys of industrial production (Cremin, 1961, p. 156).

Throughout, students were departmentalized and classified as rapid, normal, or slow learners. Interviews and tests helped individualize programs for all Gary pupils, who were allowed to work at their own pace, given coaching lessons on Saturday when they fell behind, and allowed to pursue extra work in any subject.

Examining the Organizational Structures in the Gary Plan
Using the questions presented earlier as a starting point, let us examine the kinds of elements that were formed to make that school curriculum.

1. Every curriculum structure begins with a set of intentions. Sometimes the intentions embedded in the curriculum are labeled *expectations* or *aims,* but more commonly the curriculum intentions are called *objectives.* Can you list some of the principal objectives of the Gary plan?
2. It would appear from the curriculum that Mr. Wirt had a theory about the kind of a society the Gary pupils would enter after they finished their education. From the evidence that you were presented, what was Wirt's social philosophy? Which of the four curriculum strands influenced Wirt the most? How do you know that?

3. Based on your examination of the Gary plan, how did the developers think that children learn best in school?

4. What kinds of school environments did Wirt and his followers believe facilitated children's learning?

5. What kind of subject matter was of primary importance in the Gary plan? What was the optimal organizational structure to present subject matter?

6. How did diagnosis and testing fit into the Gary plan?

7. How could the effectiveness of the Gary plan be tested?

8. What kinds of mechanisms were built into the Gary plan to make it efficient?

9. Would the Gary plan work as a model for a curriculum today? List three impediments to its success today.

10. After considering this case, what do you think are the most important organizational elements of any school curriculum?

11. Imagine it is the year 2525, and you have landed with 1,000 other people on the planet Jupiter. It is your task to develop the organizational elements of a school curriculum. Outline the steps you would go through.

THE CONTENT OF THE CURRICULUM

▶   As we just saw, the curriculum begins with an idea. Organizational structures translate the idea into expectations called *educational objectives,* which describe what the student will be like once the school is finished with him or her. Both the ideas and the objectives are influenced by community values and expectations concerning the public schools. Curriculum makers in the local community are permitted the free exercise of their craft within clearly defined boundaries. Whenever developers exceed the community's "zone of tolerance," they run the risk of opposition and controversy (Boyd, 1978).

As we described previously, on the national stage, a consensus forms periodically around one of three values—efficiency, equity, or freedom of choice. Our society generally permits only one of these values to soar at a time. The dominant value is a product of the struggle for the control of educational policy. The struggle, which is ceaseless, is fought out between various interest groups. The group possessing superior resources and tactics is allowed to define educational "common sense" at that time. The common sense can evaporate quickly. At all times, there is an organized opposition who refuses to accept the consensus, no matter how humane or efficient the program it supports.

Subject matter brings the abstract educational objectives to life.

The most important subject matter considerations involve the choice of which subjects to study, and how to present those subjects to the students. The curriculum's organizational structure specifies the form, defines the value, determines the scope of the subject matter, and allocates the time, place, and duration of the students' experience with each subject matter. However, the content of the school curriculum is more than mere subject matter.

The content of any classroom is dependent on two fundamental systems of knowledge: lesson structures and subject matter structures (Leinhardt and Smith, 1985). Lesson structures include elements such as the knowledge required to construct and conduct a lesson. These kinds of systems of knowledge were discussed in Chapters 5, 6, and 8. In the remainder of this section, we will concentrate on the second general system of knowledge—knowledge of the content structures of the school curriculum.

Although there are many different schemes that define conceptions of subject matter, two large and loosely organized families of educational thought can encircle most of these conceptions (Jackson, 1971). In most curriculum structures, the content of the school curriculum either springs from one or the other side of the child-centered or discipline-centered dichotomy. The various dimensions of this dichotomy will be explicated in the next chapter. Here, it is sufficient to note the dichotomy, and to provide an illustration to illuminate the subsequent discussion.

The best way to provide a concrete illustration is through intellectual profiles of the two principal exponents of the respective positions. There are, of course, several champions of each of the positions. However, only two individuals (one in each of the categories), who by the sheer force of their personality and writings, managed to dominate discussions about the nature of the content of the school curriculum from their respective corners. These two individuals are John Dewey from the child-centered persuasion, and Jerome Bruner from the discipline-centered orientation. Let us begin by examining Dewey's thinking on the content of the curriculum.

▶ John Dewey and the Child-Centered Curriculum

John Dewey is the most influential, most misunderstood, and most difficult philosopher of the twentieth century. His ideas about child-centered curriculum sparked three generations of curriculum development and arguments. For nearly one hundred years, educators have treated the vast corpus of his work almost as if it were a menu in a Chinese restaurant, picking and choosing items that were familiar and easy to digest, and ignoring the others.

Some of the difficulty with Dewey can be attributed to his literary style. After reading one of Dewey's books, Supreme Court Justice Oliver Wendell Holmes exclaimed, "It was incredibly ill-written but [it] showed a feeling of intimacy with the inside of the cosmos that I found unequaled." It was, he went on to say, "how God would have spoken had he been inarticulate but keenly desirous to tell you how it was" (Mayer, 1961, p. 68).

Central to Dewey's philosophy was the belief that the curriculum was a social invention. Education, Dewey said, is the fundamental method of social reform. The primary purpose of such an agency was to equip the young to live in and participate actively in the democratic society that surrounded them.

Looking around him from the vantage of the 1890s, Dewey saw a rapidly changing society and a series of inert school systems where the emphasis was primarily intellectual. As the anecdote that traced Dewey's search for desks revealed, the conventional wisdom dictated that the ideal school must be remote from society, and it must emphasize subject matter that was contained in the organized bodies of knowledge.

Dewey objected to this kind of curriculum conception because he believed that traditional education was wrong in assuming that the mind was purely intellectual when it also involved emotion, purpose, and action — a union of thought and practice. The mind, Dewey maintained, was not individual but social, and learning was a by-product of social activities.

Dewey believed that all curriculum must be generated out of social situations. This sort of a curriculum would not be based on the organized disciplines, but founded on the twin pillars of the capacities of the child and the demands of the environment. The required curriculum must be constructed to help the child "grasp the connection between their homes and . . . the wider community, and hence to perceive the essential interdependence of an industrial society" (Cremin, 1961, p. 139).

The teacher in Dewey's curriculum conception had a difficult role to play. Teachers needed to know which opportunities to use, which impulses to encourage, and which social attitudes to cultivate in their curriculum, yet they could not do this without a clear sense of what was to come later. In order to produce a fully educated individual, the teachers themselves had to be very well acquainted with the bodies of organized knowledge. In short, as Cremin says, "The demand upon the teacher is twofold; through knowledge of the disciplines and an awareness of those common experiences of childhood that can be used to lead children toward the understandings represented by this knowledge" (1961, p. 138).

The task for a teacher employing a Deweyan conception of subject matter is formidable. The tendency to oversimplify and streamline inevitably creeps into an individual's conception of the complex set of ideas. Dewey's curriculum is not immune from that process. At various points in recent educational history, ideas masquerading as Deweyan streaked across the educational landscape, caricaturing Dewey. Illustrations abound. The scene in the movie, *Auntie Mame,* where the protagonist visits the progressive school in which she has enrolled her nephew, and finds all of the children running around naked in the name of freeing up their impulses, is typical of such renderings.

► ## Jerome Bruner and the Discipline-Centered Curriculum

Jerome Bruner claims that he got into education by accident. Despite his lack of attention to education, he claims, "It was completely in the cards that I got into it one day." He attributes this inevitability to the fact that he had spent most of his adult life involved in studies of cognitive science or, as he says, studying how the mind begins.

Bruner was one of the first cognitive psychologists and the founder of the Center for Cognitive Studies at Harvard University in 1960. Bruner is also a literary stylist of the first rank. This latter characteristic probably got him into education because he was chosen to write the summary report for an important conference of mathematicians and scientists who gathered at Woods Hole, Massachusetts, in September 1959 to discuss how education in science might be improved in the primary and secondary schools.

The report was published as Bruner's first education book, *The Process of Education.* In that report, Bruner articulated his position regarding the disciplines, and set forth a strong argument favoring the idea of structures of the disciplines. In brief, Bruner maintained that the object of education "was to get as swiftly as possible to that structure—to penetrate a subject, not cover it" (1966).

You do this, Bruner argued, by spiraling into the great disciplines like physics, mathematics, history, and the dramatic forms in literature. It is necessary to do this because the structures of these disciplines are less repositories of knowledge than methods to use the mind. Bruner defined *spiraling* as first taking a pass through the discipline to obtain an intuitive sense of the subject. Subsequent forays into the same domain involve exploring the discipline more deeply and formally, he claimed (1983).

Using the structures of knowledge, Bruner believed, was the proper emphasis for the curriculum because it gave meaning to what children learned, and made possible the opening up of new realms of experience. The great organizing concepts that inhere in the structures of the disciplines permitted children to understand, predict, and possibly change the world in which they live (1966).

Bruner asserted that Dewey's child-centered curriculum conception was outdated and simplistic, because it misunderstood what knowledge was and how it was mastered. For example, in a discussion of how children learn mathematics, Bruner said, "If set theory—now often the introductory section in newer curriculums in mathematics—had to be justified in terms of its relation to immediate experience and social life, it would not be worth teaching. Yet set theory lays the foundation for the understanding of order and number" (1966, p. 121).

Rather than making the school less intellectual, as Dewey seemed to argue, Bruner wanted the school to be more intellectual because it gave children "the informed power of mind and a sense of potency in action which are the only instruments we can give the child that will be invariable across time and circumstances" (1966, p. 122). Bruner asserted that this intellectual power, rather than any amount of content covered, will prepare the child for the unpredictable future.

In sum, these profiles presented two general structures of curriculum content. The two sides are not mutually contradictory. Each advocates the development of children's intellectual power. Neither is opposed to fostering children's emotional growth. For example, in several publications, Jerome Bruner has written admirably about John Dewey. (Dewey, who died in 1952, was not aware of Bruner's work for the simple reason that Bruner did not enter the educational arena until 1960.)

Whichever side the teacher comes down on in this dichotomy is of course extraordinarily important, because this decision—probably more than any other force—shapes the content structure that organizes that teacher's classroom. The nature and form of classroom content is the subject of the next section.

COMPONENTS OF THE CLASSROOM CURRICULUM

► It is in the classroom where the curriculum comes to life. On the broadest level, the curriculum appears quite simple—it is taught by teachers and it is studied by students. The curriculum is more complex, however. There are formal aspects to the curriculum that determine what, when, where, and how subject matter is taught. There are also the informal or hidden aspects to the curriculum that shape the manner in which teachers and students interact. In the following chapters we study in detail the formal curriculum and the hidden curriculum, but to bring the study of elements of the curriculum to a close, four major areas can be delineated: content, concepts, skills, and values.

► **Content**

Curriculum content refers to what is specifically taught in the classroom. Examples of curriculum content are the American Revolution, the human body, and Victorian English writers. Content generally equates with systematic organized bodies of information. How this content is organized varies widely across the content areas. For example, some teachers organize content in a chronological manner; others might organize the content from simple-to-complex. Chapter 11 details how these organizational patterns bring order to the curriculum.

► **Concepts**

The second structure in any classroom relates to the development of important concepts. A concept is an idea or an abstraction about particulars. For example, if two students engage in a fight at school, they are involved in a conflict. The fight represents a particular event bound by time and space, but it is an example of the concept *conflict*. Concepts help students make sense out of the world around them, and have widespread application. Concepts transcend time and space and can be transferred to new situations. Concepts provide common threads of comparison and contrast that enable the learner to organize data in a logical and coherent manner. If learned, concepts can be powerful tools for the student, and can be used as organizers for the content.

► **Skills**

Skills are a third structure of the classroom curriculum. Like concepts, skills are content-free and can thus be applied or transferred to new and unforeseen settings. The *Oxford English Dictionary* defines a skill as the ability to do something well. All areas of the curriculum lend themselves to skill development. Some, however, are more noted as skills subjects. Language arts and mathematics, for example, are considered by many to be the domain of the "basic" skills of reading, writing, and arithmetic.

A common orientation to skills in the curriculum is provided by Benjamin Bloom's Taxonomy of Educational Objectives in the cognitive domain. Bloom's taxonomy is a hierarchical construct that classifies learning into six levels in ascending order: knowledge, comprehension, application, analysis, synthesis, and evaluation. Perhaps the most propitious instructional use of the taxonomy is as a means of structuring learning activities in such ways as to ensure that students not only acquire and understand information, but that they are able to apply and examine ideas divergently as well. Thus, one obvious value of the taxonomy is that of accounting in advance for a range of skill development across an intellectual continuum.

When teachers fail to employ some sort of hierarchical system in planning for skill development, it becomes all to easy for instruction to settle at the memory and explanation levels. A case in point comes from the mathematics curriculum. The recent National Assessment of Educational Progress tests showed conclusively that although many students across the nation had a reasonably good grasp of computational skills, relatively few could *apply* those computational skills in problem-solving situations that called for analytic, synthesis, and evaluative skills (Mackey and Appleman, 1985).

▶ Values

Values represent the least planned for and yet the most pervasive element in the curriculum simply because they are unavoidable. Productive work, respect for others and for property, openness to ideas, reasoned thought and expression, and so on, are among the many values differentially held and differentially explored daily by teachers and students. Edwin Fenton (1967) has identified three types of values related to learning. Effective curriculum must consciously take all three types into account. The three types of values are:

1. *Behavioral values* or values related to conduct in the classroom; for example, the right of students to be heard, and the expectation on the part of the teacher that students will follow instructions. These are values that elementary students are perfectly capable of formulating with some help from the teacher.
2. *Procedural values* or the values consonant with the rational manner of the investigator; for example, respect for evidence, critical thinking, and willingness to participate in rational discussion. Inquiry learning has as one of its major objectives the development of procedural values.
3. *Substantive values* or those beliefs held by individuals as a result of their family, ethnic, religious, or cultural experience; for example, attitudes toward divorce or political and religious beliefs. Teachers need to help students clarify these values through discussdion and self-examination.

Following are some *behavioral* values a class might develop with their teacher's help. These values (rules) would be examined critically by the students periodically and would be subject to modification if the majority of the class so desired.

1. Students have one thirty-minute free period during the week when they can work on anything they choose.
2. Students may meet with the teacher privately from 11:15–11:30, Monday through Friday.
3. Parents and other adults may attend any of the classes by appointment with the teacher.
4. The class will provide monthly newsletters explaining their activities to parents.
5. Students may volunteer to teach mini-classes if they schedule a time for them.
6. Students recognize and support the teacher's right and responsibility to maintain order in the classroom.

Here is a sample listing of *procedural* values subscribed to by scientific investigators:

1. A scientific investigator has respect for evidence (recognizes data sources, selects relevant sources of information, gathers data, classifies and processes data, and makes inferences from data).
2. A scientific investigator values opinions of others (listens to others' comments, accepts divergent views in a rational manner, helps others to clarify their views, and works cooperatively in groups).

The following are examples of issues on which *substantive* value positions will differ.

1. The prettiest color
2. The appropriate number of children in a family
3. Whether it is better to work alone or in a group
4. Whether or not students should be given letter grades in social studies
5. The best uses of free time

Figure 10–2 further defines this discussion of the four dominant curriculum strands.

SUMMARY

► This chapter attempted to define the elements of the school curriculum. The account showed that the curriculum elements were often not clear or concrete. In addition, it was revealed that curriculum structures frequently change, often fairly quickly. At the root, curriculum structures are based on values. Those values that are the most strongly held

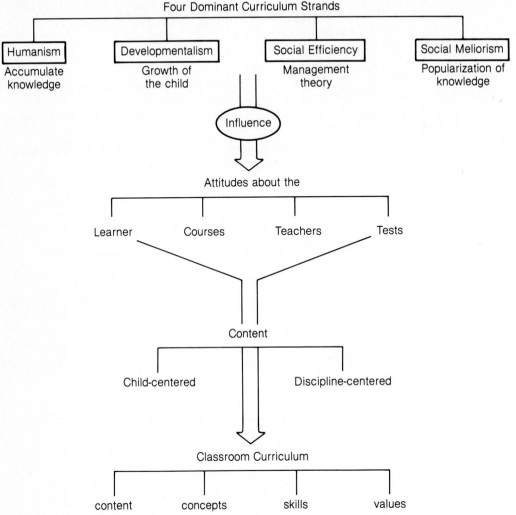

FIGURE 1O-2 Basic Elements of the Curriculum Further Defined

in the community at any given time are most likely to dominate and to shape the school curriculum.

The analysis revealed that three values, egalitarianism, efficiency, and freedom of choice, were most likely to be the foundational values on which a curriculum for an American school is constructed. Furthermore, an historical examination showed that it is possible to identify four curriculum strands or theories that describe the goals of most curriculums. These strands were labeled *humanism, social efficiency, social meliorism,* and *developmentalism.*

The chapter used a case study of the founding of the Gary,

Indiana, school curriculum to provide an opportunity to make the curriculum strands more concrete. In regard to the selection of curriculum content, the chapter contended that there were two essential positions, identified as discipline-centered and child-centered. Since the ideas inherent in the dichotomy were somewhat abstract, profiles of the leading advocates of the alternative positions were developed. The protagonists of the intellectual profiles were John Dewey, representing the child-centered orientation, and Jerome Bruner, representing the discipline-centered ideology.

The chapter then proceeded to define the dimensions of subject matter. Four elements—content, concepts, skills, and values—were identified and explicated.

ACTIVITIES

1. What were the principal elements of any school curriculum?
2. Imagine that you are appearing before a local school board meeting to defend one of the four strands of the school curriculum. Select one of the strands that we identified, and then present a rationale for its use. What makes the strand you selected superior to the others?
3. Suppose that a new community springs up in an isolated area of this country in 1990, and almost overnight it has a population of 100,000. You are selected to organize the school curriculum for the new community. Would your procedures differ from those William Wirt employed ninety years ago? How?
4. As the country moves toward the twenty-first century, what kinds of questions may be raised about what students need to know, and how will these questions influence the curriculum?

REFERENCES

Bobbitt, J. F. (1981). *The curriculum*. Boston: Houghton Mifflin.

Boyd, W. L. (1978). The changing politics of curriculum policy-making for American schools. *Review of Educational Research, 48,* 577–628.

Bruner, J. S. (1966). *On knowing: Essay for the left hand*. Cambridge, Mass.: Harvard University Press.

Bruner, J. S. (1983). *In search of mind: Essays in autobiography*. New York: Harper & Row.

Counts, G. A. (1982). *Dare the schools build a new social order?* New York: John Day Co.

Cremin, L. A. (1961). *The transformation of the school: Progressivism in American education.* New York: Vintage Books.

Cremin, L. A. (1975). Curriculum making in the United States. In W. Pinar (Ed.), *Curriculum theorizing: The reconceptualists.* Berkeley, Calif.: McCutchan Publishing.

Dewey, J. (1899). *The school and society.* Chicago: University of Chicago Press.

Fenton, E. (1967). *The new social studies.* New York: Holt, Rinehart and Winston.

Fitzgerald, F. (1980). *America revised: History schoolbooks in the twentieth century.* New York: Vintage Books.

Ginger, R. (1958). *Altgeld's America: The Lincoln ideal versus changing realities.* Chicago: Quadrangle Books.

Jackson, P. (1971). How teachers think. In G. Lesser (Ed.), *Psychology and educational practice.* Glenview, Ill.: Scott-Foresman.

Kliebard, H. M. (1982). Education at the turn of the century: A crucible for curriculum change. *Educational Researcher,* 16–24.

Leinhardt, G., and Smith, D. A. (1985). Expertise in mathematics instruction: Subject matter knowledge. *Journal of Educational Psychology, 77,* 247–271.

Mackey, J., and Appleman, D. (February 24, 1985). Student tests fail as worthy measure of school effectiveness. *St. Paul Pioneer Press and Dispatch,* 3G.

Mayer, M. (1961). *The schools.* New York: Harper and Brothers.

Shane, H. G. (1981). Significant writings that have influenced the curriculum: 1906–1981. *Phi Delta Kappan, 62,* 311–321.

SUGGESTED READINGS

Bruner, J. S. (1966). *On knowing: Essays for the left hand.* Cambridge, Mass.: Harvard University Press.

Dewey, J. (1899). *The school and society.* Chicago: University of Chicago Press.

English, F. (1983). *Fundamental curriculum decisions.* Washington, D.C.: Association of Supervision and Curriculum Development.

Goodlad, J. I. (1979). *Curriculum inquiry: The study of curriculum practice.* New York: McGraw-Hill

Gress, J. R. (1978). *Curriculum: An introduction to the field.* Berkeley, Calif.: McCutchan Publishing.

Kliebard, H. M. (1986). *The struggle for the American curriculum: 1893–1958.* Boston: Routledge and Kegan Paul.

Pinar, W. (1975). *Curriculum theorizing: The reconceptualists.* Berkeley, Calif.: McCutchan Publishing.

Toner, J. (March 5, 1987). Judge rules textbooks promote secular humanism. *New York Times,* 1.

Tyler, R. (1949). *Basic principles of curriculum and instruction.* Chicago: University of Chicago Press.

Wirt, W. (1916). Foreward in Bourne, R. *The Gary schools.* Boston: Houghton Mifflin.

Wise, A. (1979). *Legislated learning.* Berkeley, Calif.: McCutchan Publishing.

11

The Content of the School:
Its Formal Curriculum

▶ ───
─── ◀

OVERVIEW

▶ Chapter 11 discusses the formal curriculum of the school. It examines
what students are expected to know as they progress through their school
years, and discusses the issues related to the development of the school's
formal curriculum. After reading the chapter, you should be able to
define formal curriculum, describe issues related to its development,
and discuss current pressures that are calling for the reform of the
curriculum.

INTRODUCTION

▶ It is early morning. As the nation slowly awakens from east to west
it is bound together by one common occurrence. Large yellow vehicles
begin slowly moving across the landscape. They appear in urban areas,
sprawling suburbs, and the quiet, misty outreaches of rural America.
Each has one purpose: pick up America's students and deposit them
at school. For some, the ride is a few blocks; for others, it will take
them across town or several miles through the country. The trip will
be filled with talk, laughter, shouts, and occasional tears. At the end

of the school day the cycle is repeated, but in reverse. The buses now lumber away from the school to deposit their charges in the vicinity of their homes.

For approximately 180 days out of each year this cycle is repeated over and over again. Students are picked up at a certain time each day, driven to school where they follow a set schedule of classes and activities, and then loaded onto buses at a set time to be delivered home. School and the students' lives are directed by the clock — bus pick-up at 7:10 A.M., school at 7:45, lunch at 11:30, last class at 2:45, first bus at 2:55, and the final activity bus at 4:00 P.M. This scenario, or one very similar to it, regulates the lives of most elementary and secondary school students. In between the beginning of school at 7:45 and its conclusion at 2:45, the students receive instruction in the formal curriculum of the school. The formal curriculum is composed of specific planned activities for students, which are designed to achieve the overall goals of the school. At the elementary school, most of these activities take place in a self-contained classroom with the teacher determining what and when certain subjects will be taught. At the secondary level, students shift from one class to another after about one hour of instruction.

THE FORMAL CURRICULUM

▶ A typical hour of instruction includes about forty-seven minutes of instructional activities. During a class period, about 70 percent of the time involves verbal interaction between the teacher and the students, with the teacher doing most of the talking. Students, for the most part, listen to the teacher lecture or explain, complete written assignments, and prepare for or clean up after assignments. Another 12 percent of the hour may be devoted to class discussions, group activities, taking part in a simulation, individual reading, or the use of audio-visual equipment. The remainder of the hour is usually taken up by maintenance activities such as taking attendance, making announcements, and other school business. Children in the primary grades are more likely to be involved in at least five different types of learning activities during the day, whereas senior high-school students will probably be involved in only two.

During the class the teacher remains in control. Although there may be disruptions, overt student misbehavior is minimal in most classrooms. Instruction is usually directed to the total class, with occasional small-group or individual instruction taking place. In fact, most classrooms are designed for large numbers of students rather than small groups or individualized instruction.

Each class period is usually organized around a specific category within a subject area (spelling, handwriting), various topics to be studied (parts of speech, the legislative system, mammals), or specific skills (map reading, long division, squaring lumber). The course is designed for students in a specific grade and assumes that certain prerequisites have been mastered. The teacher has received training in the area and is certified by the state to teach the course. The teacher relies heavily on the textbook to provide the basic content of the course and the questions needed to have students remember basic facts.

The formal curriculum, as presented in most schools, encourages students to listen, respond when called on, read short sections in textbooks, write short essays, and choose from among alternatives on quizzes. The curriculum content is geared to reach the maximum number of students within a given time and space. Teachers are charged with the task of transmitting a set body of knowledge and skills, and the student is supposed to acquire this knowledge and related skills in order to meet the requirements for moving to the next grade or for graduation.

What is quickly established in the school is a set of expectations concerning teacher behavior, student behavior, and the kind of learning that is to take place. Students learn that their job in school is to take the courses and earn the grades to get credit for the work. A rhythm exists. The successful student becomes a part of this rhythm; the unsuccessful one does not.

THE NATURE OF THE FORMAL CURRICULUM

▶ Throughout American history, schools have been buffeted by a multitude of social, economic, and political forces. The calls for reform have been many. Special interest groups have sought to mold the school to some particular image. Nationwide concern created by various political, economic, and social issues permit critics to lament the poor conditions of today's schools and, in some cases, call for drastic reforms. In the face of all these charges, however, the school's formal curriculum has remained quite stable.

As noted earlier, the formal curriculum is composed of specific planned activities for students. These activities are designed to achieve the overall goals of the school. Therefore, the formal curriculum is the most fundamental concern of the school, and it centers on *what* is taught and *when* it is taught. How these activities are organized reflect the overall goals and philosophy of the school. Most schools do not adhere to one particular point of view, but instead combine organizational structures into a general curriculum pattern. It is still possible, however, to discern two basic organizational plans for the formal school curriculum.

▶ Subject Area Organization

The oldest and most common organizational plan views the curriculum as a body of content or subject matter. This subject matter is designed to help students achieve specific cognitive outcomes. The roots of the subject-centered curriculum may be traced to the Common School movement of the 1820s, in which the elementary school was to teach: "common subjects and common values and . . . to enroll every single child in the United States in order to socialize him" (Church and Sedlak, 1976). The reformers wanted all students to have the same set of learning experiences; therefore, they decided what should be taught and when it should be taught during the years of schooling. Reading, writing, and arithmetic, with a robust dose of "proper" moral conduct formed the basis of this early formal curriculum.

William Torrey Harris, superintendent of the St. Louis, Missouri, school system in the 1870s, established a subject orientation to the school curriculum that has dominated American schools since that time. Harris organized the curriculum into content areas that focused on a set of common courses for all students—specific courses for the development of particular knowledge or skills, and elective courses from which a student could choose a course of interest. Common courses were English, mathematics, science, and the social sciences. All students from grade one through at least grade ten would take courses from these disciplines. Other courses, such as those related to art, music, foreign language, and industrial arts, were to be used to develop special skills or to meet particular interests. This pattern still exists today in schools across America. Reading, writing, and arithmetic form the center of the elementary school curriculum. At the secondary level, students enroll in courses in English, science, mathematics, and social studies. But they may also take special courses, such as business mathematics, chemistry, or other electives.

The subject area curriculum has remained the most popular and most dominant form of curriculum organization for four basic reasons. First, most teachers, especially at the secondary level, are trained in the subject areas. For example, secondary teachers most often think of themselves as biology teachers, algebra teachers, or American history teachers. Even at the elementary level, teachers-in-training study social studies, science, and mathematics as separate subject areas more often than as interdisciplinary subjects. Second, organizing the school by subject matter makes it easy for parents to understand their child's education. Most adults attended a school that was organized in such a manner. Third, subject matter organization permits teachers to develop curriculum and goals. The content serves as an organizer and provides the focus needed in planning. Finally, over the years textbooks and other curriculum materials have been developed for subject area courses. These materials, which form the mainstay of the course, continue to provide stability and continuity to the manner in which the school is organized. The emergence of textbooks has also provided uniformity in what is taught in schools all across the nation. As a consequence, the formal curriculum of an elementary school in Pasco, Washington, may look much like the formal curriculum of an elementary school in Sabetha, Kansas.

► **Child-Centered Organization**

The second general category of curriculum organization focuses on the learner, the acquisition of process-oriented skills, and meeting the needs of the child. The progressive education movement served as the cornerstone of the student-centered curriculum approach. The integrated curriculum, the core curriculum, and the experience-oriented curriculum are all organizational patterns designed to focus on the student as learner and the exploration of real-life issues. The goal of the student-centered curriculum is to motivate and interest the learner in the learning task. In order to do so, the student-centered classroom has to be built on the real-life experiences of the child.

Historically, schools have used variations of both organizational patterns for the formal curriculum. Elementary schools have tended to be more student-centered and secondary schools more subject-centered. It appears that as the learner proceeds through the schooling process the emphasis changes from that of the individual to a more detailed study of a particular subject area. In fact, one of the reasons for the creation of the junior high school and middle school was to provide a school setting between the student-centered curriculum of the elementary school and the subject-centered curriculum of the high school.

Whatever the curriculum organization, the formal curriculum of the schools has remained constant over the years. The curriculum of the 1980s is much like the curriculum of the 1960s. As John Goodlad (1983) noted after an in-depth study of schools in 1983, there is ". . . a sameness of form in the substance and design of the curriculum." Why? A variety of reasons may be offered.

First, the school is an institution with a history of accepted practices and procedures. To radically change these established practices and routines is most difficult. To change the curriculum—what is taught and when—means changing the lives of all the personnel in the school (schedules changed, teaching assignments altered, room assignments shifted, new materials purchased, etc.). Also, parents and community members must be convinced that change is necessary and the cost worth the effort. To many administrators and school people, changing the curriculum is like throwing a rock into a pool. The ripple effect will have far-reaching effects. Changing the curriculum should not be done without considerable thought and planning.

Second, the call for change usually comes from outside the school. For example, the curriculum reform movement of the 1960s was essentially led by university scholars who had few ties to the public school classroom. As Charles Silberman (1970) noted in his book, *Crisis in the Classroom*, most reformers "tended to ignore the harsh realities of classroom and school organization." As a result, their expectations were unrealistic when thrust upon a classroom teacher who was not academically prepared to implement such changes or given enough time to prepare to try. The new materials and teaching strategies were then thrust upon the teacher in "teacher-proof" packages. The end result was that most teachers remained untouched by the efforts of those from the outside.

This is not to say that the formal curriculum has not changed. It has. The most common method of change has been to add new courses and teaching methods to the existing curriculum. Career education, consumer education, drug and sex education, bicultural and bilingual education, and environmental education have all been included in the formal curriculum. Team teaching, individualized instruction, computer instruction, and programmed instruction are all methods of instruction implemented in varying degrees in schools across the nation. Another change that has affected the curriculum is the emergence of textbooks across all subject areas that are based on sound academic knowledge and a view of American and world society that is more realistic and less ethnocentric.

The changes that have been recommended for the formal curriculum have most generally accepted the basic organization of the school's curriculum. Responses have tended to call for better content, better teaching methods, and better test scores. Therefore, underlying all the additions to the curriculum is a set of courses that has stayed the same since William Torrey Harris first organized the St. Louis schools in 1870. If there is a basic curriculum, what are students taught?

WHAT DO STUDENTS NEED TO KNOW?

 To attend school is considered a basic American right. In all fifty states students are required by law to attend school until the completion of ninth grade or upon reaching sixteen years of age. In 1980 the over-whelming majority of children between the ages of six and seventeen were enrolled in schools. Legislation and court decisions have mandated that each child has the right to a public education and it is the task of the school to provide that education. This belief requires that the school establish a formal curriculum that provides for the education of each student so that each one is literate, moral, healthy, occupationally competent, and socially skilled! The formal curriculum must provide an adequate education.

Adequate education means attention to the content that is taught and the evaluation of the learning outcomes as a result of studying the content. To ensure that each student receives an adequate education in 1983, forty-two states dictated that students must complete a set of core courses. The Carnegie report found that most American young people graduate from high school after completing three years of English, two years of social studies, one year of math, one or more years of science, two years of physical education (including health), and a smattering of specific local requirements. The most commonly required course was one course in social studies, usually American history. The most common local requirement is often driver education.

Eight states in the Carnegie report did not require core subjects for graduation. Nebraska and Vermont simply listed the number of credits needed to graduate; California, Colorado, Connecticut, Florida, Massachusetts, and Wisconsin had no statewide requirements. In these six states the local districts determine the graduation requirements.

Although these requirements have remained fairly stable since the 1970s, most students graduating from school today take fewer courses in the core curriculum and an increased number of elective courses. Students in 1981 took fewer courses in science, social studies, English, and mathematics. In their place, courses categorized as "personal service and social development" were taken—most popular being physical education, music performance, remedial English, driver education, cooperative education, general shop, and training for marriage/adulthood. This trend toward taking fewer academic subjects may be changing. Since the mid-1980s more and more states are reviewing graduation standards and requiring more traditional courses.

When selecting a course of study, a student chooses from one of three programs: general, academic, or vocational. At a comprehensive high school the academic program is more rigorous because it requires more courses from the traditional academic subjects and it is designed to prepare a student for college. The general program requires fewer academic courses and allows the building of an elective program to fit the needs of the student. The vocational program is for students who plan to enter the work force upon graduation. Within each program, requirements are set and contribute to the adequacy of the student's education.

To prepare the student for the completion of the core program and the other courses needed to graduate, each school system designs a set of expectations for students at each grade level. This set of expectations is usually stated in a document outlining the district's philosophy and general goals. A sample goal is presented in Table 11–1. Notice that the goals address academic and social needs of the students. They are a response to society's charge to educate the whole child and to prepare the individual for a positive role in American society. If taken seriously, the goals represent a formidable task for the school. This is especially true when one realizes the diversity of backgrounds from which the school population comes.

Based on these general goals, district officials then develop specific guides for each of the grade levels. Although districts vary in the delination of these goals, common expectations for the grade levels may be described in the following manner.

Primary School

Young children begin learning the rudiments of reading, writing, and mathematics in grades one through three. The formal curriculum in the primary grades is limited to the basics of education. Social studies, science, and physical education receive less attention. Children who complete the primary grades are expected to have acquired the fundamentals in reading and mathematics to enable them to continue the exploration of these two critical areas. They should also have acquired the needed social skills to be able to participate in the school.

TABLE 11-1 Sample Goals of a School District

The goals of K-12 programs in District X are to help each student:
- Learn the skills of effective communication–reading, writing, listening, speaking, and observing.
- Learn the skills of computation and mathematics concepts.
- Develop skills needed for effective problem solving and decision making.
- Develop the knowledge, skills, and attitudes needed to function in society.
- Develop an awareness of how the past influences the future.
- Be aware and responsive to the needs and values of other people.
- Develop an understanding of individual capabilities.
- Develop an awareness and capability to use technology.
- Develop and use good health practices.
- Understand the value of creative expression and explore its various forms.
- Understand, use, and conserve the natural resources of the environment.
- Prepare for choosing a career.
- Develop an interest in lifelong learning.
- Develop interests that will lead to the effective use of leisure time.

Intermediate School

Children in the intermediate grades continue to build their skills in reading, writing, and mathematics. Greater emphasis is also placed on social studies and science. For example, history and geography are usually introduced at the fourth-grade level as students begin to explore the world outside their neighborhood. The science curriculum also takes on a more formal nature as students begin to study concepts from biology and chemistry. By the end of sixth grade, students are expected to have specific learning experiences in each of the core areas of the curriculum. Also, the nature of their study should have prepared them for entrance into the junior high school's formal curriculum and for the learner behaviors that will be needed to succeed in junior high. It is during the latter part of the intermediate school years that the formal curriculum in most schools shifts from a student-centered approach to a more subject-centered orientation. The formal curriculum becomes more centered on the study of the various academic disciplines.

Middle School and Junior High School

Although these two organizational patterns represent different philosophical positions about the role of the learner, in practice the formal curriculum for both is much the same. Conant (1960) recommended that the subject-matter curriculum of these institutions follow a specific pattern and have a strong academic orientation. Students in seventh and eighth grades should take English (reading and composition), social studies (history and geography), mathematics, science, and other general education courses. At the ninth-grade level, those students who have the ability should be introduced to advanced mathematics. Other students should conclude their studies with a final general mathematics course.

Some middle schools and junior highs may organize the formal curriculum into a "unified studies" or "core" curriculum in which English and social studies courses are taught together during a longer block of time. Other schools may center the content around problem-solving issues and use an interdisciplinary approach. Such arrangements for the formal curriculum are the exception rather than the rule.

The junior high school often serves as the point in a student's academic career when a choice is made between a more academic-disciplined course of study and a more vocationally oriented curriculum. At the end of the ninth grade, many students select a particular path to follow through the formal curriculum.

Senior High School

The American comprehensive high school seeks to provide the final public education experience for students who will be going in a variety of directions. At a minimum, students are expected to be able to read, write, compute, and be knowledgeable of American history and government. To ensure that students have these minimal skills, many states now require basic skills tests prior to graduation.

The public's expectations of the school to serve broad educational needs has led to the establishment of a formal curriculum with two tracks. One focuses on the academic disciplines and is often called the *college preparatory curriculum*. Students in this track enroll in additional courses in mathematics, science, social studies, English, and a second language. These courses are designed to teach students specific aspects of the discipline and to expand their knowledge beyond the general knowledge level. For example, the mathematics curriculum may be divided into algebra, geometry, advanced algebra, and calculus. Students take the courses in a particular order, with each one becoming more complex. After completing such a course of study, students should have an advanced knowledge of mathematics.

Students may also enroll in courses that are more *work-related*. Business education, wood and automotive programs, art, and electronics are examples of courses in this area. Although not without specific content, these courses often focus on the development of specific skills that will enable the student to apply them either in the workplace or as a citizen. As a consequence, vocational courses emphasize more hands-on learning than the discipline-centered courses.

Both sets of courses are offered in the traditional senior high-school setting. Students select a series of courses for a quarter or semester and usually attend each class each day be rotating through a schedule. The curriculum goals for a district set the general direction for the formal curriculum. The goals represent the district's response to pressures from the society as a whole as to what schools should be doing, and to the unique demands of the local neighborhood. The goals provide the threads that hold the K–12 curriculum together. Although the goals are important, they do not solve all the problems for a district.

PROBLEMS IN DECIDING WHEN TO TEACH SPECIFIC COURSES

► Once a school district has reached agreement concerning the purposes and goals of the district, the next tasks are to determine *what* is to be taught at each grade level and *how* the content and skills at each grade level are to be related to those taught prior and following a specific grade. Traditionally these tasks fall under the problem of determining the "scope and sequence" of the formal curriculum. Determining the scope and sequence is not an easy task because it involves several important issues.

Ralph Tyler (1949) defines the scope of the curriculum as the breadth of the curriculum—the content, topics, learning experiences, and organizing threads or elements. The scope of the curriculum can be visually represented as a horizontal line that provides the organization for a class, a grade level, and a school and district. Along this horizontal line are the facts, concepts, skills, and attitudes that are included in the curriculum. For example, Table 11–2 shows how a

TABLE 11-2 An Example of Curriculum Goals

Development of Skills for Using Technology and Problem Solving		
Level A	*Level B*	*Level C*
Understand how technology can be used in solving problems.	Use technology to solve problems in both an academic setting and in daily life situations.	Develop a plan, make decisions, and evaluate the result.

Each of these levels may be then broken down into the following areas:

Information Technology Learner Outcomes

Level A: Knowledge and Comprehension
Goal:
1. Students will understand how technology can be used in solving problems.
Outcome:
   a. Students will understand problem-solving processes and identify appropriate technology to assist in the process.

Level B: Application
Goal:
1. Students will use technology to solve problems in both an academic setting and in daily life situations.
Outcome:
   a. Students will use the calculating ability of a technological tool to organize information.
   b. Students will use the visual communication ability of a technological tool to record and organize information to present ideas.

Level C: Evaluation
Goal:
1. Students will develop a plan, make decisions, and evaluate the result.
Outcome:
   a. Students will be able to use various information technology to study career opportunities and conduct job searches.
   b. Students will use problem-solving skills to develop and evaluate a "real world" problem, such as a school event or a traffic problem.

school district might think about basic skills for using technology and problem solving.

As shown in Table 11–2, there are three levels of this skill. Level A is the lowest level in which students understand that technology can be used. Level C, the highest level, has the students develop a plan, make a decision, and then evaluate the results. By identifying levels of sophistication, educators can begin to break learning into smaller categories.

PROBLEMS IN CHOOSING WHAT SHOULD BE TAUGHT AND WHEN

▶ The problem of selecting content for the curriculum must be made after considering three key issues (Oliva, 1982).

1. *Relevance:* If learning is to be meaningful and applicable, the content learned must be meaningful to the student. The student must see how what he or she is learning relates to life. This major issue is demonstrating how abstract knowledge is relevant to the student's life. For example, students who dislike mathematics often say, "No one I know ever talks 'algebra' in the real world. How is knowing algebra going to help me?"

2. *Balance:* In selecting the experiences to be included in the scope of the curriculum, balance also becomes an issue. Balance refers to the equilibrium between the experiences the student has during school. For example, how is the formal curriculum balanced between student-centered and subject-centered courses, individual needs and the formal disciplines, and societal needs and individual learner needs? Most educators would agree that balance is critical; determining the balance is the issue.

3. *Integration:* Hilda Taba (1962) believed that learning is more effective when facts and principles from one field can be related to another. Therefore, selecting the formal curriculum involves trying to build a unified view of the disciplines so students can see how the knowledge and skills in one discipline can help them understand a problem in another area. The problem in the traditional subject-centered curriculum in which the disciplines are taught as separate entities is that it becomes most difficult for students to see the interrelationships among the disciplines. For example, how does understanding the scientific method in biology help solve a problem in social studies?

Once having determined the general scope of the curriculum, the next issue confronting the curriculum developer is establishing a sequence to these activities to maximize learning.

THE SEQUENCE OF THE FORMAL CURRICULUM

► Every formal curriculum must have some form of orderly, progressive arrangement of the subject matter. This order of planned activities is the sequence. How this sequence is determined often falls to commonsense judgments about the objectives, content, and the learner. The most common sequencing patterns are chronology and difficulty. Most people learn history in a chronological fashion, starting with the early inhabitants and progressing to the discussion of recent events. Mathematics is often taught by introducing simple concepts and then moving upward in difficulty level.

Jerome Bruner (1960) is credited with the idea of the spiral curriculum. A spiral curriculum introduces the basics of the disciplines, then repeats them with increasing levels of complexity and sophistication throughout the learning experience. For example, an important social science generalization is that all societies must develop a means of enforcing laws (or rules) and developing new laws if the society is to continue. Scope and sequence issues focus on where in the K–12 social studies curriculum this concept should be taught and at what level of complexity. Using the idea of a spiral curriculum, the social studies generalization would be introduced at its most simple state early in the curriculum, then taught again later with additional objectives added to introduce more complex ideas. Table 11–3 illustrates how the scope and sequence for this particular generalization might be taught in a K–12 curriculum.

As we examine Table 11–3, we find that the generalization is first introduced in the third grade, along with three other important objectives. The major generalization is reinforced in grades four through seven and again in ninth and twelfth grades. By indicating that this generalization is to be taught at a particular grade level, the district or the curriculum specialist indicates to the teacher *what* should be taught and *when* it should be taught. If we look at the table once again, we would expect that social studies units of grades three, four, nine, and twelve would talk about governments, governing, and conflict. Upon examining most social studies curriculum patterns, one would find that it is at these grades that discussions of government begin at the local level in the early grades, moves forward to civics education at the ninth grade, and culminates with the study of American government in the twelfth grade. The scope and sequence is designed to provide order, a focus as to what content is to be taught, and an indication of the level of difficulty. The learning outcome for a student progressing through such a curriculum would be a more sophisticated understanding of governments and how they deal with conflict.

The challenge for the school is to develop a scope and sequence for each of the subjects taught in the curriculum. General district goals provide insights into what the district seeks to achieve for its students.

TABLE 11-3 Generalizations

	K	1	2	3	4	5	6	7	8	9	10	11	12
All societies develop means of enforcing laws (or rules) and working out new laws.				X	X	*	*	*		X			X
a. Every society must have some minimum of order or regularity of behavior if chaos is to be avoided.								#		X			
b. Some norms are considered so important by a society that they will be enforced through the use of force if necessary; other norms are considered less important.				X						X			
c. All societies have potential conflict and must develop means of trying to settle disputes and accommodate differences; in every society there is some means of making authoritative decisions where people's goals differ.				X			X			X			X
1) All societies have potential conflict and must work out some means of accommodating differences if violence is to be avoided.				X			#		X				
d. The greater the population density and the more complex the technological system, the greater the need changing laws.				*		X	*			X			

X = Objective of unit in course.
* = Subgeneralization related to this generalization is objective of unit.
# = Taught in unit but not listed as objective.

It is through the specification of these goals into content-specific goals and objectives that the formal curriculum comes alive. The final translation is then by the individual classroom teacher who reviews the district's scope and sequence for a particular subject and translates that into a series of lessons to be taught to the students.

The development of meaningful district-wide goals is a difficult task. Schools rely on professional educational societies in the various disciplines to provide important insights and direction as to the scope and sequence for a particular discipline. These learned societies draw members from a national constituency, serve as sounding boards for discussions about the goals of the discipline, and interpret the implications of research findings for the discipline. In addition to the national groups, most districts have key personnel from the district who are involved in exploring the particular needs and goals of the district. The task of the district personnel is to translate national ideas about what should be taught into specific action plans for the district.

In addition to directives from the national societies and the local district, the public (represented in a variety of ways) also tells the school what should and should not be taught. These nonacademic pressures also have a voice in what is taught and when it is taught.

PRESSURES FOR THE REFORM OF THE FORMAL CURRICULUM

▶ Our nation is at risk. . . . For the first time in the history of our country, the educational skills of one generation will not surpass, will not equal, will not even approach, those of their parents (*Education Week,* 1983).

"A nation at risk" became the watchword of the mid-1980s. The National Commission on Excellence, an eighteen-member panel appointed by Secretary of Education Terrel H. Bell, examined the American educational system and found it wanting. The commission's report was soon followed by books entitled *A Place Called School* by John Goodlad (1983) and *High School: A Report on Secondary Education in America* by Ernest L. Boyer (1984). Each new study reported on an in-depth analysis of academic health of the schools, and each one found the schools not meeting the challenges of today's students.

Public school critics found the formal curriculum and the American high school providing a warmed-over version of old principles. Paul Hurd was quoted in the National Commission Report as saying that the American schools are "raising a new generation of Americans that is scientifically and technologically illiterate." All reports indicated that the standards of achievement had fallen, that more and more American high-school graduates were functionally illiterate, and that scores on standard achievement tests had fallen to a twenty-six-year low. Each study indicated that the public was demanding that educational and political leaders act effectively and quickly to bring American education into the forefront once again. But what was to be changed?

Most critics attacked the formal curriculum and the manner in which it was taught. All agreed that it had become "watered-down" with too many electives and open choices for students. There was a general call for a return to a core curriculum with academic rigor based on the disciplines of English, social science, mathematics, and foreign language.

Bringing about change in an institution, such as the school, is a slow and evolutionary process. The call for the reformation of America's schools is not new. It is a constant echo across the land. Educators, sitting in a most vulnerable position, move slowly in answering the call. To improve the education of American students involves a strong public commitment demonstrated through the allocation of the resources to achieve these ends.

It must also be recognized that while the voices for reform were the most vocal in the mid-1980s, there were others who were deliberately seeking to keep the school system stable. Through nondecision making, simply not doing anything, some educators will adopt a wait-and-see attitude. Others will use conflict avoidance strategies to avoid responding to issues that the local community may feel are too controversial, whereas other groups will use controversy to keep the school from making a decision. If these techniques fail to delay major curriculum changes, the "trickle down" theory will affect what actually happens in the classroom. This concept, called *loose coupling*, recognizes that those goals set by reformers may not always be achieved in the day-to-day existence of the classroom. Evidence from the studies of the past would seem to support the position that reform imposed from the outside may never make its way to the classroom.

Does this mean that schools are doomed to remain the same as they were in the 1960s and before? No. The formal curriculum will change as the demands of the school's constituents require and support them.

SUMMARY

► The formal curriculum of the school describes what is taught and when it is taught. This complex task is accomplished through a variety of learning activities, usually organized around a specific category within a subject area controlled by the teacher. The teacher—who does the majority of the talking in most classes—is charged, primarily, with the task of transmitting the formal curriculum. There are two basic frameworks for presenting the formal curriculum: subject matter organization and child-centered organization.

Subject matter organization, the most common curricular orientation, defines what is to be learned as a body of knowledge derived from the academic disciplines. For example, the social sciences are simplified for pedagogical purposes depending on the age and the ability of the pupil.

The second basic orientation, child-centered organization, tries to motivate the child into learning by concentrating on his or her needs and concerns. Ideally, the child-centered curriculum revolves around the real-life experiences of the student. The child-centered curriculum concept is difficult to implement and organize, and is thus the less common of the two orientations.

The formal curriculum is under almost constant criticism from the American public because they have a nearly insatiable desire for better content, better teaching, and better test score results. The dilemma of deciding when to teach what content is never solved, but it is customarily resolved through the formal curriculum which expands across two dimensions: scope and sequence. The scope of a curriculum describes its breadth—the content, topics, learning experiences, and organizing elements. The sequence is the order of planned activities of the curriculum.

Each year, every school is confronted by the challenge of developing a scope and a sequence for each of the subjects taught in their curriculum. In the end, the ultimate success of their formal curriculum depends on how successfully each of these schools deals with this crucial task.

ACTIVITIES

1. Based on your reading, define each of the following terms:
   a. formal curriculum
   b. scope and sequence
   c. spiral curriculum
   d. curriculum balance
2. The formal curriculum may be subject-centered, student-centered, or a combination of each. What are the basic characteristics that differentiate the two approaches to curriculum organization?
3. Why has the subject-centered approach to curriculum organization been the most popular approach used by schools?
4. Changes in the formal curriculum have occurred very slowly. Describe what you think are three important factors that impede rapid change in the formal curriculum.
5. In your opinion, what is the biggest challenge confronting the formal curriculum of the school?
6. Based on your reading and your own experiences, what common set of knowledge do you think a graduating senior should know? First, make a list of the knowledge and skill outcomes. Then list the specific formal curriculum experiences the student should have in order to achieve the goals. Finally, given your goals, what are the implications for the formal curriculum in the earlier grades?
7. Obtain a curriculum guide from a local school district, review it carefully, and answer the following questions:

    a. How do the goals you developed for activity 6 compare with the goals of the district?

    b. Is the district's curriculum primarily subject-centered or student-centered? Why?

    c. Can you find examples within the district's curriculum to include experiences relevant to today's students? If so, cite them.

    d. How might the district's curriculum be improved? How might your set of curriculum goals be improved?

    e. If possible, visit the school whose curriculum goals you have examined. What specific examples can you observe to support the fact that the goals are being implemented in the day-to-day life of the school?

8. Examine three popular news magazines. Look at the issues for the past two months and read the stories related to education that are contained in the magazines. What are the basic themes of the stories? Review the calls for reform discussed on pages 225–226 of the text. Are the same concerns still evident in the magazine articles? What different issues have emerged?

9. Based on the response to questions 6 through 8, what changes would you make in your formal curriculum that you developed for activity 6? Why?

REFERENCES

Boyer, E. L. (1984). *High school: A report on secondary education in America.* New York: Harper and Row.

Bruner, J. (1960). *Process of education.* Cambridge, Mass.: Harvard University Press.

Church, R. L., and Sedlak, M. W. (1976). *Education in the United States.* New York: The Free Press.

Conant, J. (1960). *Recommendations for education in the junior high school years.* Princeton, N.J.: Educational Testing Service.

Education Week. (April 1983). "An open letter to the American people, A nation at risk: The imperative for educational reform," pp. 12–13.

Goodlad, J. I. (1983). *A place called school.* New York: McGraw-Hill, p. 396.

Goodlad, J. I. (March 1983). Study of schooling: Some findings and hypotheses. *Phi Delta Kappan,* pp. 465–470.

Oliva, P. F. (1982). *Developing the curriculum.* Boston: Little, Brown, pp. 464–465.

Silberman, C. E. (1970). *Crisis in the classroom.* New York: Random House, p. 180.

Taba, H. (1962). *Curriculum development: Theory and practice* New York: Harcourt Brace and World.

Tyler, R. W. (1949). *Basic principles of curriculum and instruction.* Chicago: University of Chicago Press.

SUGGESTED READINGS

Craft, A., and Bardell, G. (1984). *Curriculum opportunities in a multicultural society.* New York: Harper and Row.

Clark, C. M. (ed.) (1987). Part one: What should I teach? In *Educators' handbook: a research perspective.* Virginia Richardson-Koehler, ed. New York: Longman.

Goodlad, J. (1983). *A place called school.* New York: McGraw-Hill.

12

The Hidden Curriculum

▶───────────────────────────────◀

OVERVIEW

▶ This chapter describes some of the critical elements of the hidden curriculum. Particular emphasis is placed on teachers' behavior, concept of role, management techniques, and feedback. Key questions ask the reader to think about specific teacher actions that influence the classroom environment. A concluding activity involves a careful analysis of a school environment.

INTRODUCTION

▶ The gymnasium is packed. It is hot and it is noisy, but it is *great!* Down on the floor the cheerleaders are yelling, "Go Cyclones, go State, go Cyclones, beat the Tartans!" Over and over again the cheers fill the gym. The coach comes to the microphone and tries to get the crowd's attention, but they don't listen right away as the kids, teachers, and parents continue to chant, "Go Cyclones, beat the Tartans!" Finally, the coach gets everyone's attention and the crowd quiets.

Over the cracking sound of the public address system the coach says, "This is what we've worked for all year. The team has given 110 percent all season and now we are off to win the state title. It will be tough, but our team is tougher and it knows what to do with such a challenge. I am so proud of these fine athletes, our school, and our student body. I hope you are as proud of our school as I am."

The crowd erupts into thunderous applause, shrill whistles, and screams. Again, the chant is heard, "Go Cyclones, beat the Tartans. Go Cyclones, beat the Tartans!" The coach steps back from the microphone and helps lead the band in the school fight song. Soon he steps back to the microphone.

"Let me introduce the kids who have given their all to this season. Please hold your applause until all the team has been introduced."

One by one the team members are introduced. The obvious stars receive applause and shouts. When everyone has been introduced, the crowd stands in mass and applauds, screams, and whistles, and the band plays on and on. The coach shouts into the microphone that everyone should come to the game and that student support is critical to a victory. But it is impossible to hear exactly what is said. The team members wave to the crowd and leave the floor to a crescendo of noise.

Ms. Wainwright, the principal, tries to tell the students that buses will be leaving the school at 8:30 in the morning. Not many people are listening. She finally signals the band director to play the school song. He strikes up the band and everyone stands to sing. Some students are so excited that they can't sing; instead, they dance around with their hands high in the air signaling that we're number one! Others are so emotional that tears stream from their eyes.

Today, in this crowded, hot gymnasium there are no losers. Everyone is a winner. They're off to state! Today, they're number one! No school is better. Go Cyclones, beat the Tartans! Win, team, win!

This gymnasium, filled with students and teachers, also represents the school's curriculum. This curriculum stands in sharp contrast to the formal curriculum described in Chapter 11. But its impact on teachers and students is profound and longlasting. It is the hidden curriculum that exists in every school.

THE HIDDEN CURRICULUM

▶ The hidden curriculum is the complex set of teacher and student behaviors and their resultant effects. Borrowing from the research directed by Lawrence Letzotte and his colleagues, the *hidden curriculum* may be defined as the norms, beliefs, and attitudes reflected in the school's practices and the behavior of teachers and students.

The formal curriculum focuses on what is taught—the courses, the grade levels, and student organizational patterns. The hidden curriculum focuses on the expectations that are developed about learning, and are self-based on the interactions that take place in the school between the teachers and students, students and students, and students and materials. These expectations are developed by following explicit rules and implicitly by subtle messages received from many sources.

Although the formal and hidden curriculum are inextricably tied, it is possible to examine key aspects of the hidden curriculum. Our attention will be on the teacher and student in the learning environment.

THE LEARNING ENVIRONMENT

▶ Two schools may show great similarities on the surface. The buildings are basically the same. Both have about the same number of students and are located in similar socioeconomic environments. They have similar resources with respect to libraries, science materials, and other facilities and equipment. Each has a principal, other key administrators, and support staff. The teaching staff is organized by grade level and subject matter. The teachers in each building are certified and have college degrees. The formal curriculum is subject matter-oriented for both schools. But the schools are different. Teachers' attitudes are different. Student achievement is different. And the relationships that exist between teachers and students are different. One school is successful, whereas the second is not. In one school there is a positive feeling. Teachers and students feel good about being in the school. Student achievement is better in one school than in the other. Also, an overall positive school spirit can be felt in one school but not in the other.

Why do these differences exist? Although it is quite difficult to pinpoint the exact reasons, we do know some of the possible reasons why schools and classrooms differ. The formal curriculum may be important, but it is the hidden curriculum that contributes the major differences. Examining the school as a social organization can provide important clues.

An important text by Robert Dreeban (1968) contends that schools and classrooms have a particular pattern of organizational properties, and what children learn derives from the nature of their experiences in the school. It is in this environment that students learn to accept principles of conduct, or social norms, and to act according to them (p. 44). It is also in this social arena that students learn about roles and values (Letzotte et al., 1980, p. 27). Before exploring the impact of the learning environment, let's define each of these key concepts.

Norms are shared expectations of or attitudes toward ideas as to what are appropriate procedures and behaviors in the school environment. They prescribe some actions and behaviors as appropriate and carry power to sanction behavior that deviates from expected patterns. In schools there are norms for students, teachers, administrators, and support staff. These behavior norms are related to a particular role.

Roles refer to the behaviors of members of a social system. For example, in a school system people have certain positions and behave according to a conception of what is expected in that role. In schools, the positions people hold are very clear. There are four major roles: students, teachers, administrators, and staff members. Each role has certain responsibilities. The students are there to learn. The teachers are the instructors of the students, and the principal serves as the manager and instructional leader. The staff members help the teachers and principal run the school. Although these are universal roles and everyone generally knows what each one means, they can vary markedly from one school to the next and create different learning environments. The roles held by the members of the school determine how one acts. These actions are also influenced by values.

Values are those things that people feel are important. They are standards used to decide whether things are good or bad, right or wrong, important or worthless. Values guide people in deciding how to live and serve as standards for deciding between alternatives. Values help us understand ourselves, our relationship with others, and with the society as a whole. In the school, the overarching values reflect those of the society as a whole; however, within each school system there are values that may set the school environment apart from others.

As students, teachers, administrators, and school staff interact, various messages are sent to everyone in the school. A particular climate is developed for the school as a whole and within particular classrooms. The school climate is important, but our attention will be on the classroom and the actions of the teacher and students.

► The Teacher and the Classroom

In the typical secondary school a student may have as many as seven different teachers during the day. Each teacher's classroom is different—the norms, roles, and values are not the same. In Mr. Ehman's class, no one acts out, no one talks without being recognized, and no one dares to cheat. Ms. Lowinski's class is more relaxed and people cooperate a lot. She is considered tough, but nice by most of the students. And so it goes. In each class the student must adjust to the overall climate and the rules of the game. Just as teachers talk about the characteristics of students, students talk about the teachers. "Oh, Ehman, he is really tough. He won't let you say or do anything." "Ms. Lowinski's cool, man, but she still gives hard tests." The informal network of friends and advice from brothers or sisters to younger siblings keep the messages alive in the school. Students play an important role, but it is the teacher who sets the initial tone. Teacher behavior, concept of role, management techniques, expectations of students' work and behavior, and feedback of students will set the climate and influence the hidden curriculum.

Research studies by Lezotte et al. (1980), Schmuck and Schmuck (1971), and Rutter et al. (1979) all found that a positive learning environment is critical to the development of a student's self-esteem and academic performance. Students must have an environment in which learning is possible and one in which they are not physically or emotionally threatened. In developing such an environment, the teacher makes many choices about the rules, both formal and informal, that will govern behavior. The teacher sets the tone for the classroom by establishing rules to guide interpersonal relationships and by determining how much structure is needed to enable students to succeed at various academic tasks. The teacher's decisions in these areas, whether made consciously or unconsciously, are critical.

For example, as students enter a classroom they are confronted by a set of formal and informal rules that the teacher has established. Formal rules may vary from something as simple as having everyone raise their hand before they talk, to very specific rules about how all assignments must be completed. Most teachers go over these basic rules at the beginning of a new class, and take particular care to enforce them during the early part of the course. Often, rules of behavior will be posted in the room along with certain penalities for breaking a rule.

Informal rules also influence the classroom environment. Informal rules are ones between the teacher and students that tell students how much talking the teacher will permit before asking people to be quiet, or how much students can cooperate before the teacher will tell them to work alone. Informal rules also set guidelines for student behavior for some groups as compared to others. For example, in one class it might be acceptable for one group of students to talk a lot but unacceptable for another group. These rules are never explicitly stated. They are established by watching and listening to what the teacher says and does.

Students are very quick to pick up the teacher's expectations about their academic and personal performances. Students critically examine the teacher's behavior during the early days of class. Students read the rules, listen to what is said, and watch the behavior of the teacher. Here is a simple example.

> Ms. Larios explained to her third graders that no one was to leave his or her seat without permission. It would be disruptive for other students if people were walking around the room. But, after several weeks, Sally, Nang, and

Roberto were able to leave their seats and do things. When Willie got up he was told to sit down and finish his work. When he asked why, Ms. Larios said he never got his work done.

Ms. Larios established a rule, but her behavior gave a different message. The students in her class soon learned that for Sally, Nang, and Roberto, the smart students in the class, the same rules did not apply. There were rules and then there were the real rules. They may not have been fair, but they were the rules.

The messages of the hidden curriculum may also influence student attitudes and beliefs. What type of message is being given by this social studies teacher?

> The ninth-grade social studies class was studying voting. The class had just completed a series of activities on the importance of voting in a democracy. Mr. Averyt, their teacher, had been telling the students that voting was critical if a democracy was to survive.
>
> In the hallway before class, Mr. Averyt talked to Mr. Goldstein about the upcoming election. Several students overheard Mr. Averyt say, "No, I'm not going to vote. In this one-party state my vote doesn't mean a thing. I haven't voted in the last two presidential elections."

What message did these students hear? The books and lessons said voting was important, but the teacher had not voted in the last two presidential elections. Why should a student vote when the teacher doesn't? The formal curriculum says voting is important, but an important component of the hidden curriculum gives a different message.

As a teacher, it is important to realize the impact of behavior on student attitudes and beliefs. Additional points will be made later in this chapter, but at this point we raise the following key questions for consideration:

1. Do you talk about respect as an important part of class behavior, but do not treat students with respect?
2. What does your behavior say about your feelings regarding the principal, other teachers, the school, and the community?
3. What do your words say about the importance of learning?
4. What does your behavior say about expectations for student achievement?
5. How does the structure and physical appearance of your classroom influence student attitudes about themselves and the importance of learning?
6. Do you talk about the importance of writing and spelling but hand out materials that are poorly written and that contain misspelled words?

Why is the teacher's behavior so influential? Because the teacher has a wide base of influence over the lives of the students. There is *legitimate power* simply because of the role. There is *expert power* because of knowledge of the subject matter. And, there is the *power to reward* students and to punish them. The teacher may also have what is called *referent power,* the closeness that students feel toward the teacher. How the teacher uses these sources of power can have considerable influence over the behavior and attitudes of the students.

A teacher enters the classroom with certain types of bases of power. Students usually assume that a teacher has legitimate power and some power to reward and punish them. How the teacher uses these bases of power has direct implication on the learning environment. The research by Abraham Maslow (1962) and Richard and Patricia Schmuck (1971) provides some useful insights into the uses of personal power.

Maslow's work focused on human needs. He viewed these needs as fitting into a hierarchy from basic physiological needs to needs related to self-actualization. Maslow had a vision of a good teacher as a good helper. He was convinced that good helpers are the "most fully human" persons because they possess such characteristics as compassion and genuine concern for others. Therefore, according to Maslow, the best path to becoming a better teacher is to become a better helper and thus a better person.

Maslow postulated that an effective, helping teacher is one who can manage to harmonize an apparent dichotomy within individuals. There is the urge of a healthy organism to stretch, and to venture out. At the same time, there is a polar urge to remain in the safe and familiar. The teacher's job is to encourage and actively support attempts at intellectual and emotional risk taking and freedom, while at the same time provide a safe, supportive environment.

Schmuck and Schmuck's research supports many of Maslow's claims. After reviewing a variety of research reports, the scholars suggest that a teacher may enhance the classroom environment if students are given specific tasks, have a degree of independence, and feel free to communicate with the teacher (1971, p. 30). Teachers who have too tight a control over the class tend to develop students who are dependent, resist authority, and have problems with interpersonal relations.

Maslow and the Schmucks point to the major issue confronting the classroom teacher. The issue centers on the relationship between the amount of structure provided in a classroom and the amount of interpersonal relationships that exist.

Remember, a classroom is a social setting. Teachers and students live together in close proximity hour after hour. The ostensible reasons for placing students in classrooms are academic, but the outcomes reflect a combination of academic and social experience.

In any classroom there must be a balance between the structure needed to provide a learning situation for students and the establishment of warm, interpersonal relations that create a positive learning environment. Within the class there is an environment that fosters cooperation, competition, or individualistic behavior. It is the teacher who has the major responsibility for creating the balance between structure and relationships determining the goal structure for the class. Three classrooms illustrate these relationships. In each class the teacher is successful and students learn the materials.

> *Classroom A:* Mr. Jones runs a very organized and structured classroom. In his class he is the leader. He determines what is done, when it is done, and how it is done. He is a pleasant man, but he doesn't worry much about knowing his students or encouraging them to work together. Most of the time he tells and they listen. Although students cooperate from time to time, they are mostly responsible for their own work.

> *Classroom B.* Ms. Johnson also has an organized class. She has carefully laid out lesson plans and rules. However, she works hard at getting to know her students and having them work together on various projects. There is a warm, friendly atmosphere in the class, yet it is clear that she is the instructional leader. Ms. Johnson sells her class to her students. There is also a lot of cooperation among students on various class projects; however, grades are still individualistic.

> *Classroom C:* Mr. Buckland has concluded that his students can take more responsibility in their education. He provides little structure in determining the content and allows his students a lot of freedom to determine what they should study. Whether students work together or work alone is pretty much left up to the students. Some work together quite a lot, but there are some who prefer to work alone most of the time. Mr. Buckland supports each student's choice.

Determining the balance between structure and personal relationships is a difficult task for any teacher. Research by Paul Kersey and Kenneth Blanchard (1976) provides some important clues for the teacher. Kersey and Blanchard suggest that the balance between these two important ingredients of management should be determined by the maturity of the group and the specific task to be completed. *Maturity* is defined as the ability of a group of students to establish goals and take the responsibility for the achievement of the goals. Let's look at the classes just described.

Mr. Jones's class is a highly structured one in which tasks are emphasized over relationships. He may have determined that the maturity of his students is such that at this point they need very specific direction. Given that the class is successful, he is probably fair and well liked by his students. Mr. Jones chooses to provide only the structure they need to complete his assignments.

On the other hand, Ms. Johnson has a class that she feels can have more freedom in completing various learning tasks, but the class still needs structure. So she provides direction in what should be done yet also gives a lot of personal attention to her students. The students in her class are given more freedom to do an assignment on their own without specific directions, but she is ready to provide more structure if needed.

If Mr. Jones and Ms. Johnson are structured, Mr. Buckland, who is the most unstructured, must have students who are more mature and have the ability to complete assignments on their own. His role is really that of a facilitator for his students.

These three classes also differ in the type of goal structure that exists. The research of Roger Johnson and colleagues (1983) has focused on these differing goal structures. Research suggests that the choice of a classroom goal structure has serious and abiding ramifications for academic achievement, for broad socializing forces, and for the development of the individual student's self-concept.

Johnson and associates contend that most classrooms are individualistic. Thirty students may be given the same assignment, but each student is expected to complete the assigned work on his or her own. Each student takes the same unit test or weekly quiz, but each is expected neither to give nor to seek help from fellow students. Students are to learn primarily on their own, with minimal help from their classmates. If the class is highly competitive, students might cheat in order to get a good grade.

Individualistic and competitive classrooms can be very stimulating environments. Some students respond very favorably to competitive environments. However, before structuring a class solely on a competitive model, it is wise to bear in mind two simple truths. First, competition must be fair. When the same people "lose" all the time because they can't read, spell, or compute as well as others, then the competition is unfair and damaging. Second, a teacher's function is to help students learn and it is difficult for students to learn in an environment in which they constantly lose. All students need to "win" in the classroom. Although some students don't expect to win all the time, they need to win occasionally.

A different classroom goal structure is one based on cooperative learning. The key concept in cooperative learning is interdependence. Interdependence implies a recognition of the fact that no one needs to stand alone in the classroom. The hallmarks of a cooperative classroom include groups of students working together to find the answers to questions. Students are grouped together and do not compete with other groups. Peer teaching occurs. The teacher's role is to design instructional activities that have students work together, facilitate group progress toward the completion of a task, and ensure that individual learning occurs.

The hidden curriculum is also influenced by the teaching methods that are used. Two people teaching United States history might well use widely different approaches. One uses a lecture-discussion-reading approach, and the other uses a project-oriented method. Thus, the role of the teacher is quite different in each room even though both classes are studying exactly the same subject. The point here is not to say that one method is superior to the next, but to indicate that both have an impact on how students feel about the course. As we noted in Chapter 8, a good teacher uses a variety of approaches. The point we are making is that *how* you teach interacts with, or even supersedes, *what* you teach. A brief exchange between a daughter and mother illustrates this point.

> Mary Beth is telling her parents about school. She says, "Science is my favorite. I just love it."
>
> Mary Beth's mother exclaims, "I thought you hated science. Remember last year when you wanted to drop the course?"
>
> "Oh," Mary Beth replies, "Not this year; it's different."

Mary Beth is saying that *what* is taught may not be as important as *who* teaches it and *how* it is taught. Teacher behavior, classroom structure, and methods are important, but so is the feedback students receive from the teacher.

Feedback is what students receive about what is and what is not acceptable behavior. Earlier in the text we discussed the impact of feedback on academic learning; however, feedback is also related to personal factors related to academic learning. This type of feedback may be direct and immediate—"Good answer, Robert. That shows you are thinking." "Dale, sit down and get to work." It may be less direct and delayed—a good grade in a course or an award for athletic prowess. Or the feedback might be very indirect—posting student work on the bulletin board. Feedback may be verbal, written, or nonverbal. For example, work by Mary Budd Rowe (1969) on teachers' responses to students suggests that too much praise may limit student participation, and that teachers often do not wait long enough for students to respond to questions before asking another question. This is especially true when the students are perceived to have lower academic skills. The teacher might not be aware that messages are being sent as well as subtle feedback.

Research on effective schools suggests that teachers who provide verbal and nonverbal feedback that focuses on high expectations, efficacy, and pervasive caring send positive messages to their students (Hersch, 1984). A teacher who has high expectations for students' work is essentially saying, "I think you ought to and can achieve." The teacher is also telling the class, "I have high expectations for you because I care about you and want you to learn." And finally, messages of high expectation tell students, "You are really more capable than you think."

When such messages are supported by a teacher's attitude, students may indeed begin to feel that they can learn. Then when these actions are supported by a caring environment in which students are supported, the message is clear: Students learn in this class. Hersch's contentions are supported by other research teams. For example, Lezotte and colleagues suggest that the hidden messages are often quite clear.

> Nearly every type of activity in a classroom represents an opportunity to communicate expectations to students. Many teachers wrongly believe that expectations can be communicated only by formal written and spoken statements. While such vehicles for communicating expectations are important, teacher expectations are also communicated to students in extremely subtle ways. The strategies teachers use to structure reading groups, allocate status roles, ask questions, evaluate student performance, and communicate to parents are all indications of the expectations they have for students (1980, p. 103).

When thinking about giving feedback to students, consider these questions:

1. What types of comments do you make to students?
2. What kinds of written comments do you place on students' work?
3. Is student work displayed in the classroom?
4. How do you assign work groups in the classroom?
5. How do you pick people to do special tasks?
6. What kinds of messages do you send home to parents?

These questions ask the teacher to reflect on specific actions. The formal curriculum organizes the content, and specific teacher behaviors contribute significantly to the hidden curriculum.

A discussion of the hidden curriculum cannot conclude without a brief comment about the role of students in this complex set of interactions.

▶ The Student and the Classroom

Robert Dreeban (1968) contends that schooling forms the linkage between the family life of children and the public life of adults. Young children enter the school with a set of prior experiences and attitudes. The school, in a normative sense, provides the experiences needed to learn the principles of conduct and patterns of behavior appropriate to being an adult (p. 4). It is through the schooling process that students add to the things they have learned in the family setting, form new social relationships (some of which might be quite different from family acquaintances), learn about social position, and acquire group behavior patterns and a sense of group identity (pp. 21–22).

Throughout educational history, much has been written about the impact of the family on school achievement. Two general views predominate. One is that schools cannot make a difference in school success because of the tremendous impact of the home and family. A series of early studies by Coleman et al. (1966), Jencks et al. (1972), and Hauser, Sewell, and Alwin (1976) indicated that influence of low socioeconomic status is so great that the school can do little to overcome these effects. According to these studies, children from these families lack the prior training and the orientation toward schooling that will allow them to succeed.

Teachers who accept these conclusions often reinforce the beliefs by various decisions. Students may not only be placed in less difficult formal curriculum settings but they are also not expected to achieve as much as other students. The messages received from the hidden curriculum are ones that say repeatedly, "You really can't succeed; you really are not as capable; you are not as smart."

A more positive view about the impact of schooling has gained in status during the last several years. Lezotte et al. (1980) and Rutter et al. (1979) report data that indicate a low correlation between socioeconomic status and school achievement. Their work indicates that with appropriate instructional strategies, students from all levels can achieve academically. The effective teaching research reported in Chapter 8 also supports these conclusions.

It is possible to assume that with proper instruction, students from all socioeconomic classes can achieve academically in school. However, it is not valid to assume that all students bring the same set of attitudes and beliefs to the school. They do not. For example, children from different socioeconomic backgrounds and family environments have different attitudes about learning, authority, and the importance of schools. Some of these differences were highlighted in Chapter 8 where we suggested that the research on effective teaching indicated that children from lower socioeconomic environments need more order and structure in order to achieve. Middle-class students, on the other hand, may need less structure in their learning environment. Why?

Part of the reason for these differences may be related to the environment in which children live. A classic study by Fred Strodtbeck (1971) suggests important differences between middle-class homes and lower-class homes. He contends that two important variables need to be considered when understanding the learning needs of different students. Most schools are characterized as seeking to impart dominant middle-class values and orientations. Included are those that focus the use of verbal language, behavior models that encourage students to be self-directed and willing to explore ideas. The problem, of course, is that not all children come from middle-class homes and their training and concepts of acceptable behavior may be quite different.

Strodtbeck found that because lower socioeconomic families lived in areas where security was a dominant issue, verbal exchanges and behavior expectations were quite different. For example, many children from less affluent environments must contend daily with the fear of something bad happening to them. Strodtbeck suggests that before learning can take place, students must be in a secure, safe environment.

Strodtbeck's early study provided the groundwork for later research about the relationship between environment and instructional strategies. In our earlier discussions about effective teaching, it was noted that more structured teaching strategies may be most effective for achieving some learning outcomes with students from lower socioeconomic homes. These research studies suggest that all students may learn *if* the teacher is aware of important environmental factors *and* makes adjustments in teaching strategies.

As the student population in the United States continues to change, with more and more students coming from minority populations and with more students who have special learning needs, it is critical that the teacher have a better understanding of the environment from which these students come. The *at risk student* has become the term used for this growing cohort of students. The challenges they present to the teacher are many. However, although an awareness of background differences is critical, the teacher must guard against developing attitudes that suggest to the students that they cannot learn or succeed in school.

THE HIDDEN CURRICULUM IN THE FORMAL CURRICULUM

▶ The interactions between teachers and students and students and students form the heart of the hidden curriculum. Important messages are also sent by the organization of the formal curriculum. In Chapter 11 the formal curriculum was described. The discussion focused on the division of the curriculum and one focused on preparation for work. One is academic; the other is vocational. Students in most schools take courses in both areas, but sooner or later in their secondary schooling they choose one track upon which to concentrate their studies.

This formal tracking system also creates two classes of students in the school. One group is "college bound" because they are taking courses in that part of the curriculum. The other group is "vocation bound" because of their course selection. These two tracks often give hidden messages to students, teachers, administrators, and parents.

"Smart" students are in the college preparatory courses; the others are not. Teachers' expectations of a student's academic and social performance are often influenced by the formal curriculum decisions made by the student. Status and prestige are often linked to a particular curriculum. Some students, not wanting to be stereotyped in one particular group, sometimes enroll in inappropriate courses. Parents often encourage a son or daughter to take a particular set of courses because it "looks" better. Such courses might not be appropriate for the student; however, the *message* given by enrolling in the courses is more important.

In today's climate, in which educators, parents, and community members are calling for higher standards, pressure is being place on students to enroll in more academically oriented subjects. Vocational and technical programs across the country are being faced with declining enrollment because of pressure by parents and community or by increased state standards for graduation. This push away from vocational education will continue to contribute to the messages of the hidden curriculum contained within the formal curriculum.

Informal messages are also given by the materials selected to be used in the teaching of the formal curriculum. Materials should be selected because they are the most appropriate means of teaching the students the content of the course. When appropriately selected, the materials meet the needs of both the teacher and the student, and the outcome is a successful learning experience. On some occasions, materials may be used that indicate lower expectations and a belief that students are not capable of learning. Selecting very simple texts for a group of secondary students and then teaching at a very simple level when both are inappropriate tells the students that they are not capable of better work. Avoiding more demanding work, such as term papers and oral presentations, because of the belief that students are not capable of handling such demands, also sends important messages to the students. Also, showing films continually in a class indicates a perspective on the abilities of the students and the teacher's expectations. Learning materials send important messages to the individual student and to other students.

Finally, the opportunities provided within the organizational structure of the curriculum send messages to teacher and student alike. Is there a strict tracking system in which students are hindered from exploring various subjects? Is there a tracking system that establishes homogeneous groups rather than heterogeneous groupings? Is the formal curriculum organized in such a manner as to facilitate the exchange of ideas and to foster intellectual growth and independence among all students? Is the school curriculum organized in such a way as to recognize a wide range of student contributions? All of these contribute to the school's impact on the lives of both the teachers and the students.

IMPROVING THE HIDDEN CURRICULUM

▶ Many of the studies conducted during the early 1980s offered specific suggestions concerning the improvement of the school's climate as an integral part of the hidden curriculum (Felt, 1985). Specifics include the following:

1. Many studies recommend making schools smaller: fewer students per teacher, fewer students and teachers per school, fewer subjects, and fewer goals. Smaller schools would permit
   a. a better diagnosis of learning problems so students can succeed.
   b. a closer student-teacher relationship which can help motivation.
   c. a decrease in anonymity.
2. There should be many routes to reward for students. More rewards for larger numbers of students means a greater involvement in the school culture and a feeling of being an important part of the school.
3. School environments should be personalized so that teachers and students know each other well.
4. The school environment should focus on a high level of academic expectations for all students, but not so high as to create an environment filled with anxiety.
5. A climate should exist in classrooms where students are not afraid to make mistakes.

Although these five recommendations cannot affect all the factors of the hidden curriculum, they point to the importance of the intangibles of the curriculum. How students and teachers interact is just as important as the structure of the formal curriculum.

SUMMARY

▶ The hidden curriculum is composed of the norms, beliefs, and attitudes that are reflected in the school's practices and the behavior of the teachers and students. It is often difficult to pinpoint key elements of the hidden curriculum, but it is possible to sense the feeling of a school after just a short visit. The feeling that exists in a classroom has an important influence on the lives of all those who are teaching and learning there. The formal curriculum focuses on what is taught; the hidden curriculum focuses on the expectations that are developed about learning and self. They are closely tied and both are critical if effective teaching is to take place.

ACTIVITIES

1. Based on your reading, define each of the following terms.
   a. formal curriculum
   b. hidden curriculum
   c. norms
   d. role
   e. teacher sense of efficacy
2. Classroom goal structure is an important part of the hidden curriculum. Describe the differences between a competitive goal structure and a cooperative goal structure.
3. Design a learning activity that uses a cooperative goal structure.
4. Having high expectations for students is an important part of the hidden curriculum. Without using verbal clues, how might you indicate to students that you have high expectations for each of them?
5. Understanding the background of your students is critical. Describe four ways that could be used to gain insights into students' background.
6. An important skill for any teacher is to be able to analyze the school and classroom environment and the students who populate the school. This extended activity is designed to help you analyze a school. Arrange to visit a classroom of a school of your choice. Observe carefully. When you leave the school, write down your observations in as much detail as you can. Use this outline as a guide:

   I. Looking at the School:
   You can learn a lot by carefully looking at the school building and the surrounding environment. Look at: (1) the conditions of the grounds surrounding the school; (2) the condition of the halls, cafeteria, and bathrooms; (3) the neatness of the building; and (4) signs, posters, and information displayed in showcases and on bulletin boards. What did you see that helps you gain an insight into the school and the people who go there?
   II. Sensing the Socioemotional Climate:
   What is the "feeling" in the school? Listen to what is said and how it is said. Look and listen to: (1) student talk in the halls and cafeteria; (2) student behavior in the halls; (3) teacher talk in the lounges; (4) student talk and behavior in the classroom; and (5) talk between teachers and students.
   III. Observing in the Classroom:
   A. The Students
      1. Classroom norms: What do students do prior to class?

How do they behave during class lectures, discussions, and seat work? What do students to at the end of class?
2. Peer Groups: Who associates with whom? Who are the "leaders"? Who doesn't seem to fit? Are there behavior problems? Who contributes and who does not?

B. The Teacher
What does the teacher do? Look at the following key behaviors:
1. What kind of instructional strategies does the teacher use?
2. What type of feedback does the teacher give to the students?
3. What kind of expectations are given by the teacher either in verbal or nonverbal messages?

Complete the task by synthesizing your observations into a written report. The focus on your report should be on providing insights into the hidden curriculum of the school.

REFERENCES

Coleman, J.; Campbell, E.; Hobson, D.; McPartland, J.; Mood, A.; Weinfield, F.; and York, R. (1966). *Equality of educational opportunity*. Washington, D.C.: U.S. Government Printing Office.

Dreeban, R. (1968). *On what is learned in school*. Reading, Mass.: Addison-Wesley.

Felt, M. C. (1985). *Improving our schools: Thirty-three studies that inform local action*. Newton, Mass.: Educational Development Center.

Hauser, R. H.; Sewell, W. H.; and Alwin, D. F. (1976). High school effects on achievement. In W. H. Sewell, R. M. Hauser, and D. L. Featherman (Eds.), *Schooling and achievement in American society*. New York: Academic Press.

Hersch, R. H. (1984). *What makes some schools and teachers more effective?* Eugene, Ore.: Center for Educational Policy and Management.

Hersey, P., and Blanchard, K. (1976). *Situational leadership*. LaJolla, Calif.: Center for Leadership Studies.

Jencks, C.; Smith, J.; Acland, H.; Bane, M.; Cohen, D.; Gintis, H.; Heyns, B.; and Michelson, S. (1972). *Inequality: A reassessment of the effect of family and schooling in America*. New York: Basic Books.

Johnson, R.; Johnson, D.; Roy, P.; and Holubec, E. (1983). *Cooperative lerning*. Alexandria, Va.: Association for Supervision and Curriculum Development.

Lezotte, L. W.; Hathaway, D. V.; Miller, S. K.; Passalacqua, J.; and Brookover, W. B. (1980). *School learning climate and student achievement*. Lansing: Michigan State University.

Maslow, A. (1962). *Toward a psychology of being*. Princeton, N.J.: Van Nostrand Reinhold.

Rowe, M. B. (1969). *Science, silence, and sanctions.* New York: Columbia University.

Rutter, M.; Maughan, B.; Mortimore, P.; Ouston, J.; and Smith, A. (1979). *Fifteen thousand hours.* Cambridge, Mass.: Harvard University Press.

Schmuck, R. A., and Schmuck, P. A. (1971). *Group processes in the classroom.* Dubuque, Iowa: Wm. C. Brown.

Strodtbeck, F. L. (1971). The hidden curriculum in the middle-class home. In R. D. Strom (Ed.), *Teachers and the learning process.* Englewood Cliffs, N.J.: Prentice-Hall.

SUGGESTED READINGS

Cohen, M. (1987). Improving school effectiveness: Lessons from research. In Virginia Richardson-Koehler (Ed.) *Educators' handbook: a research perspective.* White Plains, N.Y.: Longman.

Lezotte, L. W., Hathaway, D. V., Miller, S. K., Passalacqua, J., and Brookover, W. B. (1980). *School learning climate and student achievement.* Lansing: Michigan State University.

Mergendoller, J. R., and Marchman, V. (1987). Friends and associates. In Virginia Richardson-Koehler (Ed.) *Educators' handbook: a research perspective.* White Plains, N.Y.: Longman.

Part **IV**

Emerging Concerns

13

Curriculum, Instruction, and Literacy

▶────────────────────────────────◀

OVERVIEW

▶ Why include a chapter on literacy in a text on curriculum and instruction? Our answer to that question is simple and unequivocal: Every teacher in every curricular area at every level needs to make literacy his or her primary educational goal. Teachers need to read, write, and use quantitative and qualitative thinking more than they apparently do. Students needs to read, write, and use quantitative and qualitative thinking more than they do. Improved literacy must be the quest of every school in the land. The school library/media center needs to become the *centerpiece* of every building, not an appendage. As our culture changes and as the technological revolution continues at a quick pace, the definition of literacy will keep expanding from its center of reading, writing, and arithmetic. What it means to be literate now and what it will mean to be literate in the future will surely change. This chapter explores the meaning of literacy and the demands of a literate society on teachers and students.

LITERACY

▶ The term *literacy* has come to signify the single most important concept in the process of education. Literacy rates are recorded by nations as a part of our planet's statistical profile. Rate of literacy, along with per capita income, caloric intake, doctors per thousand people, infant mortality, and life span are prime indicators of a nation's level of development.

What is meant by literacy? What are the characteristics of a literate person? Are there levels of literacy? What are the respective roles of schools and families in the promotion and nurturing of a more literate society? And how do changes in society (for example, the introduction of television, the video cassette recorder, and the microcomputer) affect the meaning of what it is to be literate? In this chapter, we will suggest some answers to these difficult questions.

Take a few moments to clarify your thoughts on the issue of literacy by responding to the following questions:

1. Write a brief definition of literacy.
2. What are some attributes or characteristics of a literate individual?
3. What are the benefits of literacy to the individual and to society?
4. How do societal changes (e.g., in technology) affect the definition of literacy?

We don't expect you to have definitive answers to the preceding questions at this point, but we do expect that you will continue to consider the centrality of the literacy issue in education. All other educational questions, such as methodology, grouping patterns, school organization, and specific content, are ultimately subordinate to the question of literacy.

► Literacy as a Coping Skill

The question of literacy was moot in the dim and distant past when there was no written word. Even as objects were given names and speech emerged, no one had any need of reading or writing. But from the time when someone drew a picture on a rock (the first book) or made a set of drawings on a cave wall (the first library), the literacy issue emerged. Over time, as direct representations of objects gradually became stylized representations of objects, not everyone could "read" or interpret them. Thus, people became labeled as "literate" or "illiterate."

As literal drawings gave way to pictographs, which gave way to words composed of letters, writing (and therefore reading) became more abstract, complex, and powerful. It also became harder to learn. Hence, in time, the division between the literate folks and the illiterate folks became one of few and many. But, on a day-to-day basis, it was no great handicap to be unable to read the relatively few "publications" written on stone, clay, sheepskin, or papyrus.

The invention of the printing press in the fifteenth century changed the possibilities for the masses to become literate. Eventually, government support of libraries (where books were accessible to ordinary people) came to play a role in the development of literate populations. Commerce and industry were catalysts toward enlarging the scope of literacy because of the need for workers who could read and write. The need for better educated workers brought about the creation of institutions to instruct large numbers of people. Schools, in the form that we know them, were born.

The technology of the printed word has expanded greatly in the twentieth century. Written messages are everywhere — in newspapers delivered to homes, in bookracks at grocery stores, on cereal boxes, and on television screens which carry satellite-beamed messages such as stock market reports.

Technology has also advanced the potential for oral and pictoral communication. Thus, movies, television, radio, tape recorders, and telephones have made it possible for individuals to acquire a wide range of information without being literate in the traditional sense of the word. In fact, it has been argued that literacy has suffered from the intrusion of television into people's lives. On the basis of his synthesis of educational research literature, Walberg (1984) has concluded that more than 10 hours of television viewing per week is harmful to academic progress. And although statistics vary, surveys indicate that American children watch an average of 25 to 35 hours of television per week. Senator Paul Simon of Illinois has assembled evidence that shows that the average child watches 27.3 hours of television per week and has seen 20,000 hours of television by the time he is sixteen years old. Simon states:

> Violence on television has risen more than 100% since 1980. From January to April (1985), prime time television averaged 13.8 acts of violence per hour. The average child between the ages of 2 and 11 views television 27.3 hours each week. By the time a person is 16, he or she has watched more than 20,000 hours of television, including 200,000 acts of violence, 50,000 of which are murders.

Teachers and parents who ignore such information do so at their peril. It is ironic that in a nation of free public libraries, more books per capita than any nation in history, and a school system open to all, we face a problem of a literacy rate lower than that of a generation ago.

Our definition of literacy is an expanded one that also includes mathematical literacy or what is sometimes called *numeracy*. Ancient methods of computation, such as placing stones in a jar to keep track of the number of sheep in a flock, or carving a niche in a piece of wood in order to make a record of the number of inlets the Eskimos had kayaked from home, were primitive but effective computers. Simple one-to-one correspondence methods of quantitative expression were improved upon with the invention of numerals, particularly the zero, which permitted greatly expanded forms of calculation. Numeracy was then able to take on abstract proportions somewhat analogous to the transformation from the pictograph to the written word. Mathematics, of course, is more universal in form than any written language, and for that reason, several mathematical equations were placed on the platinum record disk sent aboard the Voyager spacecraft with the hope that it might be intercepted by intelligent life forms beyond our solar system.

The invention of the transistor, the silicon memory chip, and advances in miniaturization have made generalized access to hand-held calculators and microcomputers possible in recent years. This new technology challenges old assumptions about repeated years of drill and practice in computation (adding, subtracting, etc.) as opposed to more conceptually oriented skills such as estimating and problem solving. The microcomputer, which will be further miniaturized and much more capable than its present-day counterpart, may eventually provide the student with complete libraries of information at his or her disposal. The emergence of the phrase *computer literacy* carries with it a watershed expansion of the term *literacy*.

▶ **The Literate Student**

Colonial America placed few demands on its citizens with respect to literacy. Some could read and write, but most could not. The birth of the nation as a sovereign and independent state brought few changes in this regard. To be sure, there were among the citizenry people whose advanced state of literacy seems remarkable even to this day. But for every Washington Irving or Thomas Jefferson, there were hundreds who simply were illiterate. This was true of the white, middle-class population in general, but it was nearly absolute in terms of the sizable slave population. But, as we noted earlier in this book, the mission of developing a literate society was clearly in place, and the mission's chosen vehicle was and is the public school.

But what happens when the complexity of the mission expands exponentially? Ichabod Crane's job description was a picture of clarity, compared to Michelle Comstock's, the teacher introduced in Chapter 3. At the center, the public expectation of each of these two imaginary teachers is pretty much the same: teach the children to read, write, and compute. It is the flying away from the center that makes Michelle's task so much less clear than Ichabod's. To illustrate this point, consider the fact that Michelle services a school community that is heterogeneous with respect to race, ethnicity, family structure, religion, socioeconomic status, and sense of purpose. Ichabod's clientele was far more similar than different in terms of these variables.

The student who emerges from today's schools (about 70 to 75 percent graduate from high school) will qualify as literate if he or she can demonstrate acceptable proficiency in what the Education Commission of the States calls the "Basics of Tomorrow." These basics are a useful guideline and springboard for discussion of the definition of literacy as a curricular goal in the latter stages of the twentieth century.

If we were to sketch a profile of the "literate student," that person would possess those skills and abilities listed in Table 13–1, which, at least from an academic standpoint, represent the quest. These basics give teachers an idealized standard toward which to strive. They are the shining, golden prize of teaching and learning. They are the ultimate educational reward because they are usable and salable in any unforseen context.

But for these basics to become reality, the curriculum must change and instruction must change. Whereas all of us would prefer to see things not as they are, but as they might be, the realities of classroom life speak to a less spirited commitment to literacy. Goodlad (1984) writes:

> A disturbing surprise in our data is the limited amount of time students in our sample were observed writing and reading. In the eyes of some people the reason for having schools is to teach reading, writing, spelling, and mathematics. A substantial amount of student time in the early school years is spent in writing. But much of this, as we know from other studies, is answering questions in workbooks, filling in blank spaces in short narratives, and so on. The frequency of even this kind of writing at the secondary level was about two-thirds as much in junior high and half as much in senior high classes, as compared with elementary classes. Students' experience with writing decreased, then, as they moved from the upper elementary to the senior high school grades.
> The state of reading in the classrooms we observed seemed quite dismal.

TABLE 13-1 The Basics of Tomorrow

Evaluation and analysis skills
Critical thinking
Problem-solving strategies
Synthesis
Application
Creativity
Decision making
Communication through a variety of modes

Source: Educational Commission of the States, 1982.

Exclusive of the common practice of students taking turns reading orally from a common text, reading occupied about 6% of class time at the elementary level and then dropped off to 3% and 2% for junior and senior highs, respectively. If our young people are not reading in school, where are they reading, and how much?

▶ A Goal Structure for Literacy

There is widespread agreement in our society on the issue of literacy. All of us desire an educated citizenry comprised of people who read, write, speak, and listen well. The road to literacy begins at home, but the schools must ensure that the road is broadened and extended to far horizons. An overriding goal of all classroom teachers is to determine how *best* to provide literacy to their students. However teachers accomplish that formidable task, they will need to think through their (1) curricular goals, (2) instructional strategies, and (3) methods of evaluation. All three of these considerations require careful planning.

▶ Instructional Objectives

▶ The first step in planning is to clarify instructional objectives. The most basic questions one can pose in this regard are:

1. What should students *know* about language as a result of instruction?
2. What language *skills* should students gain as a result of instruction?
3. How should students feel about the power of *language* as a result of instruction?

These three questions address the basic issues of knowledge, skills, and values. Of course, students learn from a variety of sources, including the home, other institutions such as clubs and church, television, theater, newspapers, magazines, and friends. It would be misleading to assume either all the credit or all the blame for their progress or lack of it in the area of literacy. But school instruction does represents the only consistent, nonrandom source of learning for all in our society.

▶ Growing Concern for Literacy

A growing concern exists among both professional educators and the public over the issue of literacy. When United Nations' statistics reveal that the United States fails to rank in the upper one-third of a list of more than 150 nations of the world with respect to literacy, the concern appears to be appropriate and justified (1986). Although the purposes of formal education are many, few would argue that literacy's place is at or near the top of any list. Literacy has been a primary goal of American education since the early days of colonial schooling when masters were paid to teach children to learn to read the Scriptures.

In the most basic sense, the definition of literacy is the ability to read and write. Such a definition, however, merely begins to clarify the issue of literacy from a pedagogical standpoint. A level of literacy called *functional literacy* is sometimes used as a "least common denominator" to describe the ability of adults to carry out such tasks as to follow the directions on a medicine bottle, to complete a job application form, or to read an election ballot.

Another sense in which the term *literacy* is used is with reference to the "literate" individual. Such a person is well-read, writes with fluency, has a wide range of general knowledge, and is able to use mathematics with problem-solving proficiency. This expansive description, however idyllic, vague, and elusive, is the one to which the schools must naturally aspire. It is important to note here that the definition of literacy is a condition that implies a breadth of knowledge and abilities and not a depth of specialization in a subject or skills area. The latter represents advanced study, training, or coursework necessary for particular vocations or special interests that an individual may pursue.

We have established three conditions or levels of education in the development of an enlightened citizenry. It is well to note them for the purpose of establishing a clearer educational philosophy. They are basic literacy, the literate individual, and specialization.

Basic Literacy
Basic literacy represents the acquisition of the skills of reading, writing, and mathematics at a certain level. To distinguish someone who has those skills from someone who does not (or who is, in fact, illiterate), it is necessary to specify what is meant by basic literacy. For example, such an individual would have the ability to read at a sixth-grade level of comprehension; to solve simple mathematical problems involving addition, subtraction, multiplication, and division; and to write a paragraph. (We will pursue this topic later in this chapter with a focus on the controversial issue of teacher literacy.) There is, of course, no universally agreed upon level of what constitutes basic literacy.

Basic or functional literacy is crucial at two levels: individual and societal. Basic literacy represents a utilitarian goal in that, for the individual, it is typically considered a prerequisite for all but the most menial jobs. At the societal level, the person lacking basic literacy is perceived as dependent on others for his or her welfare. No absolute cause and effect correlation exists between functional literacy and success in the job market. Certainly other factors beyond literacy are contributors to a person's success or lack of success at earning a living. Pragmatic Americans have often been accused of attempting to tie formal education to the market place as though jobs were really the ultimate reason for learning.

Basic literacy exists on a continuum of gradually increased sophistication rather than as a state of skill development. The purpose of teaching the skills of basic literacy is not one of ends, but one of means by which an individual is set free to pursue an independent, self-directed course of learning. The transition from the acquisition of basic skills toward deeper levels of literacy is obviously a difficult one for many individuals to make. It is clear to even the most casual observer that, for example, the number of people who *can* read is greater than the number of people who *do* read in any depth. One of the most perplexing challenges facing any teacher is that of helping students move beyond the skill level of literacy to the values level of literacy. Once someone internalizes the *value* of reading, writing, and problem solving, he or she is well on the way to becoming a literate individual.

The Literate Individual

The desired outcome of our educational system is the literate individual. It is a successful teacher who has directly contributed to a student's desire to learn. The many hours devoted by our schools to instruction in basic skills are meaningful only if they lead to a greater dividend than skills mastery. Yet, research tends to indicate that classroom instructional time is overwhelmingly devoted to teaching students at levels of rote memorization and factual information, and that it rarely transcends this plane toward the exploration of ideas and values or even toward the simple applications of skills to students' everyday lives (Lipman, Sharp, and Oscanyan, 1980).

It can be reasonably assumed that without basic skills, people are denied the opportunity to improve their levels of literacy. But it is also reasonable to assume that students who are taught to view learning as a catalogue of facts and skills unrelated to applications, ideas, and values will probably develop little love of independent learning. If this point were a minor one or one obvious to all, we could pass over it rather quickly. But the evidence is clear that this idea has not been incorporated into the curriculum except by a few perceptive teachers.

Ironically, the goal of advanced literacy is widely subscribed to by professionals and the public. The contradiction occurs at the instructional level, and it will take a major restructuring of the school curriculum in order to improve the linkage between classroom reality and the idealized goal of an increasingly literate society. If our educational goal is to develop better and more involved readers, writers, and problem solvers, then instruction and curriculum will have to be more directly linked to this goal than is presently the case.

Specialization

A third aspect of literacy, in-depth skill and knowledge in a specialized area or subject, is important to the well-being of an individual from both a personal growth standpoint and with respect to vocational success. Such literacy ought to be encouraged and prepared for at the public school level. However, we feel that specialized training is not the proper function of the public school, and that vocational tracks or attempts at in-depth academic specialization prior to high-school graduation are, in fact, generally counterproductive to the development of a truly literate society. On the other hand, the teacher who exposes a student to the beauty of mathematics, the enjoyment of good literature, the thrill of scientific exploration or discovery, and the power of art and music may well be responsible for initiating rewarding careers and lifelong leisure pursuits.

CULTURAL LITERACY

▶   In a recent article titled, "Student Ability to Look It Up Isn't Enough," syndicated columnist James J. Kilpatrick articulated to the public an issue that has drawn increasing attention among professional educators. That issue is the perceived, documented, and lamented decline in an area of student learning which has come to be called *cultural literacy*. A powerful lineup of critics thinks that the skills orientation to the reading, history, and language curricula as advocated by the vast majority of teacher educators and classroom teachers has failed miserably. The critics include such luminaries as Diane Ravitch, Alan Bloom, E. D. Hirsch, Bruno Bettelheim, Mortimer Adler, Chester Finn, and Lynne Cheney.

Basically, what these critics of "process-based" (as opposed to "knowledge-based") approaches to learning are saying is that American students don't know very much, and that their ignorance dooms them to a level of cultural illiteracy which threatens the standard set forth so eloquently in *Losing Battles* by Eudora Welty, who had her teacher protagonist, Miss Julia Mortimer, feel, "She didn't ever doubt but that all worth preserving is going to be preserved, and all we had to do was keep it going, right from where we are, one teacher on down to the next."

Graduates of teacher education programs have for years basked in the assurance (given to them by their methods professors) that "facts" and "dates" and "names" are not at all the essence of good teaching. What is crucial, they were told, is the ability to look up information. Beyond that, they were told to teach skills and concepts, not mere knowledge. Now the point is made that cultural literacy, knowledge held in common by the people of a society, is in fact the essence of meaningful learning. Of course, there is nothing new about the process-versus-product debate. It has been around at least from the time of Socrates. What is new is the recent evidence marshalled and articulated by those who advocate more "traditional," knowledge-based learning.

Before we took at some of the emergent research findings related to the topic of literacy, let us examine the results of test taking by American students. The Congress has mandated the administration of nationwide assessment procedures in the form of the National Assessment of Educational Progress (NAEP). Results of recent pilot testing of seventeen-year-olds' knowledge of American history indicate that two-thirds of the students tested could not place the Civil War within the period 1850–1900; half could not identify Churchill or Stalin (NAEP, 1987). Further, the College Board (1984) has documented that the breakdown of scores over 600 between 1972 and 1984 has shown a decline from 11.4 percent to 7.3 percent (Hirsch, 1987) on the Scholastic Aptitude Test.

These results will come as no surprise to the reader. For years, we have read of declining test scores. The data are explained away in a dozen different ways by those who defend the job the schools are doing in the face of impossible odds. The data are used by others to condemn "progressive" education (a form of education in the tradition of Rousseau and Dewey that is actually hard to find in today's schools).

Writing in *The American Scholar* (1984), Diane Ravitch observes:

> What the various task forces and national commissions are now saying is that our educational systems must take on the job of making all young people literate, and their definition includes both cultural and scientific literacy. No one knows whether it can be done, because we have never tried to do it on a mass scale. If we make the attempt, it should be done with full knowledge of where we have gone astray in the past. At one extreme, the perfervid traditionalists have been content to educate those at the top without regard to the welfare of the majority of students; at the other, the perfervid progressives have cooperated in dividing and diluting the curriculum, which left the majority with an inadequate education.

Few teachers and administrators take extreme positions on issues of curriculum philosophy. As practitioners, they tend to be susceptible to fads because their persuasion comes more from the media and societal whims than from educational research. Because fads are so readily and often replaced by succeeding fads, little real improvement can be realized short of "philosophical commitment to education that is sound enough to withstand the erratic dictates of fashion" (Ravitch, 1984).

Research by R. C. Anderson, P. D. Pearson, and others at the University of Illinois has led to the development of a meaning-driven model of reading comprehension (and thus a great step forward in the quest for literacy) based on a phenomenon known as *schema* theory. *Schema* theory suggests that we use words as referent points for larger categories of meaning. Thus, if you were to read the word *whale* in a sentence, there is much more at stake than decoding the word. Images, experiences, recollections, and abstract thought are also brought to bear, in varying amounts by the reader. In other words, preexisting information is crucial in order for the reader to move beyond a mere mechanical exercise. As Anderson and Pearson observe:

> The full development of schema theory as a model for representing how knowledge is stored in human memory had to await the revolution in our conception of how humans process information spurred by the thinking of computer scientists doing simulations of human cognition (1985).

Thus, the stage is set for the persuasive argument that the context established by the reader's memory is the crucial link to comprehension. This point is illustrated with the following passage, quoted in Hirsch (1987):

> The research . . . has just shown that our minds have a remarkable ability to change initial schemata according to the situations in which we find ourselves. Such adjustments are largely unconscious, but one can perceive the pattern of the quick adjustments we make even with isolated sentences, as Anderson has suggested in the following passage (Anderson, 1980):
>
>   1. The punter kicked the ball.
>   2. The baby kicked the ball.
>   3. The golfer kicked the ball.

Because, as Anderson suggests, we interpret the world through a basic set of schemata, the adjustment from football, to a large baby ball, to a perhaps angry golfer, is relatively easy and automatic.

Now consider the following paragraph that is designed to illustrate the role of the structure of a reader's knowledge in doing the information processing necessary for comprehension to occur, in other words, the set of schemata that the reader must possess.

When Ulysses S. Grant and Robert E. Lee met in the parlor of a modest house at Appomattox Courthouse, Virginia, on April 9, 1865, to work out the terms of surrender of Lee's army of Northern Virginia, a great chapter in American life came to a close, and a great new chapter began. These men were bringing the Civil War to its virtual finish.

Regarding this passage from his book, *Cultural Literacy,* E. D. Hirsch (1987) writes:

These words are like the leaves outside my window. If I do not know how they connect with larger schemata, I cannot make sense of them. On the other hand, the schemata I need are rather abstract entities that do not require profound knowledge. Consider how little detail there is in the schematic information needed to read the passage:

1. America fought a Civil War.
2. The two sides were the Union and the Confederacy.
3. Grant was the chief general for the Union.
4. Lee was the chief general for the Confederacy.
5. The Union won.

The points that Hirsch and others who subscribe to the idea of schematic information processing are: (1) in order to comprehend a passage, you must bring information to that passage; (2) the better informed you are about what you read, the easier it is for you to comprehend what you read; and (3) there is a cumulative effect to this process over time which expands one's cultural literacy. Significant research evidence that this is the case has been developed across a variety of situations (Bartlett, 1932; Ross and Bower, 1981; Hirsch and Harrington, 1978; Spiro, 1980; Anderson and Pearson, 1984).

Think about your own schemata as you read a book like this one. References have been made throughout to such educational leaders as John Dewey, Jerome Bruner, Rousseau, Jean Piaget, and many others. What level of information do you bring to your reading about these people? Obviously, the more information you possess about them, the easier it is for you to comprehend and recall allusions made to them from time to time in this text.

Thus, the road to cultural literacy for children is taken by giving them a rich background of useful, culturally enriching information through stories, films, their own reading and other sources. One of the abiding criticisms of school textbooks is that in their quest for "readability" they have been "dumbed" down to the point of inanity (Ravitch, 1985).

In the report of the National Endowment for the Humanities titled *American Memory,* author Lynne Cheney (1988) writes,

By their nature, the humanities disciplines ought to be the easiest to bring to everyone. While some students will need more help than others with the language of Shakespeare's plays, for example, the themes that animate the plays—love, honor, betrayal, revenge—are familiar to all and interesting to all. . . . 'To make the best that has been thought and known in the world current everyone' is the Matthew Arnold stated the goal. No other ambition suits a democracy well.

All teachers and administrators support the idea of a literate generation of students. Who would not? That literacy is the number-one task of the schools is a point that we have tried to make not only in this chapter, but throughout this text. The teacher's role is pivotal in such a quest. The time has come to put the "process-product" controversy behind us and to find the appropriate curricular balance that will achieve this fundamental goal.

PROMOTING LITERACY

► The following is a list of seven broad suggestions for the promotion of literacy. Taken seriously and implemented across the curriculum, they will pay dividends.

1. Teachers and administrators need to show students that *they themselves read*. Share ideas with them from books you have read. Display books and quotations from books around the room. Allow for reading time in class (not from the textbook but from books that relate to the subject(s) you teach, e.g., biographies). Occasionally read stimulating book excerpts to the class.
2. *Discuss ideas.* Athletics, mathematics, music, or any subject has controversial and philosophical ideas embedded in it. Try to promote open discussions that will draw out students' thoughts. You may need to work on structured discussion procedures such as having students paraphrase answers, increase their response time, author questions, work as partners, and so on.
3. *Make applications.* Interesting ideas ought to lend themselves to interesting applications. It is useful to attempt to relate mathematics, geography, biology, or whatever, to the real world. The daily newspaper, for example, will furnish applications to almost any subject(s) you teach. Curricular subjects themselves are seldom connected

to one another by teachers. If they were, all kinds of applications of science to English, social studies to math, art to science, and so on, could be readily made, thus giving a "wholeness" to learning.

4. *Increase students' opportunities to express themselves.* This can best be accomplished by restructured group sizes. Experiment with groups of two, three, or four in size. Give students questions to discuss in the less threatening, greater-individual-input atmosphere of small groups. Even with a small group strategy you can lead a discussion by bringing the class together every ten minutes or so for sharing of ideas.

5. *Promote reflective thought.* Students spend far more time *doing* English, science, social studies, and so on, than *thinking about* what they are learning. Allow students time to share, orally or in written form, their thoughts and feelings about assignments and activities. It is useful to set aside a few minutes toward the close of a class period or at the end of the week to provide opportunities for reflection, analysis, and synthesis. By doing this, you signal students that you want them to be thinkers and appraisers, and that you are willing to provide an open atmosphere in which their ideas count.

6. *Expect students to read.* Reading requirements need to be a part of every school subject. Agreed-upon, school-wide goals must exist to promote reading by students. Class time must be set aside for reading because it may be, for some students (those who most need it), the only affordable opportunity they receive.

7. *Expect students to write.* Writing requirements need to be a part of every school subject. Note taking, journals, essays, and written reports must be expected of all students. Teachers whose instructional area is something other than English should actively support the idea that writing is crucial for every student in every subject.

These seven strategies are simple and relatively easy to put into everyday practice. We encourage you to try them. If you do, the result should be favorable.

SUMMARY

▶ In this chapter we have attempted to persuade you that literacy is the most fundamental, pervasive goal of the school curriculum. Literacy is the responsibility of all teachers at all levels and in all subjects. It is the thread that weaves its way through academic, affective, and psychomotor skills. We define literacy from its most basic skills of reading, writing, and arithmetic, to its more complex forms that involve application to literature, the arts and sciences, humanities, and social sciences. We stress the point that literacy is a changing, dynamic concept, and that cultural and technological transformations bring about a restructuring on its very definition. In that sense, literacy is the most basic tool we have for coping with the demands and challenges of our society. Although the establishment and expansion of a literate society is not the teacher's job alone, the school does play a key role in fostering an enlightened citizenry. In this sense there must be a trickle-down effect from teacher to student where teachers model the very attributes of the literate individuals they would have each of their students become.

ACTIVITIES

1. What are five things teachers can do to increase the level of literacy of the students they teach?
2. How would you assess your own level of literacy? What are some specific steps you can take to make yourself a more literate person?
3. The microcomputer has contributed to an expansion of our definition of literacy. Select any area of the curriculum and speculate on the potential impact of the microcomputer on teaching and learning in that subject.
4. How can schools and families work together to promote literacy?
5. Why do you think literacy levels are not higher than they are presently in the United States? What do you think are the long-term consequences to a society of a declining literacy rate?

REFERENCES

Anderson, R. C.; Hiebert, E. H.; Scott, J. A.; and Wilkinson, I. A. G. (1985). *Becoming a nation of readers: The report of the commission on reading.* Urbana: University of Illinois Center for the Study of Reading.

Anderson, R. C., and Pearson, P. D. (1984). "A schema-theoretic view of basic processes in reading comprehension," in P. D. Pearson (Ed.), *Handbook of research research.* New York: Longman.

Bartlett, F. C. (1932). *Remembering.* Cambridge, England: Cambridge University Press.

Bourne, L. E., et al. (1986). *Cognitive processes,* 2nd ed. Englewood Cliffs, N.J.: Prentice-Hall.

Cheney, L. V. (1988). *American memory: A report on the humanities in the nation's public schools.* Washington, D.C.: National Endowment for the Humanities.

Gardner, H. (1983). *Frames of mind: The theory of multiple intelligence.* New York: Basic Books.

Goodlad, J. I. (1984). *A place called school.* New York: McGraw-Hill.

Hirsch, E. D. (1987). *Cultural literacy: What every American needs to know.* Boston: Houghton Mifflin.

Lipman, M.; Sharp, A. M.; and Oscanyan, F. S. (1980). *Philosophy in the classroom,* 2nd ed. Philadelphia: Temple University Press.

Ravitch, D. (Spring 1984). "The continuing crisis in education." *The American Scholar,* 183–193.

Resnick, D. B., and Resnick, L. B. (August 1977). "The Nature of Literacy and Historical Exploration." *Harvard Educational Review,* 370–385.

Ross, B., and Bower, G. (1973). *Human associative memory.* New York: Wiley.

Spiro, R. (1980). "Constructive processes in prose comprehension and recall," in R. Spiro et al. (Eds.), *Theoretical issues in reading comprehension.* Hillsdale, N.J.: Erlbaum.

United Nations Education, Scientific, and Cultural Council. (1986). *Figures for literacy rates.* New York: United Nations Publications.

Walberg, H. J. (May 1984). Improving the productivity of America's schools. *Educational Leadership,* 19–36.

SUGGESTED READINGS

Anderson, J.; and Tierney, R. J. (1984). *Learning to read in American schools: Basal readers and content texts.* Hillsdale, N.J.: Erlbaum.

Anderson, R. C.; Hiebert, E. H.; Scott, J. A.; and Wilkinson, I. A. G. (1985). *Becoming a nation of readers: The report of the commission on reading.* Washington, D.C.: National Institute of Education.

Cooperman, P. (1978). *The literacy hoax.* New York: William Morrow.

Hirsch, E. D. (1987). *Cultural literacy: What every American needs to know.* Boston: Houghton Mifflin.

Huey, E. B. (1968). *The psychology and pedagogy of reading.* Cambridge, Mass.: MIT Press (originally published in 1908).

Nist, J. A. (1966). *A structured history of English.* New York: St. Martin's Press.

14

Critical Thinking

► When teachers are asked, "What are you really trying to accomplish with these students?" the answer is inevitably, "I'm trying to teach them to think." All teachers have multiple goals for their students, including knowledge of subject matter, a sense of abiding moral purpose, and mastery of basic skills. But thinking is always at or near the top of any list of priorities.

As popular as thinking appears to be on teachers' agendas, there is widespread speculation that it is seldom taught in any concerted manner. If indeed thinking is taught, it is as a by-product of content and of such "basic" skills as computation, decoding, and grammar. Thus, one is left to assume that teachers feel that effective thinking follows naturally from a study of such content as mathematics, history, or biology. One assumes that teachers think that addition and division skills lead logically to mathematical problem solving; that learning to sound out words leads one ultimately to literary analysis; or that a knowledge of spelling, syntax, and punctuation leads one ultimately to literary expression. These are enormous assumptions that, in fact, defy simple logic. They are assumptions that at the very least represent a confusion of means and ends in the process of articulating the curriculum. Human beings can hardly be kept from thinking. A classroom filled with students is also filled with thoughts. But we are referring here to task-related or subject-related thinking that is of the higher order, known by such labels as *critical thinking, problem solving, creative thinking,* and *reflective thinking.* Many teachers espouse these kinds of thinking in their goal statements but they appear to be taught only in the most random and miscellaneous fashion.

This concept is supported by a long list of descriptive studies based on classroom observations. Among the most current research is John Goodlad's book, *A Place Called School* (1983). Goodlad has concluded, for example, that rarely do teachers help students make connections between facts and ideas. He notes that only about 1 percent of teacher talk invites such open student response as reasoning or opinion. This finding is consistent with those of Philip Jackson's (1968) research of the 1960s and with dozens of other lessor known descriptive studies of classroom behavior.

Additional documentation of the failure by most teachers to teach effective thinking is found in student test results. Scholastic Aptitude Test scores showed a steady decline from 1963 to 1983, and when scores finally did begin to show improvement, in 1984, the improvements were found at basic levels. Higher level outcomes such as reasoning and application skills continue to decline.

CRITICAL THINKING: WHAT IS IT?

▶   The report of the Education Commission of the States (1983) concluded that " the pattern is clear: the percentage of students achieving higher order skills is declining." Declines in test scores on the National Assessment of Educational Progress (NAEP) tests were demonstrated by seventeen-year-olds in reading, writing, and mathematics. The percentage of seventeen-year-olds who could analyze a written passage for mood dropped from 51 percent to 41 percent between 1971 and 1980. The percentage of seventeen-year-olds who were judged competent on the NAEP in their ability to write persuasively dropped from 21 percent to 15 percent during this time period. And the percentage of these students who could apply mathematics in problem-solving applications declined from 33 percent to 29 percent. The report of The National Institute of Education (NIE) on *Becoming a Nation of Readers* (1984) concludes that:

> Students seem satisfied with their initial interpretations of what they have read and seem genuinely puzzled at requests to explain or defend their points of view. Few students could provide more than superficial responses to such tasks, and even the "better" responses showed little evidence of well-developed problem solving strategies or critical thinking skills.

The evidence is clear, abundant, and irrefutable: Higher level thinking skills are not being acquired by students. The argument that what is learned does not necessarily equal what was taught is perhaps a way of acknowledging that teachers may be doing more than we give them credit for. These poor educational outcomes might also be attributed in some measure to the pervasive influence of television, the disintegration of traditional family life, the increased percentage of minorities in the public schools, or a host of other factors. In fact, test scores for both the SAT and ACT have shown slight improvement through the years from 1982 to 1986.

But it is the case that most classes in the elementary and secondary school curricula are devoted to learning the most basic skills and the most fundamental levels of subject matter. Analytical thought, planning skills, critical thinking, real world applications, and reflective thinking are seldom taught directly to students. Take a moment to consider the following list of topics generated by the Education Commission of the States as the "Basics of Tomorrow":

1. Evaluation and analysis skills
2. Critical thinking
3. Problem-solving strategies
4. Organization and reference skills
5. Synthesis
6. Application
7. Creativity
8. Decision making given incomplete information
9. Communication skills through a variety of modes

These basics are simply not dominant in the curriculum of the average classroom in the average school.

It is easy, of course, to point the finger of blame at teachers for the obvious lack of intelligent energy present in the classrooms. After all, the classroom is where the rubber meets the road, and if students aren't being challenged there, then any encounters with higher level thinking are random, left to enrichment classes or to the occasional home where probing discussions take place around the dinner table.

Without necessarily excusing teachers for failing to connect facts to concepts or to challenge students to reason and to offer thoughtfully considered opinions on important issues, let us turn our attention to a dimension of this problem that may be beyond teachers' grasp alone to solve.

It may well be that a large part of the problem lies within the deep structure of the school setting. If this is so, then flights of creativity by individual teachers, while admirable and helpful, can never amount to much more than isolated, idiosyncratic efforts against a less inspired backdrop. For the moment, let's explore this alternate hypothesis by examining some aspects of the structure of schools themselves. There is certainly reason to suspect that teachers may be restricted by the very context in which they perform their daily chores.

In his book, *The Third Wave,* Alvin Toffler (1981) wrote of the profound changes that came about as Western societies moved beyond the first wave of agrarianism into the second wave of industrialism. Many of these changes have had lasting effects on the structure of our schools. Schools are dismissed during the entire summer presumably so that students can do farm work, although less than 5 percent of our population lives on farms. But other than that, our schools stand as monuments to another revolution — industrialism.

The industrial revolution occurred in North America during the nineteenth century. It brought with it far more than the mass-production factory system, but that was its most tangible result. The population of the United States and Canada increased greatly during this time, partly due to immigration. Schools became more necessary than ever because parents were working away from home, and there was little else for young people to do, particularly in the expanding urban centers.

Industrialism brought about a standardized, synchronized, specialized society. Not only were mass-produced products standard-ized, and therefore interchangeable, but so were the workers, who responded in Pavlovian style to the synchronization of the time clock, the eight-hour shift, and the bells that sounded the call to work. Specialization at the professional level eventually became more and more significant. Bigger became synonymous with better, as people, energy, production, and power were concentrated and centralized. With the larger, more concentrated systems of production (whether factories or schools), specialists could give their complete attention to small parts of a whole system. Experts were free to deal with their speciality in depth, while completely ignoring the broader issues.

This fragmentation of learning into subject matter compartments taught by specialists is obvious to anyone in secondary-level educa-tion, but it is just as real at the elementary level. The same teacher who teaches children math at 10:00 A.M. rarely connects that subject to the social studies he or she teaches the same children at 1:00 P.M.

The preceding list of the "Basics of Tomorrow" is much more applicable to an interdisciplinary approach (where subjects are in-tegrated) rather than to the separate-subjects curriculum, which is the real foundation of the daily curriculum of the schools. But against the apparently insurmountable odds of changing the basic structure of the schools, we will offer in the following pages, a modest, workable agenda for the implementation of higher level thinking skills. The several recommendations that we will make are based on research findings generated from classroom settings. Systematic, widespread efforts to implement conceptual skills in classrooms are the most realistic hope for improving students' abilities to think more effectively and productively.

What can teachers do to improve students' thinking? How can they help their students to, in Jerome Bruner's words, "cross that barrier from learning into thinking"? The first two steps on the road to improvement are (1) a clarification of one's own thoughts about teaching thinking and (2) a commitment on one's part to develop a teaching-learning environment conducive to effective thinking.

A THEORY OF EDUCATIONAL PRODUCTIVITY

▶ It is simplistic and misleading to assume that teachers alone are ultimately responsible for students' effective thinking or lack of it. It is true that the teacher's role in the promotion of productive thinking is basic in that he or she has direct access to young people for considerable periods of time each day. But researcher Herbert Walberg (1984), whose review of over 3,000 studies in education has enlarged the scope of the factors of educational productivity, indicates that we may be failing to take into account some variables that have largely untapped potential for effective learning. Walberg separates these variables, some of which are obvious, into three categories: (1) student aptitude, (2) instruction, and (3) environment.

▶ Student Aptitude

One student aptitude variable affecting achievement is *ability* or *prior achievement,* as measured by the typical standardized tests such as the Iowa Tests of Basic Skills or the California Achievement Tests. Many people mistakenly believe that the abilities students evidence on these tests are largely inherent or fixed in place, but the fact that the Japanese have raised their mean IQ scores in recent years ought to put that notion to rest.

A second student aptitude variable is *development,* as indexed by chronological age or stage of maturation. Why is it that a six-year-old fails to acquire expected reading skills and is referred to a remedial program? Perhaps it has nothing to do with ability and everything to do with development. In Sweden, where boys begin school at age seven, initial reading instruction is less traumatic simply because of the maturation factor. *When* we teach a concept or skill is probably as important as *how* we teach it, but given our age-graded system of curriculum and instruction, little is actually done to diagnose and prescribe learning on the basis of an individual's developmental level.

The third student aptitude factor is *motivation,* as evidenced by a student's willingness to persevere intensively on learning tasks. Often teachers "measure" student motivation by such random observations as the tendency to raise one's hand in response to teacher questions, willingness to turn in assignments on time, or showing evidence of a "cheerful" attitude. But motivation to learn, especially at a level of perseverance in the face of complexity and difficulty, must be teacher-enhanced. This was demonstrated conclusively by a problem-solving curriculum for children developed by the National Science Foundation, where it was discovered that the primary reason that the units failed to be carried out to completion was a loss of teacher interest in the unit (USMES, 1975)!

▶ Instruction

Instructional variables affecting learning outcomes include: (1) the *amount of time* students are engaged in learning and (2) the *quality* of instructional experience, including psychological and curricular dimensions of teaching and learning.

Amount of learning time as a curricular variable quickly engages us in the old time-wasting argument over quality of time versus quantity of time. We will treat quality in a few moments, but for now, let us focus on the ratio of time teachers *have* for instruction versus time they actually *use* for instruction. Because of the vast differences in ability, motivation, and efficiency among students, it is axiomatic that much of a student's time is spent waiting—waiting because he doesn't understand how to proceed or waiting because she finished the work in less time than was allotted. Also, announcements, attendance, transitions between classes or subjects, discipline problems, and other factors serve to reduce actual instructional time. Research indicates that engaged learning time is often as low as 50 percent of the time allotted for instruction. Teachers rarely are trained in techniques of effective time management, and even a five-minute loss per class hour per day results in a net loss of about 15 to 20 days of instruction in a 180-day school year (Goodlad, 1983). Arguments for lengthening the school year are probably appropriate, but far more can be done with the time that is presently available.

The second instructional variable, *quality,* is far more elusive. But even here, there are some simple steps that can be taken to enhance effective thinking. Teachers need to commit themselves to the consistent use of those psychological concepts that have been proven to enhance instruction. For example, Walberg's (1984) research shows that

Skinnerian reinforcement in the learning process, which can mean anything from a pat on the back to a carefully conceived long-term record-keeping system for charting a student's spelling progress, is of paramount importance. Students who are learning new material with apparent ease need to have their work regimen accelerated so that they can, in Madeline Hunter's words, "learn more faster." Quality of instruction is also enhanced when teachers make every attempt to connect facts to ideas, something Goodlad (1983) says they rarely do. To learn that in 1492 Columbus sailed the ocean blue is to learn a fact. But to connect his epic voyage to the technological revolution that brought about the Caravelle type of ship and improved instruments of navigation, with the revolution occurring in space travel today is a way of teaching concepts. Thus, in addition to a curriculum filled with content, it is necessary to have a curriculum that encompasses motivation, transfer, reinforcement, concept formation, and key ideas.

▶ Environment

The third cluster of factors, which Walberg (1984) labels *environment,* encompasses the largely overlooked curriculum of (1) the home, (2) the classroom social group, (3) the peer group outside of school, and (4) use of out-of-school time, especially television watching.

Our culture has done a marvelous job of fragmenting peoples' lives to the point that we often fail to consider that there might be meaningful relationships among school, home, church, youth activity groups, the neighborhood, and so on. If students are to think more effectively and productively, teachers are going to have to intervene in the home environment. Two obvious interventions are (1) the assigning of meaningful homework so that academic learning time is reinforced and increased and (2) letters home to parents informing them of ways they can be supportive of and involved in the curriculum at school (Gray, 1984).

The classroom social group is a powerful tool for good educational effects if it is properly harnessed. Out of control, it is incredibly damaging to productive learning. The work of David and Roger Johnson (1984) in the area of cooperative learning illustrates the positive social and academic effects that accrue when students are taught to help each other. In addition, the literature of effective teaching supports orderly, teacher-controlled environments. The report to the National Science Board, *Educating Americans for the 21st Century* (1983), states that the:

> breakdown of order in the classroom is one of the more disturbing manifestations of today's educational crisis. . . . Action should be taken to maintain a classroom environment that is conducive to teaching and learning that includes:

► the adoption by schools of vigorous discipline policies which reflect goals and expectations.

► clear, written statements of the rules.

► greater support by parents of discipline in the school and classroom.

The message is clear: Teachers, not anyone else, need to run classrooms. They must be humane, they must solicit students' ideas and feelings, and they must develop links with administration and community. But let there be no ambiguity about the teacher's authority as director of curriculum and instruction in the classroom.

The peer group outside the school and outside the home has become an increasingly influential force in our culture in recent years. For the most part, it is counterproductive to the educational process. The schools would undoubtedly benefit greatly from a renaissance of young peoples' groups such as 4-H, YMCA, YWCA, Boys and Girls Clubs, Boy Scouts, Girl Scouts, church activity groups, and so forth, where positive goal structures are espoused by young people and adult volunteers. The Soviet Union, China, and Japan are leading examples of nations that have managed to create such positive youth programs that instill pride and a sense of worthwhile activity needed so desperately by children and adolescents.

The effects of television viewing on children's thinking have been widely argued. Studies indicate that young people watch an average of between twenty to forty hours of television per week. Walberg's (1984) own conclusion is that viewing in excess of ten hours per week is harmful to academic progress. If teachers want to raise academic standards, they are going to have to convince parents to limit their children's television viewing time.

These nine factors of the curriculum, some obvious, others less so, identified by Walbert are a significant point of departure for any teacher who says to himself or herself, "I'm going to resolve from this day forth to make effective thinkers out of every one of these kids."

THE COMMITMENT TO CRITICAL THINKING

► A commitment to higher level thinking is worthy because it functions as a goal structure for planning, teaching, and evaluation. It is also important for teachers to decide what *they* mean by higher level thinking. An example of what we mean by this is illustrated by the definitions of three related but different types of higher level thinking operations: critical thinking, creative thinking, and problem solving (Costa, 1985).

► *Critical thinking:* using basic thinking processes to analyze arguments and generate insight into particular meanings and interpretations.

► *Creative thinking:* the act of being able to produce along new and original lines by employing flexibility, originality, elaboration, etc.

► *Problem solving:* defining or describing a problem, determining the desired outcomes, selecting possible solutions, choosing strategies, testing trial solutions, evaluating outcomes, and revising where necessary.

ODYSSEY: A CURRICULUM FOR THINKING

► Let us turn our attention to a specific curricular model for the teaching of thinking. The model we have chosen, somewhat arbitrarily because there are several, is called *Odyssey: A Curriculum for Thinking. Odyssey* is a set of 100 lessons that draws on a deliberately eclectic approach to teaching thinking. In her summary of the program, Elena Wright notes:

> Program materials reflect the more persuasive aspects of a number of theories of epistemology and cognitive development. Some lessons involve a Socratic inquiry approach, while others are based on a Piagetian-like analysis of cognitive activities. Still others emphasize exploration and discovery in a way reminiscent of Bruner. The overall design reflects the multifaceted nature of intellectual performance and the focus on long-term effects that will transfer to content-area subjects as well as beyond school (Wright, 1983, p. 224).

Odyssey is aimed at middle-level students. The curriculum was developed by a team of Harvard University researchers (1983) in cooperation with the Venezuelan Ministry of Education. *Odyssey's* goal is to develop a broad range of general thinking skills in students. Specifically, those skills include foundations of reasoning, understanding language, verbal reasoning, problem solving, decision making, and inventive thinking.

Odyssey was originally developed for use in Venezuela in connection with the nation's Project Intelligence, an ambitious curricular adventure in making the students of Venezuela better critical thinkers. Studies conducted for the project showed impressive gains toward that goal (Harvard, 1983). The assumptions of the *Odyssey* curriculum are that performance on intellectually demanding tasks is influenced by factors of ability, strategy, knowledge, and attitudes, and that some, if not all, of these factors can be enhanced by a teaching approach that engages students actively and intellectually (Wright, 1985).

Odyssey placed emphasis on class discussion and active student involvement in problem solving, reasoning, decision making, and creative activities. As a subject in the school curriculum, *Odyssey* requires from three to five forty-five-minute lessons per week. *Odyssey* materials include six teacher manuals and six students books; it does not depend upon expensive, elaborate kits, which would make the program prohibitive in an era of reduced budgets. Information about *Odyssey* is available from Mastery Education Corporation, 85 Main Street, Watertown, MA 02172.

TEACHING YOUR STUDENTS TO THINK*

▶ There are several key reasons why subjects exist in the school curriculum. These reasons include an acquisition of knowledge of a wider world and an exploration of their own and others' values by students. Learning to think effectively must be included on any list of reasons for the existence of various subjects. It's easy to get agreement on this issue. Parents and teachers all want young children to become independent thinkers. In spite of this widely agreed-on desire, little evidence exists that students are, in fact, even taught to think, except perhaps in random instances. For example, nationwide tests indicate that even though students do learn the rudiments of computation, they cannot apply what they learned to practical problem-solving situations. Consider this:

The National Assessment of Educational Progress (NAEP), a government-supported project that surveys the academic progress of nine-, thirteen-, and seventeen-year-olds, posed the following problem: "An army bus holds 36 soldiers. If 1,128 soldiers are being bused to their training site, how many buses are needed?"

Only about 24 percent of the thirteen-year-olds gave the right answer (32 buses). Many students (29 percent) worked the problem as a math exercise and came up with 31⅓ buses (as though you could have one-third of a bus). Would calculators help these students solve the problem by freeing them from the mechanics of division? Apparently not, because the number of thirteen-year-olds who got the right answer with the assistance of a calculator dropped to 7 percent.

According to the NAEP, the problem was that the students didn't know what to do with their answer once they had divided. The calculator was of little help because, as NAEP said, "it is still necessary to know what questions to ask and how to use the results." Test results show

*From Arthur K. Ellis, *Teaching and Learning Elementary Social Studies,* 3d ed. (Boston: Allyn and Bacon, 1986), pp. 190–193. Used with permission.

that these findings can be generalized to other areas (English, social studies, science) in which problem-solving and thinking skills are also crucial.

True problem solving is not mathematical computation, nor is it a knowledge of the crops of the United States and Canadian prairie regions. Knowledge and computational skills are important tools in problem solving, but they are too often treated as ends in themselves. The problem solver needs to learn how to ask good questions, how to keep an open mind, how to make guesses and play hunches, how to give reasons, how to make decisions, and how to make corrections. We will say more about each of these skills later in this chapter, but now, let's try some problem solving. Try solving each problem. After you come up with a solution, discuss your answer (and how you derived it) with one or two others. The answers are found on page 280.

▶ *Problem 1: The Lily Pad Problem*
The number of lily pads on a pond double each day. On the thirtieth day, the pond is completely covered. On which day will the pond be half covered with lily pads?

My answer: _____

How I figured my answer to the problem: _____

_____

_____

▶ *Problem 2: The Horse-Trading Problem*
Some people brought a horse. They paid $50 for the horse. Thinking they didn't want to keep it, they sold the horse for $60. They changed their mind and bought the horse back for $70. Then they decided to sell it again, which they did for $80. How did they come out financially?

My answer: _____

How I figured my answer to the problem: _____

_____

_____

▶ *Problem 3: The Bottle of Wine Problem*

A bottle of wine costs $10. The wine is worth $9 more than the bottle. How much is the bottle worth?

My answer: _____

How I figured my answer to the problem: _____

_____

_____

On the surface, these problems may appear to be math exercises, but they are not. They are problems to solve. The arithmetic involved in any of them is quite simple. Although the arithmetic involves only adding or subtracting, the problems themselves can be difficult because of a mental process called *insight*. Psychologists Robert Sternberg and Janet Davidson (1986) have identified three types of intellectual processes required in solving insight problems.

1. The ability to encode information, that is, to understand what information is relevant (or irrelevant) to solving the problem.
2. The ability to combine pieces of information, even though those pieces may at first seem unrelated.
3. The ability to compare the problem with problems previously encountered, that is, the ability to recall similar situations and to use those skills and concepts employed in solving previous problems.

► Insight

The combination of any or all of these abilities is globally labeled *insight*. Let's examine an example of each process.

Encoding
A person has brown socks and black socks in a drawer in a ratio of four to five. How many socks would the person have to pull out to make sure of having one matched pair? The answer is three socks. In this case, the information about the ratio is irrelevant, and it is a matter of selective encoding to recognize that.

Combining
With a seven-minute hourglass and an eleven-minute hourglass, what is the simplest way to time the boiling of an egg for fifteen minutes? The essential clue is to *combine* the two timers to measure the fifteen minutes.

Comparing
What does the word *exsect* mean? By using prior knowledge, you might know that *ex* means *out* (e.g., as in *extract* and *excise*) and that *sect* means *cut* (e.g., as in *dissect* and *bisect*). *Exsect,* therefore, means "to cut out."

Sternberg (1985) suggests that these processes of insight, selectively used, are fundamental to problem solving at any level, from solving problems in puzzle books to making major scientific breakthroughs.

To the teacher, two essential questions arise: Can these problem-solving processes be taught? Can students make the transfer from solving contrived puzzles to solving real problems?

▶ Specific Strategies to Help Students

Although critical thinking, creative thinking, and problem solving involve different operations that lead to different outcomes, they clearly share a fundamental common property—that of moving students and teachers beyond memory work, textbook dependence, and the narrow confines of a contrived paper and pencil world of learning. What they have in common easily transcends their differences. Thus, their common goal structure emerges as one dedicated to helping students learn to reason, give opinions, make applications, express themselves, and make decisions. These are the basics of tomorrow. We urge you to adopt the following ten specific strategies.

Active Learning
Active learning is designed to reorient your students' process of learning from one of passivity to one of involvement. It takes on many forms. For example, the reader who is expected to take notes and to respond while reading becomes actively involved with the author of the book. The student who is expected to take notes while the teacher presents ideas will recall ideas more efficiently, will better understand what the teacher is saying, and will learn that what the teacher has to say is important.

Jerome Bruner, Jean Piaget, John Dewey, and others have noted the educational value of having students make things so that they can link the construction and design to mathematical, scientific, and social learning. Geometry, architecture, and environmental studies have obvious potential for learner involvement, yet they are sadly underused and, when they are, they are rarely applied in the curriculum. Passive learning yields a low rate of return on a teacher's investment of time and energy. The argument that not all learning should be active learning attains absurd proportions to anyone who has observed in our nation's classrooms. Task-related, conceptually based active learning is a creature so rare that it could easily be an endangered species.

Answers to problems on page 278:
Problem 1: 29th day   Problem 2: $20 ahead   Problem 3: $.50.

Question Authoring
The idea that questions might come from students and not only from teachers and textbooks is something that good teachers have known for centuries. It is an old, simple, and underused teaching-learning strategy. Having students author questions about the material they are studying will improve their comprehension and, over time, it will improve the quality of the questions they ask (Costa, 1985).

Thinking and Working Together
Learning ought to be far more socially engaging than it is. The resources (twenty-five to thirty-five students per room) are already available. It is merely a matter of bringing them together. In a working-pairs model, for example, students think aloud about problems they are trying to solve. They learn to express their thoughts, listen, probe, critique, and share ideas. Peer teaching emerges and the teacher's role changes with respect to both content and management. Here is an example: The number five thousand five hundred five is expressed 5505 as a numeral. How would you express the number twelve thousand twelve hundred twelve as a numeral? Try working on this problem alone. Then try working on it with a partner in the following way: One of you works the problem, saying all your thoughts, steps, and so on, aloud while the other person listens, probes, and seeks clarification. In what ways is working this problem alone different from working it together?

Contextual Teaching
Most subjects are taught as freestanding entities devoid of any content except their own and without linkages to other subjects or to the real world. That simply is just not very efficient. Math teachers need to talk about conflicts in everyday life. Social studies teachers need to involve students with direct experience in citizenship. Teachers' presentations should build linkages to the world and the community. Applications of skills and concepts need to be drawn by teachers and students from reality, and not left solely to textbook authors. Finally, teachers need to challenge themselves with such questions as, "How can I link what is being taught in math or English to what is being taught throughout the rest of the curriculum?"

Ill-Structured Problems
Unclear, ambiguous situations are common enough in everyday life, but they are seldom used as teaching material. Moral dilemmas, hypothetical problems, and issues from playground, neighborhood, and family life furnish us with unlimited potential for critical thinking. As an example, consider this hypothetical problem: Assume all cars will be painted yellow from now on. How many "pluses" and how many "minuses" could you list about such a change? Such problems

not only free students from worrying about "right" answers, but they also give them the opportunity to build arguments on either side of a case, thus laying the groundwork for the fundamental skills of argumentation and debate that are so crucial to the functioning of our democratic society.

Moving Outside Your Discipline

The very processes of higher level thinking are constrained by strict adherence to a single-subject approach to teaching. Nevertheless, such an approach is usually dominant at both the secondary and elementary levels. But even with this limitation, there is a great deal one can do. For example, a junior high-school science teacher gives his students extra credit for visiting nursing homes. On the surface, such an idea seems discrepant and, at best, only tangentially related to science. But the teacher knows what he is doing. He finds many opportunities to talk with his students about aging processes, about technology and its socio-medical applications to the elderly, and he has created a "laboratory" where adolescents can bring their real experiences to discussions and reflections on life itself. The opportunities to widen the scope of subject matter, to open a window of learning onto the world itself are without boundary. It is a leadership issue that teachers need to seize.

Deliberate Pacing

To the proverbial Martian visitor to classrooms, these large boxes filled with one adult and thirty young people must seem dedicated to impulsivity. A question is asked by the teacher. Depending on some miscellaneous factors, a forest of hands is raised. Someone is called on immediately and, for better or worse (that is, right or wrong), an answer is given to the question. The race is to the swift and the accurate. If the question were, "What is the capital of Texas?" a quick response (you either know it or you don't) is expected. But what if an analytical or philosophical question were posed? Such questions are important enough that they ought to be answered reflectively, and reflection can take time. The solution is easy: Slow down the pace of things.

Mary Budd Rowe (1974) has developed a concept she calls *wait-time*. It is a useful concept in the conduct of class discussion. She has reckoned that typical wait-time between the time a teacher asks a question and receives an answer is a fraction of one second. That is impulsivity. Slow the process. Ask a good question and wait for students to give it some thought. Wait until everyone who chooses to answer has had a chance to raise his or her hand. Students will begin to perceive a difference. They will begin to be more reflective simply because their teacher has created a more reflective atmosphere. In this same vein, a "question of the week" strategy is helpful. Each Monday, the teacher prominently displays a probing question and allows the class the opportunity to discuss it briefly. On Friday, the class is expected to discuss the question in depth on the basis of their reflection and "research."

Questions to be answered in oral or written form by students working in pairs, talking and listening to each other, create a more deliberate pace. This strategy also allows students the opportunity to learn from each other and to check one another's logic.

Unusual Assignments

Unusual assignments create a sense of anticipation and wonder. The predictable routine of explanation followed by boardwork and seatwork would be fine in a world of highly motivated, eager-to-learn students who just naturally love school. But research shows that in-class time is the least desirable time of the entire day for most students. One answer to this problem is variety. Presenting material in unusual ways (for example, using role play, Socratic dialogue, debate, drama, round table, construction, art) is an opportunity for teachers to model creativity to their students.

Howard Gardner (1983) argues that human intelligence is actually a host of different abilities that reside in various parts of the brain. These abilities develop more or less independently, and can bloom separately, skill by skill. Unusual, varied assignments can reach a greater range of human potential and therefore provide opportunities for growth that few teachers have thoroughly explored.

Consider the following "unusual" assignment, framed as a question to be *answered* and *acted upon* for a week (once a solution has been derived) by a class:

"What would we do if all the textbooks were ruined?" Think of the implications of this unique assignment. First of all, it would require real problem solving and creativity on the part of a teacher and the class to put together a week's worth of math, science, social studies, or whatever, with no textbooks to fall back on. Second, once the "experiment" was put into effect, it would require a great deal of reflective, critical thought to judge the effect of the experiment.

Social Structure

The teacher's single most important task along the way to developing higher level thinking is building self-confidence—the teacher's own and that of his or her students. How will teachers meet this challenge? Evidence suggests that a gradual but sure erosion of self-confidence occurs over the school years. We point this out not in order to blame teachers and the schools for a problem whose complexities transcend what is or isn't done in classrooms. Teachers are only a *part* of the larger social system. Rather, the question of what teachers can do to enhance students' self-confidence is framed as a positive challenge. Here are some techniques that seem to work. One thing teachers can do is to practice nurturing behavior. By letting students know through words and actions, teachers signal students that they care about them. Teachers need to practice a style of management that Tom Peters (1984) calls "Management By Walking Around" (MBWA). Walking around, talking to students, calling them by name, giving them verbal and literal pats on the back, and writing them notes of support will show that teachers care about them as people. A second felicitous attribute of a positive social structure is humor. It helps everyone to feel more comfortable in the confines of a classroom if they know the underlying mood is upbeat. The story goes that Thomas Edison once turned to his associates after they had all spent many frustrating hours without apparent success on their attempt to develop an incandescent light bulb, and said, "Well, boys, now we know a thousand ways not to make a light bulb." To find joy in the search and to be open to "failure" to the point that we can laugh about it and say we are at least approximating success represents a refreshing step in the direction of building people's self-esteem. And to find joy in the many successes that go uncelebrated each day in classrooms is equally significant.

Involvement
According to the research of Czikszentmilhalyi and McCormack (1983), fewer than 10 percent of the teachers encountered by students are cited by those students as having made a difference in their lives. We can all agree, that figure should be higher. What type of teacher does make a difference? On the basis of their careful analysis of student interviews, Czikszentmilhalyi and McCormack conclude that these teachers who do make a difference were strong, efficient managers of their instruction. Even more significantly, they were: (1) highly involved with and genuinely interested in the subject matter they taught and (2) approachable, easy to talk to, and ready to listen.

Now that we have outlined, in considerable detail, the various elements of critical thinking, let us exercise our own critical thinking abilities with two sets of activities (shown on pages 285–286).

SUMMARY

▶ In this chapter, we have attempted to convince you of the importance of higher level thinking as a key ingredient in teaching and learning. There is reason to be pessimistic when one looks at test scores and the status that effective thinking is afforded in the curriculum. But to quote

Critical Thinking Exercises: Working in Pairs and Thinking Aloud

1. Six thousand six hundred six is written 6606. Now write eleven thousand eleven hundred eleven in figures.

2. Which box below best completes the following series?

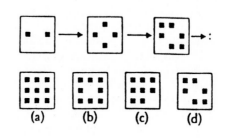

    (a)   (b)   (c)   (d)

3. If Sally's daughter is my son's mother, what relationship am I to Sally if I am male?

4. Five people competed in a foot race. There were no ties. Mary did not come in first. John was neither first nor last. Joe came in one place after Mary. Jane was not second. Bill was two places behind Jane. In what order did the runners finish?

5. If 40 pizza bakers can bake 20 pizzas in 2 hours, how many hours will it take 2 pizza bakers to make 10 pizzas?

6. On your bookshelf you have three books in a set, Volumes I, II, and III, in the usual order from left to right. You also have a bookworm who is eating them up. The pages of the books are two inches thick; the covers are each a half-inch thick. If the bookworm starts at the outside of the front cover of Volume I and eats through to the last page of Volume III, how many inches has he bored through?

*Problems adapted from *The Mensa Quiz Book* (Reading, Mass.: Addison-Wesley, 1981).

Tennyson, "Tho' much is taken, much abides. . . ." A growing body of research has given us useful ideas about how to promote effective thinking in classrooms. We have provided you with various strategies to implement such a goal. Like most worthwhile goals, the quest for higher level thinking is a difficult, elusive challenge. But as teachers and administrators, we must be eternal optimists about the possibilities.

Critical Thinking Exercises: Open-Ended

1. All cars should be painted orange. List the pluses and minuses.
2. Is the climate of our region changing?
3. What would we do if all the textbooks were ruined?
4. How can homes be adapted to use fewer resources?
5. Should the drinking age be raised to 21?
6. How would the country be different today if it had been set-tled from West to East?
7. Can you find examples of the Second Law of Thermodynamics in the local environment?
8. What is a real problem you face? How can you identify it clearly and work toward solving it?
9. How do the following affect our moods: color? music? light?
10. What evidence can you find that the relationship between the United States and China is changing? How do you predict it will change over time?
11. Is it ever acceptable to break a promise? If so, under what circumstances?

ACTIVITIES

1. Examine a school textbook in any area of curriculum and evaluate its potential for teaching effective thinking.
2. Sit down with two other people and brainstorm at least ten ways you can increase the levels of creative and critical thinking in classrooms.
3. To what extent is it possible for a teacher to involve the home in the school curriculum? What steps can a teacher take toward making schools and homes "partners" in the learning enterprise?
4. Given the range of abilities, interests, and backgrounds of students in a typical classroom, what can a teacher do to enhance the productive thinking of all his or her students?

REFERENCES

Becoming a nation of readers. (1984). Washington, D.C.: The National Institute of Education.

Costa, A. (Ed.) (1985). *Developing minds.* Alexandria, Va.: Association for Supervision and Curriculum Development.

Czikszentmilhalyi, C., and McCormack, E. (1983). The direct teaching of thinking as a skill. *Phi Delta Kappan, 65,* pp. 703–708.

Educating Americans for the 21st century. (1983). Washington, D.C.: National Science Board.

Education Commission of the States. (1983). *Action for excellence.*

Ellis, A. K. (1986). *Teaching and learning elementary school studies* (3rd ed.). Boston: Allyn and Bacon.

Gardner, H. (1983). *Frames of mind: The theory of multiple intelligences.* New York: Basic Books.

Goodlad, J. I. (1983). *A place called school.* New York: McGraw-Hill.

Gray, S. T., (1984). How to create a successful school/community partnership. *Phi Delta Kappan 6,* No. 6, pp. 405–409.

Harvard University. (October 1983). *Project intelligence: The development of procedures to enhance thinking skills.* Final Report.

Jackson, P. (1968). *Life in classrooms.* New York: Holt, Rinehart and Winston.

Johnson, D. W., and Johnson, R. T. (1984). *Circles of learning.* Washington, D.C.: Association for Supervision of Curriculum Development.

Peters, T. (1984). Management by walking around. *In search of excellence.* New York: McGraw-Hill.

Rowe, M. B. (1974). Wait-time and rewards as instructional variables: Their influence on language, logic and fate control: Part one-Wait time. *Journal of Research in Science Teaching, 11,* No. 2, pp. 81–94.

Sternberg, R. J. (September 1985). How can we teach intelligence? *Educational Leadership,* pp. 38–48.

Sternberg, R. J., and Davidson, J. (October 1986). Intelligence as thinking and teaching skills. *Educational Leadership, 38,* 18–20.

Toffler, A. (1981). *The third wave.* New York: Basic Books.

Unified science and mathematics for elementary schools. (1975). Newton, Mass.: Education Development Center.

Walberg, H. J. (May 1984). Improving the productivity of America's schools. *Educational Leadership,* pp. 19–27.

Wright, E. (1985). Odyssey: A curriculum for thinking. In A. Costa (Ed.), *Developing minds,* Alexandria, Va.: ASCD, pp. 224–226.

SUGGESTED READINGS

Glaser, R. (February 1984). Education and thinking: The role of knowledge. *American Psychologist, 39,* 93–104.

Hayes, J. R. (1981). *The complete problem solver.* Philadelphia: Franklin Institute.

Koberg, D., and Bagnall, J. (1982). *The universal traveler: A soft-system guide to problem solving, and the process of creativity* (2nd ed.). Los Altos, Calif.: Kaufman Press.

Lipman, M.; Sharp, A. M.; and Oscanyan, F. S. (1980). *Philosophy in the classroom* (2nd ed.). Philadelphia: Temple University.

Mackey, J. A. (May 1977). Three problem solving models for the elementary classroom. *Social Education, 41,* 408–410.

Rubenstein, M. F. (1975). *Patterns of problem solving.* Englewood Cliffs, N.J.: Prentice-Hall.

Sternberg, R. J. (1977). *Intelligence, information processing, and analogical reasoning: The componential analysis of human abilities.* Hillsdale, N.J.: Erlbaum.

15

Evaluation of Curriculum and Instruction

▶───────────────────────────────
───────────────────────────────◀

OVERVIEW

▶ This chapter discusses the role of evaluation in curriculum and instruction. The purposes of evaluation are discussed and the various ways evaluation can be used to assess the curriculum and instructional activities are presented. After reading the chapter you should be able to define evaluation, describe its role in curriculum and instruction, and cite specific ways to use evaluation in your own teaching.

INTRODUCTION

▶ At last the end is in sight! Teaching full-time has to be easier than living through the experiences of this final quarter. Think about it. In ten weeks there have been six straight weeks of teaching everyday with the supervising teacher looking over your shoulder, once-a-week seminars, completing a placement file, writing what seems like 1,000 letters asking for applications for a teaching position. And, now there is the teacher certification test of basic skills and content knowledge! Isn't it enough to take four plus years of college, get good grades, and pass student teaching? No, now the state is insisting that all beginning teachers have to pass a test in order to be certified. Why?

The reason for the increase in the number of states requiring the passing of a basic skills test for both teachers and graduating seniors is that many people feel teachers and students do not have the basic skills needed to be successful in today's society. Critics of education suggest that the curriculum and the instructional strategies employed are not effective and must be improved. They base their judgments on test data that are reported regularly in the press. Two national reports from the mid-1980s, the Holmes Group and the Carnegie Report, advocated the testing of all beginning teachers. To respond to the critics and as a part of an ongoing process, educators must continually gather data about student progress. These data indicate whether or not the goals and objectives of the curriculum, whether at the college or public-school level, are being met and how effective various activities may be in teaching the students the content and skills of the curriculum. From these data, educators can make judgments about the overall effectiveness of the school. This chapter focuses on this information-gathering process.

Many people think that evaluation is the same as testing. This is a common misconception because one of the most vivid memories of being in school is taking tests. There were quizzes, chapter tests, final examinations, and the big national tests that compared student achievement with national norms. In this chapter you will learn that evaluation is more than tests and that it serves a variety of important functions in both curriculum and instruction. See Table 15–1.

TABLE 15-1   Assessment

Research Finding:	Frequent and systematic monitoring of students' progress helps students, parents, teachers, administrators, and policymakers identify strengths and weaknesses in learning and instruction.
Comment:	Teachers find out what students already know and what they still need to learn by assessing student work. They use various means, including essays, quizzes and tests, homework, classroom questions, standardized tests, and parents' comments. Teachers can use student errors on tests and in class as early warning signals to point out and correct learning problems before they worsen. Student motivation and achievement improve when teachers provide prompt feedback on assignments.
	Students generally take two kinds of tests: classroom tests and standardized tests. Classroom tests help teachers find out if what they are teaching is being learned; thus, these tests serve to evaluate both student and teacher. Standardized tests apply similar gauges to everyone in a specific grade level. By giving standardized tests, school districts can see how achievement progresses over time. Such tests also help schools find out how much of the curriculum is actually being learned. Standardized tests can also reveal problems in the curriculum itself. For example, a recent international mathematics test showed that U.S. students had encountered only 70 percent of what the test covered.

Source: What Works: Research about Teaching and Learning (Washington, D.C.: U.S. Dept. of Education, 1986).

THE EVALUATION PROCESS

▶ Stufflebeam and others developed a broad definition of evaluation. They noted that evaluation is "the process of delineating, obtaining, and providing useful information for judging decision alternatives" (Stufflebeam et al., 1971). The key characteristic of this definition is a focus on the *process* of gathering useful information. Stufflebeam's definition serves as a good foundation for the definition of evaluation that will be used in this chapter. For our purposes, evaluation is the process of systematically gathering and analyzing available information concerning the curriculum, the instructional activities and materials, and student learning to enable judgments to be made about the effectiveness of the curriculum and the amount of student learning.

The purposes of evaluation are to:

1. Make judgments about the curriculum
   a. What should be revised?
   b. Which program is better?
   c. What are the educational needs?
2. Make judgments about instruction
   a. What are learning problems?
   b. What has been learned?
   c. What is the quality of the materials?

In order to make judgments or decisions about the effectiveness of the curriculum and related instructional activities, the evaluators: (1) identify and formulate educational goals, (2) select and create instruments for measuring progress toward the goals, (3) administer these instruments, and (4) make judgments based on the data collected. The evaluation process is represented in Figure 15–1.

A variety of evaluation approaches have been developed over the years; each one specifies what should be done in each of the four basic steps. The various philosophies may be placed into two broad categories.

TWO BROAD PHILOSOPHIES OF EVALUATION

▶ There is no pure evaluation model that can be used in all situations. Evaluators know the models must be adjusted to meet the constraints of a particular situation. Consequently, the evaluation that occurs in most school settings is a mixture of two general schools of thought.

FIGURE 15-1 The Evaluation Process

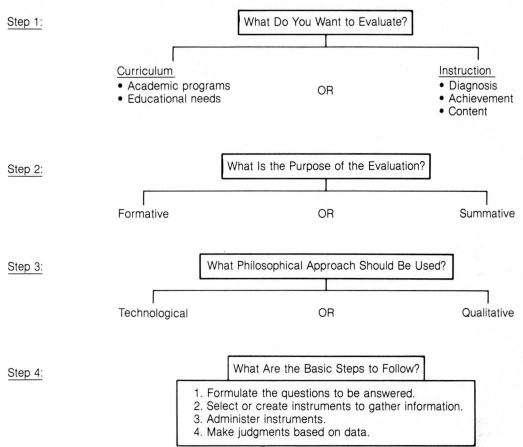

Step 1:

What Do You Want to Evaluate?

Curriculum
- Academic programs
- Educational needs

OR

Instruction
- Diagnosis
- Achievement
- Content

Step 2:

What Is the Purpose of the Evaluation?

Formative   OR   Summative

Step 3:

What Philosophical Approach Should Be Used?

Technological   OR   Qualitative

Step 4:

What Are the Basic Steps to Follow?

1. Formulate the questions to be answered.
2. Select or create instruments to gather information.
3. Administer instruments.
4. Make judgments based on data.

▶ **The Technological Approach**

An evaluation that has had wide acceptability over the past two decades is one called the "technological" or "systems" approach. The keys to the technological evaluation model are: (1) the agreement among participants as to the goals, (2) the careful specification of outcomes, and (3) the selection of methods of collecting data to determine whether or not the objectives were achieved. By following a systematic approach, proponents contend that more reliable data may be collected and that these data will then allow educators the possibility of making better judgments about the effectivensss of a program or a set of instructional activities.

The cornerstones of the technological approach are the identification of the goals and the specification of the objectives needed to achieve each goal. Robert Mager (1975) was one of the early educators who wrote about the methods of specifying objectives. According to Mager's philosophy, each objective should specify an observable student behavior, a standard by which to judge the behavior, and the situation in which the student will have to demonstrate the behavior. An example from social studies will illustrate a typical behavioral objective:

> When given an outline map of the United States with state boundaries marked, the student will be able to identify and correctly spell each state.

The specific behavior in this objective is the identification and spelling of each of the fifty states. The conditions are "when given an outline map of the United States with state boundries marked." The standard for acceptable behavior would be that the student would have to identify and spell correctly all fifty states.

Using the behaviorally stated objective as a guideline, the evaluator following the technological approach would then select a method for determining student learning of the objective and also determine what would be a passing mark. The testing would be more straightforward because the objective would dictate the test item. The example objective used above can illustrate this process.

To measure student learning an evaluator could give each student a blank outline map of the United States and ask the student to put each state in its proper location and to spell it correctly. In order to pass the test the student would have to locate and spell each state correctly.

The use of objectives to determine testing is called criterion-referenced testing. A criterion-referenced test is designed to ascertain whether or not the student has learned a specific task. The test items match the set of instructional objectives developed from the goal statement. The student either demonstrates mastery of the objective or does not. A passing mark is based on criteria established prior to testing and not on how well other students do on the test.

The criterion-referenced method of evaluation has been the most influencial philosophy of evaluation during the past several years. It has been instrumental in shaping evaluation policies in schools and classrooms.

▶ **The Qualitative Approach**

A different approach to evaluation is represented by those educators who favor a qualitative, pluralistic or humanistic approach. These educators contend that relying on measurable learning outcomes is not sufficient because it is too simplistic and too narrow. This narrow focus limits the whole evaluation process. Instead, the proponents of a pluralistic approach suggest that evaluators must collect data from a much broader base.

Qualitative evaluators assume the following:

1. The school is an enormously complex and subtle institution. One aspect of the institution cannot be studied in isolation. It must be studied holistically.
2. Evaluation must occur over a long period of time; it is longitudinal in nature.
3. Direct, on-site, face-to-face contact with people and events is the most effective way to study a given phenomenon.
4. A researcher must understand the attitudes, values, and beliefs of those being studied.
5. The basic function of the researcher is to describe the situation in the richest, fullest, and most comprehensive manner possible.

Instead of focusing on specific objectives and testing for the achievement of these objectives, qualitative researchers attempt to provide a broader information base for curriculum decisions and the determination of the success of the curriculum in reaching its goals.

Evaluators who follow the qualitative model would not avoid the use of specific criterion-referenced tests, but they would also seek out additional information. Using the objective noted earlier concerning the ability to locate and spell the fifty states, qualitative evaluators might use blank maps and ask students to locate and spell the states. However, they would also observe students using the information in other activities, and describe how the information was used in the curriculum after it had been taught. Qualitative evaluators would seek to determine whether or not students could use the knowledge more than in just a one-time testing situation.

▶ **Some Basic Differences Between Evaluation Philosophies**

Both evaluation philosophies seek the same goal — providing useful data to help educators make decisions about the curriculum and instruction. As evidenced by the preceding discussions, the differences are in the types of data collected and the manner in which these data are gathered. Vincent Rogers (1985) points out some of the basic differences between these two approaches. He notes nineteen different assumptions that guide most typical evaluation studies. Five are most important. In most traditional studies:

1. There is an emphasis on using words to name, describe, or define; a minimum value is placed on visual, auditory, and kinesthetic modes of learning.
2. The evaluator assumes that learning takes place in formal settings and can be assessed at various points in time.
3. Grades and test scores give a reasonable picture of school performance, and tests have no impact on overall student learning.
4. Evidence obtained through direct observation of or interaction with the learner is assumed to be inferior to that obtained by tests.
5. Objectives must be stated clearly before evaluation can take place.

These five assumptions indicate the basic differences between the two philosophies. Followers of the technological approach seek to create a more systematic and controlled evaluation process. Clearly stated objectives, controlled testing situations, and objective tests provide accurate reflections of learning. On the other hand, qualitative evaluators seek other sources. Critics of this approach suggest that the data collected through such evaluation techniques are too "soft"; that is, they are open to bias, not reliable, and difficult to evaluate.

► Evaluation Philosophies and Classroom Evaluation

Most classroom teachers do not purport to be experts in evaluation. Although making decisions about the effectiveness of a particular set of instructional activities and a student's success in learning the materials is an important part of a teacher's role, classroom teachers learn about evaluation more through experience than instruction. Consequently, few teachers follow a specific philosophy; instead they use combinations of both approaches.

Final decisions about how to evaluate curriculum and student learning are also influenced by several other factors. Four are of particular importance.

Skills
Developing an effective evaluation plan means that a teacher must have an understanding of the basic characteristics of each philosophy.

For example, a teacher who wishes to follow a technological approach to evaluation would have to have an understanding of the systematic approach, the ability to develop goal statements and appropriate instructional objectives, and the ability to create tests that would measure the objectives. The skills needed to complete these tasks are significant and usually beyond the level of many beginning teachers.

Time

It takes considerable time to develop a careful evaluation plan, create appropriate measures, and collect relevant data. For example, to create a series of multiple-choice questions to measure higher level learning is a most difficult task. The development of such tests usually must be done after the school day. (Few teachers have more than one hour per school day to prepare lesson plans, grade papers, develop testing instruments, and complete other administrative tasks.) As a consequence, learning about and acquiring the skills related to a particular philosophy often compete with time and the necessity to meet an immediate need.

District Policies

Most school districts have specific policies about evaluation. For example, many school districts give basic competency examinations to determine student learning. These tests have either been developed by outside testing agencies or by district personnel. Some districts also have specific "benchmark" tests to determine whether or not students should be promoted to the next grade level. With the advent of such testing policies, classroom teachers often have little impact on overall evaluation policies.

Political Decisions

As we have discussed in other chapters, the school is a part of a larger social system. As a consequence, political pressures often influence how evaluation procedures are developed, the type of evaluation techniques used, and the manner in which the data are used. District policies reflect such pressures by the public for increased accountability and a concern about student learning.

Hence, factors influence the approach followed in a school district and in a particular school. All these ensure that no one philosophy is followed in its purest form.

Whatever the philosophy, evaluation plays an important role in the school and for the teacher. Educators must decide on what type of evaluation must be used and for what purposes. Let's turn our attention to these two issues.

TYPES OF EVALUTION

▶ Educators are interested in two very broad issues: (1) how the curriculum or instruction can be improved and (2) how to determine if the curriculum is effective in achieving goals and whether or not learning took place. Based on these two issues, two types of evaluation techniques, formative and summative, have been developed. Lee Cronbach (1963) and Michael Scriven (1967) have provided the leadership in these areas.

▶ Formative Evaluation

Formative evaluation is the process used by instructors and curriculum developers to obtain data in order to revise instruction and make it more efficient and effective (Ehman, 1974). Formative evaluation refers to evaluating something in its beginning stage or as it is developing. A key consideration in the process is the collection of sufficient data. Dick and Carey (1985), representing a systems approach to development, suggest that at a minimum the following data ought to be included in any formative evaluation:

1. Test data on students' entry behaviors, pretests on knowledge and skills, and post-tests (What do students know?)
2. Specific comments made by students about the materials or activities (What did students say about the materials and activities?)
3. Data collected from attitude surveys and debriefing comments in which students reveal their overall reactions to the materials and instructional activities (Did students like the activities?)
4. The amount of time needed for students to complete the various activities (How long did it take to complete the activities?)
5. Reactions from subject matter specialists (What should be included in the unit?)

Vincent Rogers (1985) and Elliot Eisner (1985), who favor a qualitative approach to evaluation, would contend that a particular class or curriculum would need to be studied in the context of the total school, not in isolation. They also suggest that little reliance should be placed on the use of paper-pencil instruments; instead, there should be more direct, face-to-face contact and a better effort made to describe the total learning environment in the richest, fullest, most comprehensive description possible.

A teacher's interest in formative evaluation usually focuses not on how the overall curriculum can be improved in a particular subject area but on individual courses. The teacher wants to know how the course can be improved the next time it is taught or what changes need to be made during the course to improve the unit as it is being taught. A teacher seldom has a chance to field test a course before teaching it to a class of students. A teacher must field test and teach-for-real, both at the same time.

Too often a teacher relies on an analysis of a unit's test scores to make judgments about the effectiveness of the instruction. This really is not enough information because most tests measure only what students remember about the content. To gain insights into instructional activities and materials, the teacher must ask more specific questions. The answers to questions 2, 3, and 4 on the preceding page can provide useful insights. In addition, students could be asked the following questions in order to gain a more complete picture of the effectiveness of the materials and instructional activities.

1. Was the instruction interesting?
2. Did you understand what you were supposed to learn?
3. Did you get enough practice so you could learn the things you needed to know?
4. Did you get enough feedback about your work?
5. Did the tests measure what you knew about the learning objectives?
6. Did you get enough feedback about your mistakes on your test?

In addition to these general questions, students might be asked very specific questions about selected activities. For example, the teacher might ask:

1. Did you like the role-play activity about the Civil War?
2. Which short story was more realistic?

Remember, formative evaluation occurs throughout the development or learning process. It is good practice to ask students throughout the unit how things are going. Do not wait until the end. Formative evaluation should facilitate curriculum construction, improve teaching, and support learning.

► Summative Evaluation

Summative evaluation is designed to determine the value or worth of a set of instructional activities. The evaluation takes place at the end of the learning process. Stated in another way, Did the students achieve the learning outcomes established prior to instruction? The most common use of summative evaluation techniques is the use of test results and other information to assign individual grades. Grades are given at the end of instruction to signify a level of achievement related to the goals of the course.

At the broader curriculum level, formative evaluation would be appropriate during the time the curriculum was being developed, and summative evaluation would occur to evaluate the completed curriculum.

The distinction between formative and summative evaluation techniques is the purpose of the evaluation. Data-collection techniques might be similar, but when evaluation occurs at the conclusion it is referred to as *summative,* whereas evaluation of an ongoing program is called *formative.* The ultimate goal of both is to determine the worth of something. Evaluators from both a technological or systems approach are interested in formative and summative evaluation. Their interests would be directed toward both the curriculum and instructional practices.

THE ROLE OF EVALUATION IN CURRICULUM AND INSTRUCTION

► The heart of the formal curriculum is the subject area classroom. Evaluation techniques can be used to gain a better understanding of the classroom. In fact, the most important roles of evaluation are in the area of improving courses and determining the level of student achievement of instructional goals. Evaluation, therefore, plays an integral role in both curriculum and instruction.

► Evaluation and Curriculum

The formal curriculum encompasses those planned activities that are designed to achieve the goals of the school. Since the school is a reflection of society, it is an ever-changing institution. The most common way in which change is introduced into the curriculum is through the revision and comparison of courses. As a consequence, evaluation techniques can assist the educator in: (1) evaluating the courses he or she teaches in order to improve them, (2) comparing different educational programs, and (3) gathering needs assessment data.

Evaluating Classroom Activities
How successful was this lesson? What might be changed in the instructional unit to improve it? These are questions that are important to the classroom teacher. A teacher continually strives to develop instructional activities that meet student needs and teach the material.

Thus, classroom teachers are interested in gathering data about the effectiveness of a particular activity, a set of materials, and instructional strategies.

The key for the teacher is to collect information that will provide sufficient insights into what modifications need to be made to improve the curriculum. It is important for the teacher to use formative and summative evaluation techniques and not to limit the evaluation to the goals and instructional objectives that provide the focus for the unit. A variety of textbooks are available to guide the teacher in the revision process. They range from very specific systematic approaches suggested by Walter Dick and Lou Carey in *The Systematic Design of Instruction* (1985), to the goal-free model of Michael Scriven (1967) which utilizes a variety of techniques to gather information. Many of the techniques described earlier during the discussion of formative evaluation are appropriate for evaluating classroom activities. The key is to remember to ask the questions *during* the unit and at the *end* of the unit. Answers to both sets of questions can be used to gain insights into the effectiveness of classroom activities.

Comparing Educational Programs

Throughout American history educators have been bombarded with information about new educational programs and practices. For example, during the late 1960s, mathematics, science, and social studies curriculum materials were developed and each one claimed to be better and more effective than existing programs. Although some of the claims were based on little more than the opinions of the developers, some projects conducted studies to provide information to educators to enable them to compare an existing program with a new alternative.

Evaluation continues to play an important role in curriculum development. Federal, state, and local agencies demand that evaluation plans be a part of all projects. School personnel want to know that a particular curriculum will be effective in their district before they spend funds to implement the program in the school. Why? Because any curriculum change is accompanied by significant outlays of resources for materials and training.

As a result, a variety of evaluation models and research designs have been developed. In addition to those already noted, statisticians Donald Campbell and Julian Stanley (1963) have devised a set of research procedures to aid evaluators in designing experimental studies. The advances in computer technology have also enabled researchers to analyze data in a much more sophisticated manner. The goal is to enable the evaluator to confidently suggest that the findings of the research study may be applied to schools in various settings, and that educators may use the same materials and procedures and expect similar results. Educational journals are filled with the reports of various experimental studies that compare various educational programs and strategies.

The paradox in the attempt to compare different curriculums is that no matter how sophisticated the evaluation design and how powerful the statistics, the data are still inadequate in the decision-making process for a number of reasons. First, most curriculum studies are conducted in the schools; as a result, it is impossible to provide the controls necessary to make generalizations to a broader context. These are not laboratory studies, and even though sophisticated statistical techniques exist, conclusions must be accepted with a good deal of restraint. A study conducted in New York City may not be applicable to students in Portland, Oregon. Educators don't make cars on an assembly line; they work in a human environment with many more variables than they can ever control. Consequently, the selection of one curriculum plan over another is often aided by evaluation studies, but other factors enter into the decision — public pressure to adopt, financial considerations, and the current popularity of the idea within the educational scene.

Another factor that hinders curriculum comparisons is that in order to collect sufficient data to draw valid conclusions, a variety of studies over a long period of time would be needed. Data collected from a study that was conducted for a short period of time, in one location, and with a few students usually results in conclusions that must be considered very cautiously. However, longitudinal studies that take several years are not always useful to decision makers because they need to act now. Most districts do not want to wait several years to make a decision. An example illustrates this point.

During the 1980s, schools were under considerable pressure to acquire microcomputers for use in the school. Parents and educators were suggesting that students who did not have access to computers would not be able to meet the demands of the emerging technological society, and that computers could improve instruction and student learning. Educators who sought information about the impact of computers on instruction and student learning were left with very little data. Few studies had been conducted on the use of the microcomputer as an instructional tool. However, the number of computers in schools dramatically increased as educators responded to the pressures from both inside and outside the system. Decision makers could not wait.

Decision makers often do attempt to understand the desires and educational needs of their constituents. This desire to know involves yet another type of evaluation.

Needs Assessment

School districts and curriculum developers are confronted with many complex issues. For example, a school district may be thinking about a major revision of the mathematics curriculum. This change would be a major shift in the math program. On what basis should they decide? As noted above, evaluation data from the study of the new curriculum in other schools would be useful. But, before making a change of such magnitude, more information would be needed. In another situation, a curriculum developer may be contemplating the creation of a new set of social studies materials for civics education. The developer has been asked to create these new materials because there have been many complaints about the poor quality of the current materials. What exactly should the developer do? What is the nature of the problem?

The school district and the curriculum developer must either make the decision based on their own reasoning or provide a better basis for their judgment by collecting relevant data. This procedure for identifying and validating needs and establishing priorities among the needs is called *needs assessment*. Needs assessment involves collecting both opinion and factual data from a wide variety of sources both within and outside the school setting. It may begin with a general assessment of needs or with a particular problem that needs solution. If the needs assessment is general in nature, the question may focus on the human needs served by the school. If the needs assessment is more specific, the question may focus on identifying specific needs related to the problem. For example, a school district may be thinking about introducing an international, global perspective to its social studies curriculum. As a part of the needs assessment process it might complete the following activities: (1) collect information from the literature about global education to gain an understanding of what educators believe should be the imporant components of such a program, (2) review the district's social studies curriculum to assess its global perspective, (3) meet with the social studies teachers to discuss the topic, (4) administer a questionnaire to a sample of students in the district to assess their knowledge and attitudes, and (5) hold an open meeting with the school board to enable the board and interested citizens to present their views about global education. Based on the information from all these sources, school district personnel should have a clearer picture about what should be done in the area of global education.

In general, needs assessment data might be collected from students, teachers, administrators, parents, academic specialists, taxpayers, employers, graduates, and dropouts. To collect the information, evaluators might use questionnaires, interviews, school and classroom observations, public hearings, and a critical review of the pertinent educational literature. If the problem is narrower in scope, data from such a broad base might not be collected.

To assist the evaluator in formulating a needs assessment plan, analyzing the data, and forming a set of conclusions, several philosophical models may be followed. A well-known configuration, the rational model, is represented in the writings of Ralph Tyler (1950). Tyler focuses his model on gathering data from students, subject area experts, and society in order to understand those factors that influence and shape the needs and goals of the curriculum. Most districts seldom follow all the procedures outlined in Tyler's model. Whatever the model, however, each involves the evaluator in a careful step-by-step process for determining the final set of goals.

Needs assessment procedures have become very popular during the last two decades. Some groups have seen the needs assessment process as a means of clearly identifying what the school should be teaching. These groups see needs assessment as a method to enhance the efficiency of the school. Other groups believe that needs assessment is a way to bring more people into the schooling process. It can be used to increase a feeling of cooperation and sharing among those people involved with the schools. Still, other groups see needs assessment as a method of finding out the values and beliefs of various subcultures in American society so that they may be included in the school's curriculum.

Although needs assessment procedures have provided important insights into educational problems, conclusions based on needs assessment activities are not without their problems. A major problem is articulating the meaning of goals and issues to a variety of individuals so that everyone is using the same definition as a referent point. For example, if the same question is asked to students, parents, employers, and taxpayers, it is very important that everyone has a similar understanding of the question. A question like "Do you believe (you/your students/students today) have an understanding of the social, economic, and political problems of Africa?" can be asked to students, teachers, parents. The answers from various groups may then be compared. A question like, "Do you favor more literature in schools?" would be more difficult because various groups of people may have different definitions of the word *literature*.

A second problem is the amount of information that is created by a needs assessment. With so much data to analyze, researchers may then choose to examine those data that they feel are most useful to their needs. Such bias behavior dramatically limits the conclusions that may be drawn.

An additional problem is that public opinion remains stable over relatively short periods. A needs assessment is a snapshot of people's views at a particular point in time. The same individuals might have different opinions a short time later due to some event that occurred in society.

Finally, the school must focus on the future. Needs assessment data must be analyzed with the future needs of the curriculum as a reference point. Most respondents have difficulty anticipating future needs.

As a result of these and other problems, the values of the evaluators cannot help but influence the conclusions that are made. Although one would expect the researcher to bring an unbiased approach to the needs assessment process, it is critical to remember that individual values influence any interpretation of data. The critic might suggest that the researcher looks for the data to support already held beliefs.

Needs assessment, however, plays an important role in the overall evaluation of curriculum issues. It is also closely related to instructional issues.

▶ Evaluation and Instruction

Evaluation plays an important role in instruction. Three areas are of major importance: diagnosing student/teaching problems, determining whether or not objectives have been achieved, and checking the validity of the content.

Diagnosing Problems

Diagnosis, used here, means the collection and use of information to help solve teaching problems. The goal is to diagnose the problem in order to prescribe some type of treatment to solve it. For example, an eighth-grade teacher finds that her students are having difficulty working with maps. In order to find out more about this problem, some type of diagnosis is needed. Information from several sources might be useful. The teacher might ask the class to explain various features of a map. Or she might ask a series of questions to determine student knowledge. These questions could be asked orally to the class or as part of a written exercise. For example, she might ask, "What are the functions of a map's key? What does *scale* mean? How far is it from point *a* to point *b*? Which roadway on the map is a freeway?" As students answer these questions, the teacher gains some insights into potential problems. She might plan some additional exercises to help students learn the important skills.

Diagnosis might also include a careful examination of the instructional activities the teacher used to teach map skills. Students may not have learned the required map skills because the teacher really did not provide adequate instruction. By examining the learning activities, the teacher might find that not enough practice was provided for students to acquire the skills. Or perhaps she will discover that the examples used during instruction were too abstract for the students in the class.

The goal of the diagnosis process is to collect data that will provide sufficient information that will allow the teacher to make the changes needed to solve a problem for the class as a whole or for an individual student. Diagnosis takes place throughout instruction. Some educators who advocate a competency-based or goal-centered instructional model suggest that preassessment of student knowledge should be completed prior to the formulation of instructional objectives. Preassessment enables the teacher to adjust the specific goals for the class and related instructional activities. If students already know about specific aspects of the content, then it is not necessary to teach them. Instead, the teacher can move to higher level objectives or to different content.

Diagnostic evaluation techniques have been used extensively in special education to diagnose and prescribe learning activities for students with special learning disabilities. Carefully prepared tests are used to measure a student's particular learning problems or knowledge related to selected learning goals. Based on the results of tests, educators then devise an Individual Educational Plan (IEP) for each student. The IEP is usually developed by a team of educators who are involved with the student. The plan identifies specific strategies for teaching the student the knowledge and skills in a particular content area. The IEP is then implemented in the classroom. The success of the plan may vary with the abilities of the teacher to carry out the tasks, the support services available, and the materials available. Although the idea behind the concept was not new, IEPs were introduced by Public Law 97–142, a law outlining the rights of students with special learning problems. Consequently, IEPs are most often used in special education. They are also used with gifted students to outline special courses of study. It is important to note again that the success of the IEP depends on the correct assessment of learning needs, the development of a workable plan, and the implementation of the plan in the classroom. It is a difficult task.

Diagnostic evaluation is also used extensively in measuring specific reading problems. For example, a group-administered test such as the Nelson Reading Skills Tests (Houghton-Mifflin) is used for students in grades 3–9, or the Stanford Diagnostic Reading Test is given to students in grades 1–2 (Harcourt, Brace, Jovanovich). Another diagnostic test, administered to individual students is the Diagnostic Reading Scales (CTB/McGraw-Hill). This test is designed for students in grades 1–8. The results from the tests provide educators with information about a student's reading ability.

With advances in computer technology, more sophisticated techniques are being developed. Computer courseware materials are available to test a student's level of competence and to provide an assessment of his or her weaknesses. The teacher may then use this information to prescribe additional learning activities. Some computer-assisted instructional packages not only diagnose but also lead the student through appropriate remedial lessons.

In the most traditional classrooms, formal pretesting and the adjustment of learning goals seldom take place. Instead, teachers rely on informal assessments of student knowledge, skills, and attitudes. A teacher may ask a student to explain something, demonstrate how to do something, or describe how various pieces of knowledge fit together in a real world phenomenon. Or a teacher may have a student complete a worksheet or take a quiz. All these activities are diagnostic in the sense that they provide information to the teacher that may be used to determine potential learning problems.

Teachers must rely on both formal and informal methods of diagnosis in order to change instructional activities. For example, a test might be administered to formally check students' knowledge of how to add two-digit numbers. Based on the scores the teacher could develop a classroom instructional strategy and special lessons for students who had problems with the addition. A more informal method might be to ask students, as a class, what they do when they add two-digit numbers. By listening to the responses the teacher might be able to draw some general conclusions about the class's knowledge.

Determining the Achievement of Objectives
A critical part of schooling is making decisions about whether or not a student has learned the facts and skills that form the core of a particular course. Student progress from one grade to the next is determined by the evaluation of the student's work at that grade level. To determine student achievement, teachers collect a variety of information about student work. Worksheets, papers, reports, special projects, quizzes, chapter tests and unit examinations are all typical ways in which a teacher attempts to measure student learning. The cornerstone of the evaluation process in most secondary schools is the formal written examination in which a student responds to objective questions and essay questions. In elementary school formal evaluation techniques vary; however, written tests are very common.

An approach used for many years to evaluate student learning is norm-referenced testing. Norm-referenced tests are designed to compare the performances of individual students to the performance of some normative group. It assumes that some students will learn less than others. If used in a class, norm-referenced testing uses other students' test scores as the norm.

In the 1960s norm-referenced testing came under considerable criticism. Educational leaders questioned the value of evaluating students in this manner and they suggested a more objective approach. The argument followed these lines: Schooling has a purpose. Because it has a purpose, it should be possible to identify its goals. If goals can be identified, specific statements that illustrate these goals should be available so that it is possible to determine whether or not students achieve them. If these assumptions are correct about education, evaluation should serve as a means of determining whether or not a student has achieved the goals. The demonstration should not depend on other students' achievements. This movement to specify learning outcomes has received considerable attention over the last twenty years and has caused educators not only to rethink evaluation but also to reexamine the whole instructional process.

The philosophy that all students should have an opportunity to learn the material and be evaluated against clearly specified objectives is best represented by mastery learning.

Mastery learning proponents followed a technological evaluation model (see pages 291–292 of this chapter for a discussion) based on clearly written objectives. The specification of the learning objectives lead to a different type of evaluation test—the criterion-referenced test. A criterion-referenced test is designed to ascertain whether or not the student has learned a specific task rather than make comparisons with other students in the class or some other norm. The test items match the set of instructional objectives. The student either demonstrates mastery of the objective or does not. A passing mark is based on criteria established prior to testing and not on how well others do on the test.

The mastery learning approach and the specification of instructional objectives has led to many changes in both evaluation and instruction. Supporters contend that evaluation can be more objective and less subjective in nature. By specifying objectives at the beginning, instruction may be more precise, and evaluation techniques can more accurately assess student learning. Critics of the mastery learning approach suggest that following a behaviorialist approach leads to narrowly defined learning outcomes that require the learning of trivial material. As a consequence, critics suggest that tests tend to focus on multiple-choice items that ask students to recall factual information. The emphasis is on material that is easily forgotten.

The specification of learning outcomes has had a dramatic impact on the evaluation process. Although the educational claims of success have yet to be met, educators over the last two decades have sought to develop test items that measure more precisely what students have learned. Criterion-referenced testing has had an impact on how educators evaluate the success of instruction.

Checking Content Validity
An integral component of the schooling process is the materials that provide the focus and direction for the overall curriculum and for instruction. The selection of these materials has important implications for comprehensive curriculum goals.

One of the first areas of evaluation of materials is examining the validity of the content. A social studies textbook, for example, may not present a valid picture of the world. The content may either project an inaccurate picture of social reality or it may misrepresent the basic concepts of the discipline. Alan Tom (1967) suggests that in order to judge the validity of the content of materials, the educator must carefully examine them. He says that the teacher:

> . . . must not only read the intentions stated by the curriculum developer but especially the student materials. Only after looking at student materials can one estimate to what extent the curriculum conveys to students accurate conceptions of the social reality and valid structures of the discipline (p. 91).

Tom's statement suggests several areas that should be examined when evaluating curriculum materials. First, do the materials represent a realistic view of the world? For example, what about stereotypes? Are women presented as having limited role possibilities? Are minority groups presented in an unfavorable manner? Are controversial issues avoided or presented as one-sided issues? To assist in the evaluation of materials, professional organizations and local districts have developed checklists. A sample checklist is presented in Table 15–2. As you examine the criteria, remember they are just examples of questions one might ask about a set of materials. Another group with differing values might create an entirely different list.

Tom also suggests that the validity of the content goes beyond the view of the world presented in the materials. One must examine the basic concepts presented in the material. Do the materials represent the key concepts of the discipline? For example, does the seventh-

TABLE 15-2 Sample Criteria for Reviewing Materials

1. *Content:* What is the purpose of the materials? Who is the audience? Is it appealing?
2. *Reading Difficulty:* Using a standard reading test like the Fry or Dale-Chall, what is the reading level? Is there technical vocabulary? What is the interest level?
3. *Learning Outcomes:* Are goals and objectives clearly stated? What are implicit goals?
4. *Organization:* How is the text presented? Is there a logical scope and sequence to the materials? How long will it take to cover the material?
5. *Layout:* How does the book look? Check type, pictures, charts, graphs, use of color, and maps. Do the materials present a balanced view of society? Also, does the book use interesting ways to draw students' attention to key ideas? If multimedia materials are present, what is the quality?
6. *Instructional Philosophy:* After reviewing the teacher's materials, are there suggested teaching strategies? Are there suggested student activities?
7. *Evaluation of Student Learning:* What methods and materials are provided to help the teacher assess student learning?
8. *Support Materials:* Are other materials available? For example, are there manuals, workbooks, films, handouts, and tests, and materials for students with learning problems?
9. *Development Information:* Were the materials field tested? What information is available about the authors?
10. *Curriculum Issues:* How well do the materials fit into the overall curriculum? Are there interdisciplinary linkages with other subject areas? Do the materials link with the previous year's curriculum and prepare students for the following year?

grade mathematics book present the basic concepts and skills that are critical for students at that age? To assist developers and educators, professional organizations have developed guidelines. For example, the National Council for the Social Studies has guidelines for assessing key concepts, generalizations, and skills at various grade levels, and for determining the validity of computer courseware. Similar guidelines exist for mathematics, science, art, English, and second language professions.

The validity of the concepts also introduces their appropriateness for the students. It is generally accepted that some students pass through a series of developmental learning stages in which they move from being able to think at a concrete level to being able to think more abstractly. The challenge that confronts educators is matching the conceptual difficulty of the materials with the conceptual level of the students. Student often fail to understand difficult concepts and generalizations because these ideas are not presented at an appropriate cognitive level. To assist in evaluating the conceptual level of materials, three important areas may be examined:

1. *Use of examples:* Are the discussions of major concepts tied to real-life, concrete examples? In a social studies text, for example, how does the author present the word *culture*? Would a student at the concrete operational level be able to "see" examples of culture? Or are concepts in the text presented as vocabulary words in which the student simply memorizes the definition? Concept acquisition is more than being able to define a word; it is using the concept to explain. By carefully looking at how the author explains the major concepts through the use of examples, it is possible to gain insight into the conceptual level of the materials.

2. *Use of visuals:* How are visuals such as pictures, graphs, drawings, and maps used to further explain and stimulate students' interests in the concepts and materials? The printed word is not sufficient. An educator may check the visual materials to determine how the materials are integrated into the written text. A better understanding of key concepts can be achieved by presenting the concepts through more than one medium.

3. *Use of prior learning:* Robert Gagne (1965) believes that learning occurs heirarchically. According to this theory, an individual learns something new when he or she has mastered the prerequisite knowledge of skills. If this is accurate, the review of a text needs to consider what has been learned about the materials or concepts prior to the presentation in the materials. What is assumed about prerequisite skills or knowledge?

Another important area is the readability of the materials. Students must be able to read the words if they are to understand the content. Although strides have been made in assessing student abilities and in developing better materials, most teachers find that the range of reading skills is quite wide. Various reading assessment instruments are available for determining the reading level of a set of materials. Tests such as those developed by Dale Chall can be used to determine the general reading level. In addition to paper-pencil instruments, computer-assisted evaluation programs also make the evaluation of materials faster and easier.

Finally, materials must be evaluated to determine whether or not they are appropriate for the background of the students who will use them. The materials may be valid, teach key concepts, and use appropriate strategies, and still not be the right materials for the students in a particular classroom. At some point, academic soundness may not be enough. The materials must relate in some way to the lives of the students. This is a difficult area to evaluate, but if materials are remote from the lives of the students, special efforts must be made to make the content of the materials relevant to the students. Indeed, this is one of the most challenging tasks in education—making the materials come alive to the students who use them.

ISSUES IN EVALUATION

▶ A major concern during the 1980s was how to determine the success of the schools. Critics asked, "What is the school teaching?" Study after study examined this question with the underlying belief being that American students were growing less educated.

In 1985 Marilyn Clayton Felt (1985) and staff from the Education Development Center reviewed thirty-three studies of schooling in America. Included in their analysis was a section on evaluation in schools. After reviewing the conclusions from these studies, the authors offer the following suggestions concerning evaluation:

1. Formal tests should be used as teaching tools. Much less emphasis should be placed on multiple choice, true/false, and short-answer tests. More emphasis should be placed on essay tests that have students using information rather than simply reproducing it.
2. Evaluation techniques should be more individualized to enable students to demonstrate that they have mastered the required course of study.
3. Standardized tests should be used at key points in the education process to determine whether or not students have the needed skills to go on.

These recommendations suggest that important changes need to be made in the construction and usage of tests. Criticism is directed toward the type of tests that are currently being used in the classroom. The recommendations focus primarily on the evaluation of learning outcomes. More formalized testing, however, has caused concern among some groups. Although critics acknowledge the importance of such evaluations, they point to the narrow spectrum of skills usually measured, the low correlation between what is taught in the classroom and what is tested, and the many tests that are culturally biased against certain minority groups. These concerns have led to the enactment of state laws to provide more information about tests. As tests continue to grow in importance in determining student success and access to educational opportunities, this area will become more and more controversial.

As technology continues to make information more readily available, the collecting, storing, analyzing, and sharing of data will become easier. If the recommendations for standardized tests are accepted, tests will become important in determining the school's success, and new technology will enable data to be shared with many different sources. Such actions may have a dramatic impact on education and the debate noted in the preceding paragraph.

The differences between those who favor a systems approach and those who favor a qualitative approach will continue to add fuel to the controversy about how best to gain a picture of curriculum and instruction. Because each approach has a different focus, the answer is not a simple one and the debate will continue.

Overriding all of these concerns will be the events that take place in society that will cause new issues to be brought forward as concerns of education. No matter what the issues, however, evaluation will be at the core.

SUMMARY

▶ Evaluation is the process of systematically gathering and analyzing information. Its goals are to help educators understand and judge the outcomes, and to pinpoint ways to improve the educational process. Evaluation may be formative or summative in nature and may follow a technological or qualitative philosophical approach. Evaluation techniques may be used to assess classroom activities, to compare educational programs, and to assess educational needs. Evaluation may also provide pertinent information about student learning needs, the achievement of learning objectives, and the content of educational materials.

Evaluation plays a central role in curriculum and instruction. The data gathered during the evaluation process provides insights into how well the school's curriculum is achieving its overall goals, and how successful specific instructional activities are in teaching students the knowledge and skills deemed important by the teacher. Because evaluation is a critical component of the educational process, it is often at the center of discussions concerning what should be done to improve education. Proponents and critics of education both use evaluation techniques to support their claims that the schools are of are not doing their job. Issues surrounding evaluation often focus on the type of knowledge and skills being tested and the instruments used in assessing students abilities.

ACTIVITIES

1. Based on your reading, define each of the following terms:
   a. evaluation
   b. formative evaluation
   c. summative evaluation
   d. norm-referenced testing
   e. criterion-referenced testing
2. Two popular approaches to evaluation are a technological or systems approach and a qualitative or pluralistic approach. What are the basic differences between these two approaches? Give an example of the kinds of data each approach would use in studying a school problem.
3. Suppose you were a curriculum developer and you were asked to develop a new curriculum for the seventh-grade English course. What would you do to find out the needs in this area? Describe your plan.
4. A fourth-grade teacher gives each student a mathematics worksheet before she begins a new unit. The worksheet has twenty questions. Given what you have read about evaluation, why might the teacher choose to do this?
5. What are some of the problems with norm-referenced tests? With criterion-referenced tests?
6. National examinations are used by most school districts. Visit a local school district or the college's library or resource center and examine samples of these examinations. Look specifically for the Iowa Basic Skills and the Student Achievement Test (SAT). What type of knowledge and skills are being measured by these examinations?

7. During a visit to a local school, ask teachers about the procedures they use in evaluating the curriculum in a particular content area. If possible, collect samples of instruments they use.

8. It was discussed in this chapter that special education and reading use diagnostic tools to assess potential learning problems. Make an appointment with a special education or reading instructor and ask to examine examples of diagnostic instruments.

9. Go to the library and examine *The Handbook on Formative and Summative Evaluation on Student Learning* (edited by Bloom, Hastings, and Madaus). This volume gives an extended rationale and description of the mastery learning concept, and specific chapters on each of the content areas. Look specifically at Bloom's Chapter 3, and then read a chapter about a content area of special interest to you.

10. Visit the resource center or a public school and examine a set of textbooks used for a particular course. Use the questions presented in Table 15-2 as a guide for your analysis. What conclusions can you make about the texts?

REFERENCES

Campbell, D. T., and Stanley, J. C. (1963). Experimental and quasi experimental designs on teaching. In N. L. Gage (Ed.), *Handbook of research on teaching*. Chicago: Rand McNally.

Cronbach, L. J. (1963). Course improvement through evaluation. *Teachers College Record, 64,* 672–683.

Dick, W., and Carey, L. (1985). *The systematic design of instruction* (2nd ed.). Glenview, Ill.: Scott, Foresman.

Ehman, L.; Mehlinger, H.; and Patrick, J. (1974). *Toward effective instruction in secondary social studies*. Boston: Houghton Mifflin, p. 326.

Eisner, E. W. (1985). *The educational imagination* (2nd ed.). New York: Macmillan.

Felt, M. C. (1985). *Improving our schools*. Newton, Mass.: Educational Development Center.

Gagne, R. M. (1965). *The conditions of learning*. New York: Holt, Rinehart and Winston, p. 25.

Mager, R. (1975). *Preparing instructional objectives*. Belmont, Calif.: Fearon.

Rogers, V. R. (1985). Qualitative and aesthetic views of curriculum and curriculum making. In *Current Thought on Curriculum*. Alexandria, Va.: Association for Supervision and Curriculum Development, pp. 103–117.

Scriven, M. (1967). The methodology of evaluation. *AERA Monograph Series on Curriculum and Evaluation,* No. 1. Chicago: Rand McNally.

Stufflebeam, D. L., et al. (1971). *Educational evaluation and decision making*. Bloomington, Ind.: Phi Delta Kappa, p. 15.

Tyler, R. W. (1950). *Basic principles of curriculum and instruction.* Chicago: University of Chicago Press.

Tom, A. (1967). *An approach to selecting among social studies curricula.* St. Louis: Central Midwestern Regional Educational Laboratory, p. 91.

SUGGESTED READINGS

Block, J., and Anderson, L. W. (1975). *Mastery learning in classroom instruction.* New York: Macmillan.

Bloom, B. S. (1975). *Human characteristics and school learning.* New York: McGraw-Hill.

Eisner, E. (1985). *The educational imagination: On the design and evaluation of school programs* (2nd ed.). New York: Macmillan.

Frederikson, N. J. (November 1984). The real test bias: The influence of testing on teaching and learning. *American Psychologist, 39,* 193–202.

Patton, M. Q. (1982). *Practical evaluation.* Beverly Hills, Calif.: Sage Publications.

Scriven, M. (1967). The methodology of evaluation. In R. W. Tyler, R. M. Gagne, and M. Scriven (Eds.), *Perspectives of Curriculum Evaluation. AERA Monograph Series on Curriculum Evaluation,* No. 1, Chicago: Rand McNally.

Wise, A. E. (1979). *Legislated learning: The bureaucratization of the American classroom.* Berkeley: University of California Press.

16

Technology in Curriculum and Instruction

▶ ━━━━━━━━━━━━━━━━━━━━━━━━━━━━━
━━━━━━━━━━━━━━━━━━━━━━━━━━━━━◀

OVERVIEW

▶ This chapter discusses the role of technology in curriculum and instruction. Technology is first defined, then it is examined as a part of the curriculum development process and as a part of the instructional process. Specific examples are provided to illustrate how technology can be used in the teaching-learning process. After reading the chapter you should be able to define educational technology and discuss its role in the curriculum of the school and in the instructional process.

INTRODUCTION

▶ The stereo system comes on with a quiet click followed by the pulsating sounds of rock and roll. Larry awakens, rolls over, shuts off the stereo, and turns on the television. The announcer, speaking via satellite from London, is describing the latest action by the Parliament to bring about a better balance of payments between England and the Arab world. Larry is not all that interested in England's problems; however, when the weather comes on he notes that it still sounds good for the weekend. He rushes out to the breakfast area and puts a couple of waffles in the microwave and calls Mel to see if he needs a ride to school.

After a quick shower, Larry removes a tape from the video recorder, which had taped a special on South Africa. He places it in his bookbag to take to school; it will make his report better. Before leaving the house, Larry prints the outline for his communication speech that he had written the night before on the family's personal computer.

Finally he is ready to go. He jumps in his old car, turns on the stereo system, and is off to Mel's house. Mel rushes out and the two of them head for the parking lot. With about five minutes to spare, they rush into their first class, and school begins.

Most of the school day is spent listening to someone talk, writing material down in a notebook, or watching a film or videotape. Once during the day Larry goes to the library, looks something up in the card catalog, and spends a few minutes reading. In social studies class he uses the computer briefly as a part of a simulation on exploration of the new world. Mostly, however, he listens and writes things down.

Larry and many of his classmates live in two different worlds. One is a high-technology world characterized by stereos, computers, video games, videotapes, and microwaves. Many of his classmates work in businesses that have some of the latest technological advances. The second world in which they live is characterized by listening, writing, and sitting in an environment that has remained almost unchanged from one student generation to the next. It is a paradox. On one hand, most young people live in a rapidly changing technological age; on the other hand, they attend a school that is only slightly affected by that same technology. As American schools move into the twenty-first century, they too will be confronted with technological changes that will undoubtedly affect the formal curriculum and the instructional techniques used by educators to instruct students.

Two important aspects of technology are discussed in this chapter. First, educational technology is examined as it relates to curriculum and curriculum development. This discussion is followed by the exploration of the ways technology may be used as a part of the instructional process.

EDUCATIONAL TECHNOLOGY: A DEFINITION

► There are numerous definitions used within the educational literature, the most inclusive definition defines *educational technology* as "the systematic application of scientific and technical knowledge to the processes of learning and teaching" (Maddison, 1983). This means that technological thinking should be used to help educators (1) organize educational activities, (2) further intellectual skills, and (3) develop the individual skills needed to use new and existing technology. This approach to the application of scientific and technical knowledge incorporates a variety of ways of thinking about technology as a means of organizing the curriculum and assisting in the instructional process.

The two critical elements to remember about our definition are: (1) educational technology represents a systematic way of thinking and (2) educational technology is designed to use techniques to further intellectual skills.

EDUCATIONAL TECHNOLOGY: ORGANIZING THE CURRICULUM

▶ In Chapter 11 we discussed the role of the formal curriculum in the school. The formal curriculum was defined as those specific courses that are designed to teach students the intellectual skills deemed important by the school. The formal curriculum focuses on *what* is taught and *when* it is taught. The formal curriculum has a purpose and rationale for its being. At its best, the formal curriculum is a tightly developed set of experiences that progressively provide for the needs of the student. At its worst, it is a loosely related set of courses that make little sense to the learner. The challenge for the curriculum developer, either at the school-wide level or within an individual classroom, is to develop a closely related set of experiences that achieve specific learning outcomes. Educational technology's emphasis on systematic thinking and careful selection of instructional technology provides a model for curriculum developers. The model can be represented in its most simple form by Figure 16–1.

In this model one begins with an examination of goals. What does the activity seek to accomplish? Based on the goals, instructional activities are developed to achieve them. During the final component, evaluation, data are collected to determine the success of the instruc-

FIGURE 16-1 Three-Stage Development Model

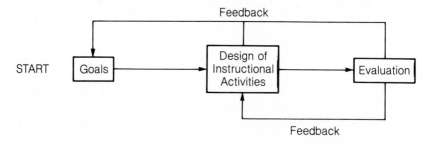

tional activities in achieving the goals. Feedback information helps the developer reassess the goals and the instructional activities.

The model as presented in Figure 16–1 is really too simplistic to be useful for most developers. A more detailed model is presented in Figure 16–2.

Figure 16–2 provides two important additions. First, educational technologists view curriculum development from a systems perspective. This means that the three-step development process outlined in Figure 16–1 cannot take place in isolation. Development occurs in a broader context in which many other factors may intervene. Although these factors or constraints are not directly related to the activities, they do influence decisions. For example, a classroom teacher must consider various characteristics about the students when determining goals, deciding on instructional activities, and creating evaluation techniques. Younger students, who lack certain skills, cannot be treated in the same manner as older students. Teaching a unit about the farms in America to students who live in urban areas is different than teaching that same unit to students who attend rural schools. Also, teaching in a school in which the periods are only fifty minutes and classes rotate so that they are not the same time everyday has important implications on what a teacher may choose to do. The constraints impinge on the decision-making process and must be considered.

FIGURE 16-2 Detailed Curriculum Development Model

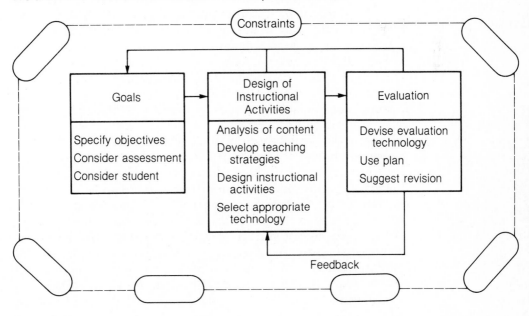

Second, the decision-making process at each stage is more detailed than represented in Figure 16–1. Work by James Popham (1969), Robert Mager, Walter Dick, and Lou Carey, for example, has provided specific steps for both the curriculum developer and the individual classroom teacher to follow. Their models attempt to provide a systematic process for the development of materials and for the use of technology during instruction. The cornerstone for all models is the development of clearly stated goals and objectives. Based on these statements, appropriate instructional materials, activities, technology, and evaluation techniques can then be created.

The technological model for curriculum development has had a dramatic impact on the education. Curriculum developers have used variations of the model represented in Figure 16–2 since the late 1960s. Between 1965 and 1975 curriculum centers, supported by large grants from the federal government, developed new materials in science, mathematics, and social studies for both elementary and secondary schools. It was one of the most active curriculum development periods in American education. Although the number of curriculum centers across the country has diminished, variations of the technological approach are still being used by developers.

Initially proclaimed to be the answer to education's problems, the technological approach is not without its weaknesses. Primary among the objections is the claim that the specification of learner outcomes leads to the identification of lower level objectives—recall of factual information and the demonstration of skills that can easily be measured. As a consequence, critics claim that more complex and sophisticated learning is avoided. A second criticism is that the development process is extremely costly in both dollars and time. For example, some of the classroom materials developed during the 1960s cost over one million dollars to create and took five years to produce! A final criticism is that no set of materials can meet the varied needs of a set of students in a particular classroom. There are no "teacher-proof" materials; that is, instructions so clear that one simply has to follow the directions and the lesson will succeed.

The technological approach to curriculum development, however, has had a profound impact on the way materials have been developed. The technologists have caused educators to think seriously about the content of specific courses, when this content should be taught, and the indicators of success as measured in student learning. The technological approach has also caused educators to think seriously about the sequence of instructional activities and which activities may be the most effective in achieving specific learning goals. These latter concerns led to the development of programmed instruction materials and computer-assisted instructional models. These newer models of instruction also incorporated new pieces of technology to achieve goals.

EDUCATIONAL TECHNOLOGY: INSTRUCTIONAL ISSUES

► Educational technology also attempts to use scientific and technical knowledge to further intellectual and technical skills. This use of technology refers to the decisions made in the second box in the planning model shown in Figure 16–2. In this designing phase the teacher examines the content, considers an appropriate strategy, creates the instructional activities, and then selects the appropriate technology to assist in the delivery of the lesson. Translated into classroom applications, this means either selecting the appropriate piece of technology to assist the teacher in teaching the lesson or establishing a technological system to deliver instruction.

Historically, technology has been most evident as the printed page. Gutenberg's press initiated a technology that disseminated visual and verbal information to millions, and it became the principal method of communication for education. In fact, textbooks and worksheets are the mainstays of today's classroom.

During the first half of the twentieth century the next major items of technology to make a dramatic impact on society and a lesser impact on education were records, film, and television. For the first time communication could include combinations of sound, movement, and other images. The printed word, which heretofore could only paint mental pictures, could now be brought to life in a new art form. These new technologies profoundly influenced education outside of the formal classroom. Students were introduced to the world as seen through the screen of the television. The electronic media of television consumed hours of time for almost all the school-aged children in America.

As a part of instruction, films, television, and videotapes allowed the teacher and student to visit places far from home and observe customs distinctly different from their own. Records, films, and television opened a window to the world, and life for most students would never be quite the same.

Since the 1960s three trends have influenced educational technology and its instructional potential. First was the trend toward miniaturization of the physical nature of technology. The era of space travel and the demands for minute pieces of sophisticated technology ushered in the transistor and then the microchip. They were extremely expensive at first, but advances in production now make sophisticated pieces of technology within the cost limitations of almost everyone. Calculators that once cost $50 are now priced under $5, are the size of a credit card, and have several times the capability of their ancient parents.

Accompanying miniaturization was the trend toward increasing simplicity. For example, early computers took a lot of space and had to be run by specialists who knew the intricacies of computer technology. Today the microcomputers can fit in a briefcase and can be used after a short period of training or study. *User-friendly* is the watchword of the 1980s for all technology.

The final technological change that has influenced education is the trend toward combining the strengths of one technology with another to form a new and more powerful tool. An interactive computer/video system, for example, merges the capabilities of the computer and the visual potency of motion and sound. When combined, these two pieces of technology form a potentially powerful teaching-learning tool. Also, satellite communication systems not only open the doors to far-away places but also the opportunities for direct communication.

These trends will continue to bring about dramatic changes in technology. Some educators suggest that the new technologies will not only change *what* is taught but *how* it is taught. Whether dramatic, revolutionary changes will continue is a point of conjecture. However, it is evident that technology has and will continue to have an impact on schooling. It will shape teacher-led instruction and technology-led instruction, and the manner in which students interact with teachers, materials, and other students.

TECHNOLOGY AND ITS RELATIONSHIP TO INSTRUCTION

▶ Educational technology seeks to apply scientific and technical knowledge to the processes of learning and teaching. In curriculum development we noted that this meant the application of a particular approach to the development of materials. From an instructional perspective technology serves another purpose—assisting both the teacher and the student in the learning process. As a teacher makes decisions about what to do, choices are made about what kinds of technology can be used to assist in achieving the goals of the lesson. In selecting the appropriate piece of technology, the teacher makes a series of important interrelated decisions about whether or not to use technology during instruction. Some of the questions are based on sound instructional practices; others are based on practical and personal choices.

Instructional Questions: (Will it help?)

1. What instructional strategies are most appropriate to teach the content?
2. Which type of technology might be used most effectively to teach the content?

3. Can technology assist me in individualizing the materials to meet student needs?
4. What materials are available to me?
5. Can my students benefit from using technology as a part of the instructional activity?
6. What pieces of technology are available to be used in the lesson?
7. How much class time will be needed?
8. Will I need to teach my students new skills in order to use the technology?

Personal Questions: (Is it worth the trouble?)

1. Do I know how to use the technology?
2. How much time will it take to get ready to use the technology?
3. What kind of management problem will occur if I use the technology?
4. How much trouble will it be to obtain the technology for my class?

The answers to these questions vary from instructional activity to instructional activity, from one group of students to another, and from one piece of technology to another. The answer to a particular question will also vary from one teacher to the next. Some individuals are always willing to try new experiences, learn new skills, and take risks. Others prefer to do what they know best.

Generally speaking, all teachers realize that different technology can assist in the learning process. Using different pieces of technology change the stimuli in the classroom. Writing on the chalkboard, using the overhead, showing a short film, and using the computer all change the interactions that occur in the classroom. All experienced teachers realize that a lecture that incorporates a videotape and an overhead projector is more effective than if the teacher talks the whole time and students write down what was said. Most teachers also realize that some students learn the material better if they can see the concepts that are being taught. Films, filmstrips, television, videotapes, and videodiscs all provide visual representation of materials and organize them in a way as to facilitate learning. More and more teachers are also beginning to see the computer and related technology as important instructional tools for use in the classroom. Most teachers know these things, but the personal questions and the potential problems often inhibit a teacher from using technology effectively. Classroom management problems and logistical problems rank high on the list. For example, why go through all the trouble to set up a time to go to the computer lab for an hour and have to worry about discipline problems when it is much easier to stay in the class and do the lesson the way it has been done before? The answer may be that more students would learn the key ideas, acquire new skills, and enjoy the learning experience; however, to do so will take time, energy, and new skills. But, let's assume that the teacher wants to use technology as an instructional tool. What can technology do for the teacher and the student? It may assist in four general areas.

► Technology May Teach Content and Skills

One of the major goals for a teacher is to teach students the content and skills that are important for the subject area. For example, teachers often see themselves as content specialists—mathematics teacher, history teacher, chemistry teacher, or special education teacher. The content provides a focus for the teacher and organizes the instructional process. Technology can assist teachers in teaching the content and skills that are central to their subject. A variety of techniques may be used. The most common are briefly described below.

Chalkboards
The chalkboard is so familiar to a teacher that it is often overlooked as one of the more versatile and convenient means of visual communication. Words, key ideas, questions, and other symbols all can be written on the chalkboard. It may also be used as a means of summarizing student discussion or as a place for students to demonstrate skills.

Still Projection
Still projection techniques include slides, filmstrips, and transparencies. Materials tend to be relatively cheap to purchase, often accompany textbook materials, are simple to operate, and are relatively trouble-free. In addition, they can be used at any desired pace. For example, a filmstrip may be shown as a total sequence or a teacher might show selected parts of the filmstrip. Transparencies, blank sheets of clear plastic, are the most versatile in that the teacher may write on them or have specific materials transferred to them. The overhead projector needed to use the transparency is an easy piece of equipment to use, having only an on-off switch.

Motion Pictures
Motion pictures and television dramatically changed the world of print. Motion pictures bring life to the printed page and provide a more engaging learning experience for the learner. Most teachers use films, live television, and videotape as occasional instructional tools. Few classrooms are characterized by frequent use of these techniques in an integrated instructional manner.

Computer
The use of computers dramatically increased in the late 1970s with the introduction of the microcomputer. For the first time the power of the mainframe computer was packaged in a small, portable machine. Since that time, the number of computers available for instructional uses has increased significantly. Microcomputers can be used to assist the teacher in teaching specific content and skills by providing drill and practice on previously taught skills, tutoring students in learning new content and skills, simulating special environments, developing problem-solving skills, and helping to analyze data. In some cases, the computer may completely manage the instructional sequence, in other situations it may be used by the teacher and students only occasionally. The most common uses of computers in the classrooms are either in a laboratory situation where students sit in front of the computer and respond to a series of questions and prompts, or in the individual classroom where the teacher uses the computer with the whole class or with small groups of students. As computer courseware improves it may take the place of many textbooks. Computer simulations in science and the social studies will also become more and more powerful tools for student learning.

Videodisc Technology
Videodiscs serve as flexible storage devices for sound, still pictures, and motion. A videodisc can store over 50,000 single frames or thirty minutes of motion with dual sound tracks on one side. When linked with the microcomputer, lessons in music, history, and language may be taught or reinforced for the student. The videodisc/computer combination will be a powerful teaching and learning tool of the twenty-first century.

► Technology May Help Develop Materials

Commercially published materials may be the mainstay of the curriculum, but most teachers still spend a considerable amount of time creating worksheets and other teaching aides. Videotapes, audiotapes, and computer technology can be used effectively by the teacher.

Audiotapes
Small, portable audio recorders now make the creation and use of sound recordings relatively easy. Commercially available materials may be purchased, but in most cases teachers can create their own audiotapes from recordings for use with a specific instructional sequence. For example, music from various historical eras may be used to illustrate a particular point of view.

Videotape

Videotape technology now allows the teacher to play commercially produced programs, record programs off the television for use in the
classroom, or develop individually designed programs to meet a specific
instructional goal. Such equipment is relatively cheap and available
in most school districts. Videotapes may be linked to other pieces of
technology, such as a computer, to create an interactive learning system.

Computer

Computers and related microtechnology have the most potential as
a technological tool to assist the teacher in developing materials. Flexible word-processing programs have changed the manner in which many
teachers and students write. They are flexible tools that have a multitude
of uses—lesson plans, letters, worksheets, tests, and reports are some
examples. Specially written computer programs can also enable the
teacher to create worksheets, readings, crossword puzzles, and tests.
These general utility programs offer the teacher who is not a computer
programmer the opportunity to use the power of the computer to create
specially designed materials. Special authoring languages, voice recognition, and flexible creation of special video and audio materials are tools
of the twenty-first century that will allow the teacher greater creativity
in the development of individualized learning materials for students.

▶ Technology May Help Keep Records

Teachers often lament that too much of their time is spent keeping
records and not enough time on actually instructing students. As federal
and state legislation has increased the demands on the schools to keep
records of student progress and learning contracts, teachers have had
to keep more and more detailed records. Traditionally, paper has served
as the main piece of technology for record keeping. More recent advances in microcomputers and related technology are changing the manner in which information is stored and retrieved. Electronic gradebooks,
for example, permit the teacher to maintain, access, and determine
student grades faster and easier than before. Computer disks have
replaced the paper gradebook and filing cabinets in the administrator's
office.

▶ Technology May Help Manage Students

Teachers spend a considerable amount of time and energy managing
students. Keeping a classroom of active students on task is a challenge.
Making sure that all students are learning the material is another

challenge. Technology systems have been developed to manage the learning process. At the core of this system are two computer-assisted instructional management techniques.

Tutorial Programs

Tutorial programs are designed to teach specific knowledge or skills to students. In most cases, these are relatively short learning experiences and are not intended for extended learning episodes. These programs are designed to take the place of the classroom teacher and to be interactive with the student. Some complex tutorial systems may include video material that can be linked to the computer tutorial.

Computer-Assisted Learning

This teaching technique allows the computer to manage the instructional process. CAI programs are descendants of programmed learning materials and the behavioral traditions characterized by the work of B. F. Skinner. Early programs were linear in nature. Later versions were more flexible and designed to evaluate a student's knowledge and skills prior to instruction and then progress through a series of prewritten programs to teach specific cognitive skills. More recent CAI and CAL programs link microcomputers and video technology, such as the laser disk in highly interactive systems. These systems have tended to be used most widely in nonschool settings; however, as the school setting becomes more technological in nature, specialized CAI and CAL programs will emerge.

TECHNOLOGY AND ITS IMPACT ON THE CURRICULUM AND INSTRUCTIONAL PRACTICES

▶ The goal of educational technology is the systematic application of scientific and technical knowledge to the process of learning and teaching. Technology can influence the curriculum as a whole and the instructional activities designed to teach the goals of the curriculum. The impact of a technological perspective and specific technological devices over the past twenty years has been significant.

Initially, curriculum materials were influenced by the technologist's point of view. Developers and textbook authors are now more attentive to goals and learning outcomes. Learning activities are designed to address specific learning goals, and tests are designed to measure specific learning outcomes. However, where development once occurred predominately outside the classroom, Madian (1986) suggests that computer technology makes it possible to develop, test, and refine instructional materials in the classroom. As an alternative to centralized, textbook-based curriculum, word processing as a curriculum design tool enables teachers / developers to initiate and implement a flexible, self-refining materials development process. Some technologists suggest that very soon there will be national networks that will allow the teacher to utilize an abundance of materials by loading them via satellite from a central storage facility. The curriculum developer of the future will be able to use selected pieces of a wide array of materials and use specific authoring systems that will permit the developer to develop creative instructional materials to meet specific needs of an individual learning situation. Whereas the curriculum developer of the past often had little flexibility in dealing with the constraints surrounding the development process, the curriculum developer of the future will be able to draw on a variety of flexible tools for the creation of instructional materials.

The demands of a technological society have also meant that the formal curriculum be reevaluated. Decker Walker (1985) suggests that the technological nature of American society is the most powerful driving force for curriculum change in our time. Some proponents of change suggest that there needs to be a reemphasis on the formal subjects of science and mathematics. Others contend that it is more important that students "learn to learn" — acquire those general strategies that can be applied to a wide array of situations. Whichever case one tends to follow, it is clear that the technological changes in America and the world have had an impact on the formal curriculum. Two examples illustrate this impact.

Technological literacy has become an important new goal for the modern-day school system. New courses have been introduced into the curriculum, and in some schools there are graduation requirements related to technological literacy. Almost all secondary schools now have at least one course in computer programming and a general course about computers in society. Most elementary schools teach the basics of using a computer and have children using word-processing systems. In some schools a carefully laid out curriculum has students studying how a computer operates, developing rudimentary programming skills, examining computer careers, learning about specific technology, studying the history of computers, and examining how technology impacts society as a whole. All of these new topics have meant changes in the formal curriculum.

One final example illustrates how technology has influenced the formal curriculum. Prior to the 1980s typing was a course offered at the junior high-school level. The microcomputer and its widespread use led to an important curriculum issue. When should students learn keyboarding skills so that they can use a computer? If students did not receive instruction prior to junior high school, they developed bad habits that were difficult to change. The result was a long-standing debate about what skills should be taught at what level and by what teacher—a typical curriculum issue. The issue has yet to be resolved.

Advocates of curriculum change suggest not only a new formal curriculum but also a new and different way of teaching those subjects. Technology has impacted instruction in two general ways. First, it has introduced different ways of teaching the content and skills of the curriculum. As we noted earlier, computers, videodiscs, and other interactive technologies have the potential to change the way lessons are taught and skills are learned. Whether a teacher uses a computer to enhance a demonstration or as a special teaching tool for an individual student, the instructional process is altered. Second, technology has also meant that many schools have focused special attention on teaching teachers how to teach using the technology. School districts throughout the country have spent millions of dollars on training teachers how to use this new technology and related instructional materials. Never before in the history of schooling has so much money been spent for training teachers how to use technology. Although the impact of these efforts are yet unknown, the commitment by schools to incorporate new instructional technology into the classroom is strong. Will such efforts pay dividends?

Supporters of the high-technology revolution suggest that the classroom of yesterday will be dramatically changed. Those in opposition to the movement look to the past and suggest that technology has had minimal impact on the classroom. Critics suggest that although phonographs, filmstrips, and films are useful techniques, they do not lead to better student achievement. Critics point to research that indicates that media do not influence learning, and at best must be considered as a vehicle that delivers instruction. In reviewing "media selection" research projects, Clark (1983) found little evidence to suggest that a specific type of media will lead to higher student achievement. Critics suggest the same will be true for the microcomputer technology.

Proponents suggest that microcomputer technology cannot be considered in the same manner as television, film, and filmstrips. Students remained passive participants when instructed using film or television, but microcomputers and interactive video systems involve the students in the learning process. A comparison of the two media illustrate the differences. A film or television show is shown to the students in the following manner: The teacher may introduce the topic, hand out a study guide, and debrief after the episode; however, the major role of the student is to observe what is being shown. The production may be extremely well done, but it remains an expository method of instruction in which students listen to all the information that is needed for them to learn. Their role is to observe and write down important facts. While involved in the learning process, they are mostly passive participants in the process.

Advocates of the microtechnology revolution contrast the above picture with research findings and experiences with microcomputers, interactive video, and satellite systems. They point to summaries of research by Kulik, Bangert, and Williams (1983) that show students who are involved with computers tend to learn key concepts faster, cooperate with each other more effectively, and like school more.

The final verdict on the impact of the new technology on curriculum and instruction will emerge over time. It is clear, however, that the changes that are taking place in society will continue to reshape people's notion of reality and will affect the school's curriculum and how students are instructed. These changes will take on several forms.

▶ The manner in which we think about knowledge will be altered.

The emphasis on recalling information from memory will be replaced by the skills needed to handle information. Students will need to learn how to manage large sources of information and how to draw conclusions from these data. This will mean that new skills will need to be learned and different teaching strategies will need to be used. Problem-solving skills and higher-order skills, long goals of education, will become more important. Educationalists such as Stanley Pogrow (1983), author of *Education in the Computer Age,* suggest that the learning of these skills is the primary imperative of a technological age. And, due to the rapid changes that are taking place in a technological age, it may be necessary for schools to help learners understand the relationships between individual and societal values and the interdependent nature of the world.

▶ The learning environment will be altered.

Sherry Turkel's *The Second Shelf: Computers and the Human Spirit* (1984) suggests that as teachers and students learn to use technology they will learn together. She also suggests that the new technology will allow students to use it in different ways to express their own individual needs and personalities. Control of the learning process may be more the responsibility of the learner rather than the teacher. In fact, Turkel contends, the advances in technology will help lead students to a clear understanding of themselves and their relationships with others.

Although this altered environment is welcomed by the advocates of technology, it will create tensions that will have a dramatic effect on the relationships between the teacher and the students. The power of the technology can change knowledge relationships in the classroom. Traditionally the teacher has been the authority. The teacher is supposed to know more about the subject than the students. If Turkel is correct, this may no longer be the case. For some teachers, such a change will be difficult to accept.

▶ Content will change.

As noted earlier in the chapter, the content of what is taught will also be altered. The most obvious example is the infusion of issues related to computer literacy — the ability to understand the impact of computers and related technology on the individual and society. Throughout the curriculum new materials have been introduced to help the learner not only acquire the skills needed to use a computer but also to understand how computers are changing the role of the individual and society. However, it is evident that due to the rapid growth of new knowledge it will be impossible to teach an individual all that he or she needs to know during the first eighteen years to become a productive citizen. What are the essential ingredients of a knowledge base for the student? How much learning must be postponed until later life? These and other questions will cause a reexamination of the content of the curriculum.

▶ Access to technology will become a critical issue.

Technology can be used in a variety of ways in curriculum development and instruction. The amount of technology in schools is increasing rapidly. However, not everyone has equal access to the technology and the learning materials developed for use on the technology. Differences between how males and females use technology are evident. Are computers predominately for males? Different instructional uses also appear. Are programs that have students use higher level thinking skills just for brighter students while less able students should only use technology for lower level learning? An important challenge facing educators is to ensure that all students have equal access to the power of technology. And finally, differences appear between those districts that have funds for technology acquisition and those that do not. Is the technological gap between wealthy and less wealthy districts widening? If so, what are the long-term societal impacts?

▶ Where education takes place may change.

There will always be schools. Schools serve important socialization and literacy functions in a society, and they will continue to do so. But, as technology becomes more advanced and learning moves beyond the school and the typical school-age years, other places — workplaces, clubs, business organizations — may begin to serve as educational centers. A mind-stretching possibility is offered by Walker (1985) when he suggests that in the near technological future education will occur through networks of people who are educating one another via telecommunications. The "learning communities" would allow people to move at their own pace. Such an environment in fraught with many problems, but the idea is interesting. The technology is present; the organization has yet to be established.

SUMMARY

▶ Educational technology as a philosophy of curriculum development and as a part of instruction plays an important part of the educational process. It has led to the creation of materials that have changed what is being taught, where it is taught, and how it is taught. Educational technology has brought into focus key questions that assist educators in determining curricular and instructional decisions.

The future of both education and technology are changing dramatically. The schools, reflecting the society as a whole, cannot escape the technological changes that are modifying society. The trends toward smaller, simpler, and coordinated technology will create more powerful tools. Technology, however, is value-free. It can determine the speed with which society moves, but it cannot determine the path society takes. Educators must be involved in determining technology's role in the education of its citizens, and they must realize that understanding the instructional process in its most complicated form is what will lead to improved student learning.

ACTIVITIES

1. Based on your reading, define *educational technology*.
2. What are the five basic components of a technological approach to the development of curriculum materials?
3. The 1980s witnessed a tremendous growth in the use of technology in schools. What three important trends have influenced this growth?
4. Why are many teachers reluctant to use technology in the classroom?
5. Describe the four basic ways technology can assist the teacher.
6. The text suggests that technology will change in three general areas. What are these areas and what other ways do you think technology will alter education?
7. Go to your computer center and find examples of each of the following sets of computer educational courseware: (1) drill and

practice, (2) tutorial package, (3) simulations, and (4) educational games.
8. Examine some of the popular technology magazines that are available at your bookstore. What are some of the latest advances in computer technology, videodiscs, and telecommunications? How might these advances influence instruction?
9. Visit a school and observe the use of technology used for instructional purposes. Ask teachers:
    a. How often do you use films, videotape, and television as a part of instruction?
    b. How often do you use computers as part of instruction?
    c. What changes need to be brought about in order for you to use technology more in your classes?
    d. Of all the pieces of technology available in your school, which one is the most useful to you as a teacher?

REFERENCES

Clark, R. (Winter 1983). Reconsidering research on learning from media. *Review of Educational Research, 53,* 4, 445–459.

Kulik, J. A.; Bangert, R. L.; and Williams, G. W. (1983). Effects of computer-based teaching on secondary school students. *Journal of Educational Psychology, 75,* 1, 19–27.

Maddison, J. (1983). *Education in the microelectronic era.* England: Open University Press, p. 112.

Madian, J. (March 1986). New flexibility in curriculum development through word processing. *Eductional Leadership, 43,* 6, 22–23.

Mager, R. (1975). *Preparing instructional objectives.* Belmont, Calif.: Fearon.

Pogrow, S. (1983). *Education in the computer age.* Beverly Hills,Calif.: Sage, 1983.

Popham, J. (1969). *Instructional objectives.* Chicago: Rand McNally.

Turkel, S. (1984). *The second shelf: Computers and human spirit.* New York: Simon and Schuster, Inc.

Walker, D. (1985). *Curriculum and technology: Current thought on curriculum: 1985 ASCD yearbook.* Alexandria, Va.: ASCD.

SUGGESTED READINGS

Hellerstein, D. (December 1985). Computers on the couch. *Esquire,* 360–365.

Papert, S. (1980). *Mindstorms: Children, computers and powerful ideas.* New York: Basic Books.

Papert, S. (January 1987). Information technology and education: Computer criticism vs. technocentric thinking. *Educational Researcher, 16,* 1, 22–31.

Weizenbaum, J. (1976). *Computer power and human reason: From judgment to calculation.* San Francisco: W. H. Freeman.

17

Curriculum Leadership

Any curriculum, any method of instruction, any amount of time a teacher spends with students represents an investment in the future. None of us wants to make a bad investment, especially where our nation's most precious resource is at stake.

You have read this book now, and we hope that we have been successful in stimulating your thoughts and providing you with useful information about curriculum and instruction. Among the themes we have discussed are critical issues in curriculum and instruction; the nature of curriculum and teaching; research and ideas about planning, instruction, and evaluation; the crucial issues of literacy and critical thinking; the formal and hidden curricula; and the emerging impact of technology on the schools.

In a spirit of optimism, we now pose a series of related questions designed to stretch your imagination, your creativity, your analytical skills, your problem-solving ability, and your vision of a shining, golden future of education. To paraphrase Gertrude Stein, the essence of curriculum lies not with the answers to perplexing issues but rather with the questions.

Imagine an hypothetical situation in which you are called upon to conceive a new school. Imagine further that the school is either elementary, secondary, or a K-12 school, depending on your preference. Imagine, as well, that the school is to be innovative in the sense that its curricular, instructional, and organizational patterns are based on ideas that have the potential to engage educational theory and practice in a meaningful way. Your answers to the following questions will draw on your personal philosophy of education as well as on your knowledge of the educational literature.

1. What will be the school's philosophy of curriculum? That is, what ought to be the sources of curriculum? What balance should be achieved between structure and freedom in the scope and sequence of the curriculum? What subjects will be taught, and how much time will be allocated for each?
2. What will be the school's philosophy of instruction? How much freedom will individual teachers have to teach as they choose? Will team instructional efforts be encouraged? Will teachers be given support in their attempts at instructional innovation?
3. What will be the school's organizational philosophy? How will the school be administered? What organizational/administrative decisions will teachers be empowered to make? How will students be grouped?
4. What qualifications and attributes should the teaching staff possess?
5. How will learning outcomes be evaluated?
6. In what ways should the community be involved with the school?

These questions are designed to probe your philosophy of curriculum and instruction. Like you, we have our biases, but we do not presume to judge yours. Rather, our intent here is to give you an opportunity to clarify your point of view as you complete your reading of this book.

ENVIRONMENT

► If you are assigned to a typical classroom, you can rest assured that too much space will not be your problem. According to state law, school classrooms must provide a minimal number of square feet per student, but there usually isn't much room left over by the time you provide everyone with a place to sit. The issue, therefore, is how to make the most of what you have.

► ## Teacher's Role

Two teachers teaching side by side in identical rooms in a building will invariably create a different environment, given four walls, a collection of desks and tables, and thirty students. The diversified character of American public education allows each individual teacher a considerable range of freedom to structure the environment. The term *environment* is used here to mean the ambience that emerges as a result of your structuring of the physical, intellectual, and social-emotional landscapes of your classroom, and collectively, of your school. Let's examine each of these crucial dimensions.

The physical environment is the geography of the classroom. The geographer studies space and spatial arrangements. The way you use the space afforded you says much about your imagination, your consideration of others, and your philosophy of teaching and learning. Viewed from this perspective, the structuring of the physical environment isn't just a chore, it's an adventure in creative problem solving. Now, before you run out to hire an interior decorator, or before you say, "Help, I'm an inferior decorator," remember that you have a powerful ally. It's called *imagination.*

To a child, a couple of throw rugs become magic carpets for reading if you call them that. A small corner table with a magnifying glass, a few science books, pencils, paper, and some leaves to examine and draw becomes a laboratory. A shelf with a few artifacts becomes a museum. A table with a few games that encourage sharing, thinking, competition, and involvement becomes a game center. An otherwise bare wall lined with maps will draw students to it as though the maps and they were magnetized. And so on. There is no excuse to have a bare, ugly room when it is so simple to create a sense of wonder.

You, the teacher, set the tone for the intellectual or academic environment of your classroom. In this context, don't ever assume that scholarship, creativity, curiosity, problem solving, critical thinking, and hard work are abstract ideas. They are, for better or worse, *you* personified. The exciting thing about the six intellectual ideas we just mentioned is that every student you teach is capable of them in large measure. Let's examine your leadership role in promoting and maintaining a stimulating intellectual environment in your classroom and school.

Scholarship

Actively discuss and promote the importance of learning new skills and ideas with your students. Support and publicize their scholarly work by posting good papers and by listing the names of honor roll students. Keep both your students and their parents aware of the fact that you are making every attempt to support academic efforts.

Creativity

Every student has far more creative potential than has been tapped. Your own creative potential is much greater than you probably realize.

Creativity begins to flower in a classroom and school where risk taking is encouraged, where discussions begin with "What if?" "How many ways?" and "What do you think?" Creativity expands when you are willing to place music, art, play, construction, design, drama, problem solving, and good literature at the heart of your curriculum.

Curiosity

This is indeed a neglected educational concept. Curiosity is seldom encouraged; it is often seen by teachers as an idle, superficial characteristic. We are curious: Can you think of at least ten ways you could promote this useful, important attribute?

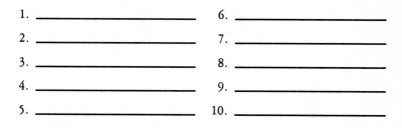

1. _____   6. _____

2. _____   7. _____

3. _____   8. _____

4. _____   9. _____

5. _____   10. _____

Problem Solving

We are not talking about the typical problems found in math textbooks. At best, those are exercises or low-level problems. The kind of problem solving that has lasting value tends to be interdisciplinary, real, open-ended, and messy. Consider this example.

A teacher and her class decided to investigate a crosswalk at their school. Everyone had known for years that the crosswalk was dangerous, but little had been done about it. This class studied the crosswalk systematically. The students timed the speed of cars through the intersection. They took photographs, made maps and models, surveyed students who used the crosswalk, conducted a safety campaign, and sent their findings to the mayor. The class ended up working with the state legislature during the time it was considering revised legislation on traffic safety near schools. And yes, the crosswalk was repainted and new warning signs were posted by the city. This is one way to teach citizenship, democratic values, and participation in the community.

Critical Thinking

Most of us appreciate disciplined critical thinking when we see it, but few teachers ever try to teach it in anything more than random fashion. It is hard to imagine a more basic, practical skill than critical thinking. You can use it to great advantage almost everywhere. To paraphrase Paul Brandwein, the critical thinker is that person who is able to place logic between impulse and action. The critical thinker analyzes issues, but thinks holistically, seeing problems in their several dimensions.

The noncritical thinker is ruled by emotion, prejudice, and lack of information, and invariably, he or she is drawn toward quick and simple solutions to complex problems. The effective critical thinker is a positive person who sees beyond the negative criticism of existing structures toward constructive criticism that builds people up and offers new insights to old problems.

Critical thinking happens at the macro as well as at the micro level. The process is essentially the same, as shown in Figure 17–1.

Item: A middle-school teacher named Willa was frustrated by the lack of reading and the reading of second-rate literature by her students. On her own initiative, she went to the library and checked out more than sixty good works of literature for young people. She set up a library in the classroom and is in the process of turning things around. She is using good literature to drive out bad literature. Our prediction is that both the long-term and short-term payoffs will be tremendous.

Challenge yourself and your class to become actively engaged as critical thinkers. Let it be said of your classroom that it was on this field that the battle for effective thought was joined.

Hard Work

Teaching is very hard work if you are conscientious. Being a conscientious student is also hard work for many. The happiest adults and children are those who know when to work and when to play. Your students need to experience success, and they need to learn from experience that success is usually a derivative of hard work. Quite frankly, the academic standards are lower in this country than they should be. No one is in a better position to raise them than you.

FIGURE 17-1 The Process of Critical Thinking

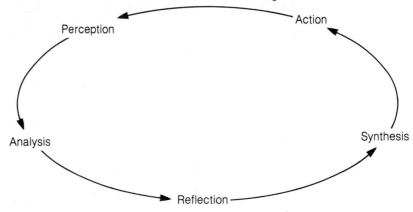

Unfortunately, many individuals perceive work to be a punishment. Such a perception damages students' chances for academic success and for success in general in adult life. Now please do not construct a false dichotomy in your mind between a grey dungeon-like workhouse and a classroom illuminated by sunbursts where the joys of childhood are perpetually celebrated. But it is a fact that nothing is ultimately as slavish, as limiting, or as imprisoning as ignorance. Nothing promotes freedom, self-confidence, independence, and a sense of efficacy like the assurance that you have the knowledge, skills, and self-discipline that result from hard work.

The social-emotional environment that you create in your classroom and in your school is just as crucial as the intellectual and physical environments. In fact, all three are parts of the whole; we separate them here only for the sake of examination. There is a sort of feeling or atmosphere that one senses immediately upon entering a classroom or school. That particular feeling is difficult to translate into words, but descriptors such as *free, fair, just, pleasant, tolerant, understanding, businesslike, friendly, caring, cooperative* (or their opposites) come to mind.

There are two different ways for you to go about establishing the atmospheric tone that pervades your classroom. The more common way, and we do not recommend it, is to play it by ear and just let it happen. You would not approach the teaching of reading, math, language, or other subjects in such a cavalier fashion, yet this aspect of the structure of your classroom and school is even more fundamental than the subjects themselves because they exist in its context. The alternative, of course, is to make careful plans for the feeling tone of your classroom.

The place to begin the process is with yourself. Your personality, your values, your characteristics, your mannerisms, and your feelings toward yourself will set the tone in your classroom and school to a deeper, more abiding extent than any protocol you decide to follow. Protocols are helpful, but they do not exist in isolation; they interact with you. Certainly, this is not a way of suggesting that if you do not have the "right" personality you ought to change it. There are many right personalities for teaching. The best advice we can give you in terms of your personality is to examine it carefully and play to your strengths. Begin with a self-assessment. The following procedure should be helpful:

Take a few minutes to list as many descriptive terms about yourself as you can. Do not be modest or grandiose; just try to be accurate. Now enlist the aid of two people who know you well. Ask each of them to independently draw up a list of words that describe you. Examine the three lists for agreement as well as for discrepancies. What do the lists say about you? How will you use your perceived (by you and two others) characteristics as strengths in the classroom?

To structure the social-emotional environment of your classroom and school, the following suggestions might be helpful:

Set aside an hour or two (about the same amount of time you might spend on a raquetball match or looking for an item of clothing at a shopping mall) and write a statement that describes your feelings about the ideal-social-emotional structure of your own classroom. Write about fairness, freedom, openness, justice, cooperation, opportunity, tolerance, and any other abstractions (which aren't really abstractions at all when they are experienced on an everyday basis in your classroom; instead, they are concrete realities). Refine your statement by discussing classroom atmosphere with others. A word of warning: In teaching, as in any profession, there are people who will advise you to set aside idealistic notions about students and classrooms and how things ought to be. Do not deny their right to their own reality, but do not let their cynicism become *your* reality. There is higher ground. Why not stand on it?

TIME MANAGEMENT

▶   Time management sounds like something you would study in a business class. The budding, young executive needs to learn to budget his or her time wisely in order to be productive and get ahead. So do you! The differences between time management for the typical person in the business world and time management for the teacher are that (1) your management job is more complex and (2) you can manage time more poorly and probably get away with it because teaching lacks a system of review and promotion that has much rigor or reward to it.

To the layperson, time management in a classroom probably seems simple enough—a little math, some reading, recess, lunch, and before you know it the day is over. But the fact of the matter is that you have managerial responsibilities for two to three dozen people who put in a full shift. You need to time-manage the effective distribution of a range and number of topics (subjects) for which you must show results (achievement gains). Therefore, your workplace is a crowded, busy shop, and as its manager, you are in a continuous process of decision making.

Time management is an area about which teachers know little. Like a number of other realities, it is just something you are expected to know how to do without the benefit of training.

Just to give you some idea of how crucial time management is, consider this: A report by the General Accounting Office concludes that improved teacher performance at the elementary level results more predictably from effective management and instructional strategies than from content knowledge:

More recent process-product research suggests that student performance can be improved by training teachers to *manage* instructional programs and student behavior (General Accounting Office, 1984).

In addition to this finding, the effective teaching literature clearly states the importance of "engaged learning time," or the percent of the school day actually spent at task (Hersch, 1984). For example, during a math class that lasts, say, an hour, how much time is spent teaching and learning math skills and concepts as opposed to taking out and putting away materials or rearranging the class into groups? Studies show that engaged learning time in some classes is as low as 25 percent. One study showed that students are actually engaged in learning for the equivalent of 81 days out of a 180-day school year (Goodlad, 1983). This represents a tremendous discrepancy in time management. This is all the more alarming when one considers the obvious (backed up by research findings): There is a high correlation between engaged learning time and academic achievement (Hersch, 1984). Learning time is gained primarily by a simple process—success in establishing a businesslike routine in the classroom and in the school. When students know what to do and when to do it, and when directions are firm and clear, classrooms become pleasant, efficient places to be.

Included here is a brief time management checklist designed to help you and your students become more efficient at manipulating this all-important variable. Know precisely what you want to achieve. If you know what needs to be done, you can tell your students. Not really knowing what needs to be done keeps most teachers from getting through the year's course of study.

TIME MANAGEMENT CHECKLIST

1. *Set goals.*   It is useful to have a "goal of the week" displayed in a prominent place. The goal is for the class as a whole and it also applies to each person (you included) in the class. The goal may be to finish a book or project, to improve a spelling score, or to help someone else. On Friday, you can conduct a brief class meeting where people talk about their progress in achieving the goal.
2. *Keep performance records.*   Older children should do this themselves. It helps them with the skills of record keeping and data analysis. It is also a learning reinforcement strategy.
3. *Set deadlines.*   William F. Buckley once wrote about the luxury of deadlines. Few of us would accomplish much if we were not given deadlines. It is also important to be firm about the deadline.
4. *Listen.*   Give your students opportunities to talk to you about their feelings, goals, and dreams. It is your single best avenue of feedback.
5. *Ask questions.*   Do not assume students are learning. Find out for sure by asking them.

6. *Practice MBWA.*   Management By Walking Around gives you better control, affords you opportunities for private conversations, and emits a clear signal that you are involved.

7. *Critique performance.*   Let students know that you care enough about them to mark their papers and to talk personally with them about their progress.

8. *Use memos.*   Send home two memos per month to parents. The memos should inform parents in a general way about what will be studied and how they can help.

9. *Use the phone.*   Place at least one phone call per year to each student's parents. Surprise them with some good news about their child.

10. *Stay on top of attendance.*   Look for patterns of absenteeism. Do not allow someone become an eventual dropout just because you let him or her fall behind in the third grade.

11. *Set priorities.*   What needs to be accomplished today? this week? this month? this year? You need to know this. You also need to discuss this with your class so that they can learn how to set priorities. Failure to learn to do so represents the greatest breakdown in effective time management.

LEADERSHIP IN THE SCHOOL AND IN THE CLASSROOM

▶ Any two given schools may bear great similarities on the surface. The buildings are basically the same, the schools are the same size, and they are located in similar socioeconomic environments. The two schools have similar resources with respect to libraries, science materials, and other facilities and equipment. Each has a principal and other administrators and support staff. The teaching staff is organized by grade level and/or subject matter. The teachers in each building have certificates and degrees. Students attend the typical array of classes, and there is little variance in the subject matter curriculum of the two schools.

Why, then, is the atmosphere different in the two schools? We might begin by raising questions about the role of the principal. How supportive is the building principal of the teaching staff? How demanding is he or she of the teaching staff? What level of academic expectations is set—excellence? mediocrity? no discernible level? Are teachers left to drift on their own, or does a spirit of leadership and caring emanate from the principal's office? Is the principal viewed by teachers, students, and the community as an instructional leader, or merely as an administrator in a more narrow sense of the word? More than any other individual, the building principal determines the tone of the curriculum. Teachers and students need to know what expectations will be placed on them and how the principal intends to insure that those expectations are met. No one individual has as powerful an impact on the hidden curriculum of the entire school than does the principal.

At the classroom level, leadership transfers to individual teachers. Teachers can be autocratic, democratic, or laissez-faire in their approach to leadership. they can be imaginative or unimaginative, supportive or uncaring, involved or apathetic, creative or dull. Seldom are teachers given specific leadership training; they are simply expected to lead. It is a curious phenomenon. Teachers are told legally what to teach, but they are infrequently told how to manage the curriculum.

The teacher as leader has several fundamental decisions to make (Hunter, 1983). Those decisions include: (1) How will I behave? (2) How will I expect the students to behave and to use their time? and (3) What methods of instruction will I use? These questions, answered thoughtfully, are the keys to classroom leadership.

The question of how students will use their time is again a function of leadership. You will set the standard on the basis of demands you make for excellence. The issue has been identified by researchers as a key variable in academic achievement. There is always the argument of amount of time versus quality of time. Without arguing that salient point, we will say only that both are crucial.

Let us look at a couple of examples of time usage. The first-grade teacher who teaches reading by using the traditional three-group method teaches one-third of the students while the other two-thirds wait. They wait for directions or help, and often stray from the task without the teacher's presence. Thus, in a one-hour reading period the academic learning time for a given student may be only about twenty minutes. This is a very inefficient ratio. In a fifty-minute high-school biology lab, the teacher spends time taking roll orally, hands out lab specimens that should have been distributed by a student assistant, disciplines students who are not sure of what they are to do, and allows students to start putting away their work ten minutes before class is over. It does not take much of this to reduce the academic learning time in a fifty-minute period by half. Now multiply that lost time by five days per week, thirty-six weeks per year. John Goodlad (1984) revealed that the academic learning time in the 34-hour school week ranges from about 18.5 hours to 27.5 hours. Such a range represents an astounding time differential.

Clear directions, efficient organization, a businesslike attitude toward school work, and a sense of order and discipline result in greater efficiency. These are factors of the curriculum that yield dramatic differences in school achievement over time. There is nothing magic about this recipe. These are merely items of common sense that you need to resolve to implement immediately in your classroom.

A third leadership issue is that of the teaching methods teachers use. For example, two people teaching U.S. history might well use widely different approaches. One teacher uses a lecture-discussion-reading approach, whereas another uses a project-oriented approach. Thus, the role of teacher and students from one room to the other could be completely different even though both classes are studying exactly the same subject. Our point here is not to say that one of these methods is inherently superior to the other. In fact, research in effective teaching supports the use of a variety of instructional strategies (Hersch, 1984). Our point is to make clear the idea that *how* you teach interacts with or even supersedes *what* you teach. The parent who sees his or her child change from hating science last year to loving it this year is seeing the powerful potential effects of the curriculum. *What* is taught may not be as significant as *who* teaches it and *how* it is taught.

Using the analogy of an iceberg floating in the ocean, we can compare the formal curriculum to the portion that is easily visible. It represents the relatively small amount of the iceberg's mass that rests above the water. Anyone could spot it a mile away. The larger and less visible curriculum, found beneath the surface, is in reality a more fundamental determinant of learning and of life-long attitudes toward continued learning. Its manifestations are subtle and often go undetected. Its effects are cumulative but difficult to assess. There is no way to count or measure the cost of the lost idealism and curiosity that can be slowly drained from learners. Contrarily, there is no salary or reward large enough to repay the teacher who communicates the joy of learning, the satisfaction of work well done, and the feeling of a healthy self-concept.

▶ The Goal Structure of the Classroom

The goal structure of classrooms is another variable that contributes to learning and to attitudes toward learning. Remember, a classroom is a social setting. Teachers and students live together in close proximity hour after hour. The ostensible reasons for placing students in classrooms are academic, but the outcomes reflect a combination of academic and social experience. There is no rational cause to assume that a student assigned to a math class learns only math. He or she also learns how to behave, whether to compete with or cooperate with fellow students, and other concepts such as responsibility, caring, and neatness.

▶ Homework and School Improvement

Homework is actually an extension of the curriculum. In recent years, it has been linked positively to academic achievement. Studies of effective teaching generally include carefully graded homework as a factor of academic success (Featherstone, 1985). Homework is considered in this discussion because in most instances it is a discretionary phenomenon. Often, there are no school-wide rules governing the amount and type of homework assigned, and when there are they are seldom enforced. Some teachers assign more homework than others; some teachers assign no homework at all. This has been especially true at beginning school levels. The problem is, though, that work habits and attitudes form early in life and are difficult to remediate later on.

It is probably the case that more and more schools will implement and enforce policies where a certain amount of homework is mandated. Recent national reports have advocated homework assignments for students beyond the primary level, and certain researchers have implied that a moderate amount would be beneficial at primary levels.

► The Promise of the Report by the Carnegie Forum

Although the rhetorical claims of teachers' organizations have trumpeted the professional status of their rank and file over the years, the fact is that the public has never perceived teachers as legitimate claimants to the mantle of professionalism at the level of, say, doctors or lawyers. Now there is reason to think that a new conception of the teaching professional is in the offering—one that promises to enhance the status of teachers through differentiated titles, greatly improved salaries, higher standards for entry into the profession, and greater teacher authority in running the schools. This new conception, one that AFT president Albert Shanker has called, "the first major move toward professionalism in teaching," comes from the prestigious Carnegie Foundation. The name *Carnegie* is associated with some of the most influential moves in the history of American education, including the Carnegie library program, which brought public libraries to almost every community; the Carnegie Unit, which remains the basic unit of high-school academic credit; and the founding of the Educational Testing Service, which has prepared the benchmark tests for college admission and the so-called teacher competency tests.

The report of the Carnegie Foundation titled, "A Nation Prepared: Teachers for the 21st Century," reads, in part:

> We do not believe the educational system needs repairing. We believe it must be rebuilt to match the drastic change needed in our economy if we are to prepare our children for productive lives in the 21st century.

The 140-page report, prepared by the Carnegie Forum on Education and the Economy, represented an attempt to explore links between economic growth and the quality of the schools. The report concluded:

> It is no exaggeration to suggest that America must now provide to the many the same quality of education presently reserved for the fortunate few. The cost of not doing so will be a steady erosion in the American standard of living.

Such a pragmatic thought from such an influential group carries with it a sense of immediacy, a clear call to reform now. The goal of the forum, according to David H. Hamburg, president of the Carnegie Corporation, is "to put teaching on a par with law, medicine, and other fields where members of the profession take responsibility for setting and maintaining high standards." The vehicle for implementing this goal, is the proposed National Board for Professional Teaching Standards. The proposed board would give practicing teachers, rather than state boards of education, primary responsibility for setting standards of the profession and for determining who would meet them. Both the American Federation of Teachers and the National Education Association were represented on the forum and their respective forum member signed the report.

Let us look briefly at the sweeping changes called for by the forum.

Do Away with the Undergraduate Degree in Education
This is not a new idea; others, the *Holmes Report* (1986), for example, have made similar proposals. Some states, California is a case in point, have eliminated the undergraduate education degree. But at present, the curriculum of teacher education for most students is composed of a degree in education. The forum proposes that students first achieve an accredited academic degree prior to their training in pedagogy. If this proposal is enacted, it will indeed mean a major overhaul of the teacher preparation process for most colleges and universities.

Create a New Master of Teaching Degree
Because students will already have an academic degree, the Master of Teaching degree will be a focused, professional degree designed to prepare teachers to work in a particular field or level of education. In some sense, the degree is analogous to a law degree in that students who study law enter law school with a degree in political science, history, or whatever. The attainment of the Master of Teaching degree would then make candidates eligible to apply for certification.

Establish a National Board to Develop Teaching Standards
The idea of a national board in a country where licensure and related standards in most professions (medicine, law, etc.) are administered

by the states appears on the surface to be a discrepant idea, especially given Americans' long-standing love of local control and suspicion of federal control. Whether the proposed board could have more than advisory status would become a condition of states' willingness to enter into an interstate compact or reciprocal agreement regarding licensure, competency testing, and so on. Nevertheless, given the transient nature of our population, there seems to be considerable merit in a single nationwide competency test for certification as well as for uniform standards of conduct by members of the profession. The deep and abiding tradition of local and regional control in this country, however, will make the realization of a politically powerful national board of teaching rather difficult.

Increase Teachers' Authority in Running the Schools

Nothing is as powerful as an idea whose time has come. In recent years, teachers have witnessed an erosion of their abilities to make decisions about curricular and instructional issues in particular. But this proposal that teachers be given new and expanded authority in running the schools has incurred the opposition of Secretary of Education William Bennett who cites research (Bossert, 1985) as saying that the principal is the key to improved academic outcomes. But the current thinking in the business community is participatory leadership, à la the quality-circles approach employed by so many successful businesses (Peters, 1984). Also, the Carnegie Forum has made it clear that teachers are professionals who must be included in the processes of decision making.

Provide More Staff Support to Classroom Teachers

Clearly a teacher's potential effectiveness is eroded by the many clerical and maintenance chores that he or she must perform during the course of a typical school day. The forum advocates greater specificity in delineating tasks that are clearly teaching tasks from those that are more properly clerical, in order to free teachers' time to work directly with students.

Increase Salaries and Career Opportunities to Make Teaching Competitive with Other Professions

It is widely acknowledged that low salaries and limited opportunities for advancement have been discouraging factors that have kept talented people from entering the profession or that have caused them to leave the profession prematurely. The forum has recommended a two-tiered career ladder concept of entry-level and advanced certification.

Entry-level certification would be granted to teachers on the basis of (1) written tests of general knowledge and familiarity with the subjects they intend to teach, (2) work with computer simulations of classroom situations, and (3) observation of their teaching by board-certified teachers (an example of greater teacher authority). Advanced certificates would be awarded under the forum's plan on the basis of demonstrated competence and leadership. Proposed salaries would range up to the $65,000 level.

The comprehensive nature of the Carnegie Forum report and its widespread support among business leaders make it the most promising of the papers in a decade enamored of reports of commissions.

SOME CONCLUDING REMARKS

▶ In summary, we can say that you are the key to effective curriculum and instruction. You are the crucial variable to the process of students' development. As a teacher or administrator, you are responsible for the positive development of the total curriculum in your classroom and school. Here are a few concluding guidelines that should give you some practical assistance with that task.

▶ Keep the focus on people.

The uplifting of human beings is what school is all about. Whatever subject(s) you teach, remember to think about the lives and the needs of your students. Show them that you care about them. Provide time for sharing, for discussing, and for helping each other. Attitude and achievement are closely linked. Do what you can to improve your students' self-images. Research shows a steady decline in students' concepts of themselves as learners throughout the school years. How ironic that in the name of learning we create situations where students gradually, but inexorably, devalue their own self-esteem with respect to their learning abilities. Resolve to turn that around.

▶ Use a variety of instruction strategies.

There is no one best way to teach or to learn. If there were, we would all use it all of the time. By employing a variety of teaching strategies, you accomplish two things. First, you make learning more enjoyable because you resist the boredom of the set routine that never varies from day to day. Second, you increase the chances of reaching the wide range of learning styles that exists in every classroom.

▶ Build relationships between facts and concepts.

Facts are bits and pieces of information. Concepts are ideas. It is crucial that you link them. Do not expect students to connect them on their own. Research shows that the relationships between facts and concepts are seldom explored in classrooms. Almost all students learn that Columbus discovered America in 1492; few are ever asked to consider the significance of voyages of discovery. Most students learn basic computational facts; few are ever asked to consider the uses of those facts in solving real problems. School learning, at its best, is based on the premise that connections among ideas do exist and that those connections are worth exploring.

▶ Teach for transfer.

Madeline Hunter (1983) reinforces this point by saying that applications ought to be built into every lesson you teach. Learning becomes easier and makes more sense when it fits into a context. Transfer represents the ability to learn in one situation and to apply that learning in other situations. It helps to keep in mind that teaching is a practical activity and, in that sense, it is dependent on practical applications.

▶ Emphasize direct experience.

School is, of necessity, an artificial environment. Lines of separation exist between it and the real world. Young children come to school having mastered tremendously difficult tasks in a very natural way, (for example, how to speak, listen, walk, etc.). In school, learning takes on an increasingly formal tone. Learning becomes more narrowly defined as the manipulation of symbolic code systems of letters and numbers. Direct, active experience, such as making things, conducting investigations, and other forms of concrete experience, build confidence, break down barriers between natural and artificial learning, and provide the tangible points of reference basic to more abstract thought.

▶ Monitor progress.

Everyone wants to know how well he or she is doing. Mayor of New York, Ed Koch, became well known for walking through the burroughs saying, "How am I doing?" Your students are learning. Capture it. Show them. Teach them to keep records of their progress. Give them the feedback they need to build their confidence. Achievement levels are enhanced by monitoring and evaluating progress. Monitoring progress raises students' levels of concern. It is one more way of showing that you care.

▶ Teach values.

Every teacher needs to model and directly teach values. Integrity, trust, cooperation, respect, and dignity can be talked about and expected in your classroom. Do not shy away from these basic values. There is plenty of evidence that knowledge without a socially redeeming value system is dangerous. You are a leader, and your ability to lead wisely depends not only on the knowledge and skills that you teach but on the moral and ethical context into which you place knowledge and skills.

SUMMARY

▶ In his excellent book, *The Discoverers,* author Daniel Boorstin (1985) pays tribute to the men and women whose breakthroughs of the frontiers of space, time, and imagination represented humankind's finest hours of boldness and creativity. Each of these people, whether Christopher Columbus, Marie Curie, or Albert Einstein, saw what others had failed to see. But each seemed as well to have discovered far more than even he or she had set out to find. These people embarked on single-minded quests, and ended by discovering new worlds.

We hope that your search for and discovery of the school curriculum brings parallel dividends to your sphere of influence. The teacher who remains after school to help a student, who is recovering from an illness, with his math lessons may have set out to help someone catch up with the class and may have, in the long run, produced a mathematician. The classroom where ideas are encouraged and examined thoughtfully can be a place of incubation for later discoveries too bold for us to imagine. Indeed, it is possible to make too much of the teacher's role. But in too many instances, the tendency has been to make far too little of it. After all, what is the curriculum beyond teacher, students, and something of value to learn?

REFERENCES

Adler, M. (1982). *The paideia proposal.* New York: Macmillan.

Bossert, S. (May 1985). Effective elementary schools. In R. Kyle (Ed.), *Reaching for excellence: An effective schools sourcebook.* Washington, D.C.: U.S. Government Printing Office, pp. 45–49.

Boorstin, D. J. (1985). *The discovers: A history of man's search for himself.* New York: Random House.

Carnegie Forum on Education and the Economy (1986). *A nation prepared: Teachers for the 21st century.* New York: Carnegie Corporation.

Eisner, E. W. (1985). *The educational imagination* (2nd ed.). New York: Macmillan.
Featherstone, H. (February 1985). Homework. *The Harvard Education Letter.*
Goodlad, J. I. (1984). *A place called school.* New York: McGraw-Hill.
Hersch, R. H. (1984). *What makes some schools and teachers more effective?* Eugene, Ore.: Center for Educational Policy and Management.
Holmes Group. (April 1986). *Tomorrow's teachers: A report of the Holmes Group.* E. Lansing, Mich.: The Holmes Group.
Hunter, M. (1983). *Using what we know about teaching.* Alexandria, Va.: Association for Supervision and Curriculum Development.
Karweit, N. (1984). *Time on task: A research review.* Washington, D.C.: National Commission on Excellence in Education.
New directions for federal programs to aid mathematics and science teaching. Washington, D.C.: General Accounting Office, 1984.
Peters, T. (1984). *In search of excellence.* New York: McGraw-Hill.

SUGGESTED READINGS

Blumberg, A., and Greenfield, W. (1980). *The effective principal: Perspectives on school leadership.* Boston: Allyn and Bacon.
Burns, J. M. (1978). *Leadership.* New York: Harper and Row.
Glatthorn, A. A. (1987). *Curriculum renewal.* Alexandria, Va.: Association for Supervision and Curriculum Development.
Hipps, G. M. (ed.). (1975). *Effective planned change strategies.* San Francisco: Jossey-Bass.
Marks, W., and Nystrand, R. (1980). *Strategies for educational change.* New York: Macmillan.
Michael, D. (1973). *On learning to plan and planning to learn.* San Francisco: Jossey-Bass.
Naisbitt, J. (1982). *Megatrends: Ten new directions transforming our lives.* New York: Warner Books.

Index